DO NOT REMOVE FORMS FROM POCKET

CARD OWNER IS RESPONSIBLE FOR ALL
LIBRARY MATERIAL ISSUED ON HIS CARD

PREVENT DAMAGE - A charge is made for
damage to this item or the forms in the pocket.

RETURN ITEMS PROMPTLY - A fine is charged for
each day an item is overdue, including Sundays
and holidays.

REPORT A LOST ITEM AT ONCE - The charge for
a lost item includes the cost of the item plus a
$5.00 non-refundable service fee.

LOS ANGELES PUBLIC LIBRARY

SEP. 0 7 1991

Corner Men

GREAT BOXING TRAINERS

MANNIE SEAMON, JOE LOUIS AND JACK BLACKBURN enter
the ring prior to Louis' one-round knockout of John Henry Lewis,
January 25, 1939.

10

Corner Men

GREAT BOXING TRAINERS

RONALD K. FRIED

OMAR CASTEDI
FUTURE BOXER

796.33 F 899

C. 004

FOUR WALLS EIGHT WINDOWS

NEW YORK

Published by:

Four Walls Eight Windows
PO Box 548
Village Station
New York, N.Y., 10014

First edition.
First printing April 1991.

Library of Congress Cataloging-in-Publication Data:

Fried, Ronald K., 1955–
Corner men: great boxing trainers/by Ronald K. Fried. —1st ed.
p.   cm.
Includes index.
ISBN: 0-941423-48-4
1. Boxing—United States—Trainers—Biography.   I. Title.
GV1131.F85   1991
796.8'3'0922   90-49705
[B]   CIP

Printed in the U.S.A.

Text designed by Cindy LaBreacht.

For L

FREDDIE BROWN AND ROBERTO DURAN
PHOTO CREDIT: PIERRE McCANN, *LA PRESSE*

CONTENTS

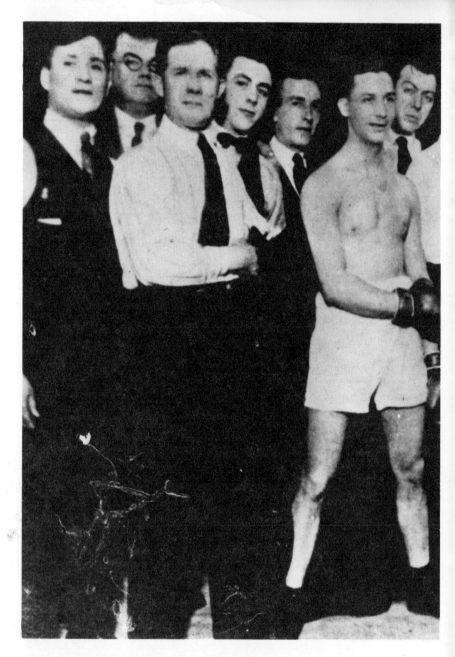

**BENNY LEONARD AND JOHNNY DUNDEE prior to their bout
on June 16, 1919. MANNIE SEAMON is furthest on the left.**
PHOTO COURTESY FAE SEAMON

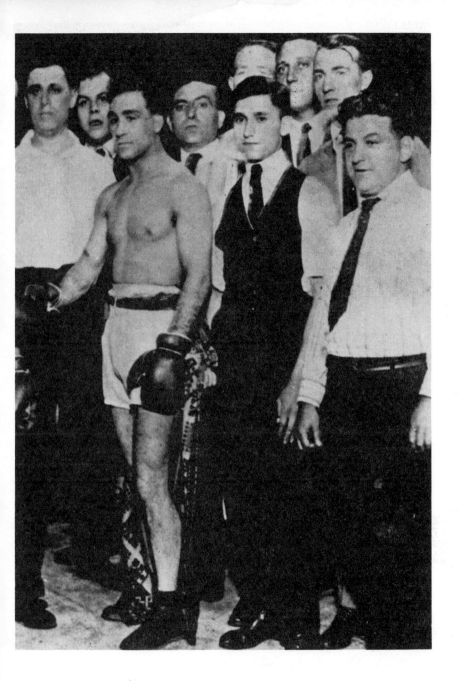

RAY ARCEL AND WHITEY BIMSTEIN
PHOTO COURTESY ADELE SHAPIRO

FREDDIE BROWN AND HEAVYWEIGHT ABE SIMON
PHOTO COURTESY MURIEL BROWN

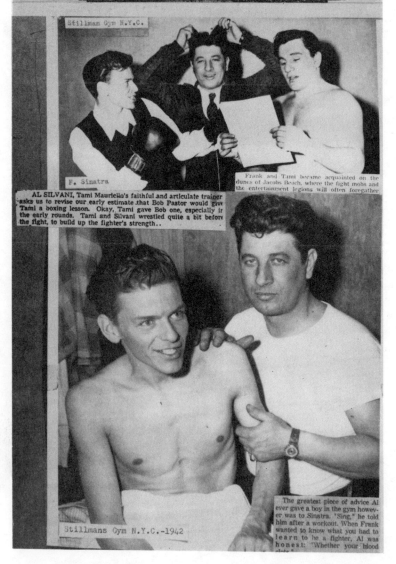

Ace Conditioner Silvani tears his hair when Sinatra boxes and Mauriello croons. NEW YORK 1942

Stillman Gym N.Y.C.

F. Sinatra

Frank and Tami became acquainted on the dunes of Jacobs Beach, where the fight mobs and the entertainment legions will often foregather

AL SILVANI, Tami Mauriello's faithful and articulate trainer asks us to revise our early estimate that Bob Pastor would give Tami a boxing lesson. Okay, Tami gave Bob one, especially in the early rounds. Tami and Silvani wrestled quite a bit before the fight, to build up the fighter's strength..

The greatest piece of advice Al ever gave a boy in the gym however was to Sinatra. "Sing," he told him after a workout. When Frank wanted to know what you had to learn to be a fighter, Al was honest: "Whether your blood clots."

Stillmans Gym N.Y.C.-1942

A page from Al SILVANI's scrapbook.
PHOTO COURTESY AL SILVANI

losing middleweight championship to Sugar Ray Robinson by a technical knockout in the 13th round. Helping Jake to dressing room after fight is trainer Al Silvani.

Al Silvani: He Finds
Success In A Corner

Boxing is surfeited with interesting characters and Al Silvani is one who can hold his own with any since becoming involved in the sport in 1936, a 42-year span in which he has trained, managed, baby-sat, fed, advised, scolded and inspired hundreds of fighters.

AL - JAKE LA MOTTA T.K.O. BY RAY

CHICAGO DAILY NEWS, Thursday, Feb. 15, 1951

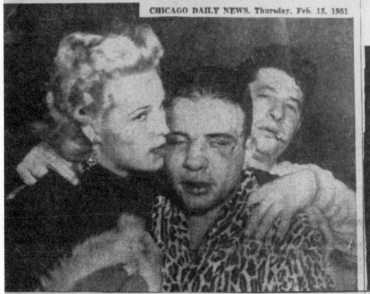

Downcast and battered, Jake La Motta gets a comforting embrace from wife Vicki aft-er losing middleweight championship to Sugar Ray Robinson by a technical knockout in the 13th round. Helping Jake to dressing room after fight is trainer Al Silvani.

A page from Al SILVANI's scrapbook.

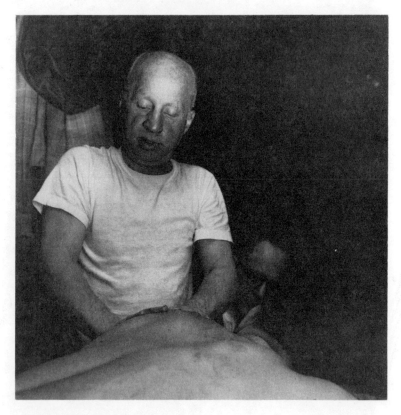

WHITEY BIMSTEIN
PHOTO COURTESY ADELE SHAPIRO

ACKNOWLEDGEMENTS

Thanks first must go to Ray Arcel, Angelo Dundee, Eddie Futch and Al Silvani, four great trainers who accommodated my repeated requests for interviews and clarifications. I hope they appreciate the depth of my gratitude.

Thanks also to the other trainers who spoke with me at length: George Benton, Luther Burgess, George Chemeres, Lou Duva, Walter Smith, Johnny Tocco and Ted Walker.

Thanks to Muriel Brown for sharing material on her husband; Fae Seamon for providing me with access to her father's invaluable scrapbook; and Whitey Bimstein's daughter Adele Shapiro for sharing her father's collection of press clippings. As I often told Mrs. Brown, Ms. Seamon and Mrs. Shapiro, my book would not have been possible if they had not shared their memories.

Both Stephanie Arcel and Mrs. Al Silvani made me feel welcome in their homes and provided me with photographs for my book.

I'm also grateful to Whitey Bimstein's son Jerry Barnes and his grandson Michael Shapiro for granting me interviews.

Members of the boxing world helped me so often that I felt

like a blind man who was escorted across the street by countless helpful strangers. Jack Fiske of *The San Francisco Chronicle* provided me with material and generously gave me leads on
old-time boxing men around the country. Irving Rudd gave me
my first interview and was available to help whenever I called.
Others deserving of special mention are Steve Acunto, Jimmy
Archer, Al Braverman, Jimmy Breslin, Harold Conrad, Joey Curtis, Billy Graham, Freddie Guinyard, Steve Lott, Peter Marciano,
Harry Markson, Marshall Miles and John Scott. They all
showed great patience in granting my requests for interviews
and suggesting others for me to contact.

Steve Lott also generously showed me vintage footage from
the late Jimmy Jacob's celebrated collection. Thanks to Al
Certo for giving me phone numbers and addresses I otherwise
could not have found.

In addition to those already mentioned, thanks to the follow-
ing fighters for granting me interviews: Vito Autuofermo,
Johnny Busso, Jackie Cranford, Vinnie Ferguson, Larry Holmes,
Dan Kapilow, Jake La Motta, Rocky Lockridge, Saoul Mamby,
Gaspar Ortega, Floyd Patterson, Willie Pep, Simon Ramos, Billy
Soose and Jersey Joe Walcott.

Thanks to these others in the boxing world who also gave me
interviews: Howard Albert, Dr. Edwin Campbell, Don Chargin,
Gil Clancy, Jimmy Glenn, Murray Goodman, Randy Gordon,
Jackie Graham, Joseph Gramby, Ben Green, Red Greb, Babe
Griffin, Don Dunphy, Norm Lockwood, Nat Loubet, Michael
Katz, Shelly Stillman and Del Williams. Thanks to Stanley
Weston for providing me with a photo he took of Charley
Goldman and Rocky Marciano.

I would never have heard of any boxing trainers if not for the
work of countless writers such as A. J. Liebling, Red Smith, Jerry
Izenberg, Harold Mayes, Dave Anderson, Ira Berkow, William
Nack, Pat Putnam, Michael Katz, Phil Berger, Gary Smith, John
Schulian, Leonard Gardner, W. C. Heinz, Frank Graham, Lester
Bromberg, Chester L. Washington, Art Rust, Jr. and Barney

Nagler. As I gratefully acknowledge throughout this book, I am indebted to the work of all of these writers, as well as many of their colleagues. I owe a particular debt to Edward Van Every of the *New York Sun* who chronicled Jack Blackburn's thoughts throughout Joe Louis' career. I'm also grateful to Chris Mead for our conversation about Joe Louis.

Dick Scalise went out of his way to find me information about Jack Blackburn's 1936 manslaughter trial in Chicago. A woman named Grace in the Hunter College Alumni Office did me a huge favor by helping me locate Whitey Bimstein's daughter.

Oscar Goodman provided me with introductions and the use of his good name. Betty Mitchell made it a pleasure to get in touch with Angelo Dundee. Kathy Duva provided help at Main Events. Andrew Vachss provided a good lead and an encouraging note. Deborah Orenstein gave me free legal advice. Bob Stein helped out with audio equipment.

On a more personal level, thanks to David and Diana Chesnoff, and Tod Mesirow and Diana Wagman for putting me up during my West Coast trip. Thanks to my father for the lift to Angelo Dundee's office and for escorting me to the closed circuit broadcast of the first Ali-Frazier fight in 1971. I should also thank Dick Cavett: If I hadn't worked for him, I wouldn't have had the chance to meet Angelo Dundee and Ray Arcel.

Thanks to Damien Bona, Susan K. Fried, Victoria Lowry, Sally McElwain, Ellen Prior, Dennis King and Chris O'Brien for reading all or part of my manuscript.

Mr. Pilla of the New York City Public Library provided an enormous amount of help in conducting research for this book.

I am also grateful to John Oakes and Dan Simon of Four Walls Eight Windows for their support.

Finally, though it feels peculiar to do so in print, I must thank my wife Lorraine Kreahling for her excellence as an editor and for enduring endless talk about boxing.

Perhaps my greatest debt of all is to Carolyn Kahn for her touchingly thorough performance as my researcher.

FREDDIE BROWN, WHITEY BIMSTEIN AND AL SILVANI
PHOTO COURTESY MURIEL BROWN

INTRODUCTION

During my first interview with Ray Arcel, the great boxing trainer offered some editorial advice. "I'll tell you something about trainers," Arcel said sternly. "I mean . . . and that includes me. You're only as good as the fighter you work with. I don't care how much you know, if your fighter can't fight, you're another bum in the park."

Reminded of his role in the careers of twenty world champions, including Charley Phil Rosenberg, Benny Leonard, Barney Ross, Tony Zale, Ezzard Charles, Roberto Duran and Larry Holmes, Arcel refrained from self-promotion. "In some instances, I was responsible for their success. In many instances, I shared the glory with them. You didn't have to be a great trainer to work with a Barney Ross or a Benny Leonard," Arcel continued, citing two fighters who are routinely rated among the handful of greatest boxers who ever lived. "I mean, these guys were natural. So if you're able to develop that, you're all right. Sometimes you can. Sometimes a guy stops dead at a certain period. So you're only as good as the guy you work with."

Arcel was clearly warning me against the temptation to over-play the roles of trainers in boxing history. But as I discovered while speaking with and studying Arcel and his most distin-guished colleagues, the best corner men always remember that before the punching starts, they leave the ring. As Angelo Dundee, trainer of Muhammad Ali and Sugar Ray Leonard, told me, "If the guy on the stool can't fight, you're in all kinds of trouble."

Fighters themselves are often eager to praise their trainers. Joe Louis spoke glowingly of Jack Blackburn; Benny Leonard raved about Mannie Seamon, as did Joe Louis twenty years later; Rocky Marciano praised Charley Goldman; Muhammad Ali has said that Dundee may have had more faith in Ali than Ali himself; and at a recent dinner in honor of Ray Arcel, champions such as Jackie "Kid" Berg, Billy Soose and Larry Holmes lined up to praise the ninety-year-old trainer. Count-less other examples abound.

Like moody adolescents reluctant to say a kind word about their parents, other boxers are less eager to credit their trainers. Former heavyweight champion Larry Holmes asked me, "Did Angelo Dundee make Ali, or did Ali make him? Did Blackburn make Joe Louis or did Joe Louis make Blackburn? . . . Nobody can make nobody fight. You could take the best trainer in the world, supposedly, and give him a kid that can't fight and that kid'll get his ass whipped every second. So fighters make train-ers, trainers don't make fighters."

My only response to Holmes is to point out that Blackburn, Dundee and their fellow trainers would be the first to agree with much of what he says.

Former middleweight champion Jake La Motta seemed at first to be in accord with Holmes. "Trainers do help fighters," La Motta said. "They do. But a great, great, great majority of train-ers, they don't know what they're talking about. . . . There's a lot of inexperienced guys out there trying to teach guys how to fight. And I don't know how they're getting away with it."

When I told La Motta which of the old-time trainers I was writing about, however, he became more sympathetic. When I mentioned Eddie Futch, trainer of Joe Frazier and Larry Holmes, La Motta said, "Well, he's a great trainer. He knows his business." Angelo Dundee? "Angelo's one of the best." Whitey Bimstein, who worked with Gene Tunney, Lou Ambers and Rocky Graziano? "He's one of the greats." La Motta's own trainer, Al Silvani? "He's a gentleman, a real respectful man." Ray Arcel? "He's the dean of them all."

La Motta then offered these encouraging words: "You got the right dope on these guys. Those are one of the handful of guys who know their business." I considered that an official blessing from the Raging Bull.

Former junior welterweight champion Saoul Mamby—anybody's idea of a quintessential ring professional—also provided something of an endorsement of my project. "Trainers work hard but they get less publicity [than managers]," he told me. "When a fighter wins a fight everybody looks at the fighter, 'Oh wow, yeah, that's good." But they never look at the trainer. You'll see 'Manager of the Year.' But he ain't did nothin'. Fighter of the Year. Yeah, he did it, but who helped him to do it? The trainer. The one who thinks about him, the one who worries about him, the one who puts up with attitudes, the one who puts up with his sarcasm. The trainer. And funny thing, whenever a fighter loses today, nine times out of ten they fire the trainer."

Although I would gladly contend that in many cases much of the credit for a great champion rightly belongs to his trainer, the argument seems fraught with dangerous generalities. It's the kind of debate I'd avoid in a bar. I'm more comfortable laying out the details of a trainer's role in a fighter's career and allowing the reader to judge its significance.

I've written *Corner Men* as a celebration of venerable men who witnessed—and influenced—a huge span of boxing history

and spoke about it in vivid and vanishing ways. If my book has
an explicit argument, it's simply that these trainers led fascinating lives and that their stories offer unique—largely undoc-
umented—perspectives on their sport. They lived more adven-
tures, learned more lessons and uttered more great lines than
the heroes of most twentieth-century novels.

Before, during and after a fight, no one is closer to the fighter
than the trainer—and trainers' observations are often more
objective and informative than those of the fighters themselves. "The trainer is the guy who knows the fighter best—if
he knows his business," Doc Kearns, manager of Jack Dempsey
and Mickey Walker, explained in 1953. "He eats and sleeps with
the boy, takes walks with him, plays cards with him, finds out
whether he's a guy that has to be needled or let alone. By the
time they get into the ring, a good trainer knows exactly what's
in the fighter, and how and when it can best be brought out. A
smart manager will let him run the corner."

Above all, trainers are professional observers. No one can
better analyze a fighter's boxing skills or psychic strengths and
weaknesses. One of the best trainers, Freddie Brown, told A. J.
Liebling in *The Sweet Science* that during a bout, a trainer's job
is "to see if he can see anything."

As Brown's idiosyncratic comment begins to demonstrate,
though trainers specialize in the fine points of brutality, they
often possess surprisingly subtle verbal gifts. They are almost
universally fine storytellers and collectors of epigrams and one-
liners.

Working with a boxer, trainers perform a variety of roles
including father figure, babysitter, motivator and, above all,
strategic advisor. Angelo Dundee has provided this job description: "To be a good fight trainer, you must adhere to a mixed
bag. You've got to combine certain qualities belonging to a
doctor, engineer, psychologist and sometimes even an actor in
addition to knowing your specific art well."

At its best, the relationship between trainer and boxer is that of mentor to student. Like the wise elders of some ancient tribe, trainers initiate their young fighters into a violent, all-male world and teach them to triumph. In some cases—though by no means all—trainers are also concerned about the condition of their disciples' souls. Journalist W. C. Heinz once wrote, for example, "Ray Arcel is more concerned with the fighter than the fight."

In less abstract terms, trainers oversee a fighter's physical preparation for a fight (roadwork, sparring, diet, making the weight); analyze the weaknesses of the opponent; create a strategy for victory; advise their fighter in the corner between rounds; improvise last-minute strategic changes; and when necessary, stop a fight before their fighter is seriously injured—as Eddie Futch did in Joe Frazier's third bout with Muhammad Ali.

Trainers must also gain the trust of their boxers, who need to have absolute faith in the authenticity of the trainer's observations and instructions. The fighter, after all, literally risks his health—if not his life—based upon the trainer's counsel.

To win this trust, trainers become experts at how to—in Angelo Dundee's phrase—"blend" with their fighter. Every trainer in this book made the same point: the trainer must not impose a style upon his fighter but must enable the fighters' natural skills and inclinations to emerge. As Ray Arcel told me, "No two men are alike. Everybody has their own style. Never change a style. Improve it, but never change a style."

The obligation to focus on the fighter's individuality and needs forces trainers to become highly skilled at suppressing their own egos. As Freddie Brown once said, "The first thing a trainer should realize is that he must let the fighter take credit for all his successes."

At times the only way to convince a fighter to do what the trainer wants is to trick the fighter into thinking that a particular innovation is the fighter's own idea. The fighter, after all, is the star, and sometimes a moody millionaire as well—particularly in these days of fantastic purses at the highest level of the sport.

Training fighters can be supremely frustrating. Charley Goldman, trainer of Rocky Marciano, explained it this way: "It's the
guys who have a good chance to win who drive you crazy.... A
fighter taking a one-sided beating can't be helped. You get
ulcers from the guy who is in a spot to become the boss and
doesn't do it." As one ex-boxer told me, "A lot of fighters broke a
lot of trainers' hearts."

But trainers are patient men, like Eddie Futch, who once
spent six months showing a young middleweight how to properly throw a left hook. In the boxing world, trainers endure;
fighters come and go. Fighters' careers are sometimes brilliant,
but always brief, while trainers continue to collect wisdom by
observing generation after generation of combatants.

When I write that a man has "trained" a fighter, I use the phrase
broadly to indicate that the trainer has acted as instructor, conditioner, chief second and cut man—phrases which require some
explaining. If a trainer's role was more limited, I make that clear.

Detailing the less glamorous aspects of the responsibilities of
an instructor and conditioner, Whitey Bimstein once said, "In
the gymnasium we have to stay with them [fighters], watch
them box, go through their calisthenics and take them in hand,
massage them and look after them like a mother would fondle a
baby. At the end of a day's work, the trainers have to weigh
their fighters and then give them instructions on what to do
until the next day, prescribe the food they should eat and how
much water they should drink. I have had a good many fighters
who would deliberately make it harder for us because they
insisted on breaking training."

The term "chief second" refers to the man who is in charge of
all activity in his fighter's corner in the sixty seconds between
rounds. In most cases, a trainer acts as chief second for his
fighter. Often the fighter's manager is also in the corner, as well
as men who assist the chief second.

The chief second controls the application of ice and Vaseline and determines how the fighter sits, when the fighter is cleaned off, when he takes in water and when he spits it out. As the actions of each trainer in this book demonstrate, of course, the chief second's responsibilities are more complex than this brief outline indicates.

"They say a second has only sixty seconds to perform the functions of surgeon, nursemaid, general and comforting friend," Ray Arcel pointed out in a 1953 interview, "but when you subtract the time spent getting into and out of the ring, you actually have little more than forty seconds."

While punches are being exchanged, the chief second never takes his eyes off the ring. Moments before the round ends, the chief second—usually with stool in hand—waits to climb the steps into the ring. Once the fighter is seated, the chief second removes the fighter's mouthpiece and wipes off his face. The chief second is usually the only one who speaks in the corner, attempting to limit his advice to clear, simple sentences. If the fighter is cut, the chief second either tends to the wound himself or has the cut man do it.

A cut man is a specialist who is responsible for closing wounds and controlling swelling on the fighter's face during the bout. Most trainers prefer to act as their own cut man, but specialists are sometimes hired exclusively for this role. Freddie Brown, for example, was Rocky Marciano's cut man during most of Marciano's championship fights.

Seconds have been known to yell at, plead with—and even strike—their fighters in order to spur them on to victory. They will do anything to get their fighter's attention, as veteran manager and corner man Al Braverman explained to me: "When a fighter looks away from you, rip his chin off 'til he looks you right in the eye. Then you know he's listening to you. Otherwise it's just window dressing. There isn't a fighter I've worked with if he don't look at me he gets a crack in the face. I take a little piece of hair out of the top of his head. I'll pinch his chin off. They gotta pay attention. I'm there to win."

Others prefer a calmer approach. An excessively demonstrative second can merely alienate a fighter. In his role as a television commentator, Sugar Ray Leonard watched a trainer berate his fighter and observed that if anyone spoke to him like that during a fight, "I would knock the guy out."

Corner men are often masters at stretching the rules on their fighter's behalf. One of today's most visible seconds, Lou Duva, told me, "I'll do anything in the world—legal or on the brink of illegal—to give my fighter an edge."

The best seconds also display a presence of mind that withstands even the notoriously chaotic conditions of championship prize fights. Where others might panic, seconds must say and do the right thing.

On occasion a chief second is brought in to run a fighter's corner even though another man has trained that fighter—supervised his daily regimen. In recent years, Angelo Dundee has worked this way.

Corner Men does not claim to be a definitive history of boxing trainers. A study such as that would have to go back at least as far as James Figg, the father of British boxing, who is reported to have been the best boxing instructor in 18th-century England. Details about Figg and other early boxing teachers can be found in Elliot J. Gorn's *The Manly Art: Bare-Knuckle Prize Fighting in America*. Readers interested in the great trainers of the early gloved era in America should seek out Nat Fleischer's 1929 pamphlet *How to Second a Fighter* for information about trainers and managers such as Bill Brady, Billy Gibson, Jimmy Bronson, Leo P. Flynn, Bill Duffy, Spider Kelly and Bill Delaney. Another pioneering trainer who deserves mention is Jimmy DeForrest, who trained Jack Dempsey when he destroyed Jess Willard in 1919. DeForrest himself put out a pamphlet promising to reveal "boxing secrets of champions." The November

1929 issue of *The Ring* advertised the work for "the amazingly small price of only $2.98—reduced from its former price of $37.50."

My own book tells the story of more recent trainers. The careers of Ray Arcel, Mannie Seamon and Whitey Bimstein pretty much began when Stillman's Gym opened in 1920, though Arcel and Seamon started out at Grupp's Gymnasium in Harlem before Lou Stillman was in the boxing business. They were later joined at Stillman's by Charley Goldman, Freddie Brown and Al Silvani, among others. In the late 1940s, Angelo Dundee began his internship at Stillman's as a bucket carrier.

The two other trainers treated at length in *Corner Men* have only marginal connections to Stillman's. Most of the trainers of Stillman's, however, saw their best heavyweights destroyed by Joe Louis. Louis' first trainer, Jack Blackburn, also receives his own chapter. Though Eddie Futch visited Stillman's in the 1940s, his start in boxing came at the Brewster Recreation Center in Detroit where one of his fellow students of pugilism was Joe Louis.

Corner Men begins with "Angelo Dundee and his Mentors," a look at the most highly publicized modern trainer. Rather than detailing the familiar story of Dundee's work in the corners of Ali and Sugar Ray Leonard, I focus on his recollections of his early days at Stillman's. I also use Dundee's comments as an introduction to the profession of training prize fighters.

"Stillman's Gym" chronicles the lore of the most famous gym in boxing history—and the home of most of the trainers treated in this book. Here Ray Arcel also provides a detailed account of how Stillman's moved downtown from Harlem to become a New York City midtown institution.

My chapter on Ray Arcel tells the story of a trainer who—after seven decades in the boxing world—has achieved something like the status of a saint.

From Dundee and Arcel, two venerable living trainers, I move backward in time with chapters on their colleagues Jack Blackburn, Charley Goldman, Whitey Bimstein, Mannie Seamon, and Freddie Brown.

The final chapters deal with Al Silvani and Eddie Futch, two contemporary trainers whose careers—like those of Dundee and Arcel—span several generations of boxers. Silvani's fighters included middleweight champions Jake La Motta, Rocky Graziano and Nino Bevenuti. Futch trained, among countless others, Joe Frazier and Ken Norton, the only two fighters to beat Muhammad Ali in his prime.

I also spoke with three veteran West Coast trainers—George Chemeres of Seattle, Washington; Ted Walker of Carson City, Nevada; and Johnny Tocco of Johnny Tocco's Ringside Gym in Las Vegas—who clearly would warrant their own chapters. I only regret that I didn't have the time to include them, and would like nothing more than to write about them at length in the future. I feel the same regret at being unable to include corner men George Benton and Lou Duva who were kind enough to grant me interviews. Their careers continued to reach new heights as I wrote *Corner Men*. An attempt to summarize their work in this book seemed, therefore, premature.

In discussing the great trainers of the era of Stillman's Gym, I have not gone into great detail about Nick and Dan Florio, Jimmy August, Chickie Ferrara, Bill Gore, Harry Lenny, Pop Miller or Izzy Kline. Again, no slights against their substantial accomplishments are intended. Like any writer, I was merely constrained by time and space limitations and the information available to me.

Also excluded, students of boxing will note, is Cus D'Amato, mentor to Mike Tyson, Floyd Patterson and Jose Torres. I've not treated D'Amato because he's fully covered in the recent avalanche of material about Tyson and because D'Amato was as much a manager as a trainer.

Other intriguing corner men such as Doc Kearns, Jack Hurley (who had Billy Petrolle and Harry "Kid" Matthews) and George Gainford (who managed Sugar Ray Robinson) were left

out also because they are thought of mostly as managers rather
than trainers. They were as famous for their deal-making skills
as their genius for coaching boxers.

In writing *Corner Men* I've tried to preserve as much of the
trainers' extraordinary language as possible. For my chapters on
Dundee, Arcel, Futch and Silvani, I've quoted liberally from my
interviews with them, as well as comments they've made to
various newspapermen over the years. In the cases of Blackburn, Goldman, Seamon, Bimstein and Brown—all of whom
have passed away—I've relied on published interviews in which
they are quoted, in addition to my own interviews with their
fellow boxing men, friends and family members.

My practice of quoting from newspaper reports raises a few
questions. First, how accurately did reporters record the words
of sports figures in the years I'm writing about? Harold Conrad,
who covered boxing for *The Brooklyn Eagle* and *The New York
Mirror* from the mid-1930s through the late 1940s, told me,
"Hey, when I was writing boxing there were a lot of giants
around," referring to the famous writers of the era. Many of the
writers "had great imaginations" Conrad added, which they
sometimes employed to enhance their reporting. Nat Loubet,
former editor and publisher of *The Ring* agreed, saying that
writers often "put words in people's mouths in order to make
good columns." Harry Markson, long-time President of Madison Square Garden Boxing, was somewhat less skeptical.
While conceding that many "good newspaper men" used their
creative powers to enhance their copy, Markson concluded, "I
would say by and large the substance of their quotes would
stand up."

Fight men who were around boxing from the 1930s through
the 1950s also report that many boxing writers were on the
payrolls of managers and promoters who paid cash to ensure
that their fighters received as much positive coverage as possible. It's safe to conclude, therefore, that some newspaper sto-

ries were inspired by something less than an objective passion for the truth.

Jimmy Breslin, who covered boxing early in his career, said he doesn't give much credence to quotes from boxers. "I never trust any of them. I mean, they make up lines for the Bush Administration ... why shouldn't they make up lines for Rocky Graziano or Rocky Marciano?"

Yet Breslin, who befriended Charley Goldman and Whitey Bimstein, says most of the trainers at Stillman's were good talkers and very likely deserve credit for the best lines that were attributed to them. With the exception of excellent writers such as W. C. Heinz, Red Smith and a few others, Breslin maintained, most writers "wouldn't know how to make up the lines" that were credited to Goldman, Bimstein and their contemporaries.

Besides, Breslin explained, trainers acted as informal press agents for their fighters and themselves, so collecting good stories was part of their job. "In those days they had to be able to tell anecdotes for newspapers—to get in the newspapers—to get space for the fighter. It wasn't just idle gossip. They were good storytellers, and would do anything to get the story in the papers. They would spend a lot of time around with these sportswriters. They were gettin' their own names in, too, but they always helped the game. It was a nice era. It's all gone now."

Keeping all this advice in mind, I've used quotes which seem historically accurate, citing the source in my text whenever possible. Although the trainers in some cases no doubt employed hyperbole when telling their tales, this seems like a legitimate device of the narrative tradition they embody.

Statements made by trainers about their own fighters should also be seen in context. When a trainer is being paid by a fighter, he obviously is unlikely to criticize that fighter in the press. If a trainer and a fighter part company, the trainer's words may be tainted by bitterness. Trainers' remarks, therefore, are sometimes best appreciated in the way a brilliant lawyer's arguments can be savored despite their obvious bias.

If trainers have one intellectual habit in common, it's a tendency to give overly rational analyses of boxing matches. Trainers always have an explanation when their man loses. Usually it's that a fighter failed to follow their advice. Like most people, trainers don't tell many stories about disasters that were their own fault.

Though the post-World War II boxing scene was a great moment in boxing history, it was also, of course, tarnished by the scandal of organized crime involvement, personified by Frankie Carbo, the man who ran boxing for the mob. Those interested in a serious treatment of organized crime influence on boxing should see *Beyond the Ring: The Role of Boxing in American Society* by Jeffrey T. Sammons.

The list of boxers allegedly involved with Frankie Carbo is long and filled with many prestigious names. The extent of Carbo's impact on boxing is, however, beyond the scope of this book. Carbo usually did his business with fight managers, demanding a percentage of a fighter in exchange for various illegal favors, though there are also stories of him directly threatening fighters unless they cooperated with him. While describing mob influence on boxing, one boxing veteran put it this way: "If your guy won the title, they were in." In 1961, Carbo—who had previously been imprisoned for manslaughter and clandestine control of fighters—was sent to jail for the rest of his life for his illegal and violent boxing-related activities.

It's difficult, however, to judge the impact of Carbo and his associates on a trainer's life. Asked about the effect of mobsters on the trainers he knew, Jimmy Breslin said, "Nobody mentioned them. It was like the hidden, secret sin—Frankie Carbo. That's the business end. Your job is just the fighter. What are you gonna do? Are you gonna make statements and change America? It couldn't be done. That's a hell of a thing to say, but it's true. It couldn't be done. . . . I mean, what shot did you have causing trouble?"

My final concern has been that I not sentimentalize the trainers covered in this book, though I clearly admire them greatly. While working on *Corner Men*, I've been haunted by a remark veteran press agent Irving Rudd made to me about "young writers" and their "sentimental stories" of boxing men who would have "stolen pennies off the eyes of a dead man."

None of the trainers discussed in *Corner Men* would steal those pennies, but I've taken Rudd's words as a warning.

Although it is easy to romanticize trainers because of their intelligence and personal charms, I've tried to remain aware that their legendary stature results from their talent for instructing one man how to best beat the daylights out of another. Within this ironic mix of civility and toughness lies the allure of their brutal yet oddly scholarly profession.

ANGELO DUNDEE counsels SUGAR RAY LEONARD between rounds during Leonard's 1987 victory over Marvelous Marvin Hagler.
PHOTO CREDIT: ASSOCIATED PRESS

ANGELO DUNDEE

AND HIS MENTORS

I know you got to blend yourself to the fighter if you're going to be of any use to the fighter. Because if you don't, then you're a stiff."

These are the words of Angelo Dundee, describing one requirement for being a successful boxing trainer—knowing when to be self-effacing.

No one speaks about boxing with more joy and exhilaration than Dundee. When the casual fight fan thinks of a boxing trainer, Angelo Dundee is no doubt the first who comes to mind. Dundee has been famous since the late 1950s, when he worked in the corner of champion Carmen Basilio, in Basilio's two brutal middleweight title fights with Sugar Ray Robinson. But Dundee became a genuine modern celebrity while serving as corner man for Muhammad Ali, the fighter who redefined ideas about just how famous a sports figure might become. Later, Dundee's association with Sugar Ray Leonard, boxing's second-most lionized figure of recent years, confirmed Dundee's role as the best-known trainer around, a beloved classic.

1

My purpose in meeting with Dundee, however, is not to coax him into shedding more light on his well-documented association with Ali or Leonard: It is to solicit his thoughts on the art of training fighters and his memories of his apprenticeship at Stillman's Gym in New York City in the late 1940s and early 1950s. This is when Dundee learned his trade by working "as the bucket guy" for the best trainers of the day. "I learned from the cream of the crème," Dundee explains, engagingly colliding the phrases "crème de la crème" and "cream of the crop."

In those days, Dundee slept in room 711 of the Capitol Hotel—a room which served by day as the office of his older brother, the powerful fight promoter Chris Dundee. The office featured a small studio couch and one closet, which was all Dundee needed. "So that was where I lived," he recalls. "And that was like six days a week—no, seven days a week—boxing, boxing, boxing, boxing."

Though he happily concedes that in New York he was merely "the available kid around that area" and that his job was only to "go here, go there," it was clearly an enchanted time for Dundee. He considered himself fortunate to be occupying the same space as the great trainers and managers of the era—"all those guys who were in New York City at that time when it was the mecca of boxing."

"I never trained nobody up in New York City," Dundee stresses. "I just observed. I worked, I worked corners. I observed. You know, fight guys are the most free-hearted people in the world." His approach to his internship was simple: "What I did was keep my mouth shut and my eyes open."

So many admiring words have been written about Dundee's prowess as a trainer and his genuine amiability, that it seems almost redundant to admire him some more. But a few stories are essential by way of introduction. Like any celebrity, Dundee has over the years accumulated a collection of standard anecdotes—often-told tales that he obligingly and lovingly exhibits in magazine profiles, television interviews and in his autobiography, *I Only Talk Winning*. And they are excellent stories, filled with instances in which Dundee's quick thinking and talent for inspiring his fighter saved Ali from danger or urged Leonard on to victory. The stories sometimes sound almost too corny—too much like an old-fashioned movie—to be true, but they certainly are.

In a bout in London in 1963, Muhammad Ali—not yet heavyweight champion and still known as Cassius Clay—was floored by a left hook from British heavyweight Henry Cooper. The knockdown came in the final seconds of the fourth round. After regaining his feet, Ali returned to the corner in a daze, his legs wobbly. The film of that fight reveals an expression of confusion, even self-doubt, that never returned during Ali's years as champion. After the first round of the fight, Dundee had noticed a small tear in Ali's glove, but, as Dundee now confesses, "I didn't bring it to anybody's attention because we were kicking the hell out of Cooper." With Ali's undefeated record in jeopardy, however, Dundee acted quickly. As he said in a 1983 interview with Randy Gordon in *Sport* magazine, "I went over to the referee and said, 'Hey, my guy has a split glove.' The referee came over to see. Sure as God made green apples the glove is split on the side. The glove had been split from the first round. The threads had come loose. But when this happened, I took my finger and pulled it over a little bit more." By the time it was determined that a replacement glove could not be found, Dundee had revived his fighter, and Ali went on to score a knockout in the next round.

Fight fans can by now practically move their lips in unison while listening to Dundee tell the story of the split glove, yet its appeal endures for obvious reasons: So great is the trainer's allegiance to his fighter that he is not above bending the rules—cheating, some might say—to ensure victory. It's as if Dundee, the benevolent mentor to the young and gifted Ali, had secured a special dispensation from above, granting momentary immunity from the rules of boxing. Who wouldn't want a protector with Dundee's poise and powers of improvisation?

Dundee again intervened in Miami in 1964 when Ali—still unproven as a professional fighter and a profound underdog in the fight—challenged that most menacing and sullen of fighters, Sonny Liston, for the heavyweight championship. While Ali appeared to be too fast and too elusive for Liston during the early going, in the fifth round, Ali was temporarily blinded, and he returned to his corner in a panic. Dundee provided something like the definitive version of the story for Randy Gordon in 1983: "Clay got something in his eyes. It was either from Sonny Liston's left eye, which was cut and had medication on it, or from Liston's shoulder, which was injured and had liniment on it. So, at the end of the fifth round, he walked back to me and said, 'Cut the gloves off! I want to prove there's dirty work afoot!' I said, 'You ain't gonna prove nothin'. Sit down.' So I sat him down and began cleaning out his eyes with water. . . . When the bell rang, I shoved Clay out of the corner as I was talking to him a mile a minute. 'C'mon now, c'mon now, box this guy. Move! Run!'" Ali's eye cleared up halfway through the round, and he won the championship when Liston quit on his stool before the start of the seventh round.

Another trainer whose resumé dates back to Stillman's Gym, Al Silvani, was at ringside for the Ali-Liston fight and credits Dundee with saving Ali. Ali "wanted to quit in the corner," Silvani recalls. "Angelo pushed him out. Clay said he couldn't see. He actually said, 'Cut my gloves off.' What does that mean? Now if you're jerky enough to cut 'em off, the fight's over."

If Dundee's efforts in Ali's fights with Cooper and Liston were his most celebrated bits of corner work for Ali, then his advice to Sugar Ray Leonard after the twelfth round of Leonard's 1981 welterweight unification bout with Thomas Hearns is surely Dundee's most famous work on Leonard's behalf.

Though Hearns had been wobbled by Leonard earlier in the fight, Hearns' blows had practically closed Leonard's left eye, and Hearns was well on his way to winning the judges' decision. Clearly, Leonard needed to come on strong to win. Working on reducing the swelling on Leonard's eye, Dundee leaned down and, in perhaps the most often quoted words of any cornerman in boxing history, presented the facts to his fighter: "You've got nine minutes," he shouted. "You're blowing it, son. You're blowing it. This is what separates the men from the boys. You're blowing it." Leonard, of course, turned the fight around and went on to knock out Hearns in the fourteenth round.

Add to Dundee's knack for quick-thinking, then, both the courage to present a millionaire superstar with the truth and the presence of mind to inspire a fighter to change a losing pattern.

Dundee's friend and fellow corner man Johnny Tocco, proprietor of the famed Ringside Gym in Las Vegas, says admiringly, "Angelo's a great motivator. He motivates these guys. If he has to cuss 'em, he cusses 'em. . . . Angelo's one of these great guys that can see what's happening, and he's the kind of guy that can say, 'Hey, now look, this is what you've been doin' and this is what you gotta do. Now let's go to work.'" Tocco speaks from experience: he's worked a corner for Sonny Liston, Larry Holmes and many other champions.

Repeating tributes to Dundee's inspirational feats must be done cautiously. No one, least of all Dundee, wants to give him credit for his fighters' deeds. Compliment him on inspiring Leonard against Hearns and Dundee will say, "Thanks, but Ray did the fighting." As Dundee carefully explains, "You know how to lick that other guy. But you gotta have the guy to do the number." That is, if a fighter can't fight, the best trainer in the world can't help him. The fighter, Dundee stresses, is "the hero. He's the guy. We [trainers] are secondary guys. We're not I, I, I. You can't be an 'I' guy. I'm not an 'I' guy."

At the age of sixty-nine, Dundee is compact and graceful. He's not a tall man, but his arms and hands appear quite powerful. Dundee's well-tanned, round face is pleasant—even jolly. He looks as if he could be the owner of a prosperous, informal restaurant which flourishes because of its proprietor's gift for making customers feel welcome. Behind the thick lenses of his glasses, he is bright-eyed and enthusiastic like a smart child. When he speaks about boxing he's full of ideas. Good quotes flow from him like foam spilling over the top of a glass of beer: his speech is carbonated with memorable phrases. At the same time, Dundee is disarmingly eager to please. He seems unspoiled by his fame.

Dundee is also an extremely sensitive man. Greeting me in his large, neat office atop a Miami office building, he immediately says he's sorry that he could not meet me a few weeks earlier in New York—sorry that I had to travel to Florida to see him. True to his reputation as the most obliging man in boxing, Dundee appears to be happy only when everyone in the room is happy. He has a joke for the waitress in the local luncheonette, and one for the elderly maintenance man at the gym where Dundee's fighters work out. "The old man, I treat him like he's the boss," Dundee confides. Dundee's endless supply of genuine modesty and charm has served him well over the years when dealing with the outsized egos that fill the boxing business. Almost everyone likes Angelo Dundee.

Behind Dundee's desk is a painting portraying his world champions: Ali, Leonard, Carmen Basilio, Sugar Ramos, Luis Rodriguez, Jose Napoles, Willie Pastrano, Ralph Dupas, Jimmy Ellis and Pinklon Thomas. Framed magazine covers feature Ali and Leonard, and there's a photo of Cassius Clay, aged 18, heartbreakingly beautiful and bulging with muscles and youthful energy.

Dundee shows his passion for his work by lovingly expanding on any aspect of the game. "The technique of wrapping hands is a study in its own right," he says, recalling what he learned from watching old-time trainer Jimmy August who handled middleweight and light-heavyweight champion Dick

Tiger. "Jimmy August, I used to watch him. He was a very smooth hand wrapper. I used to watch him wrap Dick Tiger. See, the whole key to wrapping your hands is not puttin' it up front, like loading your fist, that's baloney. What you're actually doing, you're not making a lethal weapon, you're protecting the fighter's hands. That's his bread and butter. And each hand's a different type of a wrap study. One fighter you wrap one way, another fighter you wrap another way."

To demonstrate his point, Dundee refers to a picture of Ali, whose sometimes brittle hands Dundee wrapped with, of all things, sanitary napkins. "I used to use Kotex on his hands because he had protruding knuckles," Dundee says. "Now I use this technique to this day to protect a guy's hands."

Dundee offers another brief discourse on how he sizes up an arena on the night of a fight: "You go to a fight out of town, a very important thing is to go look at that arena—where it's at. The location of the dressing rooms. Where are you at? Are you here or there? How far is it to get to the ring? If there's no john in the dressing room, where's the available john? Very important. Little things, but important. You gotta know where these things are. So when you get there you don't walk into a . . . you know, like it's all strange to you. You wanta get rid of that strangeness, you wanta make it smooth."

Dundee constantly strives for smoothness, a lack of friction. He hates the unexpected and has made a religion out of always being prepared. "I prepare my fighters for every eventuality," he says. "And you yourself have to be exactly the same way. You got to be pliable. You got to be ready for whatever's gonna happen. You don't know what the heck's gonna happen. So if a situation happens, you're prepared for it."

How does Dundee maintain his concentration—and his calm—amid the chaos and confusion that inevitably engulf a boxing ring before a big fight? "I tune myself out. First of all, with the confusion, I don't even know it's there. And all I do is centralize my thinking on the fighter. So I don't know that anyone's around. If a guy says to me, 'Geez, I was looking right at you and you didn't say hello,'. . . well, I'm not looking at him, I'm looking at my fighter. What I do is I look across the ring and I visualize what I gotta do and I contain myself within that thing that's round me."

During the fight itself, Dundee says, "You got to get the flow of the fight. Your guy might be doing things he shouldn't be doing out there, so you got to tell him, 'Hey.' Don't tell him what he's doing, tell him what he's *not* doing."

Dundee meticulously prepares for a fight by placing each piece of equipment in a pre-determined place—Vaseline, Q-tips, gauze, scissors, various coagulants for stopping cuts. "I innately know where to get my stuff. I know where it's at," he says. "You gotta be prepared. So I open everything and I make sure everything's in position. And bang. Cut. Automatic. Bing, bing. You know. Bing, bing. And I'm ready to go."

Owing no doubt to this intense concentration, Dundee recalls details and lessons learned from fights that took place twenty or thirty years ago—and takes pride in applying the lessons to the current boxing scene.

Dundee, for example, uses Carmen Basilio's 1957 victory over Sugar Ray Robinson for the middleweight championship to lead to a point about Mike Tyson, who has knocked out two of Dundee's fighters—Trevor Berbick and Pinklon Thomas. "The first Robinson fight I was like a pig in slop," says Dundee. "He outboxed Robinson. Left hand, he was poppin' him. See, a little guy can outbox a tall guy. It's where you get the positioning of your feet. 'Cause the [tall] guy's gotta reach down for you. You don't have the power when you're punching down. It's something you learn." Dundee, therefore, is not surprised that Tyson, a short heavyweight, is able to outbox many taller men.

Dundee again takes an historical leap when remembering how his left-handed fighter, Andy Arel, "raised all kinds of hell" for the legendary master boxer Willie Pep in 1955. "Learned an object lesson. Pep used to circle. See, you don't make circles with a southpaw. What you gotta do is be first with everything you do. If you circle, you give a southpaw momentum. They say, 'Why a southpaw?' Well, because a left-handed fighter comes at you from a different direction—a different balance, a different flow, a different blend. You gotta fight them different ways. In fact, I'm fighting a southpaw in New York City. And I'm going to use my teachings from that far back to make this guy lick that southpaw." (While Dundee's point was elegantly made, his fighter ended up losing to the lefty a few weeks later at the Felt Forum in New York. Historical precedence only counts for so much in boxing.)

Though Dundee likes to draw analogies between fighters from different eras, like all great trainers he stresses that each fighter is unique. "There's no two alike. You don't say, 'This guy fights like this guy.' They don't. They're all individuals. They all got their own idiosyncrasies, got their own rhythm. I've never seen two of the same fighters."

Dundee also labors to understand the needs of each fighter's psyche. "Certain guys, you cannot have the audacity to tell 'em, 'Look. I want you to do this.' Ain't gonna do 'this.' 'Why do I have to do this? I'm doing the fighting. Why do I have to do what you tell me? You can't perform like I can.' True, I can't. But certain guys will take that kind of direction—forceful direction. Other guys won't. They reject it. And what the heck, if they're talented—which they are, fighters are talented individuals—you gotta approach them from whatever angle's there. You take what's out there for you."

Training fighters, Dundee says with a laugh, "is like trying to catch a fish. It's technique, not strength. You got to play that fish nice and easy. And go with what's there."

"Nice and easy"—the words are very characteristic of Dundee. As a trainer, he says, "you gotta blend into any kind of a scene." And the word "blend" comes up again and again as Dundee describes a trainer's need to suppress his own ego to get the results he wants. The man who counseled Muhammad Ali on how to destroy Frazier, who schemed with Sugar Ray Leonard to humiliate Roberto Duran, dislikes confrontations outside the ring. It's one of the pleasing ironies of his character.

In fact, Dundee won't take on a new fighter unless he feels completely welcome in the fighter's camp. "You never like to come on a scene where you're going to create sparks. You don't want that. Because what you want—you want continuity. You want warmth. 'Cause I gel off of warmth. You can't gel off of sidelong glances and stuff like that. Not that I'm a goody-goody, but you don't get the job done. And the whole key is to get that fighter ready. And if anything like that is jeopardizing anything, you don't want to walk in on that scene. You abstain. In a nice way. Like I get offered things to do, and I turn them down, not for any reason. I just don't like to walk into a scene where I'm gonna create a problem for that fighter. Because you're not helping a fighter. Let's be realistic. If a guy's not going to be cool and comfortable with a situation, you don't walk in. So you gotta be able to blend into scenes."

This is not to suggest that Dundee can't be tough once he's working with a fighter. "You're not the same guy all the time," he says. "You can't be an even-keel kind of guy. You gotta create things that are gonna help that fighter. And if it means gruffness and it means pushing him and it means trying to put the bull on him, you gotta do it. Because the end result is you want to get that fighter juiced to try to win the fight. The name is winning. You gotta win."

Dundee once complained with mock outrage, "No one really knows what a good talker I am, 'cause I'm always with Ali, and he never shuts up." Yet his delicate way with words has been amply chronicled over the years.

Dundee's unique verbal style is reminiscent of a hip jazz musician who came of age in the big band era. A restaurant, hotel or even a country is always "a joint." To assure you that he's telling you the truth, he emphasizes that his point is "legit."

When he is excited, he's "juiced." Before a fight, he wants his fighter "loose as a goose." A victorious fighter "did a number" on his opponent. A hard-hitting fighter is always a "banger." A clever boxer is a "cutey." A boxer taking on a puncher must "play checkers with the guy." Most impressive of all, perhaps, Dundee can refer to his fighters as "my guy," "my kid," or even "son" without sounding patronizing. And that's something accomplished.

Dundee savors distinctions and chooses his words carefully. When asked by *New York Times* columnist Red Smith whether the word "luminous" properly described Muhammad Ali, Dundee replied that "opaque" was the more accurate term, "because you can't see through this kid." Asked by Smith to compare the young Sugar Ray Leonard to the young Ali, Dundee deftly refused to be pushed into a corner: "I can't compare him to Ali. . . . Ali was too intricate, too many interests. This kid is home cookin'."

Dundee can also be quite funny—even during a fight, as Phil Berger of *The New York Times* reported in his 1981 profile of Dundee. When light-heavyweight champion Willie Pastrano was in danger of losing his title against Terry Downes in England in 1964, Dundee smacked Pastrano hard on the rear end in the corner. When Pastrano got angry and lunged at Dundee, Dundee screamed, "Don't be mad at me! I ain't takin' your title! There's the chump over there you should be mad at! He's takin' your title, sucker!" Pastrano won the fight with an eleventh-round knockout.

When Dundee was accused of loosening the ropes in the ring before Ali's famous rope-a-dope victory over George Foreman in Zaire, Africa—a charge he vehemently denies—Dundee replied disdainfully, "My guy would have won if they fought in a phone booth." Before that same fight, Dundee, frustrated at a postponement of the match, told a reporter, "I was so bored I was teaching the lizards to do push-ups."

Prior to the second Leonard-Duran fight, Dundee demonstrated his verbal dexterity by showing how to conceal an accusation within a series of compliments and jokes. "Don't get me wrong," Dundee said, "I'm the biggest admirer of Duran. But the reason he has problems with tall guys is because he can't use his head against them. He uses his head as a pivot in the clinches. His head is definitely a weapon. Maybe we should put a glove on it." Another time, Dundee offered Duran a classic back-handed compliment when he observed, "Duran has his own unique way of throwing his right hand, left hook and left knee at the same time."

Though Dundee's one-liners can be so bad they're good, his more serious comments about boxing can be quite moving. His finest rhetorical flights tend to be inspired by his boxers' greatest victories and defeats. When Sugar Ray Leonard lost a fifteen-round decision in his first fight with Roberto Duran in June of 1980, Dundee responded like a quintessential good father: "Ray Leonard did not lose his title last night. In my eyes and in my heart he's still the champion of the world, and he always will be a champion. Ray Leonard was born a champion and will be a champion until the day he dies." After Leonard humiliated Duran in the rematch, Dundee was duly boastful: "We took everything away from him. . . . When he tried to box with us, Ray jabbed his head off. When he tried to muscle Ray on the ropes, my guy banged him to the body with both hands and spun him like a baby. We knew everything Duran was going to try, and we were ready for it. In the end, Duran quit like the bully he is."

But Dundee has never been more articulate or moving than on the night of Ali's 1980 doomed attempt to come out of retirement to challenge undefeated heavyweight champ Larry Holmes. Prior to the fight, Dundee expressed his loyalty to Ali while simultaneously forecasting a difficult night for the ex-champion: "I was with him in the beginning, I've been with him in every circumstance and every condition, and I want to be with him at the end."

The fight itself proved to be a disaster as Ali, age thirty-eight, seemed defenseless against Holmes who finally held back, appearing to take pity. It was Ali's worst night in a ring—surely one of the worst nights of his life and Dundee's, too.

Finally, after ten rounds, Dundee decided to stop the fight. But Drew Bundini Brown, one of Ali's seconds at ringside—the highly volatile man credited with inventing Ali's motto, "Float like a butterfly, Sting like a bee"—wanted Ali to continue. According to *Sports Illustrated*, when Bundini grabbed Dundee's sweater and begged for "one more round," Dundee screamed, "Take your goddamned hands off me. He can't take any more. He's defenseless. Get the hell away from me. I'm the boss here. It's over."

The next morning, Dundee told the press, "I didn't do good business last night. It was a horrible night. I seen an Ali, couldn't do nothing. He just wasn't there. I hope he won't fight again, but you know I don't tell him what to do. Nobody does."

One quote from Dundee, however, summarizes Dundee's importance to Ali, his immense powers of observation and his gifts as a speaker. Dundee's words were recorded in a 1975 column by Dave Anderson of *The New York Times*. Here are Dundee's memories of what he noticed before Muhammad Ali—in one of the greatest upsets in boxing history—regained the heavyweight championship by defeating George Foreman in Zaire, Africa in 1974:

> Over in Zaire, my guy trained at noon, then Foreman trained at two o'clock in the same place. I spied on Foreman from the doorway behind the stage in the big hall we used, sometimes from behind the curtain in the cafeteria at the other end. I noticed that Foreman would go for hand feints. I noticed that when he got somebody on the ropes, he could move good to his left but not to his right; he got his legs crossed to his right. I noticed that when he got his jab going, he

was all right but I knew my guy would give him too much motion. I told my guy that he could feint Foreman, that he could move him because in a clinch Foreman put both his feet together, he was off balance to be moved. I saw those things and I told my guy about them. He remembered because he knows that when I see things through my eyes, I see things.

When Dundee speaks, traditional English usage is, to say the least, stretched and malapropisms abound. Yet the language is utterly original and entirely Dundee's own—and it conveys exactly what Dundee knows in his heart. Of how many men can that truly be said?

Dundee's fame, as might be expected, has brought a few detractors. These critics—a small number of cynical boxing writers, other trainers, guys you meet at a gym—argue that no one really trained Ali. They tell you that—especially once Ali won the heavyweight title—the champion did as he pleased. To the critics, Dundee was a mere figurehead, yielding to Ali's moods, absorbing his histrionics without protest to maintain an association with the great Ali.

Former heavyweight champion Larry Holmes, who worked as a sparring partner to Ali, offers this assessment of Dundee: "Angelo Dundee never took a right hand or a left hook in his life, but he had somebody in front of him that did. Angelo didn't teach Muhammad Ali, Muhammad taught Angelo Dundee. . . . Dundee has a great philosophy, he talks a good show, he's a motivator. And that's what Angelo Dundee does: he motivates you. But Muhammad Ali's the fighter. He knew the rights and the lefts, and when to duck and when not to duck. And so Angelo Dundee became famous because of who? Muhammad Ali."

Dundee responded to his critics during his 1983 interview with Randy Gordon: "The training of Muhammad, or Cassius then, was a different blend than training anybody else. What you have to do is make the fighter feel like he's the innovator. Later on, in years to come, Muhammad would say, 'Angelo didn't train me.' Well, he was right. I didn't train him. I advised him. He'd be in the gym and I'd say, 'You're really putting your left hand into that jab. You're really snapping it.' Then, when I'd see him doing something right again, I'd say, 'Oh my God, I've never seen a heavyweight throw a left uppercut so perfectly. Oh boy!' Then he'd throw it again. And again."

The image of Dundee as a deft manipulator of Ali's legendary ego is reinforced by veteran boxing writer Harold Conrad, who became part of the Ali entourage. "Angelo was invaluable in the corner during a fight, and Ali knew that," Conrad says. Describing Dundee's approach to Ali, Conrad adds, "Angelo had it down to a science. He knew exactly when to make a point and when not to." Dundee also knew enough to "let Ali do the talking— which is what Ali wanted."

In a 1976 Red Smith column, Dundee expressed the joy of working with Ali. Here, Dundee, as always, focused on Ali's most innocent, least complicated self: "The secret is, he [Ali] truly enjoys what he does. And that's why in all these years, I never felt like walking away. With him, the scene always changes. He's the easiest fighter I ever worked with, never a moment of aggravation. I understand him. I know what turns him on. Some fighters tire of the drudgery. To him, it's dynamite."

Dundee prefers to talk about Ali the high-spirited, brilliant boxer, rather than Ali the moody upstart, the revolutionary who became a Muslim and refused to go to Vietnam. But Dundee's outlook helped Ali, and Ali has acknowledged the benefits of Dundee's unending faith. "Never told anybody, but I had doubts," Ali said in Gary Smith's 1987 *Sports Illustrated* profile of Dundee. "After Frazier beat me, after Spinks beat me. He made me believe again. Angelo really had more confidence in me than I did."

If Dundee is whispered to have been merely a front man in Ali's camp, he is also sometimes criticized for spending too little time with Leonard. Throughout Leonard's career, Dundee was in charge of selecting Leonard's opponents—which is an art unto itself requiring years of experience. "The whole thought when you got a young talent is to bring him up gradually to make him learn his profession without getting destroyed," Dundee explains. "A lot of guys make boo-boos, they take the wrong kinda opponents. You're not picking stiffs, you're picking guys to teach your fighter. How to handle height. How to handle a short guy. How to handle a quick guy. How to handle a tough guy. To be a champion, you gotta learn to handle all types, all sizes, all shapes."

Leonard's conditioning process was supervised by other trainers, and Dundee would arrive at training camp a few weeks before each fight to fine-tune strategy. Then, the night of the fight, Dundee would take over in Leonard's corner, sharing the spotlight with the talented and charismatic Leonard.

Dundee defends his methods this way: "All I really need is like three weeks. Because he's [Leonard's] gonna be training. He's gettin' in condition. And you know, I'm not a . . . I'm not a sweat wiper. So that's why I started coming in like two, three weeks before. What do I need? Just format him, or work on him—the work for the guy he's gonna be fighting. So meanwhile, I'm at home, I'm looking at tapes, going out of my mind studying the son of a bitch to see what's gonna work."

Finally, Dundee is taken to task for all of the media attention he receives, but as Dundee is the first to remind you, "in boxing you're selling just like in any other profession. You're selling your fighter." Dundee is in the business of convincing the public to pay money to see a fighter—and he needn't apologize for his considerable talent for publicity.

In his underrated book *Muhammad Ali*, novelist, critic and life-long fight fan Wildred Sheed summed up Dundee's role as Ali's unofficial press agent: "Dundee himself is a curious figure to find in the back of the [Ali] Promotion Machine. He loves publicity yet is a comfortable, homey man who'll kill a valuable hour talking fishing; he jokes with writers all day and plays poker with them at night, yet does not leave you with that slimy feeling on your hands that you frequently get from P.R. people."

Sheed's generous—yet open-eyed—appreciation of Dundee seems fair and accurate. And much of the criticism of Dundee seems like so much jealous sniping. It's easy to make the case that Dundee played a vital role in the career of Sugar Ray Leonard, as well as Muhammad Ali.

Before Leonard defeated Roberto Duran in their November 1980 rematch, Wiliam Nack of *Sports Illustrated* reported that Leonard sat with rapt attention as Dundee laid out the tactics that would frustrate the great Duran: "Keep the guy turning . . . hit him with shots coming in . . . belly jab . . . pivot off the ropes . . . spin out . . . slip the jab. . . . Move over! Don't go straight back . . . push him off you. . . . When you spin, stay there. And nail him!"

After Leonard's upset victory over middleweight champion Marvin Hagler in 1987, Dave Anderson of *The New York Times* described Dundee as a Michelangelo sculpting a boxing "masterpiece."

Anderson's assessment is backed up by veteran press agent Irving Rudd who was in Leonard's camp during the preparation for the Hagler fight. "I was in camp with Leonard for thirteen weeks, and let me tell you, Angelo Dundee won that fight," Rudd says. "Absolutely. I was there. I saw it taking shape. If Hagler had Angelo in his corner, Hagler would have knocked Leonard out."

Dundee recalls that when he arrived at Leonard's training camp, Rudd told him, "Ange, this guy don't look good. He's gonna get the shit kicked outta him." Dundee soon saw for himself that Leonard "was doing all the wrong things. A little thing like . . . in the clinch, Hagler's strength is his right side, not the left side, oddly enough. So Ray was trying to get outta the clinch to the right side. I said, 'No, go left.' He said, 'But I'm going to his left hand.' I said, 'Yeah, but the strength is his right hand. Because he's a converted right-handed fighter."

Rudd also praises Dundee's work in the corner during the fight. "What people don't remember, or couldn't hear or see," Rudd says, "is Angelo pounding the ring every once in a while, 'Hey, Marvin, where'd he go? There he is, Marvin. Look, he's behind you Marvin.' That had to have some kind of effect, you know. And if it didn't, it charged Leonard up anyway."

Leonard himself acknowledged Dundee's role in the victory. "Look at Angie! He's like a kid," Leonard told William Nack of *Sports Illustrated* as they reviewed a tape of the fight together. "I'm telling you, Angelo was great! . . . Boy, Angelo pumped me up there."

Before Leonard's next fight, Dundee and Leonard parted company owing to a dispute over a contract. Leonard then insisted that Dundee's absence had no effect on him. But Leonard's praise for Dundee immediately following the Hagler fight seems like a more accurate assessment of Dundee's importance.

The day after Leonard fought a controversial 1989 draw against old rival Thomas Hearns, Dundee—who didn't work in Leonard's corner—placed an early morning phone call to his old friend Johnny Tocco in Las Vegas. Dundee was eager to hear Tocco's expert, eyewitness assessment of the fight. "I tell you truthfully," Tocco says, "I think the guy [Dundee] still loves the guy [Leonard]."

All of the regulars from Stillman's Gym in the late '40s knew Angelo Dundee. "I remember Angelo coming out of the Army and he didn't know a left hook from a fish hook," says Irving Rudd. "I remember Angelo sleeping on a cot. That's where he slept. What he did was hang around. He carried the bucket. He carried the bags. He paid his dues. He learned. A different kind of fight game, a different kind of thing."

Dundee speaks with an abiding humility about the early days

when he resided in his brother Chris' office in the Capitol Hotel—"caddy corner to the old Garden, 51st and Eighth Avenue," as he evocatively puts it.

Sounding like a graduate student remembering his favorite professors, Dundee says, "I was lucky. I had all these guys at my disposal. We used to meet at the Ringside Cafeteria. It was across the street from Madison Square Garden, and all the guys would be there: Chickie Ferrara, Ray Arcel, Charley Goldman," Dundee recalls, citing three of the trainers to whom he became closest. "We'd all meet there because Stillman's was up the street on Eighth Avenue."

Dundee turns even a casual memory of running an errand to the office of Rocky Marciano's manager, Al Weill, into an encounter with boxing history: "Chris would send me with a message to Al Weill, and I'd go up to his office and I'd walk into a scene where he's berating the hell out of Marty Weill, his son. 'Dumb sucker, how could you put that four-round kid in without asking me . . . ba . . . ba . . . ba!' You know, that kind of stuff. But I met all these guys."

Dundee's self-effacement was both a natural inclination and a calculated strategy. "You know, bring the matchmaker at Madison Square a cup of coffee in the morning once I got to know him a little bit. 'Cause I don't want to push my way. I used to just sort of edge my way."

Edge his way he did, and today he still treasures the small lessons he learned by watching the great trainers of the era. "I used to watch all these guys," Dundee says. "You watch, you learn. You apply what you can utilize for yourself. You also watch how they work, you know, and the way they try to hustle guys. . . . Training techniques, everybody's different. God made us all different. So every trainer is different. And they're fascinatin'. You watch these guys work—how they do things. Some guys are gruff, but you got to be gruff sometimes. Sometimes you got to be wishy-washy, pat, you know, amiable. It's all according to what the project calls for."

Although Dundee frequently underplays his early boxing work by stressing that he was a mere "bucket guy," if asked, he'll discourse at length on the intricacies of working with a bucket during a fight. "You gotta know how to handle a bucket: put the bottle here, the ice there, not too much ice. Make sure it's wet enough so you can get the sponge into it—little things which are big things. I mean, if they're not done properly, you're in trouble. It's a profession. The simpler you make a thing the better off you are. 'Cause a lot guys, they got buckets, they tip 'em over. They wet newspaper guys; they don't know what they're doing. There's more to it than that."

Every experience was an opportunity for Dundee to learn. "I remember like it's yesterday, Ray Arcel working with Jackie Cranford who was a very nervous individual," he says. Arcel, of course, was one of the master trainers of the era. Jackie Cranford, Dundee recalls, was "*the* white hope then, in line to fight Joe Louis, legit. And I was around the fringes, I'm watching Ray playing cards with him, kidding with him to try to calm him down. Then finally Ray says, 'Ange, you watch him.' And I watched the store." The responsibility of killing time with a nervous fighter was a small triumph—an incremental move towards becoming a trainer.

Fondly describing the young Dundee as someone who knew how to say "please" and "thank you," Arcel remembers Dundee doing him favors and "not always sticking his hand out" for payment. "Angelo was smart and he kept his mouth shut," Arcel says. "He learned his trade."

Dundee also lingers over the story of the first time he wrapped a fighter's hands after his brother Chris sent him to the Fort Hamilton Arena in the Bronx to serve as an assistant to trainer Chickie Ferrara who was to become one of Dundee's most beloved teachers.

"I didn't know how to work with fighters," Dundee confesses. But Chickie Ferrara quickly initiated the young Dundee. "So Chickie throws two rolls of bandages and one roll of tape at me and says, 'Wrap his hands,'" Dundee recalls. "'I don't know how to wrap hands,' I said. I was embarrassed. I was looking around the room. But I wrapped this kid's hands." With a laugh, Dundee concludes, "My greatest thrill was that the kid won the fight without breaking his hands. And so, this was the beginning."

Ferrara, Dundee says with admiration, "was smooth. Chickie was good. He knew how to work. He loved boxing. Chickie Ferrara was just a nice, warm individual. Great guy. I loved him. I loved him like a brother. Chickie was the guy that brought me around a little bit. Stillman's Gym. Introduced me to people. You know, he was the ice breaker. 'Hey, this is Chris' kid brother, Angelo.' You know. And I met these people slowly and easy. Never busted into nothing."

Two of Ferrara's best-known fighters were Tommy Bell—who lost a fifteen-round decision for the welterweight championship to Sugar Ray Robinson in 1946—and Johnny Busso, who dropped a fifteen-round decision for the lightweight title to Joe Brown in 1959, though Busso had won a decision from Brown in a non-title bout the previous year.

Today, Busso, a product of New York's Lower East Side, strains to find the right words to express his debt to Chickie Ferrara. "With me and Chickie it was a personal affair," Busso says. "He brought me from a street fighter, a nothing, a nobody. Cultivated me, trained me, taught me, and I fought for the title. Which is like a guy painting a picture, let's say, and he comes up with a Picasso.

". . . All I can give for Chickie is utmost praise, and it's hard to explain the feeling," Busso says. "The guy, with me anyway, and with other people, was *devoted*—like you got a second father. The man was great. . . . Everything I ever was or am, or any success I achieved, was all to this man."

Busso also remembers Angelo Dundee's closeness to Ferrara. "Chickie taught Angelo," Busso says. Then, as if addressing Dundee directly, Busso looks into the tape recorder that is documenting his remarks and adds, "And Angelo, if you're listening to this or when you read it, I'll tell you that he taught you everything you know. He did."

But Dundee doesn't need to be reminded. Years after his days at Stillman's Gym, when Dundee was working with the hottest property in boxing, heavyweight champ Muhammad Ali, he repaid the trainers who helped him by using them in Ali's corner. Chickie Ferrara, for instance, worked in Ali's corner the night Ali was knocked down by Henry Cooper. "Chickie was working on him, putting the ice on his neck and his pants and everything else," Dundee recalls. "You know, it was so glorious in the early days of Cassius Clay. I used to hire guys. Naturally, I'd go to New York and it'd be Chickie. . . . See, I remembered all these guys. And I put 'em in the corner. Not for anything. They were always nice to me. And I'm grateful. And in my own little way I tried to repay them for their kindnesses."

Recalling the days when New York was the center of the boxing world, Dundee speaks glowingly of Stillman's Gymnasium. Each day, Stillman's, located on 55th Street and Eighth Avenue, five blocks north of Madison Square Garden, was filled with top fighters, former champions, managers, match-makers, trainers, writers, assorted characters and hangers-on.

Again, Dundee's role was humble. "I used to be phone picker-upper of the pay phones," he says. "They had about six or seven pay phones in the back of Stillman's. They would get calls from all over the world."

At Stillman's, Dundee also befriended Charley Goldman, the former bantamweight who trained heavyweight champ Rocky Marciano. "Charley and I sort of adopted each other," Dundee says. "We used to eat at the cheap joints." These included Jack Dempsey's Broadway restaurant where Dundee and Goldman were often joined by Dempsey himself.

Charley Goldman was a beloved figure, an utterly original character. Standing just over five feet tall, Goldman began fighting professionally as a street kid in Brooklyn, and was a veteran

of 137 recorded fights—and many more unrecorded fights—
between 1904 and 1914, during the "no-decision" era of boxing
when bouts were fought in the back of saloons or at private
clubs. The bouts were billed as exhibitions, and barring a
knockout, no winner was declared. Later in life, Goldman was
rarely seen without his derby, without a cigar or without a
young lady friend whom he inevitably described as his "niece."

Dundee confirms the details of the Charley Goldman legend:
"Well, I tell you. Charley Goldman used to wear that derby.
Charley used to smoke cigars. Charley was a magnificent
human being. Just a very, very warm individual. And he'd been
through . . . everything. And he knew how to get along with
everybody. He was a very, very smart individual." Is the story
about his "nieces" true? "He had more nieces than Carter had
pills, and they were all tall chicks, because he was short. Charley musta been five foot if he was five foot."

Goldman lived in Ma Brown's, a boarding house on the Upper
West Side of Manhattan. Where exactly was it? "It was right
next to where you did roadwork—Central Park. Right around
there," Dundee replies, revealing his decidedly boxing-oriented
sense of New York City geography.

One day, Goldman invited Dundee to come see a young
heavyweight prospect named Rocky Marciano. "I met Marciano
the first time he was in New York at the C.Y.O.," Dundee recalls,
referring to the Catholic Youth Organization Gym on West
17th Street where Goldman trained young fighters whom he
wanted to shelter from the spotlight of Stillman's. "Charley
Goldman said, 'Come on, Ange. I want you to see somebody.
Can't fight, stoop shoulders, bald headed, but oh, how he can
punch!'"

Marciano, Dundee says, "gave me an image of being like
Popeye—big arms, big legs, great foundation." Though Marciano was then relatively awkward and unskilled, Dundee was
struck with what he saw. What impressed Dundee most, though,
was what Goldman did for Marciano. "Charley did the most

magnificent structural job of a trainer of all time on Marciano,"
Dundee says emphatically. "There's a guy that got a fighter and
made him outta stone, you would say, etched him in stone, and
made a great champion out of him—an undefeated champion.
You know, here's a guy that never tasted defeat. Isn't that a
wonderful thing to say?"

But Goldman didn't change Marciano's natural balance. "See,
you work with what the guy's got. In other words, you don't try
to put something there that don't belong there."

What else did Goldman teach Marciano? "The other thing he
taught him is punch on the way up. I watched it. It was a
heckuva move on the heavy bag. In other words, he would get
down like on a deep knee dip, you know, straight down and
start punching on the way up then wind up with a whomp—you
know a big punch at the end of it. It's a difficult thing to do. You
try that some time. Get down, bend your knees, and start just
waving your arms, and punch on the way up, you're gonna get
winded. But it's a strenuous exercise. But he applied it to Rocky
'cause Rocky was a very strong physical individual. Even
though he was small in stature. Stoop shoulders. See, he was
deceiving as heck. But he could punch!"

Did Marciano fight out of a crouch? "Yeah," Dundee says making a fine distinction, "but not a crouch per se crouch. Like you
got Tyson—crouch, small. Joe Frazier—crouch, different bend,
though, different rhythm. Different. Every fighter's different."

From the specifics of what Goldman did for Marciano, Dundee also points out a general rule. "The thing I learned from
Charley was, 'If they're short, make 'em shorter. If they're tall,
make 'em taller.' So there's a tremendous amount of advice."

Though Chickie Ferrara and Charley Goldman were the two
trainers to whom Dundee became closest, he also remembers
fragmented details about the other "masters" of Stillman's Gym.

"I loved Bill Gore," Dundee says of Willie Pep's trainer. "I
loved him. I admired him because he had his own technique.

Big, tall guy and he used to work with Willie Pep, a small guy. He would lean over that top rope—never get in the ring. He never worked the middle. He used to work on the outside. Clean the guy up—had his own way of cleaning the guy up. Kept talking to him, got his face in the other guy's face. And he did his thing from the outside. That was his technique. That's the way he worked. And he was good—sharp, gruff instructions."

In addition to Pep, Gore also worked with lightweight champion Joe Brown and light-heavyweight champion Bob Foster.

Willie Pep today eagerly pays tribute to Bill Gore. "When I was a kid, I wanted to be a champion and all that. But it never would've happened without Bill Gore," Pep says. Crediting Gore for the sensational boxing skills that made him famous, Pep adds, "He taught boxing: jab, jab, move around, and keep your fanny off the floor. And that's exactly what I did for all them years. . . . He was a great trainer. He had his own style, and I followed his style." Turning ring historian, Pep says of Gore, "This is one of the great trainers of our time. He belongs with the great Whitey Bimsteins and Ray Arcels." Comparing Gore to other trainers, Pep adds, "Them other guys would get in the center of the ring and they'd make motions and they'd get you nervous. But Bill calmed you right down, and that was his style. And I needed someone to calm me down because I was a very nervous fella—very jumpy. And look what he did for me. He made me a champ."

While Angelo Dundee learned volumes from trainer Ray Arcel, he remembers Arcel's adaptability most of all. "Ray was great with all types of fighters. He had that type of pliable stuff," Dundee says. "I don't think anybody ever gave Ray Arcel problems. I swear to God. I just think he was adaptable to any kind of scene. He could handle any situation."

Dundee also recalls Arcel's technique in the corner. "The big thing about Ray Arcel, I used to watch him work, and a guy would come back to a corner pretty disheveled. Now, he would clean him up so where psychologically when he would come out of the corner, the guy who was fighting him would say, 'Hey. I had this guy all busted up. What's going on?' Ray would clean him up. Now this is a great psychological ploy. Because right away the guy thinks he got the guy, and all of a sudden here comes a guy all bright-eyed and bushy-tailed." Dundee also remembers the way Arcel would place his hands beneath a fighter's arms and seemingly shove the fighter off the stool. "Give him that little boost, that little lift," Dundee says admiringly. "But the thing is, he had that knack. He was good. He was excellent. He knew how to take care of that fighter. Get him back and sit him down, relax him, put the arms down."

Dundee laughs when citing a specific trick he picked up from Arcel. One of Arcel's fighters had scored a knockdown, and the referee was starting to count out the fallen opponent. "So what Ray did," Dundee remembers, "he went up the steps and put the robe on his guy." When the referee saw Arcel's fighter with his robe on, he unthinkingly assumed the fight was ending—and hurried his count. "The referee figures the fight's over," Dundee says, "the guy's putting on the robe." Years later, Dundee concedes, "I pulled the same thing."

About Whitey Bimstein, trainer of Rocky Graziano, among countless others, Dundee says, "Whitey Bimstein had a tremendous sense of humor. He was a helluva fight man. He had a knack of—you know how the hula girls move their stomach?— well, he used to move his stomach like vertically with the muscle tone in the stomach. He had a little pot belly on him. He was cute as hell. I remember him fondly."

Dundee's recollections of other, less celebrated trainers are sketchier, though no less colorful. "Yusl Grove," Dundee remembers, using a nickname for trainer Izzy Grove. "He's the guy used to spit bee-bees in the gym. He had the knack, you know, to hit you with a bee-bee, and you wouldn't know it was him. He would drive everybody up a wall."

About trainer Teddy Bentham—who worked with lightweight champion Jimmy Carter and featherweight champion Davey Moore, among others—Dundee says with a smile, "that's the guy with a short arm. Had a little short arm on him and every time he tried to describe a left hook, it would look kinda weird. He'd say, 'It's a short left hook.' He had a short left arm with a short left hook."

Stressing his respect for each corner man at Stillman's, Dundee is careful to also mention the names of trainers such as Johnny Sullo and Freddie Fiero. "Every one of the guys at Stillman's were capable of doing every facet of the training regimen," Dundee says, "everything that had to be done with a fighter." Today, by contrast, corner men tend to be specialists—which annoys Dundee. "They should be *trainers*. There shouldn't be cut man, bucket man, second man, third man, fourth man. You got to be a complete man to help a fighter. You gotta be able to do it all."

Straining his memory, Dundee apologizes for not being able to remember all of the trainers of Stillman's Gym. "See, I feel kinda funny because there was other trainers there, and I can't think of their darned names." One was "a little short fat guy used to come over from Jersey all the time," Dundee says. "Little burly sort of a guy. Geez, was a good friend of mine. I mean those guys would come over to the office at the Capitol hotel and stay there 'til fight time," he adds, trying to remember. "This guy was a good trainer, a real good trainer. I hate to forget him."

Dundee, who often calls himself one of the last of a dying breed, won't even begin to consider retirement. Having split with Sugar Ray Leonard, Dundee has not in recent years been associated with the more glamorous rising stars of boxing. As an independent operator in a sport filled with big money promoters and managers, Dundee is having trouble finding his next superstar.

But Dundee is nothing if not an eternal optimist, and he continues to love his work. "As long as that emotion is there then I know I'm not dead," he says. "And I'm juiced, and I'm ready to go. Then you can add something. When you get to where you're half dead in that corner and you're not giving of yourself, then it's time to take a walk and give it to the younger guy to do the thing. As long as you can give something, then you belong there. If you don't give, then you don't belong there."

He began by carrying a bucket in grimy arenas, and went on to work fights that are, without exaggeration, the stuff of boxing legend: Basilio vs. Robinson; Ali vs. Liston, Frazier and Foreman; Leonard vs. Duran, Hearns and Hagler.

Watching young prospects in a Miami gym, Dundee demonstrates a left jab with a genuine grace and speed that bespeaks his love for all kinds of dancing. "See, the gymnasium is fun for me," he says. "It's relaxing for me. 'Cause I can see things I can work on."

Coaching his fighters, Dundee's patter overflows with his signature phrases: "Box! Box! Box! That's it. Now get outta there! . . . Move over. Slide out. . . . You can't wait on this guy. Don't wait to get hit! . . . You gotta make angles. If you throw straightaway you're gonna miss your punches. . . . I told you, I don't like fighters who get hit." It's advice he's been passing on for years.

Dundee's fellow trainer Al Silvani observes, "I met him over forty years ago, hanging around the gym at Stillman's. And the man never changed. You see, those type of guys are real. They went through the suffering. They know."

A favorite Dundeeism comes to mind: "When I see things through my eyes, I see things." This seemingly redundant sentence is as close to a boast as Dundee allows himself—and a perfect expression of who he is.

When Angelo Dundee sees things through his eyes, he sees things.

Trainers and managers pose in the ring at STILLMAN's GYM some time in the 1930s. This photo belonged to Mannie Seamon who wrote the name of each boxing man on the picture. Top row: Doc Bagley, Whitey Bimstein, Mannie Seamon, Lou Brix, Nick Florio, Willie Beecher, Abe Katz and Lew Diamond. Seated: Ray Arcel, "Yuskee" and Doc Robb. PHOTO COURTESY FAE SEAMON

STILLMAN'S GYM

The mention of Stillman's Gym evokes almost lyrical reveries in seemingly unsentimental, old-time boxing men. "There was no other place like that in my life. No other place," says Al Braverman, a former heavyweight who today works as Don King's director of boxing. Braverman, whose family owned a pawn shop next to the gym, recalls working as a sparring partner at Stillman's for leading contenders of the late 1930s and early 1940s, including Lou Nova and Bob Pastor. "It was an institution never to be duplicated. It was run by the greatest character in the world and all the trainers, every trainer, was up there," Braverman recalls.

"Stillman's Gym was like the capital of the world," says veteran journalist Harold Conrad. "You'd go up there, you'd see everyone from the heavyweight champion to the flyweight champion. You'd see Jack Johnson fooling around—an old man fooling around with guys watching him. It was a fantastic place for fight people. And big audiences all the time. Movie stars, all kinds of people used to go up there. It was a great show."

Ted Walker, a trainer from Carson City, Nevada, first visited Stillman's in 1948. "Oh it was great," he says enthusiastically with the wizened voice of an aging cowboy in a Western movie. "Unsurpassed, unsurpassed. Everything in *fistiana* was personified there. You had all the champions training there. The contenders. A colorful bunch of managers."

For Ray Arcel, who was present at the founding of the gym in 1920, "Stillman's Gymnasium was a school; it was not a gym. You went there, you learned—you learned your lessons."

Lou Duva, who came to prominence in the 1970s and '80s as the corner man and co-manager of such champions as Evander Holyfield, Pernell Whitaker and Meldrick Taylor, remembers Stillman's as a place to observe professional fight handlers in action. During the 1950s, Duva explains, "I had my own trucking company. I used to drive a truck, and I used to work my can off just so I could go over to Stillman's. And I didn't watch the fighters. I used to watch the managers get in fights, cutting other managers out of the fights. I used to watch the trainers, the way they used to train the fighters—how they handled them after the training sessions and stuff like that. How they would instruct them. That's what I used to watch, and to me that's where I got my education."

For most of its existence, Stillman's Gymnasium was located in New York City on the west side of Eighth Avenue between 54th Street and 55th Street—a site that is now occupied by a large, white brick apartment building so ordinary-looking that it seems to mock the memory of the most fabled and colorful gym in boxing history. Stillman's address, 919 Eighth Avenue, today belongs to a small shoe repair shop on the ground floor of the apartment building. No plaque commemorates the location's distinguished history.

In the heyday of Stillman's, a sign outside the gym read:

STILLMAN'S GYM
WORLD'S LEADING BOXERS
TRAIN HERE DAILY
FROM 12 to 4pm   ADMISSION 25¢
Boxing Taught by Expert Instructors

Some time in the 1940s, the admission charge changed to fifty cents. The gym remained open, as they said around Stillman's, "Sundays, Mondays and always." This included both Christmas Day and Yom Kippur.

With wooden stairs leading from the street to the second floor, Stillman's was, as promoter Red Greb puts it, "a one-flight-up joint." It was a remarkably large gym. The main floor, which featured two boxing rings, was 125 feet long and fifty feet wide. A spiral staircase led to the second floor. Photos of famous fighters covered the walls. A loud bell sounded at regular intervals indicating the beginning and end of a round.

"All the sparring was done on the lower level," Angelo Dundee recalls. "There was a flight of steps. It musta been an old firehouse. It was steel—it was iron steps. And down below was where you came into the gym. And Jack Curley sat over there and collected money to get in—from the fans. Fifty cents. Maybe a buck if there was a bigger name there. Because, you know, you had big names there."

Jack Curley worked the front door and served as the manager of Stillman's. Vinnie Ferguson, a two-time national amateur boxing champion who trained at Stillman's when he fought professionally as a middleweight in the 1950s, says that Curley "wouldn't let Jesus Christ in there without fifty cents." Ferguson laughs as he describes the time lightweight champion Jimmy Carter—not a regular at Stillman's—tried to get into the gym without paying. "Carter wanted to see his manager. His manager happened to be standing inside there on business. Curley wouldn't let Carter in." Curley's message to the lightweight champion was simple, Ferguson recalls: "I don't give a shit who you are. You got fifty cents, you can come in here."

On the main floor attention focused on the two boxing rings which filled with fighters between noon and four p.m. In the 1950s, the hours were extended into the evening to accommodate fighters who had to work during the day to earn their living.

Spectators sat on folding chairs placed in front of the rings. Trainers worked from behind the rings, against the back wall. Trainer Al Silvani, who began at Stillman's in the late 1930s as an assistant to Whitey Bimstein and later to Ray Arcel, recalls, "You had about fifteen, twenty rows of seats where the audience paid so they could watch." Often as many as two hundred spectators crowded into the gym. Says Silvani, "Every day you had the damn place packed up. Where could you get that? When I first broke in there for twenty-five cents you saw a show—for three or four hours, the greatest fighters in the world. One after another. For twenty-five cents!" Lou Stillman, the proprietor of the gym, liked to tell interviewers, "The joint was so thick with fighters they used to knock each other down shadow boxing."

The journey up the stairs from Eighth Avenue to Stillman's could be intimidating for those who were mere civilians—not part of what was known as the fight mob. Whitey Bimstein's daughter, Adele Shapiro, rarely visited Stillman's, but she vividly recalls the atmosphere—and the smell. "When you got into Stillman's your nose knew where you were," she says. "It was a combination of sweat and some kind of liniment."

The gym attracted mobsters who owned a piece of a fighter, or gamblers with special interests of their own. Spectators were advised to hold on to their overcoats at all times. Stillman claimed that a dozen alumni of the gym went on to the electric chair.

Fighters sat on a bench next to the rings waiting their turn to spar. The wait could last three hours or longer if Stillman didn't know the fighter or was angry with him. Former featherweight champion Willie Pep recalls with great pride that he never had to wait to spar at Stillman's. Says Pep, "Stillman loved me. He let me do things that he wouldn't let anybody else do. He would hold a ring for me. He never held a ring for anybody!" Pep today still considers Stillman's special treatment "a great, great thing."

Most of the fighters waiting on the bench at Stillman's were far less celebrated than Pep. They were "flatnosed, tough kids, prideful as hell," says trainer Ted Walker. "And they would come to the gym usually with an entourage, followers from the neighborhood. Those neighborhood kids and their friends and their relatives would pull for them [the fighters] in the sparring like they were in a fight. And that added a lot to the color there in the gym. God Almighty there were some tough kids."

Relative beginners could learn volumes at Stillman's if they were properly matched with more experienced boxers. "If you were going to learn to be a fighter, that was the place to go," says middleweight Vinnie Ferguson.

Jimmy Archer, brother and manager of middleweight contender Joey Archer—and himself a lightweight boxer who frequented Stillman's in the 1950s—explains how the lessons were taught: "When you box with the best you get better. You box with mediocre guys, it's hard to improve. So four-round fighters would be boxing with eight- and ten-round fighters. They would learn little tricks from 'em and that's how they got better."

A famous row of five pay-phones stood near the entrance of the gym. Calls came in from all over the world—mostly from promoters and matchmakers trying to book fighters. If an unscrupulous manager answered the phone, he could easily exploit the situation by booking his own fighter instead of a fighter managed by whomever the caller was initially seeking. It is, of course, safe to say that Stillman's was always well-supplied with unscrupulous managers.

Trainer Eddie Futch, who occasionally visited the gym in the

1940s, remembers being advised by trainer Mannie Seamon never to receive calls from matchmakers at Stillman's. This atmosphere of mistrust made the job of answering the phones a position of great trust and responsibility. Angelo Dundee and Al Braverman are both proud to have held the job.

Managers and matchmakers congregated at the rear of the gym in an area which Stillman dubbed "the Stock Exchange of Boxing." Stillman complained that, "A million dollars' worth of business goes on there, and most of the guys look like they can't buy themselves a nickel cigar."

The main floor also featured a snack bar that offered tea, sandwiches, hot dogs, soft drinks and adhesive tape and bandages, as well as raw eggs—a favorite for boxers in training.

The entrance to the fighters' locker room was underneath the stairway leading to the second level of the gym. About twenty dressing rooms where champions and leading contenders were given rubdowns were located on either side of the entrance to the locker room. A sign in each dressing room read: "Wash Your Clothes—By Order of the Athletic Commission." One fighter recalls, "There were two or three showers. Sometimes they didn't work."

Upstairs, fighters hit the light and heavy bags, did their bench exercises and skipped rope. Al Silvani says that the small upstairs ring was used "to practice movements only."

Stillman's was famously unwashed. The grit-covered windows were kept shut. Cigarette butts littered the floor. Fighters who asked that the windows be opened were told, "Find yourself another gym." Asked how rundown Stillman's actually was, Al Braverman replies, "Terrible. You had to look out and see that the plaster didn't fall down and hit you. There was always plaster coming down." Ray Arcel says, "Stillman wouldn't paint the place, he wouldn't do anything to fix the place up. He just let it go."

"What was horrible about training at Stillman's was the fact that smoking was allowed," says Steve Acunto, currently Deputy Commissioner of the New York State Athletic Commission. Between 1938 and 1942, Acunto served as a sparring partner at Stillman's for Lou Ambers, Henry Armstrong, Lew Jenkins and other leading lightweights of the time. After a workout at Stillman's, "your clothes became infested with cigarette smoke," Acunto says with disgust.

According to one often-told tale, when Stillman had the gym cleaned up and the windows opened in deference to the wishes of Gene Tunney, the regular crowd boycotted the place in protest. It's said that featherweight champ Johnny Dundee, upon hearing of Tunney's demand, replied, "Fresh air? Why that stuff is likely to kill us!"

Every heavyweight champion from Dempsey to Louis trained at Stillman's, along with fighters like Rocky Graziano, Beau Jack, Kid Gavilan, Tony Canzoneri and Sandy Saddler. After they retired, heavyweight champions Jack Dempsey, James J. Braddock and Jack Johnson came by to watch the sparring. "So you had all the greatest names," says Al Silvani. "When you walked in there you'd see names you couldn't believe." Lesser-known ex-boxers who were down on their luck also stood around looking for handouts.

Steve Acunto, who idolized—and imitated—lightweight champion Benny Leonard to such an extent that Jack Curley started to call him "Benny," still speaks proudly of the day he met the great Leonard himself at Stillman's. Acunto was sparring with Lou Ambers, he recalls, "when I came back to the corner to get my mouthpiece washed. And Benny Leonard came up those three steps, and he said, 'Kid, where did you learn that style?'" Acunto adds quickly, "He didn't know the hours I spent watching him move and box."

Lightweight contender of the 1950s Johnny Busso also remembers the excitement a young boxer felt seeing his idols at the gym. "If you were a piece-of-shit fighter, you mingled with the best fighters in the world," he says. "I met guys who overwhelmed me. I met Kid Gavilan over there. Joey Maxim. Rocky

Marciano." Before he started boxing, Busso says, "I was, like, Johnny Busso, nothing, a kid from the neighborhood." But at Stillman's, says Busso, "Geez, this was an experience—you can't buy this. You can't buy going over and saying, 'Hey, Joe Louis, how are you?' and he goes, 'Hey, Johnny, how are you?' You can't buy this 'cause the guy don't sell his handshake for nothin'."

Lou Stillman, the grouchy, outspoken man who owned the place—and rarely appeared there without a loaded .38-caliber pistol beneath his suit jacket—presided over his gym on the first floor by announcing through a public address system which fighters were about to spar: "Now in Ring 1, Rocky Graziano." Journalist Harold Conrad recalls that Stillman was an entertaining master of ceremonies: "He would do all the introducing and the announcing—and he had a pretty good routine."

It seems impossible to overplay Stillman's eccentricities. "Anything that you've heard about Lou Stillman—double it up, triple it up, magnify it four more times, and you'll get the real, real, real, real individual, Lou Stillman," advises referee Joey Curtis who trained at Stillman's as a lightweight in the 1940s. "Sometimes he was peaches and cream. But let him get pissed off about something, man, he would take his ire out on the world. I'm including everybody and anybody—gangsters, racketeers, wise guys, fighters, trainers, anybody. If he was mad at something, everybody knew about it. And they stayed away from him—including me."

Angelo Dundee says, "I think Ray Arcel was the only guy to get along with Stillman," but then corrects himself and adds, "I got along with him. You know, I never bothered him."

Stillman once summed up his management philosophy this way: "Big or small, champ or bum, I treated 'em all the same way—bad. If you treat them like humans, they'll eat you alive." Another time he said simply, "In my place, there can be no two bosses. I . . . am . . . the . . . boss."

Trainer Ted Walker remembers that Stillman "had a big clock and a bell up over a little stand that he had built for himself up on the wall where he could oversee the rings. And this clock had been given to him by Jack Solomons from England. The great promoter. And Stillman had great pride in that clock. He would wipe it off every day when he got up there. He always carried a towel, a little short cocktail towel with him, and he cleaned that clock off." Though a prominently posted sign warned against spitting in the gym, Stillman himself would spit down from his perch with regularity.

The first word that comes to most boxing men's mind when they describe Lou Stillman is "gruff." Las Vegas promoter Red Greb, who visited Stillman's on his trips to New York, says, "I remember Mr. Lou Stillman with a voice that hasn't been duplicated by God or anybody else." In his novel *The Harder They Fall*, Budd Schulberg speaks of Stillman's "garbage disposal voice."

And Stillman could back up his tough words. "I'll tell you," says Red Greb, "Stillman could throw a mean right hand. . . . He had fights with fighters. Boy oh boy, he was a tough son of a bitch." Stillman described his approach to self-defense this way: "I can lick most guys with bluff, so I haven't gotten into a fight since I was a kid. . . . I've carried a gun all my life, used to carry two of them in the old days. But I only had to pull it out once . . . when a guy shot me." Stillman had survived being shot through the chest by a gunman in Harlem.

Don Chargin, another West Coast promoter, admits that when he went into Stillman's as a young man, he found it intimidating. "I was very young," Chargin concedes, "and the way Stillman used to yell at everybody there—it was scary for a young kid."

Another fight man with less than pleasant memories of Stillman is Jackie Graham who often watched his brother, welterweight contender Billy Graham, work out at the gym. "Cantankerous is too kind a word for Stillman," says Graham, who works for the New York State Athletic Commission. "Obnoxious is a more accurate word. He was an obnoxious man. I mean, he would scream obscenities across the gym. . . . If you owed gym dues—a lot of those guys, they were hurtin', they didn't have money—he'd scream across, 'You fuckin' nigger you owe me dues from last month'—that kind of stuff." Adds Graham with quiet precision, "That's not nice now. It wasn't nice then. It never will be nice. But it didn't bother him, he did it. And he continued to do it."

While acknowledging that Stillman was "a tough son of a bitch"—a phrase which often pops up in descriptions of Stillman—Ted Walker says with admiration, "He ran that place with an iron hand. He was a good guy, though. I became his friend. 'Cause I knew how to get along with him. You didn't have to kiss his ass, you had to do what you were supposed to do."

Murray Goodman, publicity director of boxing for Madison Square Garden from 1949 to 1960, says Stillman was "aggressive and abusive, but he was a pussycat." Harold Conrad adds, "Stillman didn't take any shit from fighters. But he had a good heart. Guys that didn't have the locker fee, he would stake 'em."

Stillman's son Shelly acknowledges that his father "was a rough person in the gym." He adds, "He had to be because if he wasn't, he wouldn't have survived. He was a good family man, he was good to his kids, and he was good to his friends."

In a 1969 obituary of Stillman, New York Post boxing writer Lester Bromberg agreed. "A gallery of his peers has voted Lou Stillman not guilty of the hard-as-nails front he tried to maintain. . . . 'Nobody took him serious when he screamed and bullied,' is the consensus on Stillman." Bromberg quoted former Madison Square Garden matchmaker Johnny Attell who maintained that Stillman's gruffness was a put-on. "I think he knew that we all knew," said Attell. "He kept it up because there were some laughs in it for him and everybody else."

This softer side could be seen in Stillman's comments about his favorite fighter, Benny Leonard, whose greatness made Stillman practically dewy-eyed with nostalgia and admiration. "Benny Leonard was the best gymnasium fighter ever came in here," Stillman said in 1938. "He was just as good out there when they turned the lights on, and played for keeps." Six years later, Stillman expressed the same sentiment. "There was a perfect fighter," Stillman said of Leonard. "All you had to do was make one mistake with Benny, and your number was up. He had brains, personality, ability and courage."

Lou Stillman was born Louis Ingber in 1897 on the Lower East Side of Manhattan. Though most accounts of Lou Stillman's early life say he was a policeman before opening his gym, Stillman's son Shelly can't confirm the story. "I heard that, too, but if he was it's news to me," he says. "I never knew he was a police officer. I don't think he could've gotten on the police department because I don't think he ever got past the second grade." Ray Arcel, however, vividly recalls Lou Stillman saying that he had been a police officer.

Shelly Stillman offers this version of how his father came to run a gymnasium: "He was a conductor on the trolley car . . . and some guy came and sat next to him and his name was Marshall Stillman. He was a banker. And they came up with this idea of opening up a gymnasium to rehabilitate people coming out of jail."

Marshall Stillman was a wealthy philanthropist. He and Lou Ingber opened the first Stillman's Gym on 125th Street in Harlem. Unfortunately, the gym was robbed by the very young men it was designed to help.

Ray Arcel, at the age of ninety-one, proves his excellence as an historian by providing a detailed account of how the fighters and trainers of his generation left Grupp's Gymnasium in Harlem in favor of Stillman's.

Following World War I, Arcel begins, Grupp's Gymnasium, located on 116th Street and Eighth Avenue, was New York's boxing headquarters. "It was the only outstanding gym in the

City at that particular time. So all the great fighters worked there. And there were many Jewish fighters because right at that particular time they were the products of the early Jewish immigrants that settled on the Lower East Side."

The incomparable lightweight champion Benny Leonard, Arcel says, was "the leader" of all the Jewish fighters, a group that also included Benny Valgar, Leach Cross and others.

In 1919, Billy Grupp, the proprietor of Grupp's Gymnasium, sabotaged his business by publicly displaying his anti-Semitism. "Billy Grupp was a Dutchman and he drank," Arcel recalls. "He was a drunkard. And he's out there one day and he's hollerin', 'If it wasn't for all the Jews there'da been no war.' He was running around. He was drunk. And he was hollering about all the Jews. The Jews are responsible for the War and everything else. And of course, the gymnasium is full of Jewish fighters."

Upset at Grupp's outburst, Benny Leonard suggested that his friends work out at Marshall Stillman's new gym. "Leonard got a few of the guys together," Arcel recalls, "and he said, 'There's a new gymnasium opened up on 125th Street. Let's go up there and take a look.'"

At the time, Marshall Stillman's gym had no connection to boxing, and the man with the straw hat and cane who ran the gym, Lou Ingber—later to be known as Lou Stillman—didn't know who Benny Leonard was. "He didn't know any of the fighters," Arcel says. "He didn't know much about professional boxing. And we told him we'd like to come up there and train. I didn't talk. Leonard did the talking." When Ingber decided to allow the boxers to work out at the gym, Arcel emphasizes, "he didn't know the value of what he was getting into."

Describing the first Stillman's Gym in Harlem, Arcel looks around his modestly sized Manhattan apartment and says, "Now the place was a little bit bigger than this living room. . . . You couldn't move in the joint. They had a nice ring, that was the main asset, a nice ring. And they had a punching bag." The great Benny Leonard's personal headquarters were also decidedly modest. "They had a toilet in the back," Arcel recalls with a laugh, "and they put a sort of a fence around the toilet—and that was Benny Leonard's private dressing room."

Lou Ingber quickly realized the commercial potential that came from running a center for a popular boxer like Benny Leonard. "When Leonard went up there to train the place was mobbed with people to watch him," Arcel says. "I mean, he was a great fighter, a tremendous attraction. So everybody went up. Now this guy, Ingber, he doesn't know what the hell's going on with all these people. So he figured he'll charge fifteen cents admission."

Ingber's involvement with boxing coincided with the passage of New York's Walker Law in 1920, legalizing fifteen-round fights with a winner determined by judges' decisions. Ingber saw that boxing was growing in popularity, Arcel says. "So he decided that he was going to build his own gymnasium." Crediting Ingber's business acumen, Arcel adds, "He had enough imagination to realize that with all these people coming in he could charge admission and make money. So he went down and he rented a hall on Eighth Avenue, 919 Eighth Avenue, between 54th and 55th Street. And it was a union meeting place. It had two floors, upper and lower."

Ingber took on a business partner, Arcel recalls, who had made money in the shoe business. "Lou needed cash. This guy had it. So they went down there and I think they had to pay a thousand dollars a month which was a tremendous move for him. It took a lot of guts in 1919, 1920—right after the War. I mean things were rough. But anyway, he went down and he built the whole thing up and he laid it all out with the help of this businessman."

After Lou Ingber moved his gym downtown, Arcel says, Ingber acquired a new name: "A lot of fighters started to call him Mr. Stillman, so he changed his name."

During the 1930s, Stillman's temporarily abandoned its Eighth Avenue address. "Things got a little rough and he had to get out of there, and he went down to 37th Street and Seventh Avenue," Arcel remembers. "He couldn't make it. Then he rented in the Hearst building on 57th Street and Eighth Avenue. And there was an elevator and you had to go upstairs and it was all right. It was big and roomy. . . . And we stayed up there for quite a while. Then he moved back to 919 Eighth Avenue."

Recalling the difficulty of earning a living working as a boxing trainer during the early days of Stillman's, Arcel concludes, "Those were bad years. They were rough and the Depression came in. A dollar bill was a million dollars. It was hard, hard to get by. It was rough. You had to be a damn fool like me to be able to stay in this thing and starve, but we worked and we developed fighters."

No one's memories of Lou Stillman are more colorful than those of Al Braverman who frequented Stillman's Gym in 1939 and 1940. Braverman offers this physical description of the gym's proprietor: "Stillman was about six-foot-two, semi-bald, a lot of big bushy hair on the side, big nose. He looked funny, like a clown." In fairness to Stillman, it should be pointed out that in many photos he looks quite well-groomed and dapper in a stylish, double-breasted suit.

Braverman takes delight in describing gags he often played on Stillman—the equivalent of pouring grease on the fire of Stillman's celebrated temper.

"We used to drive Stillman crazy," Braverman says with pride, citing the time he called Stillman on the phone pretending to be a wrestler. "I'm a wrestler. I vant to wrestle in your gym," Braverman said with a vaguely Eastern European accent. "I don't take wrestlers," Stillman replied. "I'm prepared to pay five hundred dollars a month," said Braverman. "Well, wait a minute," said Stillman, "I got a ring upstairs. What time do you want to come in? How's one o'clock?" Then came the punchline from Braverman who, like Stillman, is Jewish. "One condition," Braverman said, "I don't want no Jews around me." With that, Still-man blew his top. "You son of a bitch," he said, and slammed down the phone.

After pulling this gag, Braverman played innocent. "Imagine," Stillman told him, "some dirty bastard called me, says no Jews can watch him." "No, Lou, he said that?" Braverman replied. "Who's the guy?" "I don't know," Stillman said. "Some god-damned wrestler. I don't want no wrestlers ever in here."

Another time, Braverman called Stillman pretending to be a representative of Fox Movietone News. Braverman recreates the dialogue as follows: "'Fox Movietone News here. Are you the boss?' 'Yeah, I'm the boss. Of course I am.' 'We're coming up to shoot in your joint today.' 'Who said you're coming up?' 'We're prepared to pay you fifteen hundred for a day's shoot.' 'Oh,' he says, 'well wait a minute. When you coming up here?' I says, 'When's convenient, around twelve to three?' 'Oh geez, most of the boxers . . .' 'Well we want to get them in action. By the way, you got enough current there? You got the right volts?' 'Oh, I got all the current.' 'Well,' I said, 'You can take that current and stick it up your ass.'"

After the put-on, Stillman told Braverman, "Wait 'til I get the pricks from Fox Movietone News. . . . Them bastards, who do they think they are?"

Braverman also delighted in obscuring Stillman's view of the door, where Jack Curley collected the admission fee from the public. "I'd send guys deliberately to stand in front of Stillman because he always wanted to watch the door where Jack Curley was taking the money," Braverman says with a laugh. "He was always afraid Jack would take some money. I'd send some fight-ers or guys who were friends and say, 'Stand in front of Still-man.' He'd say, 'Get out! Get out of there! Would you mind? Get out of the way!'"

Did Stillman ever figure out that Braverman was pulling gags on him? "God forbid," Braverman says. "He'd bar me in a minute, even though he was friendly with my father downstairs."

Braverman wasn't the only one to pull gags on Stillman, Joey Curtis says, but he quickly adds: "I got news for you, when Stillman found out about the joke, the guy that pulled the joke—he was nowhere to be found. Nobody had the balls to say, 'Yeah. I did it. So what?' You were liable to have that .38 up your ass!"

Humor, gags and put-ons fill many people's accounts of Stillman's Gym. Stillman himself seems to have cultivated the comedic atmosphere of the gym. "Every bad fighter I knew always made the other boys laugh," said Stillman. "That's why we let them train up here."

Newspaper and magazine stories about the gym treated Stillman's almost like an asylum filled with characters who constantly played jokes on one another. So exaggerated and self-consciously adorable are many of these stories, that one wonders whether writers used their imaginations to heighten the gym's eccentric image—or if perhaps Stillman's regulars made either a conscious or unconscious effort to live up to their growing reputation for goofiness.

A typical story is Dan Parker's 1944 piece for *Collier's* which describes Stillman's as a "slug nutty saloon." The story details the many practical jokes the regulars played on an ex-fighter, a black man named Battling Norfolk who was employed as a masseur at the gym.

Norfolk's life was filled with hotfoots, rubber snakes, fake skeletons and telephones rigged with explosive charges. Accounts of these practical jokes are racist by today's standards: the black man, Norfolk, is reduced to the clichéd role of a pathetic fall guy.

Many of the best-known stories about the denizens of Stillman's, however, remain quite funny. The most famous, perhaps, tells of a man known as "Racehorse" who used to work out at the gym. Stillman himself told the story in a 1938 article in *Collier's*: "There was a funny guy. He drove a cab and he'd park the cab in front of the gym and come in here to work out. He'd punch the bag and skip rope and shadow box for three hours. But he'd never get into the ring. He was all the time boxing shadows. One day I kidded him and said, 'Racehorse, a promoter was in and he said he'd give you a thousand dollars to fight in a semifinal for him.' Racehorse looked at me and he said, 'Nuttin' doin'. I want ten hundred dollars or I don't fight.'"

Another often-told story concerns Jack Dempsey and heavyweight contender "Two Ton" Tony Galento, who once fought Joe Louis, knocking Louis down before being knocked out himself. Galento often pestered Dempsey to manage him. Finally, Dempsey, no longer champion and not a young man, stepped into the ring with Galento to give him a boxing lesson. After out-boxing Galento, Dempsey floored him with a left hook. "There, Tony," said Dempsey over the fallen Galento, "that's how you hit. Now go get yourself a new manager."

Perhaps the most cherished of all Stillman's gym anecdotes involves lightweight champion Beau Jack. Jack was a regular at Stillman's but decided to travel to a training camp in the country to prepare for his 1943 title defense against Bob Montgomery. After he lost to Montgomery, the chastened Beau Jack resumed training at Stillman's and won the rematch. The moral of the story, of course, is that fresh air couldn't compete with the agreeable squalor of Stillman's.

An adjunct to the scene at Stillman's was the Neutral Corner Cocktail Lounge and Restaurant. "Go down from Stillman's, make a left, you're there at the Neutral Corner," Angelo Dundee remembers. "The guys would go there to have a drink. I didn't drink. I used to go in to see all the guys."

The sign on the awning of the Neutral Corner read, "Steaks and Chops Our Specialty, Meet Your Favorite Fighters and Managers Here." The bar was opened in 1949 by Nick Masuras, a former middleweight club fighter. Two years later he took on two partners—Chickie Bogad, a former Madison Square Garden matchmaker, and a fight manager named Frankie Jacobs. Welterweight contender Tony Janiro worked as a bartender at the Neutral Corner following his retirement from the ring.

Ex-fighter and manager Jimmy Archer says the Neutral Corner, "was strictly a fighter's bar or a manager's bar in those days. . . . There was a lot of bookmakers around, too, hanging around, or gamblers hanging around the bar. And they all talked fight talk, strictly. And all the fighters hung out there. Retired fighters. And a lot of times the fighters who were fighting would come down, not that they drank, but they'd have sodas there and just hang around the fight crowd." Part of the appeal, no doubt, was that fighters were often extended credit at the Neutral.

A. J. Liebling had a special fondness for the Neutral Corner, and a visit there for a drink with Whitey Bimstein or Charley Goldman was a staple of his reports on the big fights of the 1950s. In *The Sweet Science*, Liebling describes "the Neutral," as it was called by its devotees, as a place frequented by, among others, "ex-fighters, who favor a place where somebody is likely to recognize them."

Colorful anecdotes, famous hangouts, and outsized characters aside, Stillman's Gym is best remembered by the trainers who worked there as a kind of boxing think tank. Ray Arcel describes the collegial atmosphere: "With all the fighters and the trainers that were around in those days, you could stand and talk to them and they would tell you their problems and you would tell them your problems. And sometimes you'd work with their fighters [or] they'd work with your fighters. It was a very, very friendly group of trainers. And that's why there were so many good fighters. Everyone of them—every one of the trainers in those days knew how to train a fighter."

In addition to Charley Goldman, Whitey Bimstein, Freddie Brown, Chickie Ferrara and Al Silvani, Arcel's fellow trainers at Stillman's included brothers Dan and Nick Florio, who together seconded lightweight champion Tony Canzoneri and featherweight champions Battling Battalino, Petey Scalzo and Freddie Miller. Nick, who was not much of a talker, was known as "Gabby." The more loquacious Dan was dubbed "Silent." Dan Florio went on to train lightweight champion Paddy DeMarco and heavyweight champions Jersey Joe Walcott and Floyd Patterson. Another prominent trainer was Jimmy August, whom Al Braverman describes as follows: "The sweetest little, quietest little man you could ever meet. He looked like a little Kewpie doll. He was beautiful."

Al Silvani explains that all of the trainers got along because they needed each other. "You needed the spar mates," Silvani says. "There was about seven or eight of us [trainers] taking care of ten, fifteen fighters a day."

When Charley Goodman left New York with Rocky Marciano, he told *The Ring* in 1953, he turned his fighters over to other trainers. "We have a fine crowd at Stillman's—Whitey Bimstein, Jimmy August, Dan and Nick Florio, Teddy Bentham, Chickie Ferrara and Freddie Brown—and everybody works together. Sometimes I take care of their fighters when they're away, and they return the favors when I'm out of town."

The trainers' schedule was extremely busy. Fights were held six nights a week, from Monday through Saturday—all at arenas and fight clubs within twelve miles of Stillman's, as Al Silvani points out. Silvani lists the basic schedule as follows:

> Monday — St. Nicholas Arena
> Tuesday — Broadway Arena
> Wednesday — White Plains Arena
> Thursday — Bronx Coliseum
> Friday — Madison Square Garden
> Saturday — Ridgewood Grove

Silvani adds that there were also "many, many other weekly boxing clubs" in the New York area, including Laurel Garden, Meadow Brook Bowl, Star Casino, Queensboro Athletic Club, Coney Island Arena, and the Fort Hamilton Arena.

"I got fighters at Broadway arena," Silvani remembers telling his fellow trainers. "You take care of them, and I'll take care of your fighters at White Plains." On any given night, says Silvani, "you usually worked the whole card, because that's how many fighters you had. And that's how the experience comes."

Contemporary corner man Lou Duva maintains that the trainers of the Stillman's era were better than current trainers. "When you talk about the trainers of yesteryear, they were masters—not like today," Duva says. "The trainers of yesteryear were much more dedicated to the sport. . . . Don't forget, fights back then were like every night. They'd be training these guys during the day and hitting the small clubs at night." Today, by contrast, Duva says, fights "are few and far between."

Though the trainers of Stillman's Gym are esteemed today, they were often greeted irreverently by Lou Stillman. Al Braverman recalls that from ten in the morning until noon, all the trainers would gather at the gym. "Stillman held court there every day for two hours," Braverman says. "He would abuse everybody, but he would never abuse Charley Goldman. No. And the other one he didn't abuse was Ray Arcel. Ray and Charley were the only ones who escaped his wrath. Freddie Brown got it. . . . Whoever was there got the shit blown out of them every day." Others recall that Stillman also refrained from insulting Whitey Bimstein.

Lou Stillman's celebrated gruffness—and the atmosphere of friendly insults he created—wasn't a hindrance to Ray Arcel or his elite colleagues, nor was it of much interest. Stillman, Arcel recalls, "was a rough guy to live with. But we never had any time for these guys. Stillman was the owner of the gym. I mean, we were working there—we were too busy to worry about Lou Stillman."

The best trainers, while withstanding Stillman's wrath, were extremely serious about their work. The gravity of a trainer's work is summed up by ex-fighter and manager Jimmy Archer who understands the dangers involved when boxers work out in a gym—and how good trainers can protect their fighters.

If a fighter has "a good chin," Archer explains, "after a while he doesn't feel the punches. Doesn't even feel 'em." Archer, whose flattened nose offers proof that he fought professionally for sixteen years, says that late in his career he felt himself succumbing to the delusion that he could not be hurt in the gym. "But then I realized," he says, "hey, this can't do me any good."

Many fighters, though, become accustomed to the physical beating without really thinking about it. "Guys in the gym, boxing in the gym, especially old pros, they become accustomed to getting hit, and they don't feel it anyway—in the gym," says Archer. "So they'll put their chin out and let you hit 'em."

An experienced trainer must warn his fighter against this, Archer says. Fighters should be told, "Hey, getting hit like that is no good because if I take a hammer and keep banging that wall, one day that wall's gonna fall, no matter how strongly it's built. One day I'm gonna weaken something."

Archer adds that trainers often fail to notice that their fighters are being hurt in the gym because a trainer "that hangs around a gym becomes immune to certain situations. And he doesn't realize. He's not knowledgeable enough."

Among those whom Archer counts as both knowledgeable and concerned with their fighters' well-being were the two venerable trainers who worked with his brother, Joey Archer— Whitey Bimstein and Freddie Brown. "Guys like that knew," Archer says. "There was only a few guys."

Lou Stillman sold his gym in 1959. Facing the press, Stillman was less than nostalgic. "There's no more tough guys around, not enough slums," he told *The New York Times* which reported the closing of Stillman's Gym on its front page. "That's why I'm getting out of the business. The racket's dead. These fighters today are all sissies." He did wax sentimental, however, for the old days, "when the fighters breathed bad air, ate bad food and when slums were slums." Of the 1959 crop of fighters, Stillman said, "These kids got dough in their pockets but they don't know how to laugh."

Others were saddened when Stillman's closed. "It was like you lost your heart," former lightweight contender Johnny Busso remembers. "It was like you lost a place to stay. Even if I wasn't training, I used to go up there to see my friends. . . . It was like when you were a kid, you went to the candy store on the corner. All of a sudden the candy store's closing, now what are we gonna do?"

In 1967, two years before Stillman's death, writer Ted Carroll of *The Ring* reported that Stillman still wore his famed grim facial expression. Asked why, Stillman—as quotable as ever—replied, "How can you change something that's been part of you for forty years? How long do you think a man with a happy face would have lasted in my old business, running a boxing gym? Managers and fighters would have borrowed me broke. When would they have paid their bills if I had been a soft touch with a big grin?" Speaking of himself in the third person, Stillman added, "Everybody called Stillman a grouch, a crab, cranky guy who never smiled. Well, that's what scared off the chiselers, moochers and deadbeats. A good-natured guy would have been played for the biggest sucker in the world."

Shelly Stillman says that after his father sold the gym, he missed the boxing world. "He was always in the limelight. Wherever he went, it was always, 'Lou Stillman this, Lou Stillman that.' After he retired, it's like anybody else—once you're retired and you're out, that's it. People don't even wanta know you. So basically after he retired he never really heard from anybody."

Al Braverman remembers seeing Stillman after he'd given up the gym. "It was pitiful," says Braverman. "He said, 'It's the worst thing I ever did in my life, Al.' He said, 'I'm lost, I ain't got nobody, and I can't abuse nobody anymore. It wasn't like I abused anyone. I liked them, you know. I would just tell 'em off.' It was pitiful," Braverman concludes. "It killed him. Killed him. Went out of the business. He had nobody to talk to, nobody to talk to him."

RAY ARCEL

I went in to learn a trade and I learned my trade well. And I learned one thing. The most important thing of all—and I taught it to my fighters—*boxing is brain over brawn.* Learn how to think. Learn how to think and you'll be successful. That's the most important thing—to be able to think in that ring."

With these words, Ray Arcel at the age of ninety-one distills one of the great lessons of his career as a boxing trainer.

Arcel's longevity in boxing is such that—to make a comparison with baseball—it's as if the same coach who worked with Babe Ruth went on to give instructions to Reggie Jackson. From the 1920s through the 1950s, Arcel trained such champions as Charley Phil Rosenberg, Benny Leonard, Barney Ross, Kid Gavilan, Tony Zale and Ezzard Charles, and he stood in the corner of Joe Louis' opponents fourteen times. To fight fans, Arcel's memories of these years carry the fascination of vivid testimony from a wise family elder.

After retiring from the ring for nearly twenty years, Arcel came back to second Roberto Duran and Larry Holmes, two

55

recent champions he feels warrant comparison with the all-time greats.

Manager and corner man Lou Duva speaks for many in boxing when he says of Arcel, "He's a guy who should be enshrined. He's an angel, that guy." Asked about Arcel, Larry Holmes replies, "Ray? Phenomenal. He is a phenomenon."

In *The Sweet Science*, A. J. Liebling wrote, "Arcel is severe and decisive, like a teacher in a Hebrew school." Severe and decisive Arcel certainly is. With his thinning white hair, hawk-like nose and wise brown eyes, Arcel gives the impression of being simply too ancient to waste his time with anything but the truth. He answers questions with utmost seriousness, showing deep respect for his fighters—respect for the glories they achieved, and the discipline and pain they endured.

Yet Arcel also cherishes a good joke, and he is strikingly in touch with the joy and enthusiasm of earlier days. When he smiles while remembering a favorite anecdote or a beloved friend, his eyes become playful and his boyish expression reveals how he might have looked in his youth. The music in his voice recalls a cantor in a synagogue and the sound of Gershwin tunes; it is uniquely a product of the era in which he came of age in New York City.

Anyone meeting Arcel immediately notices that he is in splendid shape: erect posture, firm handshake, superb concentration. Citing boxing matches from as far back as the early 1920s, Arcel gives the year the fights took place and the rounds they ended—and his memory inevitably proves accurate when checked against *The Ring Record Book*.

Each time I visit Arcel, he greets me as I step from the elevator into the hallway leading to his apartment, and he walks me to the elevator when I leave. His courtly—and utterly endearing—good manners inspire a visitor to be his best, most polite self. It's no wonder that Red Smith called Arcel "the first gentleman of fistfighting"—or that Damon Runyon once remarked, "Ray Arcel is the only man I ever knew who would say 'yes, ma'am,' and 'no, ma'am,' in a house of prostitution."

In 1972, Ray Arcel—along with Freddie Brown—seconded Roberto Duran when Duran won the lightweight championship from Scotsman Ken Buchanan in Madison Square Garden. This was Arcel's first appearance in a fighter's corner in New York in eighteen years.

At the time of Arcel's comeback, press agent Irving Rudd—whose friendship with Arcel dates back to the 1930s—would ask young writers, "Do you know that the world's lightweight champion is seventy-three years old?" To writers unaware of Arcel's history, meeting him must have been like stumbling upon a long-lost family friend who could tell them everything they wanted to know about their parents and grandparents.

What did you think of Jack Dempsey when you saw him fight in 1916? What was it like to befriend Benny Leonard at Grupp's Gymnasium in 1917—and later train him for his comeback in the early '30s? What kind of a man was Gene Tunney? How did Barney Ross behave during his loss to Henry Armstrong? What was it like to work opposite Joe Louis? Arcel's answers to these and other questions were polished yet unsentimental—and his opinions were utterly authentic. It only added to Arcel's considerable appeal that at the time he was handling one of the finest and most ferocious lightweights of all time, Roberto Duran.

Stories written about Arcel during the 1970s show that journalists found themselves with the enviable task of acting as jewelers, creating the proper settings for Arcel's gem-like memories. Two writers who rose memorably to the task were Red Smith who, over the years, devoted several columns to Arcel, and Jerry Izenberg of the *New York Post* who wrote a fine profile of Arcel in 1979 for *Sport* magazine.

Both Smith and Izenberg chronicled the by-now familiar story of how Arcel, after retiring from boxing in disgust in 1954, was lured back into the game by an old friend, the millionaire Panamanian Carlos Eleta who managed Roberto Duran.

In 1972, one of Eleta's boxers, Peppermint Frazer, was scheduled to fight for the junior welterweight title. Eleta had worked with Arcel twenty-five years earlier when he sent Arcel a Panamanian fighter named Frederico Plummer. Eleta now wanted Arcel's help with Peppermint Frazer.

As Arcel recalled for Jerry Izenberg, he told Carlos Eleta's representative, "I'm seventy-three years old. I do not train fighters anymore. I hardly ever even go to fights anymore. . . . I have a job and a good life and I'm not interested."

Arcel's initial reluctance to resume his boxing career somehow made his return that much more appealing—the revered wise man emerges from retirement only as a favor to a friend. Arcel had, after all, established a life outside the ring and was quite successful as a purchasing agent in the steel business. Arcel did not need boxing.

But Arcel relented and journeyed to Panama with his wife. He couldn't help Eleta's fighter, Peppermint Frazer, however, without first sizing up the opponent, the Argentianian Nicolino Loche. Informed that Loche trained in secret, Arcel donned a disguise and snuck into one of Loche's workouts. Arcel's account of what happened next speaks volumes about the subtlety of his powers of observation, his great gift for strategic invention, and the sheer joy and precision of his storytelling.

"I get inside the gym, and right away I know our man Peppermint has a problem," Arcel told Izenberg. "This Loche is excellent. He is a good mechanic but I get a feeling there's something more there. Then I see it. He is backing away and the sparring partner is moving in. Now Loche misses a left hand and leans back and he's on the ropes and I can't figure out what the hell he's trying to do.

"The kid moves to him and then I really see it for the first time—the real rope-a-dope. He grabs his kid, pulls him in, spins him around and now the positions are reversed and he's beating hell out of the kid.

"So I go back to Frazer and I watch him and I don't really say anything to him until the night before the fight. I tell Frazer that he can forget the jab because he couldn't land one on this Loche with a machine gun. Now I see Peppermint's scared and he wants to know what to do."

Arcel then gave Frazer this advice, Izenberg reported: "Now you listen, and no matter how it sounds, you do it. You walk out there in the center of the ring when the bell rings and you throw the biggest right hand you ever threw in your life. I don't even care if it lands . . . just so he knows you've got one. Then he will feint and slide back to the ropes.

"Now, you are home and you are the hero, so you remember this. There will be 20,000 Panamanians there. When he goes to the ropes you step back to the center of the ring and laugh at him. Now those 20,000 Panamanians will have seen you throw the right hand. They will know now you came to fight. So don't follow him. Make him come off the ropes. If he doesn't, 20,000 Panamanians will do it for you."

Concluding the same story for Red Smith, Arcel said simply, "Well, that first punch won the fight. The fight went fifteen rounds with Peppermint in command."

This one anecdote embodies the pattern that makes Arcel such terrific press copy: the sagacious trainer makes a shrewd, complex observation which would not be apparent to the un-trained eye; he passes it along to the fighter at the psychologi-cally correct moment; the fighter does as he's told; the oppo-nent reacts precisely as the trainer predicted; and the trainer's fighter goes on to victory.

The history of Arcel's reluctant mission to help Peppermint Frazer might have gone largely untold if Carlos Eleta had not soon phoned Arcel again. This time Eleta was seeking Arcel's help with a young boxer named Roberto Duran, who was in line to challenge for the lightweight title. "I told him [Eleta] I had another business that was very important to me," Arcel explained to Red Smith, "but I'd give him as much time as I could. I told him I'd get Freddie Brown to work with me, because I think Freddie is one of the best in the business."

Freddie Brown—eight years Arcel's junior and perhaps best known as the cut man for Rocky Marciano—had trained Bob Pastor and Abe Simon for their fights with Joe Louis, and had seconded Tony Janiro, Joey Archer, Dick Tiger and countless others.

Arcel and Brown went way back togther. They both worked at Stillman's Gym, and at different times they had both been partners with trainer Whitey Bimstein. As Arcel told Red Smith, "We were together with a lot of fighters and sometimes we were in opposite corners. I was with Ezzard Charles, you know, and the night he split Rocky Marciano's nose like a walnut, it was Freddie who stopped the bleeding long enough for Rocky to knock Snooks out. That's what we called Ezzard—Snooks."

Brown traveled to training camp with Duran and handled Duran's day-to-day supervision, a job that was at times more than maddening owing to Duran's moodiness, frequent reluctance to take sensible counsel and his outsized appetite for food that would put him over the 135-pound lightweight limit. Arcel stayed in touch with Brown, and joined the camp for the final stages of preparation. Nestor Quinones, Duran's original trainer from Panama, also continued to work in the Duran camp.

Duran's manager, Carlos Eleta, described Duran's need for Arcel and Brown in a 1978 article by Pat Putnam in *Sports Illustrated*. "Our trouble is that the trainers he [Duran] has in Panama can't handle him, they can't control him. And he knows this is not good for him. Only Brown and Arcel can control him. That is why before every fight he calls me and says, 'Where are they? I need them. Please call and get them for me.'"

The different roles played by the two trainers was best—and quite movingly—described by Duran himself in Jerry Izenberg's

Sport piece. "Freddie Brown is like my Poppa," Duran told Izenberg. "I can't even go to the bathroom without him peeking. But Ray Arcel, for him I have no words. I feel so much for him. And when he is angry, he says nothing. He only gives me the look, then I know it is time to go to work."

When I ask Arcel what he and Brown taught Duran, Arcel gives me a version of "the look"—as if he is displeased at even a vague effort to overplay his own role in Duran's career. "Nobody had to teach Duran how to fight," Arcel lectures. "The first day I saw him—not in New York, I saw him in Panama—I told everybody around him, *'Don't change his style.* Leave him alone. I don't want anybody to ever tell him what to do. Let him fight,' I said. 'He'll carry the whole gang of us.' He knew how to fight."

Describing Duran's impoverished background Arcel recalls, "He was a street fighter. And the people down in Panama . . . I tell you, poverty—it's a terrible thing to look at. And I used to go down there and it used to break my heart. And I was a perfect stranger. So how would he as a native—women coming around with two or three kids—who didn't eat . . . Whatever he had in his pocket, he gave 'em."

Though Arcel downplays the importance of his own work, he and Brown were credited with increasing Duran's patience, discipline and flexibility as a fighter. They fashioned a strong left jab to match Duran's celebrated right-hand knockout punch and polished Duran's often underrated defensive skills.

Arcel was also widely credited for the strategy Duran used when winning the lightweight title from Ken Buchanan in 1972. No fight, however, demonstrates Arcel's importance better than Duran's 1974 victory over Esteban DeJesus.

In 1972, DeJesus handed Duran his first loss as a professional, knocking him down and outpointing him in a ten-round, nontitle bout. Before the 1974 rematch with DeJesus, Red Smith reported, Arcel told Duran, "Now, listen carefully. When DeJesus knocked you down, you were starting to throw a right hand and he beat you to it with a hook. He'll be expecting the right hand again. I know you are angry, eager for revenge, want to take him out as fast as you can. Don't do it. Just stick, stick, stick and move until I give the word." Smith concisely conveyed the result of Arcel's wisdom: "Duran outboxed DeJesus for ten rounds. Finally, Ray said, 'Now!' K.O. 11."

The minute observation of opponents' weaknesses; the calm concentration in the corner; the sage advice that repeatedly proves to be uncannily correct—what is the source of Arcel's wisdom and poise? The answer, Arcel says, is very simple: "I was a very diligent pupil." If A. J. Liebling likened the mature Arcel to a severe Hebrew teacher, then the young Arcel must have been an inspired student with a passion for knowledge.

Ray Arcel was born on August 30, 1899 in Terre Haute, Indiana, the son of Jewish immigrants. He recalls that when his father's family came to America, "they were put on a train and the train stopped at Terre Haute, Indiana, and they all got off."

Arcel still speaks sadly of his mother becoming very ill when he was four years old. "You see, my mother was born in Brooklyn, so she wanted to come to New York and see her parents because she felt like she was gonna die."

Arcel's father, a peddler who eventually owned a fruit store in Terre Haute, moved his family to New York—first to the Lower East Side and then to 106th Street near Third Avenue in Harlem. Arcel's mother passed away shortly after the family arrived in the City.

In describing his life as a young Jewish boy in a tough, Italian neighborhood, Arcel displays his characteristic abhorrence of cliché: "You had to fight in those days. You lived in a neighborhood where you were challenged every day. We were the only Jewish family there, but that's an old story. Wherever you go they tell you the same story. Of course, fighting in the street meant nothing. Wherever you'd go, you'd see two guys fighting." With a smile Arcel adds, "If you didn't fight you were yellow."

Contemplating the prejudice which so frequently led to

street fights, Arcel says sadly, "People brought their hatreds with them from Europe. They didn't go to school, so they fought. It just grows, ignorance. Kids develop this hatred."

Seeking to hone their fighting skills, Arcel and his friends visited Grupp's Gymnasium on 116th Street near Eighth Avenue, across town from Arcel's East Harlem home. It was here that Arcel's fascination with boxing began. "Boxing grew on me, and I got acquainted with a very good boxer, Benny Valgar," Arcel explains, citing one of the finest lightweights of the time. "He was an exceptional boxer. I used to go up to Grupp's Gymnasium with him. He trained there. And the first time I went was about 1917." Eventually, Arcel fought eight or nine professional fights, earning two dollars per bout. He soon decided to become a trainer.

At Grupp's, Arcel also forged a friendship with the great lightweight champion Benny Leonard, who journeyed from his home on the Lower East Side to train at the gym. Leonard, a fighter Arcel never speaks of with anything short of reverence, was perhaps the best lightweight who ever lived.

"Leonard was just as great as can be," Arcel recalls with a warm smile. "And he used to talk to me, and I used to ask him a million dumb questions and he used to show me. And naturally, I absorbed all of his knowledge." Pinpointing the source of Leonard's greatness Arcel says, "His main asset was his ability to think. He had the sharpest mind. He was the one fighter that I saw who could make you do the things *he* wanted you to do. He could feint you into knots. He was a master of the feint."

Listing other outstanding Jewish fighters of the era, Arcel says, "There was Marty Cross, Leach Cross. They all changed their names in those days because it was a very—it was a shame for a Jewish boy to be a fighter, you understand." Benny Leonard's given name, for example, was Benjamin Leiner.

To illustrate the attitude of many Jewish families towards boxing at the time, Arcel tells a story about Benny Leonard, masterfully recreating the Yiddish accents of those involved.

"When he started on the Lower East Side, Leonard had a following," Arcel begins. "Because he—right from the very start—had an exceptional style and ability. So one day there was a little bus in front of his house and his mother happened to be downstairs. His father was a presser. He earned eight dollars a week. And the mother was standing downstairs, and as soon as she saw all these guys going into this little bus, she happened to say to one of the neighbors, 'What's going on here?' Told that fans were gathering to travel to see a fighter, Leonard's mother asked, 'A fighter? What is this?' The neighbor told her simply, 'Ask your son. He's the fighter.'"

Leonard's mother "went upstairs and she was all upset," Arcel continues, "and his father came home late that evening, and she started to cry and to carry on. . . . The father was waiting when Leonard came home, and he brought him into the bedroom. He said, 'What's going on? What are you doing? You're bringing shame to the family. What is this—you're a fighter?' So Leonard had boxed a preliminary and he had made thirty-five dollars. He took the thirty-five dollars out of his pocket, he gave it to his father, and his father said, 'What is this?' He said, 'That's what I got for fighting.' He said, 'That's what you got for one night fighting?' He says, 'Benny. When are you going to fight again?'"

Arcel, too, initially concealed his fascination with boxing and his ambition of becoming a trainer. "I used to go right into the gym after school," he remembers. "One day my stepmother said to me, 'Where are you running to with that bag?' So I said to her, 'I'm a salesman.' So she says, 'What do you sell?' I said, 'Hooks, jabs and uppercuts.'" Arcel laughs with delight at the memory, summoning the impish look of a young high school student pulling a gag on his stepmother.

Though Arcel's father wanted his son to become a doctor, he took pride in the young man's growing fame as a trainer. When Arcel's name began appearing in newspapers, his father always showed the clippings to his friends. Arcel describes his father as calm and quiet. He was a man who "never hollered," Arcel says, "like me." Citing his father's favorite Yiddish proverb, Arcel adds, "My father taught me, 'Without common sense you are buried.'"

Arcel's recollections of his youthful efforts to learn to be a trainer create an image of a young man in perpetual motion. "I didn't have too much money, so I used to walk or run from 106th Street and Third Avenue to 116th Street and Eighth Avenue, which is quite a distance. But it made no difference to me because I was a runner in high school, and I used to just run. And I used to go right into the gym after school." Despite all his boxing activity, Arcel managed to graduate from Stuyvesant High School.

Two well-known trainers of the time served as Arcel's mentors: Frank "Doc" Bagley, who once managed Gene Tunney, and Dai Dollings, a Welshman who had trained marathon runners and became involved with boxing around 1914. Dollings' best-known fighters included Harry Wills, Jack Britton and Johnny Dundee.

Describing his internship with Bagley and Dollings, Arcel says, "I worked with both of these men continously. I wanted to be a great trainer . . . and I learned all the tricks of the trade." For Arcel, this was a time of great mental activity—genuine learning.

A 1942 *Collier's* magazine profile of Dai Dollings by Dan Parker, sports editor and columnist for *The New York Daily Mirror*, depicted Dollings, then eighty-three years old, as "one of the physical marvels of the age"—a well-conditioned, strict vegetarian who walked ten miles a day and was "more active than the average man half his age." A veteran of over a hundred fights himself—in both the bare-knuckle and gloved eras— Dollings was the great grandson of a famed Welsh trainer of boxers. Parker also reported Dollings' claims that he could eliminate two pounds of fat from the body through massage, cure baldness, and rid the body of rheumatism with a combination of diet and hot baths.

Arcel recalls that Dollings used to boast in his strong Welsh accent, "I'm the best rubber [masseur] in the world and the best doctor in the world." While teaching the art of massage, Arcel adds with a hearty laugh, Dollings would tell him, "You bloody bastard, you'll never learn."

Describing his sessions with Dai Dollings at Grupp's Gymnasium, Arcel says, "When you're in an area like that you're in a school. You're in a college. You're watching real pros."

Foremost among Dai Dollings' lessons to Arcel was the importance of scrupulously observing the opposition. It's a lesson Arcel would employ six decades later when he spied on Nicolino Loche before his match against Peppermint Frazer.

"Dollings was a smart trainer," Arcel says, pointing to his head for emphasis. "He was a fella who'd study the styles of the different boxers. And of course when I started with him, that was the one thing he inspired me with—everyone's style is different, so you must understand the different styles of your opponents. And we used to make a great study, watching these fellas work."

Dollings also taught Arcel to treat each fighter as a unique individual. Arcel never forgot the lesson. "Each young man that came to me, I made a complete study of his personal habits, his temperament," says Arcel. "Because there are some people you could scold and some people you had to be careful with. And you treated each person as a different individual. No two people are alike. What you tell one fella, you couldn't help the other fella with. And some fellas could develop mental energy and others couldn't. And you had to find out how to teach him."

Dollings was a notoriously frugal man who was never eager to part with a nickel for a street car, so Arcel made it a practice to accompany Dollings on his long walks around Manhattan. "But in the course of that," Arcel says, "I'd talk nothing but fights—different moves, different angles."

As for Arcel's other mentor, Doc Bagley, a 1939 *Saturday Evening Post* article describes him as "a studious, gaunt, round-shouldered man in his fifties, who . . . is considered the best cut man among seconds and will usually be found in the corner of any fighter who bleeds easily."

Bagley's reputation as a great cut man was based partly on his work in Gene Tunney's corner during Tunney's 1922 loss to the legendary Harry Greb—the only loss of Tunney's career. Describing Bagley's efforts that night, Tunney later told columnist Grantland Rice, "Between rounds Doc's long fingers flew. A superb 'cut' man, he'd manage to stop the bleeding only to watch Greb bust my face in the following round. It was disgusting." Though Tunney estimated he lost "nearly two quarts of blood" during the fight—and Grantland Rice called it "perhaps the bloodiest fight I've ever covered"—Bagley managed to keep Tunney going for fifteen brutal rounds.

Arcel takes delight in passing on a story which reveals his own youthful, over-eager ambition to be the Doc Bagley of his generation. "Doc Bagley chewed tobacco, and he could stop the worst kinds of cuts. And in those days a boxing arena was the size of this living room, approximately," Arcel says, gesturing towards the living room of his apartment. "And everybody smoked and before you realized it, the place was smoke-filled. The fellas standing in the back couldn't even see the fighters.

"So we used to swing a towel in between rounds. When a fighter came back, we'd swing a towel and try to get some air into this guy's lungs. And I was a towel-swinger because I was working with Bagley and he let me work in the corner because I wanted to. I wanted to watch him, I wanted to see how he operated. And he'd say, 'Swing that towel!'

"And if the fella got a cut he'd take a piece of chewing tobacco out of his mouth and press it up against the cut. I didn't know whether it was the pressure applied or whether it was tobacco juice or whatever it was, but he was successful in stopping the cuts.

"One day . . . well, he used to handle all his fighters, whether they were four-round fighters . . . he was that diligent a man.

And he called me at home and he told me that a certain kid, a four-round fighter, was boxing in Jersey City, and would I go over with him?" Here Arcel laughs as he approaches the punch line.

"This was my first chance to become Doc Bagley. The first thing I did was I bought a plug of chewing tobacco. And I sat in the corner and I was just praying for this guy to get cut. I wanted to fix the cut. And then all of a sudden, [I saw] an imaginary flow of blood! And I bit into the tobacco ... and I must have swallowed the juice and I got sick. I fell underneath the ring and I never knew what happened to the fighter or anybody. They called an ambulance. They thought I had appendicitis."

Again Arcel laughs with the relish of a man who enjoys telling a story about himself. Whenever Bagley saw him after that, he'd offer Arcel some chewing tobacco—a running gag which still delights Arcel more than seventy years later.

The historic reach of Arcel's boxing memories is demonstrated by his account of seeing Jack Dempsey fight John Lester Johnson in New York in 1916. "In those days, you could see a fight for a quarter. So a whole gang of us went up to see this 'great fighter,'" Arcel says, recreating the skepticism he felt as a teenager intent on evaluating Dempsey for himself.

Arcel was not impressed. "He looked like anything but a great fighter. I mean, there were no decisions in those days. So you fought and when the fight was over you walked out of the ring. But Dempsey didn't look like a fighter. You know, a rough, tough guy—but he was a saloon brawler."

Later on, of course, Arcel's opinion of Dempsey changed. "As rough and tough a guy as Jack Dempsey was, he still had knowledge," Arcel says. "He still had a lot of knowledge. He knew how to get away from a punch." Yet Arcel remains aggravated over Dempsey's tendency to take off too much time between fights. "Idleness," Arcel says, "he laid off too long. Too long! I was in Los Angeles with him in 1925. I stayed at his hotel and I said to him, 'What the hell are you doing, Jack? Why don't you fight? . . . He was having problems with [his manager] Jack Kearns, then he married Estelle Taylor. And he's running the hotel. I mean, you gotta be a fighter," Arcel continues. "You gotta fight."

But Dempsey remains very high on Arcel's list of great champions. A Dempsey fight was "magic," Arcel told *The New York Times* after Dempsey died in 1983. "The minute he walked into the ring you could see the smoke rising from the canvas. You knew you were going to see a tiger let loose." Comparing Dempsey to other heavyweights, Arcel said, "Who could say anyone was better than Joe Louis? But Dempsey was as great as you'd want any fighter to be. . . . Dempsey would have had a picnic with most of today's fighters."

Talk of old-time heavyweights prompts Arcel to tell a story about Jack Dempsey's great rival and successor as heavyweight champion, Gene Tunney. The story also involves Benny Leonard—not in his customary role as a fighter, but as an adviser to Tunney.

Setting the scene, Arcel recalls Tunney's 1922 loss to Harry Greb. Greb "was great," Arcel says, "but as great as he was, that's how dirty he was—all of the dirty tricks of the game." Speaking with compassion for what the defeated Tunney went through in losing to Greb, Arcel says sadly, "This is the only fight Tunney ever lost—and he took a bad lickin'."

Following the loss, Tunney became obsessed with beating Greb in a rematch. Tunney was then managed by Billy Gibson who also handled Benny Leonard at the time. "Tunney made up his mind. He was a very determined guy—clever, determined and very difficult to talk to," Arcel remembers. "And Tunney kept harping, 'Get that guy back for me.' And he kept calling Gibson every day, 'Did you make the match?'

"So Gibson finally called Leonard up, that was his fighter. He says, 'Ben, do me a favor. Go up in the gym,' he says, 'Gene is working out. I don't have anything booked for him, but he's working out. He's tearing the bags down. And he's fighting for a return match with Greb. Go up there, look at him, influence him to take his time. 'Cause I don't want to make the match yet.'"

Because Arcel was at the gym when Tunney and Leonard met, he is able to recreate much of the dialogue between the two champions.

"So Benny went over there, and of course when Leonard walked into a gymnasium everybody stopped working. This was the great, the great . . . you know. And he walked over to Gene, and Gene is punching the bag and Leonard stood there lookin' at him and he says, 'How are you, Gene?' Tunney kept punching and he said, 'I'm all right, Ben, I'm trying to get into shape. I'm gonna knock that Greb out.'

"Leonard says, 'You're throwing a right hand. Where you gonna hit him with a right hand? On the chin? You ain't never gonna hit Greb on the chin with a right hand. If you're gonna hit Greb with a right hand, the place to try to hit him is in the body. Try to do *that*.' And he says, 'Take your time. The longer you wait to fight Greb, the better it is for you.'

"Greb had a great reputation for being a dissipater—drinking and all that. Greb was that way. He fought every night in the week. If you look at his record you see that he fought twenty, twenty-five fights a year.

"So Leonard says, 'The longer you wait, the better off you are because this guy dissipates. He drinks. He runs around with women.'

"And Leonard went up there for a few days and just talked to him. Kinda eased him, you know. And Tunney had such great respect for Leonard that he took advantage of that knowledge.

"And the second fight, Tunney destroyed Greb. *He destroyed him*. He really did. *Body punches*. He took Leonard's advice."

Telling the story, Arcel quietly repeats phrases like "he took a terrible beating" and "he destroyed him," as if in awe of the punishment absorbed by two formidable champions when they meet.

As an afterthought, Arcel also shares his memories of Tunney. "I always had a lot of respect for him. I never was very friendly with him, but I *respected* him. He was the type of guy, he was a determined guy and a very sincere and conscientious worker. And there's no telling how far he could have gone as a boxer. Of course he was never a puncher. And naturally the people go to see knockouts. With Tunney, it was ten- or fifteen-round fights. But he displayed boxing knowledge that the average guy didn't have."

Lessons, hard work, diligence—these words take on an almost sacred quality as they come up again and again in Arcel's memories of his life as a trainer in the 1920s and 1930s. Though he taught lessons that were brutally physical, Arcel was above all a supreme pedagogue. "I never considered myself a trainer," he says. "I considered myself a teacher."

Repeating the lectures he used to fix his principles in his fighters' minds, Arcel says, "Learn how to think! Don't stand there and get hit. Talk to yourself. Talk while you're shadowboxing. Make believe you got an opponent in front of you who's trying to hit you with a jab. What am I going to do? Maybe I'll throw it off and I'll counter."

If Arcel was a strict instructor, he also displayed a sensitive understanding of the frailties of the human psyche. "I had great patience. I never scolded a fighter, especially a young fighter because I learned early in my career that that's the easiest way to discourage a fighter."

Arcel understood the need to build a boxer's ego slowly. "You instilled confidence in a fighter that tomorrow was another day. Sometimes if he'd get in there and box and he'd walk out of the ring, some of them would cry, 'Geez, I didn't do good.' 'Well, tomorrow you'll do better. Don't worry about it. This is a school.' We taught them that the gym was a school. That's where you learned your lessons.

"And we never hesitated or failed to sit and talk to the fighter after the work was over: what he did wrong, how he should do it better. 'Try to do this tomorrow. Think about it when you go home. When you get up in the morning, shadowbox in front of the mirror. Make believe that your image in the mirror is your opponent. *Think* about it.' And you instill a strong influence on him to keep thinking, keep thinking."

Arcel believed strongly in positive reinforcement—so much so that he wasn't above deluding a fighter now and then. "I'd never discourage them. '*Now you're doing it.*' Even if they didn't do it. '*Now you're doing it.* Did you see how you made that guy miss? Did you see how you ducked away from a punch? Did you see how you countered?' He never did," Arcel recalls, "but that was his lesson."

Yet there is clearly steel within this supremely gentle man. As Duran remembered, "When he gives me the look, then I know it is time to go to work."

But Arcel, always careful and purposeful, used his anger in a controlled, self-conscious way designed to get results. "There were days when I would scold and walk away," Arcel remembers, stressing that he never held a grudge. "*That was the end of it.* They never heard of it again. But I left an indelible impression. And they figured, 'If Ray scolds me . . .' I sent them home *thinking.*"

Arcel remembers angrily telling fighters who had disappointed him, "When you lie in bed tonight, *you think* about what you did wrong. I don't have to tell you, you know." It was a lecture that often yielded the desired results. "Naturally they'd come in and when they'd work again it was, 'Well, is that all right?'"

As much as Arcel stresses the joys of his early days as a trainer, he also emphasizes the hard work and economic hardships. His typical day was long. "As a trainer, we used to get to the gym, maybe eight o'clock, nine o'clock and I'd never leave the gym until maybe seven or eight o'clock at night." Arcel would then work fighters' corners as often as six nights a week, seldom returning home before one or two in the morning. "I was just instilled with that strong desire," he says.

But Arcel was not alone. "Any trainer that we had in those days was a capable man because every fighter you worked with wanted to win, he wanted to make money. The family was starving. Whatever money he made—ten dollars a round—whatever money he made he had to bring home just to have as eating money. People don't realize what tough years they were. It's different than today when a guy sees he gets a hundred thousand, two-hundred thousand or fifty million."

Arcel also remembers feeling a bond with his fellow trainers at Stillman's Gym. "There was sort of a close association. There were no big shots. We were all bums starving to death! I mean, what the hell, we did the best we could."

Though Arcel was not earning a lot of money, his hard work created champions. In 1927, he trained Terry Roth, the first boxer to ever win a golden gloves title. Summing up his early ring successes, Arcel says, "In the course of three different years, I had developed three champions: In 1923, Frankie Genaro, he beat Pancho Villa for the flyweight title. In 1924, Abe Goldstein, he was an orphan, came out of the orphanage. And I worked with him. Lovely, lovely guy. Smart. And he beat Joe Lynch for the bantamweight title. So when he lost that to Eddie Martin, then I developed Charley Phil Rosenberg. I took thirty-nine pounds off him to win the title."

Arcel particularly cherishes the story of Charley Phil Rosenberg, who in 1925 had only three months to drop from 155 pounds to 118 pounds to fight Eddie "Cannonball" Martin for the bantamweight championship. It is one of the most celebrated episodes in Arcel's career.

Before the fight, Arcel became inseparable from Rosenberg while forcing the fighter to follow a strict regimen of running, sparring and walking ten miles a day. Arcel also created a spartan diet that limited even Rosenberg's intake of water. To make sure that Rosenberg didn't stray from the program, Arcel slept in the same room as his fighter. As Rosenberg lost weight, so did Arcel, so that at the time of the fight, Arcel says, "He weighed 116; I weighed 116."

"I remember Rosenberg being so dried out and his throat so parched that I would let him gargle to cool his throat while I stood a few inches away watching his Adam's apple to make sure he didn't swallow any," Arcel remembered in a 1950 interview with Nat Loubet of *The Ring*. "At night I would give him a couple of spoonfuls of calf's jelly, which is cooling to the throat but not fattening. I recall making Charley work out in a rubber girdle which I made from baby's rubber panties." Arcel added, "I dragged thirty-nine pounds off Rosenberg many a time and it didn't appear to affect his health, but it sure played hell on his temper . . . what he called me you can't print . . . but I got him in shape."

Expanding on the fine points of taking weight off of fighters, Arcel told *The Ring*, "Weight making is an art. It is generally bad for a fighter but a lot of it depends on the build of the man. You must know the complete makeup of the fighter you're attempting to take the weight off. A short, chunky guy like Jake La Motta or a Charley Rosenberg is easy, but take a guy like Abe Goldstein, he was a wiry, slim kid and all he had to do was take a shave and he was at his fighting weight. To take anything off Goldstein was impossible without hurting him."

From 1925 through 1934, Arcel was partners with Whitey Bimstein. Together they became known as "The Siamese Training Twins," and handled such fighters as junior welterweight champion Jackie "Kid" Berg; middleweight champion Lou Brouillard; and bantamweight champion Sixto Escobar.

While they were partners, Bimstein and Arcel each worked with their own fighters separately. "You know, we'd have certain fighters that Whitey would handle and certain fighters that I would handle. Whitey was a good trainer—an excellent trainer. I mean, there were days when we wouldn't say two words to one another because from ten to six we'd be working with different fighters. If we started with a kid, we'd stay with him. There were days when he might lose patience or I might lose patience—and we'd switch."

Arcel and Bimstein also often faced each other in opposite corners during fights. No one, however, seems to have accused the two of a conflict of interest.

Al Braverman, who remembers both Arcel and Bimstein from his days as a young heavyweight at Stillman's, contrasts Arcel and Bimstein this way: "Whitey was well-liked. Outgoing. Ray was different. Ray was like a principal in a school. Whitey was like one of the students."

In discussing his work with Bimstein, Arcel stresses the hard times the two went through together. "It wasn't a question of making money. There was no money around. I mean there was a little money. But the amount of money the trainer earned was minimum compared to what a fella would earn today."

During the depression years, Arcel recalls, "There were no days off. You had to try to pick up a five-dollar bill some place. You learned how to starve quietly." On many days, Arcel adds, "I'd walk into the gym, maybe I'd have a nickel in my pocket." He'd approach a young fighter about sparring only to be told, "Ray, I didn't eat." Inevitably, Arcel wound up using his credit at the Stillman's snackbar to buy the starving pugilist a roll and coffee.

In 1934, Arcel and Bimstein decided to dissolve their partnership. "You couldn't make any money, and finally Whitey and I sat down, and I said, 'Look, Whitey, let's go on our own. If I make ten dollars, I gotta give you five dollars. If you make ten, you gotta give me five. And it hurts. This way we can still work together and keep what we make.'"

After Bimstein died in 1969, Lester Bromberg of the *New*

York Post asked Arcel about rumors that he and Bimstein had "parted enemies." Arcel responded, "Who could fight with a sweet guy like Whitey?"

One fighter Arcel handled without Bimstein was Benny Leonard. "I worked with him alone because Leonard was a very peculiar fella," Arcel explains. "And Whitey had a different disposition than me."

Though Arcel had befriended Leonard early on, he did not work as Leonard's trainer until Leonard—who had retired as champion in 1925—was forced back into boxing in 1931 after losing his money in the stock market crash. "Bad investments," Arcel says, explaining Leonard's economic woes. "He retired with a million dollars and he thought that that was all the money in the world. Well, it was in 1925."

Of his association with Leonard, Arcel says, "He honored me by saying, 'I want you to look after me.'"

Arcel also vividly remembers his incredulous response to a phone call from the great Leonard. "I was in Los Angeles, and I got this call, it was Benny. 'This is Benny Leonard.' I said, 'Who?' He says, '*Benny Leonard.*' I says, 'Oh, come on, stop.' He says, 'No. Ray, this is Benny.'"

When Arcel returned to New York he learned that although Leonard had begun his comeback under Jack Dempsey's manager, Doc Kearns, Leonard wanted to make a change. Arcel then agreed not only to train Leonard, but to book the fights, too.

In 1931, Leonard was thirty-five years old and a veteran of nearly two-hundred fights—nowhere near the great Leonard of old. "I knew he had nothing," Arcel remembers. "He was washed up. But he was dead broke. I knew he wasn't gonna make any money, so I figured if he was that great a fighter, he rates much consideration."

Rather than putting Leonard in against leading contenders, Arcel booked matches against ordinary fighters in small clubs. "If you wanted big money fights, you could've fought name fighters and gotten hurt," Arcel says. "But he wasn't that equipped. As fast a thinker as he was and as good a fighter as he was, his reflexes were gone and his coordination was way off, and he had to have constant work in order to be able to re-establish himself mentally and physically—and regain his confidence. I don't care who you are, you're away from the business for six years, you might kid the world, but you can't kid yourself."

Opponents were easy to find for Leonard. "Managers loved him. 'Put my kid in with him.' They knew he wouldn't hurt 'em. You know, he wasn't gonna look to make a knockout record."

The financial rewards were modest. "I booked him in these various small clubs and he got a pretty good percentage. You know, everybody wanted to see Benny Leonard. We didn't make any money. He was getting five, six, seven-hundred dollars for a fight. And that was all the money he had. That's what he was living on. It cost him one-hundred dollars to get in shape, you know. We went to a training camp and you had to pay forty or fifty dollars a week. But I went along with it and traveled with him. Fights in Albany and all over. He was making enough money to get by."

As Leonard's comeback progressed, the boxing commission became concerned. "The commission called us down," Arcel recalls. "You know, there's always somebody that will interfere with your progress. You don't bother anybody. You go along, but there's always some s.o.b. who can't mind his own business who'll file a complaint. And the complaint was, what do you allow a great fighter like this to make a fool out of himself in these small clubs? So I went down and talked to the commission with Leonard. And I told them, I said, 'He's broke.' And they said, 'Look, Ben, get yourself a shot of money and call it quits. We don't want you to fight.' So he said all right. By this time he felt like he'd had it, too. 'Cause he wasn't making any headway."

On October 7, 1932, Leonard lost by a sixth-round knockout to future welterweight champion Jimmy McLarnin in Madison

Square Garden. It was the sixteenth fight of Leonard's comeback.

"They charged one dollar to five dollars," Arcel says. "Five
dollars ringside. And Leonard got as much as McLarnin—
twenty-five percent. There were no guarantees in those days.
Jimmy Johnston [the head of Madison Square Garden boxing]
said they could draw $60,000, which they did. Sold out com-
pletely." Leonard's purse, Arcel recalls, was $15,000.

Film of the fight shows the young Arcel in Leonard's corner,
his hands beneath Leonard's armpits as he lifts the fighter off
the stool at the start of each round. It is exactly the same
posture Arcel would use almost half a century later when
sending Roberto Duran out against the likes of Ken Buchanan
and Sugar Ray Leonard.

Benny Leonard "nailed McLarnin" in the first round of the
fight, Arcel says, "and that was all. He couldn't do it." Recalling
the following rounds, Arcel says somberly, "Leonard to me was
like a brother. I just took care of him as much as I could. And I
kept saying, 'Are you all right? Are you all right?' Arthur Donovan [the referee] was given instructions to please don't let him
get hurt. That was his instructions. Don't let him get hurt. And
he kept watching to see if McLarnin nailed him. McLarnin
nailed him in the sixth round, and was ready to nail him again,
and Donovan stopped it."

Arcel's fondest memories of working with Benny Leonard,
though, are of training sessions, when Leonard would be surrounded by young admirers. "I used to tell Leonard, 'Get into
the ring—box with these kids, teach them.' I said, 'I don't want
you to get hit. You don't need any sparring partners. Get in the
ring and teach these kids.' They all wanted to box with him.
He'd never hurt them. And he taught them, and he moved, and
he boxed. He was a great guy. And oh what a smart person! He
had tremendous thinking powers. And he was a wonderful
influence on a lot of these kids."

When I make a casual comparison between Benny Leonard

and Sugar Ray Leonard, Arcel stops me cold. "Sugar Ray Leonard never would come *one step* with Benny Leonard," Arcel states emphatically. "He was only an imitation, you know."

If Benny Leonard is universally considered the greatest Jewish fighter who ever lived, then another of Arcel's fighters, Barney Ross, may very likely be the next greatest. Leonard and Ross, Arcel says, "were the kind of people that you had to love. They were decent human beings, considerate. It was just a pleasure to be with them—joke, kid around. They knew what they were doin'."

Arcel worked with Ross because he was very friendly with Ross' managers, Art Winch and Sam Piam, who had handled Ross in Chicago since his fifth professional fight. "And, of course, they needed a little help . . . and they asked me to work with 'em," Arcel says, explaining how he came to be in Ross' corner in 1933 when the fighter successfully defended his lightweight crown against Tony Canzoneri in New York.

One of Arcel's prized memories of Ross involves his 1937 defense of his welterweight title against future middleweight champion Ceferino Garcia. The story is central to the legend of Barney Ross. Two days before the Garcia fight, Ross, who had won two decisions from Garcia in 1935, fractured his right thumb. Despite his manager's pleas, Ross refused to delay the fight. Finally, Piam and Winch asked Arcel to convince him to postpone.

As Arcel remembers his words to Ross, his voice is gentle and imploring. "I says, 'Barney, why sacrifice?' He says, 'I don't sacrifice anything.'" Ross then told Arcel of his fight plan: He was out to prove "I don't need the right hand."

For fifteen rounds, Arcel remembers, Barney Ross out-boxed Garcia who was "an excellent, excellent boxer." How did Ross do it? "Just with the left hand—*and a brain*," Arcel says with pride. "He made him miss. He looked like a Benny Leonard in there. And he wasn't looking to knock the guy out. He'd just make believe he was gonna throw the right hand. Maybe he did throw it but he didn't put any force behind it. But that's the way he fought. And that's what most of my fighters were able to do—*think.*"

Arcel was also in Ross' corner in 1938 when Ross lost his welterweight title to Henry Armstrong. Known alternatively as "Hammerin' Hank" and "Homicide Hank," Armstrong was the only man to simultaneously hold titles in three weight divisions—featherweight, lightweight and welterweight. The Armstrong-Ross fight is considered one of the most brutal in history—and Ross's refusal to quit on his stool is part of ring lore.

"Well, Ross was hurt in the twelfth round and we were gonna stop the fight," Arcel says. "Because there was no sense in him getting hit. And he told us, 'You stop this fight and I'll never talk to you for the rest of my life.' And he meant it! And the referee was standing there, and he heard it, and he said, 'All right, you're on your own!' But he was a tremendous, tremendous person, Ross."

For the next "three days and three nights," Arcel recalls, he stayed with Ross in a New York hotel room, ministering to the defeated boxer, "putting hot towels on this man's face."

The late 1930s also provided Arcel with his first glimpse of perhaps the finest fighter who ever lived—Sugar Ray Robinson. One day, George Gainford, Robinson's long-time manager, asked Arcel to come up to the Salem Crescent gym in Harlem. "George and I were good friends," Arcel says proudly. "I said, 'What? You got another bum you want me to look at, George?' He says, 'Come up and look at this guy. This guy's gonna make me a millionaire.' I went up there, and I saw *a fighter,*" Arcel says with awe in his voice. "I said, 'You got something.' I said, 'Where d'ya build *this?*'"

In the 1930s and 1940s, Ray Arcel hauled Joe Louis' victims from the ring with such frequency that he earned the nickname "The Meat Wagon." Arcel first stood across the ring from Louis in Chicago in 1934 when he seconded Charlie Massera whom Louis knocked out in three rounds. Arcel gained his only victory over Louis sixteen years later when his fighter Ezzard Charles won a fifteen-round decision from Louis to defend the heavyweight title.

Along with trainers Doc Robb and Whitey Bimstein and manager Joe Gould, Arcel was in heavyweight champion James J. Braddock's corner when Louis beat Braddock for the title. Recalling Braddock's surprising first-round knockdown of Louis, Arcel says, "Louis was looking to score a one-round knockout—which was a mistake. He did that a couple of times and he got hurt. And Braddock could punch."

The Louis-Braddock match marked the first time a black man had fought for the heavyweight title since Jack Johnson lost it in 1915. Asked if race was an issue at the time of the fight, Arcel replies, "No, that wasn't an issue. The issue was money. Braddock was broke. And they were lookin' to get money."

After Louis won the title, Arcel was faced with the daunting task of preparing opponents to do battle with an awesome champion. How did Arcel help his fighters overcome their natural fear of Joe Louis? "Oh I mean, that's the hardest thing in the world to be able to overcome because any time—I don't care who the man is—there's a certain amount of nervousness," Arcel says. "If you are training three or four weeks to fight *Joe Louis* and you go to bed with Joe Louis every night and you're laying there and you can't sleep and that's on your mind—I mean, that deprives you of energy and the ability to think properly and it takes everything away from you." As Arcel put it in one of his most memorable similes, many of Louis' opponents "folded like tulips."

Joe Louis' boyhood friend Walter Smith—who went on to second fighters such as Thomas Hearns at the Kronk Gym in Detroit—remembers with a laugh, "All those fighters he [Arcel] brought to Joe got dragged out of there. He's a helluva trainer, though, Ray Arcel" Smith adds with respect. "Good man in the ring, knew what to do in the ring. Ray Arcel, I'd go to bat for him. He's one helluva corner man."

Perhaps the most often told Ray Arcel anecdote involves a mid-ring comment made to Arcel by Joe Louis. "It was about the fifth or sixth fight I had against Louis," Arcel recalled for Ira Berkow of *The New York Times* in 1988, "and when I took my fighter—might've been Nathan Mann—to the middle of the ring for instructions, Joe looks at me and says, 'You heah again?' I burst out laughing."

Reminiscing about the effect Louis had on his victims, Arcel told Berkow, "I remember in 1940 I walked Johnny Paychek into the ring against Joe, and his knees were actually trembling. He wasn't a live body." Paychek lasted into the second round. Another of Arcel's fighters, Lou Nova, lasted six rounds in 1941. "Lou knew how to fight," Arcel told Berkow, ". . . but he lost all control of his whole system. He didn't know who he was."

Arcel's fighters occasionally fared better against Louis. In 1941, challenger Buddy Baer succeeded in knocking Louis out of the ring in the first round. Louis fell through the ropes and didn't make it back into the ring until the referee reached the count of four.

"Louis fell out of the ring because the ropes were loose," Arcel says. "It was a wrestlers' ring. Fortunately, there was a platform there and he fell on the platform. But Baer made a good fight that night. Louis was not Louis." Baer, whom Louis accidentally hit after the bell at the end of the sixth round, was disqualified by referee Arthur Donovan after failing to answer the bell for the seventh.

By the time Buddy Baer lost to Louis in one round in their January 1942 rematch in Madison Square Garden, Arcel had developed a sense of humor about his habit of lugging Louis' victims from the ring. The morning after the fight, *The New York World-Telegram* ran a story under Arcel's byline with the headline, "Baer Haulage Arcel's Best: Ray At Peak While Re-trieving Buddy."

Arcel's story read in part: ". . . I am happy to say I retained my title as champion hulk carrier last night in the Garden. I handle big propositions best and Buddy Baer, at 250, gave me a chance to prove that I haven't slipped a bit. Of course, I was in great shape. I never underestimate Joe Louis. I was ready to pick up whatever came my way. I can divulge now that I underwent secret practice before the fight. I worked with [heavyweight contender] Abe Simon at Stillman's Gym and set an unofficial record of two seconds flat in bringing him across his locker room. Unfortunately, there was nobody holding a clock on me last night. I think I was sharper than I've been in some time."

Self-mocking humor aside, Arcel's respect for Louis is bound-less, as is his sympathy for the opponents who crumbled in Louis' presence. Arcel has often said that the idea of a "bum of the month club"—unqualified boxers challenging for Louis' title—was a misnomer. The opponents were often fine fighters, Arcel maintains; the truth is that Louis was simply overpowering.

Film of the conclusion of Ezzard Charles' 1950 decision vic-tory over an aging Louis shows the fighters patting each other on the back after the bell rings to end the bout. Arcel, rising out of Charles' corner, walks to the center of the ring and puts his arms around both fighters. Louis then returns the embrace. Describing his feelings when Charles defeated Louis, Arcel told Michael Marley of the *New York Post* in 1988, "As glad as I was that Ezzard beat Joe, I was sad for Joe. I was very fond of Joe. He was an outstanding man, a real man."

During the Joe Louis era, Arcel was by no means solely occu-pied with opposing the heavyweight champion. His champions in those days included bantamweight Tony Marino and middle-weights Freddie Steele, Ceferino Garcia, Billy Soose and Tony Zale.

Billy Soose, who won the middleweight crown in 1941 with a decision over Ken Overlin, remembers making the decision to have Ray Arcel in his corner. In June of 1939 Soose and his

manager, Paul Moss, were in New York when Arcel seconded
Lou Nova in his knockout victory over former heavyweight
champion Max Baer. "After the fight we went back to the hotel
and Ray invited us to his room," Soose recalls. "And I watched
Ray fixing up Lou Nova's ear. His ear was torn and Ray stayed
with Nova for three days, applying compresses and the like to
Nova's ear. And I told Paul, 'Ray is the man for me as my
trainer.'"

In his first fight with Arcel in his corner, Soose faced the
legendary Charley Burley. Burley is ranked as one of the all-
time greats by such authorities as trainer Eddie Futch and
former light-heavyweight champion Archie Moore, who lost to
Burley in 1944. Burley, however, was one of the outstanding
black fighters of the era who was never given the chance to
fight for a title.

Asked about Burley, Arcel says, "The best. The best! Ray
Robinson wouldn't fight him. Charley Burley was a welterweight, a middleweight. He had to fight heavyweights in order
to make a few bucks. This guy was a master."

Arcel then recalls being approached at Stillman's Gym by
Soose's manager Paul Moss, who said, "I made a match in Pittsburgh, and I'm not sleeping nights because everybody tells me
that my fighter will get knocked out." When Moss told Arcel
that Soose was to face Charley Burley, Arcel thought, "This guy
[Moss] is a nut!"

Arcel recalls giving Soose the following advice about facing
Charley Burley: "Remember one thing, in this guy's mind you
are nothing. And what he's going to try to do is to knock you
out as fast as he can. But we're gonna fool him. Let him try. You
are on the defense all the time. Just move and box like you're
shadowboxing. If you hit him, all right; if you don't hit him it's
okay, too, as long as you don't get hit. Jab and see what he's
gonna do. He's gonna get wild at times. Jab him. That's all. Don't
look to knock him out because you're not gonna do it. Just let
him do all the work and you be on the defensive."

Remembering the fight, Arcel says, "He [Soose] went ten rounds. He lost the decision, and he went into the dressing room and he started to cry. I said, 'What are you crying about?' I says, 'I'm the happiest guy in the world. You went ten rounds with the greatest fighter that's living today. This guy can fight Joe Louis.' I says, 'You're gonna be a helluva fighter, Billy. You did a wonderful job.'"

For his part, Soose today says that Arcel was far more than a trainer. "He taught me many things other than boxing. We were together for three years. He taught me a lot of other values." After citing several of Arcel's lessons about boxing and life, Soose says, "Above all he taught me that love and faith and trust were the most important things in the world."

Soose adds that Arcel was "a very compassionate man" who seemed almost not to belong in boxing. "For him as a trainer in the boxing world back during our time, you know when it was pretty tough . . . He was much too good for the game at that time. He had too much compassion and respect for his fighters."

Following World War II, Arcel worked in Tony Zale's corner for Zale's three celebrated middleweight championship fights with Rocky Graziano. Arcel says that the key to Zale's ability to win two out of three three bouts was his dedication to conditioning. "He was in the Coast Guard for four years. He was down in Puerto Rico. And he was a devout Catholic. He never would go out when they had a night off. He'd go in the gym and spar. And that's what carried him through. So that when he went out [of the Coast Guard] he was able to make some money."

Jackie Cranford, a heavyweight contender in the late 1940s, remembers Arcel as a demanding teacher. "He would train you, and he was tough," Cranford says. "He said, 'Do this, do this'— and you did it. The guy was so businesslike about boxing. He knew the darn thing so well. You just followed along with everything he told you to do."

Arcel often criticized Cranford. "If you did wrong, if you messed up and didn't follow his directions, he told you about it," Cranford says. "If he showed you something in the ring, and you got back in the same position and didn't do it, he'd stop and say, 'What's the matter with you? Why didn't you do it?' He knew how to handle it—not making you mad, not in a grouchy way, but just so firm that this is the right way."

Another of Arcel's fighters from the 1940s, welterweight contender Dan Kapilow, focuses on Arcel's compassion. "His greatest asset to me was his care—caring for you as an individual, as a person, beyond the fact that you might earn some money for him."

Kapilow, the retired president of a New York City Teamster's local and an active member of the boxing veterans' organization, Ring 8, still seems touched by Arcel's concern: "When you got finished with a day in the gym or the night of a particular fight, he wouldn't just leave you putting your shoes on by yourself. He stayed with you 'til you were home practically."

But Arcel "was no patsy in the corner," Kapilow says. "No, he was a strong advocate in the corner. He would throw insults at you and do anything to wake you up—to get you moving.

"He was always making you think that perhaps you were better than you were. I remember a couple of nights when I thought I couldn't make the next round because I was too tired, and at that point he would get pretty tough on you, too. You know, almost threatening to slap you in the face, but instilling in you the ability to get out there and go on. And before you knew it, you were doing it—and he was right. You had plenty of energy left. You had plenty of strength left.

"He was a very . . . how the hell should I put it? He was very sympathetic. He was a good buffer between you and the manager who was usually no good."

One of Kapilow's favorite memories of Arcel involves a fight that took place when Arcel was no longer his trainer. "One night I was fighting a critical fight in Pittsburgh—and this is after the war—against Gene Burton," Kapilow explains. "And in the first round I hit the guy a good left hook, and didn't know I had hurt him. And suddenly out of the corner of my eye, there's Ray Arcel running down to ringside shouting instructions, '*Linka! linka! linka!*' which means 'left hand' in Yiddish. And I'll never forget that night. He came out of the blue. I didn't even know he was in Pittsburgh. That was a one-round knockout for me. That's something that sticks out in your mind, you know, like a photograph. Yeah, I caught him out of the corner of my eye and it was as if he was up in the corner shouting the old instructions."

A detailed account of Arcel's working methods as a trainer during these years is contained in a 1940 profile of Arcel for *Collier's* by Dan Parker of *The New York Mirror*.

"The successful second must be able to double for a mother, a psychologist, a physician and a mind reader," Arcel told Parker. "After you've worked behind five or six-thousand fighters, like I have, it becomes second nature to you, like swimming or typewriting. You've got only about forty seconds to work on your fighter between rounds. Often you have to stop a hemorrhage or bring a fighter back from unconsciousness in that fleeting interval. That's where a second who knows his business can save a fight and where a mere water-bucket toter can lose it."

The story listed the variety of items that Arcel in those days brought into a corner during a fight: "a pail, sponge, bottle and supply of ice . . . a bottle of smelling salts, a little brandy and a mixture of honey, brandy and lemon." Dan Parker explained, "The brandy stimulates the heart without intoxicating, honey supplies energy and lemon juice chases away the nauseous feeling a fighter gets when tired."

The image of Arcel as a consummate professional is verified by scores of boxing men. Asked to name the finest cut man he's ever seen, Al Braverman says immediately, "There's only one— Ray Arcel. He was the best cut man of them all put together. By that I mean in the time allotted to you to work a cut—to do everything—he was the best, barring none."

West Coast trainer George Chemeres' memories of Arcel in the 1940s focus on Arcel's conversational skills. "He'd talk so great," Chemeres says. "So beautiful."

Promoter Don Chargin recalls, "Arcel was always considered, oh, like a cut above, you know. He was always like an elder statesman that people would go to for advice and all that. Arcel always had time for everybody."

Arcel's expertise, of course, by no means guaranteed victories for his fighters. Describing his work in Henry Armstrong's corner when Armstrong was stopped in twelve rounds by Fritzie Zivic in 1941, Arcel told reporters: "There wasn't a thing I could do. Henry was dead set on going out fighting. I had to use adrenaline and a venom solution to stop the blood. After that, all I could do was pray for a lucky punch."

Though boxing was always a serious business for Arcel, he also has a taste for the humor that so often accompanies boxing men's memories of their violent—and potentially lethal—sport. Arcel's stories, though, never rob their subjects of their dignity. No boxer is ever humiliated in a Ray Arcel anecdote.

"The wit! I mean, this was the East Side wit," Arcel says. "Well, the greatest comedians, where the hell did they pick it up? In the streets of Brooklyn or the Lower East Side. There are five million quotes, how can you remember all those things?" Arcel, though, possesses something like a genius for remembering stories.

Arcel provided Murray Rose of *The Ring* with this tale about Benny Valgar, the outstanding lightweight of the 1920s: "Benny was a great boxer. But he couldn't punch. He was on the way down and we were taking a trip around the country. One night Benny looked around the arena and saw only a handful of customers. Benny looked at me and said, 'Ray, what's the matter? Why ain't we drawing?' I said, 'Benny, the fans want action.

They don't want to see any of that fancy jab and run stuff. Get out there and slug.' Benny said he would do that.

"The round started. Benny went out with a rush but did nothing but box. When the round was over, I said to Benny, 'Why didn't you go out there and slug?' Benny turned to me and said, 'I tried, Ray, honestly I did. My arms were willing but my brain wouldn't let me do anything wrong.'"

Another fighter that Arcel remembers with particular fondness is Englishman Jackie "Kid" Berg who won the junior welterweight championship from Mushy Callahan in London in 1930 with Arcel in his corner. Arcel's nickname for Berg was "Yidl." When Arcel first laid eyes on Berg—who had just come to America from England—he told the slim fighter's manager, "My God, you're going to get arrested. He [Berg] looks like a little girl." Arcel soon discovered, however, that the little man could fight.

Berg, also known as "The Whitechapel Whirlwind" is perhaps best remembered for his 1930 victory over future junior lightweight champion Kid Chocolate in New York's Polo Grounds. Before losing to Berg, Chocolate was undefeated in sixty-six professional fights. Arcel, who helped Berg shed twenty-eight pounds before the bout, calls Berg's victory over Chocolate "one of the most sensational fights I ever saw."

Born Judah Bergman, Berg carried "tzitzis" into the ring—what Arcel describes as "sort of a holy cloth." "He used to come down the ring and he used to wave them," Arcel says with a laugh. "Most of the fight fans were Jews. They used to go crazy. And he used to take the tzitzis and put 'em right on top of the ring posts. And the commission called me down one day, and they said to me, 'We can't allow this.' I says, 'Well, Commissioner, he does this the same way as a Catholic boy would go to a corner, kneel and bless himself. It's the same thing,' I says, 'only he does it to get the crowd cheering him.'"

Arcel again laughs when describing Berg as "God's gift to women." Because of Berg's affection for female company, Arcel says, "I had him living with me. I used to take him home with me. If I didn't, he'd just be in some woman's bed." After Berg flirted with gangster Legs Diamond's girlfriend in a New York hotel lobby one day, Berg and Arcel received a visit from Diamond's henchmen who made it very clear that Berg should look elsewhere for companionship.

Berg was also an extremely superstitious man. On the night before one of his big fights, Berg returned to his bed in Arcel's home and found Arcel's black cat asleep there. Assuming that Berg would take this as a bad omen, Arcel recalls, "I was ready to choke the cat." Fortunately, Arcel's mother-in-law had the presence of mind to say immediately, "That's good luck, Jackie. You'll win tomorrow." Berg seemed to accept the comment, but Arcel was worried. "I was awake all night," he says.

Perhaps Arcel's favorite Berg anecdote involves one of the fighter's matches against the formidable lightweight Billy Petrolle. Telling the story to Red Smith in 1972, Arcel recalled, "Billy Petrolle hit him a left hook in the body and I swear I saw the punch come out of his back. Sol Gold, working in the corner with me, ducked under the ring. 'Yidl,' I said when the round ended, 'How do you feel?' 'Lovely, thank you,' he said. 'And you?'"

One of the most devoted collectors of stories about Arcel is press agent Irving Rudd. Though press agents are sometimes seen as a writer's nemesis, Rudd is beloved by writers, including Red Smith, who gave Rudd the name "Unswerving Irving." Rudd first met Arcel in 1935 when Arcel trained Rudd's boyhood friend, Bernie "Schoolboy" Friedkin. Rudd has been talking about Arcel ever since.

Rudd relishes telling a tale which illustrates Arcel's well-known intolerance of drinking. It concerns Lenny Mancini, father of former lightweight champion, Ray "Boom Boom" Mancini. The elder Mancini was a lightweight contender trained by Arcel before World War II.

During the war Mancini was wounded and found himself on leave in Paris with a friend. Picking up the story, Rudd says:

"Lenny Mancini gets shot up and now he's in Paris on R & R. And he goes out—and nothing wrong, he's not bothering anybody, but a couple of sheets to the wind, and the MPs are making a sweep along the Champs Elysees. And what they're doing is they're just picking up these kind of guys and taking them back to their base. No arrests, no brawl or nothing. 'Come on, soldier, come with us,' you know. So he's weaving around with a snootful and the two MPs are taking them away. This man just got shot up in the Battle of the Bulge and all. And he turns around to [his friend] and he says, 'Don't tell Ray Arcel about this.'" Savoring Mancini's line, Rudd adds, "That tells it all—tells it all."

Adding that Arcel never drank and was always careful about what he ate, Rudd employs the Yiddish word for "garbage" when he explains, "Ray always was a stickler, never a slop guy, never a *hazeri* eater."

Arcel also kept himself in shape by doing roadwork with his fighters—a practice that led to an incident which took place in 1947, outside of London, where Arcel was preparing heavyweight Joe Baksi to face Bruce Woodcock. Baksi was reluctant to do his roadwork, so Arcel made sure he ran with Baksi each morning. Arcel was then forty-eight years old; Baksi was twenty-four. "Oh how he hated me when I used to wake him up," Arcel told *The Ring*. "We had miserable weather all the time we trained in England. This one day was the worst of all. It was drizzling and it was cold. I woke Joe up and he looked at me with hate in his eyes.

"He finally got up and I could see I had trouble ahead. I found out he was determined that this was going to be the last time I'd do any roadwork with anyone. He started out as if he was on a sprint. He ran me ragged for four miles. With about a half a mile to go, he stopped running, and started jumping up and down. He shadow-boxed. Then he looked at me to see if I was dying.

"Believe me, I was. But I knew if I let on, he would know he had me and wouldn't do any more work. So I told him, 'Let's finish this last half mile with a sprint.' . . . Then he yelled: 'Even a work horse gets tired!' We ran back together. I didn't have any more trouble with him on that trip. And, if you remember, he knocked out Woodcock in seven rounds."

When I ask Arcel about the incident, he says of Baksi, "He wanted to kill me." Arcel then remembers a sad twist. A few days after the April 15, 1947 fight, Arcel and Baksi were walking in London when they saw a newspaper headline: "Great Champion Dies." Baksi immediately feared that his opponent had died from injuries sustained in the bout. Looking at the paper, however, Arcel discovered that his beloved Benny Leonard had died from a heart attack while refereeing an evening of fights at the St. Nicholas arena in New York.

Though Arcel's years in boxing provided many laughs, he also witnessed countless incidents of the discrimination and indignities visited upon black fighters. "The blacks of the '30s were the best fighters," he says with a sense of outrage. "There were no better fighters ever lived than those fighters. But they never got work. They were in that gym waiting to substitute. And they could do everything." As always, Arcel sees waste of talent as an unforgivable sin.

To illustrate the obstacles faced by black fighters, Arcel cites an incident in the early 1940s in Washington, D.C., when he was handling Jimmy Bivins, a black heavyweight from Cleveland.

"The room that they got him in a colored hotel, a black hotel, was a steambath," Arcel recalls, explaining that it was a particularly hot summer. Arcel quickly approached a friend who managed the whites-only hotel where Arcel was staying. "I'm gonna ask you for a favor," Arcel told the friend. "I brought my valet with me." The alleged valet, of course, was Jimmy Bivins.

"I said, 'Look, I'm gonna ask you as a special favor. I got a room up there with two beds,'" Arcel recalls in a quiet voice. "'Let him sleep up there. Let him stay here.' I said, 'The joint they put him in is murder.'"

"He says, 'Now listen to what I'm tellin' you. I'm gonna let you do it. But when you order his meals, you order for *yourself*. Don't let anybody see him. Put him in the bathroom. When they come up to take the dishes out, put him in the bathroom. No hanging out in the lobby. When he goes down that elevator—*out*, out of the hotel. 'He made a delivery. Know what I mean?'"

With bitter irony Arcel adds, "Washington, D.C. this is, the capital of the United States!"

Arcel faced many similar situations while working with Ezzard Charles, whom Arcel trained together with Jimmy Brown, Charles' trainer from his amateur days. In 1952, shortly after Charles had lost his heavyweight title to Jersey Joe Walcott, Arcel went through an elaborate ordeal finding facilities in the state of Utah when Charles fought heavyweight Rex Layne.

"But the trouble with Charles was he carried ten guys with him," Arcel says. "I don't know why, but this was his gang. He carried ten guys. And of course going around the country, I was the advance man. Aside from being his trainer, I had to see that he had a place to eat and sleep and everything else. It was tough enough trying to get a room for him, but you had to get a room for him and ten more guys—black guys!"

Arcel begins, "We went to Ogden, Utah, and the mayor of the town was supposed to have made arrangements. The mayor told me that everything was all set. I was there two days before Charles. Charles wouldn't fly. So he was coming in on a train. So I went up to the manager of the hotel, the owner, and he sat there with a gun on his hip. And I said to him, 'My name is Ray Arcel, I'm from New York. The mayor told me to see you, and that you would give us some rooms.' 'Give who rooms?' I said, 'Ezzard Charles and his entourage.' He says, 'Is he a nigger?' I said, 'Well, he's a black man.' He says, 'I don't allow any niggers in my hotel.' I said, 'But the mayor told me that he had spoken to you and made arrangements.' He said, 'The mayor doesn't own this hotel, I do.'" As if apologizing for the language in his story, Arcel adds, "He didn't say, 'black.' 'Niggers'—that was his pet word."

Following the hotel owner's suggestion, Arcel went to a newly opened motel and paid the husband and wife that ran it cash in advance for six double rooms. "I always carried five or ten-thousand dollars with me," Arcel says. "I had to in order to be able to get accommodations."

When Arcel arrived with Charles and his entourage, he says, "This man and his wife, I will *never, never* forget, they stood there and they *froze*. They were absolutely . . . You think white is white? They were whiter than white. And I knew right away what the problem was. So I went over and I figured, well, I have to con 'em. I said, 'Look, this man is a champion prize fighter.' He said, 'No music?' 'No.' 'No girls?' 'No.' I said, 'He goes to bed at nine o'clock, half-past nine. Gets up in the morning, we leave. No hangin' around here.' So I eased them."

Arcel's problems were not over: "I had to find a place to train, I had to find a place to eat." Looking for a restaurant, Arcel returned to the hotel owner, who had rejected his business earlier, and arranged for Charles' group to eat breakfast and dinner at tables that had to be set up in two private rooms. Arcel told the owner: "When we eat steaks, I like the best. Whatever you charge me, I will pay you. You have to hire waiters, I will pay them."

But Ezzard Charles still had no place to train. "So there was a roller skating rink, and we had to go in there," Arcel recalls. "The guy who was supposed to be the promoter, he was some schlump. And he had a ring that we could put up and take down. And we had to do that for several days. We had to put a punching bag up. And I'm walking down the street and I bump into this friend of mine who's in uniform. I said, 'What are you doing here?' He says, 'I'm at the air base.' He says, 'It's a beautiful spot.' I says, 'What recreation?' He says, 'We got a beautiful gym there.' That's all I had to hear! I said, 'I'll bring Ezzard Charles up there to work out.' He says, 'Would you do that for the guys?'

Would I do that? So I went up there and the guy who was a master sergeant, he was in charge of the gym. Big black fellow. Nice guy. And I told him that I was going to bring Ezzard Charles. He says, 'Boy oh boy!' And we worked there all the while. They did everything to make it comfortable for us."

With an ironic laugh, Arcel says, "It was very rough. And the reason that I worked with Charles, I guess, is that I was able to accomplish what the other guys weren't able to accomplish. I fought for him."

Though Arcel's life as a trainer was certainly fraught with a variety of struggles, he emerged in a 1953 *Newsweek* survey of fight seconds as a prosperous man at the top of his profession: "In Boston a few weeks ago," *Newsweek* wrote, "Arcel, freshly manicured, gray, and dapper in his thirty-seventh year of handling boxers, made it seem that his bloody trade had become a highly scrupulous profession. It hasn't, of course. The main qualification demanded by too many commissions for a position involving ring experience, first-aid knowledge, coolness, and some degree of unselfish judgment is still only the $5 license fee. But Arcel, studying the trade with an artist's conscience, now commands as much as $5000 for a single assignment."

As Arcel headed off for "another night of ministering to Ezzard Charles," *Newsweek* added, he "resembled a trim-figured doctor en route to a catastrophe."

Charles, however, was the shyest and most enigmatic of boxers—and Arcel's work with him was never easy. "I've never known a fighter like him," Arcel told sportswriter W. C. Heinz in 1952. "I wake him up in camp and we go out on the road. It's six o'clock in the morning, and I say to him, 'How did you sleep last night?' He says, 'All right.' Maybe he didn't sleep all right, but he won't complain to anyone, and that's the extent of our conversation."

In *The Sweet Science*, Liebling records Arcel's observation that Charles was "like a good race horse who won't run for you."

Today, though, Arcel speaks of Charles as a great fighter who could do anything in the ring. Charles had been "underrated," Arcel says, and was "never given the real credit due him."

A boxing fan with a casual interest in Arcel's career after his return to the ring in 1972, would gather that Arcel had left boxing in the 1950s owing to some vaguely defined disgust with the corruption in the sport.

Arcel's remarks in Jerry Izenberg's 1979 *Sport* article offered a hint of Arcel's feelings. "Boxing can bring out the worst evil in people," he told Izenberg. "It can be cruel. Fighters sweat and bleed and usually die broke. Nobody cares. It shouldn't be that way. The good ones are artists. The very art form is self-defense. But there are so many people who kill it for them . . . the politicians . . . the commissions made up of political appointments . . ." At this point, Izenberg reported, Arcel's "voice trailed off."

A specific incident in 1953, however, most likely contributed to Arcel's decision to leave boxing. On the afternoon of September 19, 1953, as Arcel stood in front of the Hotel Manger in Boston, he was struck on the forehead by an assailant wielding a lead pipe wrapped in a paper bag. Arcel had just returned from Yom Kippur services at a local synagogue. The assault landed Arcel in a Boston hospital with "a brain concussion and severe scalp lacerations," according to an account published in *Look* magazine. Arcel spent nineteen days in the hospital and "was lucky he wasn't killed," *Look* reported. "He doesn't want to talk much about it, but he hovered between life and death for about a week," an old colleague of Arcel's explains.

The assault took place after Arcel had set himself up as a promoter and initiated a package of "Saturday Night Fights" which appeared on ABC television. This put Arcel and his business partners in direct competition with the International Boxing Club (IBC), which was controlled by Jim Norris of Madison Square Garden. The IBC promoted championship fights in nearly every weight division and controlled the television rights to the bouts. It's widely reported that Norris was closely associated with the organized crime figures who permeated the boxing world at the time. These mobsters controlled many of the important fighters of the day and many of the managers in the International Boxing Guild.

The *Look* article, written by Tim Cohane and Harry Grayson, portrayed Arcel as a man with a reputation "for fair dealing and decency" who was "outspoken in his contempt for criminal elements" in boxing. Arcel himself revealed that he had been threatened prior to the assault. "I got a telephone threat in New York last March," Arcel was quoted as telling the police from his hospital bed where he received around-the-clock protection against further attack. "A man's voice said: 'Get out of the TV racket, if you know what's good for you! That's all. Then he hung up. But my show isn't big money. I get a fair week's pay. Nothing to compare with the two weekly fight programs run by the International Boxing Club, which go into big figures."

Following the attack on Arcel, Dan Parker of *The New York Mirror* wrote, "All of the evidence points to the conclusion that the brutal assault was motivated by revenge for Arcel's refusal to be intimidated by one of the several factions which resented his Saturday night television boxing show." Parker also praised Arcel for his "clean record in the professional boxing field where few can tarry long without being sullied."

No one was ever arrested for the near-murder of Arcel. *Look* put it this way: "If Arcel knows or suspects the identity of his assailant, he is keeping silent for reasons of his own."

"He went through some really bad times," Arcel's friend and former fighter Dan Kapilow says. "But you never heard him bitch about it, either. You never hear a word out of him." Boxing in the '50s, Kapilow concludes, was filled with "wise guys and they were up to doing things that this man wouldn't think of doing in six zillion years. And they almost did him in."

It's significant that as the promoter of "Saturday Night

Fights," Arcel was supporting small boxing outlets throughout the country—clubs which were then floundering because fans preferred to stay home to watch fights on television.

Arcel explains, "I was the one that actually introduced these fights all around the country. Because the only place a guy could get a fight was in New York, in the Garden. The small clubs were dying because they couldn't pay the rent. Everybody wanted to fight in the Garden that Jim Norris was running. And I ran 104 shows, and they were all successful shows. We didn't make a lot of money, but we had success." Among the fighters who rose to prominence through the "Saturday Night Fights" were future middleweight champions Carmen Basilio and Bobo Olson.

After two seasons on the air, Arcel's "Saturday Night Fights" lost its sponsor, a Philadelphia cigar company. "But when the show was over I tried to operate in the same places where I promoted on TV," Arcel says. "You know, go into those towns with pretty good fights—and I lost money. I couldn't make it. Expenses were high."

With corruption spreading in the boxing business and the loss of a sponsor for his television productions—and the assault doubtless weighing heavily on his mind—Arcel reconsidered his choice of professions.

"I just sat down and took inventory of myself," he says when asked why he left boxing. One night in Toots Shor's restaurant, Arcel encountered his good friend, Harry Kessler. In addition to being one of the best fight referees of the time, Kessler was a millionaire metallurgical engineer who invented a metal-casting process and owned three steel foundries.

"I tell ya, I don't know what to do," Arcel remembers telling Kessler. "My mind isn't made up. I don't want to go back to training fighters."

Kessler responded by offering Arcel a job. "He made me a very decent offer," Arcel says, "to go into his purchasing department and handle that." So Arcel became a purchasing agent for the

Meehanite Metal Corporation. "It was a lucky thing for me to do it. I never stepped away from boxing. I was always with the boxing people and the newspaper men. But I was earning a nice living and it was more money than I could make in the boxing game."

And so Arcel retired from boxing for eighteen years.

If Arcel's comeback as Duran's trainer in 1972 made him famous again, Arcel—and his co-trainer Freddie Brown— became virtual fixtures of fight coverage in 1980, when Duran fought two celebrated bouts with Sugar Ray Leonard.

Leonard, then an undefeated Olympic gold medalist adored by the media, was often compared to Muhammad Ali in terms of slickness, speed and personal charm. Leonard's sweet smile, good looks and lack of one-punch knockout power, however, led some to charge he was less than authentic—a media invention rather than a true champion.

No one, however, doubted Duran's authenticity: he was a genuinely ferocious former lightweight champion who had won celebrated battles with champions such as Ken Buchanan and Esteban DeJesus. His relentlessly aggressive style led sportswriters and fans to describe him as a force of nature. Duran was said to be a fighter who—as Arcel himself acknowledged— could have stood beside the likes of Benny Leonard or Harry Greb. Like all potentially great fights, the first bout between Leonard and Duran promised to answer fundamental questions about both of its participants.

Arcel prophetically framed the main questions about Sugar Ray Leonard when Arcel was interviewed before the fight by William Nack of *Sports Illustrated.* "Look," Arcel said. "Leonard is an excellent boxer. He's a master craftsman. He can do anything, but we don't know one thing. Can he stand up under the body-battering that he's going to get from Duran in the early rounds? If Duran hurts you and you're backing up on the ropes, I'm telling you, he don't let you alone. He sticks to you like a plaster. He's that vicious. And he has the unique ability to get stronger as the fight goes on. When he's in top shape, after the seventh round, you got to watch yourself. He gets his second wind and he can go like hell. You can't avoid punches when you're in there. It's the highest form of individualism there is. You're in there all alone. When you take a punch to the belly, you can't say, 'Time out!' You've got to be able to weather the storm. Can Leonard stand up? Can he take what Duran has to offer? That's the question."

Arcel felt that Duran had won a psychological advantage over Leonard as early as the press conference at which the fight was announced. According to a story by Vic Ziegel in *Inside Sports*, Arcel embraced Duran after the press conference and said, "You won the title right there. The other guy was full of crap. He's scared. As soon as he goes back to his room he's going to go in the bathroom." Arcel's words, of course, may have merely been a psychological ploy to bolster Duran's confidence.

Working across the ring in Leonard's corner, was Angelo Dundee who, as he cheerfully told reporters, had learned his profession in the late '40s by carrying a bucket for Arcel and Brown.

Arcel says that there was no bad blood between himself and Dundee even though their fighters disliked each other. "I have great respect for Angelo, and he's looking to·make a living. He does the best for his fighter, and good luck to him. There never was any hard feelings because I root for Angelo. I think that Sugar Ray Leonard owes Angelo an awful lot." (Arcel was a bit less magnanimous before the second Leonard-Duran fight when he responded to Dundee's prefight gamesmanship by saying, "Angelo is trying to make up five-million excuses. He picked up all this stuff hanging around Muhammad Ali too long.")

Facing his mentors, Dundee was duly respectful. "Going in, I've got to be a big underdog," the fifty-eight-year-old Dundee told Dave Anderson of *The New York Times* in a reference to the combined ages of Arcel and Brown. "With their 154 years against me, I'm outwisdomed by almost three to one." Dundee also told reporters, "Hey, those two guys are as old as water."

In the days leading up to the fight, the combined wisdom of Arcel and Brown was needed when Duran underwent a pre-fight physical examination and was found to be suffering from a heart condition. At the time, Duran's handlers had no way of knowing that the diagnosis was erroneous.

"The Monday before the fight, the fight's on a Friday, is a press conference and a weigh-in," Arcel recalls. "And we go to the gym after the weigh-in, and they call me on the phone, the commissioner. He says, 'I'm very sorry to tell you that Duran won't be able to fight. The fight's off,' he said. I said, 'Why, what's happened?' He said, 'Duran's got a heart condition.' I said, 'Duran's got a heart condition? He doesn't even have a heart.'" This one-liner would become one of Arcel's best-known witticisms.

"I got a hold of Carlos Eleta," Arcel continues, referring to Duran's manager. "So he called Panama and the government sent up a special plane with the best heart specialist in Central America. They pushed him on that plane and sent him up."

Though Duran's heart was found to be normal—and he was given permission to fight—the ordeal of a three-hour medical examination left Duran emotionally shattered.

"Duran walked out of that," Arcel says, "I'm telling you, my heart dropped. I just was looking at a washed-up guy. I mean, what they put him through! So I took him and put him in bed." Arcel's instructions to the members of Duran's entourage were, "Stay away from him. Let him lay there. I don't want anybody to come into this room. Leave him alone."

Arcel and Brown then treated Duran gently: "In the evening, we went in, saw that he had a nice dinner. The next morning, we took him for a walk. I'm talking about a couple of days before the fight. Went over to the gym just to shadow box. Just, you know, let him keep active. Friday, roadwork and that's all."

Besides lingering worries about Duran's heart—and the effect the false alarm might have on Duran's psyche—Arcel and Brown were also troubled by the referee who had been chosen for the bout. Carlos Padilla had recently worked a bout in which one of Brown's fighters, Vito Antuofermo, lost his middleweight title to Alan Minter. "Damnit, let 'em fight," Brown had screamed at Padilla throughout the fight in a vain protest against the referee's habit of breaking the fighters and preventing Antuofermo from fighting on the inside. Arcel and Brown knew that in-fighting was a central part of Duran's plan for dominating Leonard.

A glum Arcel told the press, "We are in the camp of the enemy." He and Brown launched a very vocal campaign aimed at influencing Padilla. "The one thing I fear and dread," Arcel told Dave Anderson before the fight, "is if the referee doesn't let Duran fight inside. If that happens, Duran won't be able to fight his fight."

Moments before the fight began, two almost frail-looking men stood amid the chaos and melodrama of the crowded ring giving referee Carlos Padilla a talking-to. They were, of course, Arcel and Brown. Following Duran's victory—a triumph of aggression and in-fighting for Duran—Arcel told Red Smith what he had said to the referee during this pre-fight lecture: "You're a good referee, one of the best, but you've got to let these boys fight. They're good fighters. Remember, the whole world is watching you."

During the fight, though, Arcel held Duran back. "I couldn't press him," Arcel recalls. "I had to hold him back because I figured, this is fifteen rounds. All right, he might win two, three rounds in good style and then blow his load. Couldn't afford that. I wanted him to be able to finish—and finish in good style. So you had to guide him. 'No rush. No rush. Take it easy. Take it easy. Take it easy. You're doin' good, good, good. 'Cause this is a bum! He's a bum!' And I said, 'Take it easy, take it easy. Every once in a while, dig.' And he would dig."

When asked if Duran could have knocked Leonard out when

he had him hurt in round two of the fight, Arcel says, "In that round, yes, if I woulda sent him, and he woulda really let loose." But as Arcel told Red Smith, ". . . I kept fearing he would come back to the corner and say he was tired. Then what would we do? Take a chance on his heart?"

In the hours following the bout, a proud Arcel told Dave Anderson, "This night compares to when [Barney] Ross beat Jimmy McLarnin, and when he beat Tony Canzoneri the second time." Arcel again sounded pleased when he told *Sports Illustrated*, "Duran did what he was told. He fought the kind of fight he was told to fight. Leonard wouldn't jab. We never let him execute. And Roberto set a hell of a pace." Arcel also praised Leonard, saying, "Leonard surprised me taking some of the punches he did."

Asked for an assessment of Leonard, Arcel tells me, "The guy's a good fighter. That's all. That's all he is. A good fighter: not great but good."

The first Leonard-Duran fight was likely the high point of Arcel's comeback as a trainer, but November 25, 1980, the night of the second Leonard-Duran fight may have been the most baffling—and painful—Arcel ever endured in a fighter's corner.

"*No más* . . . no more box," Duran said that night in New Orleans, uttering what are perhaps the most infamous words in the history of boxing. The sight of Roberto Duran turning his back on Sugar Ray Leonard after Leonard had clowned and taunted—and made Duran miss—must have seemed precisely like a nightmare to Ray Arcel and Freddie Brown. "Nobody quits in my corner," Arcel was famous for telling any boxer who displayed a distaste for combat. Yet now one of Arcel's greatest fighters had surrendered.

The night of the fight, Arcel was as straightforward with the press as he could be. "I wish I could give you an honest answer," he said. "I always thought this guy would fight until he dropped. I just can't figure it out. I've got no answer now. I don't know.

I don't know. He had been so sharp in the last week of train-ing . . ."

Arcel also announced his retirement from the ring. "I've had it," he told *The New York Times*. "People don't understand the rigors of handling a fighter. As for Roberto, there's a lot of people who live off him. I just hope he doesn't go broke."

In a 1988 *New York Post* column, Jerry Izenberg recalled that after the "No Más" fight, Arcel, with tears in his eyes, was the only member of Duran's entourage to attend a pre-dawn hearing called by the local boxing commission. Asked why he went to the meeting, Arcel said, "Why? Because he was my fighter when he came here. He was my fighter last night. Until he gets on a plane today, he will still be my fighter. Why did I go? How could I not?"

In the weeks following the fight, Arcel continued to be both-ered by the press. "Some of my friends in the newspaper field, they wouldn't leave me alone," he recalls. "They thought I knew something. I said to them, 'What do I know? What you saw, I saw. I know as much about it as you do.'"

As the years passed, however, Arcel discussed the fight openly with reporters. In 1987, he told Ira Berkow of the *Times*, "I told Duran, 'Don't let Leonard move, keep him on the ropes. If he moves he gains momentum, and he's got the ability to make a sucker out of you.' And he did." But Arcel always refrained from the sort of psychological speculation that many in the press indulged in while attempting to explain Duran's actions. In another Ira Berkow column in 1988, Arcel said, ". . . No one can explain that 'No Más' fight. No one really knows all the things that go on inside a fighter. But I was terribly upset when Roberto quit the fight, and it took me a long time to get over it—if I ever have."

Arcel's voice is still somber when discussing Duran's actions. "I never experienced anything like that in my life," Arcel says. "I mean, it was just unbelievable. I thought maybe he broke his hand or something. . . . This is the last guy in the world that I thought I'd ever see quit in the ring. He would commit murder and he wouldn't quit." Later, almost whispering, he adds, "The only thing I said to him when I left, I says, 'I am very sorry.' That's all. He broke my heart."

Arcel, though, harbored no bitterness toward Duran. When Duran came back in 1983 to beat Davey Moore for the W.B.A. junior middleweight title, Arcel told *Sports Illustrated*, "Ah, he was an artist. That performance could be compared to that of any great fighter who ever lived. It was masterful."

Six years later, during another of Duran's remarkable comebacks, he beat Iran Barkley for the W.B.C. middleweight title. Arcel was delighted. Smiling proudly, he says that while watching the bout on television, "I just sat there . . . and I mean, I was laughing. I mean, this is my baby." Then he adds, "Duran knows how to move you out of position. He knows how to make you miss. Takes a good punch. That's why a guy like Duran, if he was five years younger . . . he could . . . well . . . he could be light-heavyweight champion. I mean just on his knowledge alone."

In an article which appeared in *The New York Times* on Arcel's ninetieth birthday in 1989, he paid Duran something like the ultimate compliment when he said, "I think he may know more than I do about boxing."

Arcel's last appearance as a second came on June 11, 1982, when he worked Larry Holmes' corner as Holmes defended his heavyweight title against Gerry Cooney. At the time, Holmes was trained by the venerable Eddie Futch, then age seventy-one. Eddie Futch recalls, "Larry came to me and he said, 'How do you get along with Ray Arcel?' I said, 'Oh, well. He's a good friend of mine. I've known him for years. I have a great deal of respect for him as a man and as a second. I'd be happy to have him work with us.' So I called Ray and he came in and it was perfect. We complemented each other. Since that time, we've been very close."

Explaining why he wanted Arcel in his corner Holmes says, "Well, it was the experience that he had being around the fighters—all the great fighters, and training them—Roberto Duran—watching them work, getting to know them, liking them, and I wanted someone that knows boxing to talk boxing. And that's what prompted me to bring him in."

The day before the fight, Arcel compared Gerry Cooney unfavorably to Primo Carnera, the heavyweight champion whose career was built on fighting stiffs and set-ups. "Carnera could jab and move, and by the time he fought for the title he had about eighty fights," Arcel told Dave Anderson. "To me, Cooney is absolutely inexperienced."

On the night of the Holmes-Cooney bout, Arcel wore an expression of seriousness and disapproval. When Cooney repeatedly landed low blows, Arcel looked as outraged as if his own middle had been violated. "Don't let that bum take your title," Arcel told Holmes in the late going before the champion scored a knockout.

"He [Cooney] showed me he's better than I thought," Arcel told Dave Anderson after the fight. "But he hadn't developed any sense of pace. The only way a fighter develops that is in fights. The gym is your school. The gym is where you learn what you're supposed to do. But it's only in the actual fights that you learn how to do it."

Arcel later recalled that he expected Cooney to come back a better fighter after losing to Holmes. "When the fight ended, I looked across the ring at Cooney, and right away, I thought of Joe Louis against Max Schmeling the first time around," Arcel told writer Thomas Hauser in Boxing Illustrated in 1990. "I thought Gerry had it in him to come back, beat Holmes, and become one of the most popular heavyweight champions of all time."

As for Holmes, Arcel rates him among the finest heavyweights of all time. "How can you help but rate him?" Arcel asks. "Nobody ever gave him the credit because he lived in the shadow of Muhammad Ali. Larry Holmes was a hell of a fighter. People don't realize how good he was. Maybe he wasn't a sensational performer, but he was a hell of a fighter. Sometimes a guy's personality works against him. You have to rate him with the top ten heavyweights."

Arcel goes on to acknowledge the show business aspects of boxing. "I mean, what made Muhammad Ali? His personality, you know. People like to see that. They like to see a lunatic. And if you behave like one ... I mean like with Tyson, they love to see a wild man."

Despite Arcel's retirement, his presence continues to be felt in the boxing world as writers seek out his memorable, expert opinions, and he plays the role of a highly quotable senior statesman of boxing.

Throughout the 1980s Ira Berkow of *The New York Times* chronicled Arcel's opinions on the passing fight scene. Berkow, for example, recorded Arcel's telling analysis of Hagler's brutal, three-round knockout of Thomas Hearns in 1985: "When I saw the Hagler-Hearns fight, I knew that Hagler would not fight Hearns again. He took murderous punches. When Hearns hits you, you kinda stay hit. Hagler was subjected to more punishment than Hearns, but Hearns didn't have the stamina or endurance that was needed. Once the cork comes out, there's no putting it back. Hagler knocked out Hearns in the third round, but he got hurt. He wouldn't want to walk on the same side of the street with Hearns again."

Following Leonard's stunning 1987 upset of Hagler, Arcel told Berkow, "It was a case of brains over brawn. Leonard had too much mental energy for Hagler. He outsmarted him and outpunched him."

Arcel expressed his disapproval of Leonard's continued comeback in 1989 when the second Leonard-Hearns fight was announced. "What's wrong with them? Do they want to be richer than Rockefeller?" Arcel asked Berkow. "All those punches take their toll. Even if Ray and Tommy get all that money, they may not be able to count it."

When another contemporary star, Mike Tyson, knocked out Michael Spinks in ninety-one seconds in 1988, Arcel said, "He [Spinks] fell apart, he just went to pieces. You see sudden changes in a fighter, in their makeup. And I know Spinks for a long time, and admired his courage and determination, but he was simply in there with someone who, well, who is the nearest thing to Jack Dempsey in his prime. He could hit you once on the top of the head and finish you."

After Tyson was upset by James "Buster" Douglas in 1990, Arcel told Dave Kindred of *The National,* "Tyson was not himself. And why? Because Tyson betrayed himself. I don't blame his corner. . . . I blame only Tyson." Arcel added, "In my sixty-five years in boxing, I have learned that in order for a man to walk into the ring, he must be in top fighting shape. He must live like a saint. This, Tyson does not do. He's a pretty sensible kind of guy, but he's young, he's got a lot of money and there are a million whores in New York. He probably figures, 'What the hell, I can overcome it.'"

When I ask Arcel what advice he'd give Tyson, following his loss to Douglas, Arcel says simply, "The most important thing I would tell him is, 'Don't overrate yourself and underrate everybody. And learn how to live a clean life.'"

Writers are by no means the only ones who seek out Arcel's wisdom. Young boxers such as welterweight Mark Breland visit Arcel to soak up knowledge, and today's corner men also seek his counsel. At the age of seventy-five, veteran Seattle manager and trainer George Chemeres, who has known Arcel for nearly half a century, says he still telephones Arcel "when I need an answer."

Shortly after Ray Arcel's eighty-sixth birthday in 1985, Governor Mario Cuomo of New York declared "Ray Arcel Day" in the state, and issued a proclamation which read, in part, ". . . to be a successful handler of people a person must have special qualities. He must be able to instill confidence, gain their respect and win their trust. He must be above all else a man among men. This Ray has been and more. . . . He exemplifies without doubt the saga of the sport of boxing, the supreme trainer and maker of champions."

Arcel received another honor that year when *Ripley's Believe It or Not!* column reminded readers that Arcel had "guided nearly 2,000 fighters, twenty of whom became world champions . . . and not one of them was ever hurt."

In November of 1988, the boxing veterans' organization Ring 8 named Ray Arcel its "Man of the Century" at a dinner at the Downtown Athletic Club in New York City. Bill Gallo, longtime sports columnist for the *Daily News*, called it, "absolutely the best boxing dinner I ever attended." Those present included Jersey Joe Walcott, Willie Pep, Rocky Graziano, Larry Holmes, Jake La Motta and Eddie Futch. Jackie "Kid" Berg flew in from London. "He paid his own way," Arcel reports. "He said, 'I met you sixty years ago and I'll never forget you.'"

Arcel himself was delighted by the dinner. "I tell ya, I haven't gotten over it yet," he says more than a year later. "I was in a trance. I really mean it."

When I ask Arcel to explain his longevity and his superb health he says with a smile, "I guess I owe it to boxing. I was a cross-country runner. I did roadwork every day. I walked miles. I didn't dissipate. I didn't drink. I didn't smoke. So I owe it to boxing. I owe it to boxing." Arcel still includes walking—"vigorously, not a stroll"—as part of his regimen.

Arcel also continues to serve the sport of boxing by actively participating in Ring 8, sponsor of the Ray Arcel Medical Center, which provides medical care to former boxers. When great former featherweight champ Sandy Saddler was found to be receiving inadequate medical care while suffering from Alzheimer's disease in the psychiatric ward of a hospital, Arcel, along with Irving Rudd and Dan Kapilow of Ring 8, led the effort which moved Saddler to a nursing home.

I first met Ray Arcel in 1986 when I produced his appearance as a guest on "The Dick Cavett Show" on ABC-television. The unflappable Arcel arrived at the studio in his customary tweed jacket and striped tie. After taping the interview, he was approached backstage by a woman who had been charmed by his comments. "How old are you?" she asked Arcel. "Eighty-six," came the reply. "Eighty-six fucking years old!" the woman said, and with that, Ray Arcel, the man who had flourished since 1917 in the toughest sport in existence, blushed beet red.

Upon leaving the studio, Arcel and his wife Stephanie insisted on giving a researcher from the show a ride to Grand Central station in the limousine that had been provided for them. When the car stopped to drop the young woman off at Grand Central, Arcel exited the car on his side and hurried to open the door for her.

Arcel's superb manners, dignity, dedication and integrity would be somehow lessened, though, if they were not combined with an abiding sense of irony. "It was great. I had a great career," he says. "I never have any regrets. There were days we didn't eat. It made no difference. I was only part of the mob."

A final tribute to Arcel comes most appropriately from one of the boxers he trained. This is what middleweight champion Billy Soose said at the Ring 8 dinner for Arcel: "Arcel is one of the finest men I've ever met and what he taught us was not only boxing but also the true values of life. He was my trainer, my father, my psychologist, my teacher, my friend, my mentor."

To Mamie

From

_____ Blackburn.

JACK BLACKBURN

Ray Arcel speaks with great seriousness and respect as he provides an assessment of Joe Louis' trainer, Jack Blackburn. "We became very close friends because I used to have a lot of fighters in Pompton Lakes, and he was up there," Arcel says, referring to the famed New Jersey training camp. "And we used to sit and talk. Blackburn had a rough life. He was a bad guy. He used to get drunk and have fights. He killed a couple of guys. He was a great trainer," Arcel stresses with solemn intensity. "You talk about trainers! *He was a great trainer.*"

Arcel is not a man who uses the phrase "great trainer" lightly. He clearly feels that Blackburn, a difficult man, was also awesomely competent and knowledgeable—that Blackburn was in his own class.

"Well, he was a good fighter himself," Arcel adds. "He was a lightweight and he fought heavyweights. It didn't make any difference. In those years, the black boy didn't have a chance at all. They didn't have any scales. He told me, 'I never cared what they weighed. As long as they had two hands.'"

A portrait of JACK BLACKBURN autographed to Mannie Seamon.

Asked what made Blackburn a great trainer, Arcel offers a prized memory. "I used to watch them work. See, Joe Louis would work out and he [Blackburn] always used to say to me, 'I don't care. He's shakin' his behind in there for the newspaper men. Talking to them.'"

When the reporters left camp, however, the real work began. "He [Blackburn] used to take him [Louis] in the gym and lock the door. I think that I was the only one who ever was allowed in there," says Arcel. "And I stood way over in the corner. And he made Louis punch that bag! And they'd fight like cats and dogs. He [Blackburn] says, 'You're not in the ring up there with those bums now.' He says, 'You're here with me. We're here alone. And you do what I'm telling you to do.' And he made Louis develop the best left hand of anybody that I ever saw. Louis could knock you out with a left jab. And this used to go on for *hours*. They used to scream at one another. But, you know, there was a brotherly feeling there. He was a trainer, boy, I'm telling you! He was the boss and he didn't care about anybody. He was fearless."

Jack Blackburn was born in Versailles, Kentucky on May 20, 1883. Some reports say he was born Charles Henry; others say he was born Charles Henry Blackburn. His father was a preacher. When Blackburn was ten years old, his family moved to Indianapolis and then Terre Haute, Indiana. Blackburn began fighting in Indiana in 1899. He soon ran away from home and found his way to Pittsburgh, where he continued his boxing career. At the time, it should be remembered, boxing was an unregulated, largely illegal sport.

Blackburn was one of the countless black boxers of his generation deprived of the glory and financial rewards a white fighter with the same talent would have received. Early in his career, Blackburn fought mostly in Pittsburgh and Philadelphia, as often as two or three times a week. He was either five-feet-nine-inches or five-feet-ten-inches, according to various reports.

Either way, this made him relatively tall for a lightweight. He never grew beyond the welterweight limit of 147 pounds—which didn't stop him from facing fighters in all divisions right on up through the heavyweight class.

Blackburn's list of opponents includes several all-time greats. According to some reports, Blackburn faced the legendary Sam Langford—the "Boston Tar Baby"—six times, earning two fifteen-round draws, a ten-round draw and a twelve-round draw, as well as two no-decision outcomes. To put this feat in perspective, it should be noted that Langford boxed heavyweight champion Jack Johnson to a draw in 1906 and that Johnson then avoided Langford for the rest of his career.

It's said that Jack Dempsey's manager, Jack Kearns, continually turned down Langford's requests to fight Dempsey even when Langford was an aging, half-blind fighter. When Blackburn and Langford met, Blackburn reportedly weighed 136 pounds to Langford's 180 pounds. *New York Journal American* columnist Bill Corum reported that Joe Louis used to say of Blackburn and Langford, "They fought more draws than a man draws his breath." Later in life, Blackburn would tell journalists, "I'd say Langford was the greatest of them all."

Blackburn also faced Joe Gans three times. Gans, known as "The Old Master," was the first black lightweight champion. His record included a forty-two-round victory over Battling Nelson and a twenty-round draw with welterweight champion Joe Walcott. Blackburn twice fought Gans to a draw in six-round contests in 1903 and in 1906. In 1904, Blackburn lost a fifteen-round decision to Gans. This was the only loss in the first eight years of Blackburn's career—a period during which he was not knocked off his feet once. All of the Gans-Blackburn fights were non-title bouts. According to a report in the *Pittsburgh Courier* by journalists Chester L. Washington and William G. Nunn, Gans once told a Minneapolis newspaperman that Blackburn was the only man he refused to meet in a championship bout.

Another tale from Blackburn's boxing career involves the time Blackburn out-boxed and embarrassed a 200-pound-plus heavyweight who, in desperation, turned to the referee and said, "Make him stop that!"

Blackburn's other career highlights include a 1903 fifteen-round draw with future welterweight champion Mike "Twin" Sullivan; a 1904 victory over future welterweight champion Jimmy Gardner; a 1907 victory over leading middleweight contender Jack Lewis; a 1909 no-decision contest with light-heavyweight champion "Philadelphia" Jack O'Brien during which Blackburn, according to *The Ring*, "gave . . . O'Brien plenty to remember him by"; and a six-round no-decision bout in 1915 against legendary middleweight champion Harry Greb. Washington and Nunn reported that in Philadelphia in 1907, Blackburn became "the only man in the world who ever fought six men in one night, one round apiece, and knocked three of them out."

It is also said that when outweighed by his opponents, Blackburn sometimes "loaded" his gloves by dipping his bandaged hands in plaster of Paris, turning his fists into rock-hard weapons—a not uncommon practice among boxers of that era.

In Philadelphia in January of 1909, Blackburn went on a shooting rampage, fatally wounding a man and shooting two women, one of whom was his common-law wife. According to newspaper accounts, Blackburn shot Alonso Polk and injured Polk's wife, Mattie, after the couple had quarreled with Blackburn and his "white wife or paramour," Maude Pillion, whom Blackburn also shot. Blackburn was found by a policeman standing over the fallen bodies. After a chase and a struggle, the policeman reportedly used a club to knock Blackburn unconscious. Blackburn was convicted of manslaughter and sentenced to either ten or fifteen years in prison, according to various reports. While in prison, Blackburn is said to have become a boxing instructor to the warden and his three sons, and to have taken his meals at the warden's table.

Ray Arcel remembers that Blackburn often spoke about the problems he'd encountered in his life. "I was just another nigger," Arcel remembers Blackburn explaining. "If I walked into a saloon, the wise guys would pop [off] . . . I had to walk out because there was only one solution, I'da had to kill 'em." A long scar on the left side of Blackburn's face also testified to Blackburn's violent past.

Later in life, Arcel adds, Blackburn learned that "it was easy for him to get into trouble . . . and he knew that the smartest thing to do is to keep your mouth shut."

When he was released from prison in 1913, Blackburn continued his boxing career. A fight poster from 1917 described him as "The Man Who Came Back." In 1923, in his final professional bout, Blackburn lost by a knockout to Roy Pelkey. According to The Ring, in a career consisting of 167 fights, most of which were no-decision affairs, Jack Blackburn lost only twice. Blackburn claimed in a 1936 interview, however, that he'd had "about 385 fights." In 1940, The Ring summed up Blackburn the boxer this way: "Fearless, clever, snappy puncher, good jabber and had a powerful left hook."

Another part of the Blackburn legend is that he showed up Jack Johnson in a sparring session in a Philadelphia gym before Johnson became heavyweight champion of the world in 1908. According to the story, Blackburn bloodied Johnson's nose and angered him, though Johnson was unable to retaliate by hurting Blackburn, who was a much smaller man. Repeating the anecdote in his autobiography, Joe Louis: My Life, written with Edna and Art Rust, Jr., Louis wrote that Johnson continued to hold a grudge against Blackburn. When Blackburn got out of prison, according to Louis, Johnson refused to take part in a benefit for Blackburn. Johnson called Blackburn "all kinds of sons-of-bitches," Louis recalled, "and let this information get around."

In 1935, according to a U.P.I. report, Blackburn, responding to Jack Johnson's public criticism of Joe Louis, claimed that Louis was the greater fighter. "Louis would whip Jack Johnson sure,"

Blackburn said. "We would not be a bit afraid to take him on were Johnson in his prime. Johnson was a defensive fighter—he'd fool around until you made a mistake, and then he'd pop you. Louis would get him first."

In private, however, Blackburn seems to have taken the opposite view. Louis' boyhood friend Freddie Guinyard, who became Louis' secretary and traveling companion, recalls that Blackburn told him that Johnson would have defeated Louis. "Blackburn and I were roommates," Guinyard says affectionately, recalling that while at training camp, "Jack Blackburn and I had twin beds—I was on one side of the room and he was on the other. We would go to bed any time after dark—nine, ten o'clock. And for two old streetwise characters, nine o'clock was a little bit early for he and I to go to bed, so we'd lay there and talk for a long time. And one thing he told me, he said, 'Young man'—that's what he used to call me—he said, 'Young man. Jack Johnson would've whipped his [Louis'] earlocks off. Because he's a standin' target. Jack Johnson was a movin' target.'"

Asked if Blackburn ever discussed his fighting career, Guinyard says, "He sat up and talked to me about fighters like Harry Wills, other fellas like that." Wills, of course, was the great black heavyweight who was denied a shot at Jack Dempsey's title.

Blackburn also spoke about his old rival Sam Langford. "He talked about this fella, Blind Sam, Blind Sam," says Guinyard. "And he would talk about these fighters who were little—and they fought so hard until they made a big man look a little bad. Jack Blackburn told me that when he was fighting, he wore a size eight-and-a-half shoe, but he had to put on a ten. The promoters used to pay him in silver dollars and twenty-dollar gold pieces, and he had to put it in his shoe, otherwise the promoter woulda been gone when the fight was over."

When Blackburn turned to training, he often worked with white fighters because of his conviction that black fighters would never be treated fairly and allowed to make money.

Before his association with Louis, Blackburn had produced two champions—bantamweight Bud Taylor and lightweight Sammy Mandell. Taylor, who won the bantamweight title in 1927 with a victory over Tony Canzoneri, also recorded wins over such champions as Jimmy McLarnin, Abe Goldstein and Charley Phil Rosenberg. Mandell won the lightweight title from Rocky Kansas in 1926, and defended it against Jimmy McLarnin in 1928 and Tony Canzoneri in 1929. In 1930, Mandell lost the title to Al Singer by a first-round knockout. A 1953 report in *The Ring* recalled that Mandell "absorbed Blackburn's canny stuff so well, that although lacking a punch he was the best lightweight of his time."

Summing up his early career as a trainer in a 1935 article credited to him in the *Pittsburgh Courier*—and prepared with the help of writers Chester Washington and William Norman—Blackburn stated, "I've trained two boys to win the championship, taking Sammy Mandell when he was just a school boy and making him the lightweight king, then I helped Bud Taylor win the bantam crown." Among the other fighters Blackburn said he'd handled were heavyweight contender Art Lasky, welterweight champion Jackie Fields and lightweight contender Lew Tendler.

While working out of the Arcadia Gym located at 13th and Cherry Streets in Philadelphia, Blackburn also tutored a promising welterweight named Arnold Cream, who eventually became heavyweight champion fighting under the ring name of Jersey Joe Walcott. In *The 100 Greatest Boxers of All Time*, Bert Randolph Sugar reported that when Blackburn accepted the offer to train young Joe Louis, Blackburn had intended to bring Walcott along to Chicago to continue working with him. When Walcott fell ill with typhoid and took a year to recuperate, however, "the men in Chicago had forgotten all about him," Sugar wrote. Walcott would have a measure of revenge on Blackburn's prize pupil in 1947, when Walcott gave Louis so much grief while dropping a controversial decision to the heavyweight champion in Madison Square Garden.

If Walcott harbors any resentment toward Blackburn, it's not apparent. Blackburn "was a great fighter and a great teacher," Walcott says. Asked if Blackburn was stern, Walcott replies, "No, he was more of a diplomat. He knew how to get his points through without being excited, without being boisterous. He was a wise man."

Another of Blackburn's fighters in the late 1920s was Joe Gramby, a young featherweight who went on to become a venerable trainer in his own right, managing and training lightweight champion Bob Montgomery, among others. Gramby agrees with Walcott that Blackburn was more of a diplomat than a tyrant, calling the trainer "a good teacher, a great teacher." Gramby saw Blackburn's early champions Bud Taylor and Sammy Mandell in action and remembers them as "very smart" fighters with "very good left hands"—two qualities that marked all of Blackburn's pupils. "Blackburn had a helluva jab," Gramby says. "That was one of his mainstays."

Blackburn often preached about proper balance. Paraphrasing Blackburn, Gramby intones, "Be in the right position, both feet in the right position. And don't be off balance when you throw a punch. Be in a position where you can follow through with another punch if you miss one."

Rather than criticize a fighter in front of others in the gym, says Gramby, "Blackburn took you aside. But one thing, if you didn't do what he told you, he would get in there and whup you—and show you. Yes he would."

Gramby also recalls that Blackburn was not pleasant when he was drinking. "A lot of people were afraid of Blackburn. He was a nice person, but when he was drinking, he was hell. We used to come in the gym, it was on the third floor, and we would come up on the elevator, and if we heard him talking loud and all, we wouldn't train that day."

The story is often told that when Blackburn was first approached in Chicago in 1934 by one of Joe Louis' managers,

John Roxborough, he was skeptical in the extreme about the opportunities awaiting a black heavyweight.

Louis' managers, themselves black, were younger and less cynical than Blackburn. Roxborough, though he came from a middle class family, earned his living by running a numbers operation in Detroit. Roxborough's partner in handling Louis was Julian Black, who ran a speakeasy in Chicago at the time and was also involved in the local numbers racket.

Blackburn told the story of his first conversation with Roxborough in a 1936 interview with the U.P.I. during which he explained that "Joe Louis ain't no natural killer; he's a manufactured killer." Although Blackburn's words in the interview are presented in an exaggerated southern black dialect, they're presented here in a more standard form. "You see, I ain't heard of this Joe Louis when John Roxborough comes to me in June, 1934, and asks me to handle a good heavyweight prospect he's found," Blackburn explained. "That was in Chicago. So I says for Roxborough to bring around his white boy and I'll look him over." Roxborough, of course, immediately told Blackburn that Louis was black. "Soon as I heard that, I tells Roxborough I won't have no truck with a colored boy," Blackburn recalled, "because I figures colored boys ain't got much chance fighting nowadays—unless they just happen to be world-beaters. Roxborough he laughs and says that's exactly what he's got. That's what everybody says when they gets a fighter, so I'm not impressed. Well, John brung this colored boy 'round to . . . [the] gym. I gives him the eye, and I'm still not impressed."

In a 1937 interview in *The Ring*, Blackburn said, "When Black and Roxborough brought Joe to me, he was just a big, easy-going Negro boy with high water pants and too much arms for his coat sleeves. 'So you think you can get somewhere in this fighting game?' I says to him. 'Well, let me tell you something right off. It's next to impossible for a Negro heavyweight to get anywhere. He's got to be very good outside the ring and very bad inside the ring. Mr. Roxborough, who has known you quite a while, is convinced that you can be depended on to behave yourself, but you've gotta be a killer, otherwise I'm getting too old to waste any time on you.'" Louis' response, Blackburn recalled, was, "I ain't gonna waste any of your time."

Though Blackburn was only fifty years old in 1934, he already thought of himself as an old man. His years of tough living and drinking were no doubt already catching up with him. As Freddie Guinyard remembers, "Blackburn had been training around Chicago, but he had arthritis pretty bad and he was kinda out of the business." Blackburn, in fact, only took the job of handling Louis when he was guaranteed a weekly salary of thirty-five dollars for the initial four weeks he worked as Louis' trainer. According to Chris Mead's biography of Louis, *Champion: Joe Louis, Black Hero in White America,* Blackburn's response to John Roxborough's offer of a regular salary was, "This will be the best job I ever had. Usually got to whip my man to collect my pay. I got to tell you, you'll never make a success of this kid, but I need the job. He ain't going to make no money worth shaking your finger at. Remember he's a colored boy."

In the U.P.I. interview, Blackburn said that he was not impressed with Louis until the young fighter had been working with him in the gym for about a week. "I began to figure maybe Roxborough was right. Maybe this Louis boy has real talent. He had a good body, hit fast and learned fast. And he was nuts about fightin'."

Blackburn was concerned, however, that Louis might be "too easy-going—too nice a fella" to succeed as a professional boxer. Louis "didn't have any blood in his eye," Blackburn recalled. "He didn't go out to murder the boys in the gym. Didn't have the killer's instinct. So I knows right then what I got to do and I does it."

What Blackburn did was convince Louis that he would have to be a sensational knockout artist if he had any hope of succeeding. "You can't get nowhere nowadays trying to out-point fellows in the ring," Blackburn recalled telling Louis. "It's mighty hard for a colored boy to win decisions. The dice is loaded against you. You gotta knock 'em out and keep knocking 'em out to get anywheres. Let your right fist be the referee. Don't ever forget that. Let that right there be your referee."

"I painted the picture for Joe and I kept painting it for him," Blackburn told his interviewer. "Fightin' is a tough business. Nobody knows that better than me. I fought 'em all for twenty-five years—lightweights to heavyweights. . . . You just gotta throw away your heart when you pull on those gloves, or the other fella'll knock it outa you. That's why Joe Louis is a killer in the ring today."

A well-known piece of the Joe Louis story which warrants repeating is the celebrated list of rules which Roxborough and Black established for Louis as he began his professional career. According to Louis biographer Chris Mead, Roxborough presented these rules to Louis in conversation and later formalized them for public consumption as a public relations device. The formula was designed to assure the white public that Louis would not run into the problems encountered by Jack Johnson, who flaunted his success by grinning over fallen opponents in the ring and shocking white society by associating with—and twice marrying—white women.

The rules specified that Louis never be photographed alongside a white woman; never go to a nightclub alone; take no soft or fixed fights; never gloat over a fallen opponent; maintain a 'deadpan' expression when photographed; and live and fight cleanly.

In Louis' autobiography, Louis recalls that Blackburn also warned him against behaving like Jack Johnson. "You know, boy, the heavyweight division for a Negro is hardly likely," Blackburn told Louis when the two were working together in Trafton's Gym in Chicago. "The white man ain't too keen on it. You have to really be something to get anywhere. If you really ain't gonna be another Jack Johnson, you got some hope. White man hasn't forgotten that fool nigger with his white women, acting like he owned the world. And you got to listen to everything I tell you. You got to jump when I say jump, sleep when I say sleep."

In his 1937 interview in *The Ring*, Blackburn also argued that Louis would not have succeeded if he'd copied Johnson's masterful, defense-oriented boxing style. The boxing fans of the 1930s, Blackburn said, would not have appreciated a skilled boxer like Jack Johnson because he was "not enough of a killer." Blackburn said, "The fans wouldn't have stood for the Johnson style of fighting today, not enough action."

During the first week Blackburn and Louis worked together at Trafton's Gym, Blackburn would not permit Louis to enter the ring. Louis merely hit the heavy bag as Blackburn held it and spoke to him. Blackburn recalled in the *Pittsburgh Courier* in 1935 that when Louis and he began working together, "Joe needed correction in everything except hitting. I had to teach him to back up his punches with the proper timing [and] accuracy, and to instruct him in the important art of balance."

The young Joe Louis, a shy Alabama native with a subtle sense of humor and a slight speech impediment, was by all accounts somewhat intimidated by Jack Blackburn, the hard man who had served time in prison and reportedly carried a knife.

Marshall Miles, who took over as Louis' manager in 1944, first met Louis in the early 1930s, and often observed Blackburn and Louis together. "Blackburn was entirely a different kind of a trainer than you ordinarily see," says Miles. "He was very mean. And he wasn't soft with a fighter. In fact, Joe was kinda a little bit afraid of him, put it that way. Because he was a very nasty guy. But a nice guy, sincere—but he wouldn't take any foolishness."

Trainer Walter Smith, from the Kronk Gym in Detroit who grew up with Louis in Detroit and watched him box from his first days as an amateur at the Brewster Recreation Center, remembers Jack Blackburn as a stern taskmaster. Smith, who accompanied his friend, light-heavyweight Dave Clark, to Louis' early training camps, says Blackburn was also a quiet man. "The only time he would say anything to Joe is when Joe wasn't doing something that he thought he should be doing," Smith recalls. ". . . He was a real quiet man. He was a hard man, he was a hard man." Smith adds respectfully, "You had to have discipline to box for him [Blackburn]. He required that."

Veteran West Coast promoter Babe Griffin calls Blackburn "one of the greatest" trainers ever. "Some guys are trainers, but they're not teachers, but you gotta get somebody who can teach along with it," explains Griffin, who as a young fighter was taught by one of Jack Dempsey's trainers, Dolph Thomas.

Griffin observed Blackburn and Louis working together before Louis fought Donald "Reds" Barry in San Francisco in 1935. "I furnished him with heavyweights for sparring. And I got acquainted with Blackburn then," says Griffin. "I was there every day. He used to call Joe Louis 'Chappie.' While they were out in the gym there was very little talking because Louis done everything that Blackburn wanted. And that's why he was a great fighter."

Asked if Blackburn was a tough man, Griffin replies, "He might have been when he was young. But he was an older man. He had got out of prison, you know. He was very mellow. He never said . . . only a few words and that was it. But he was, at the time I met him, he was a terrific man."

Freddie Guinyard also depicts the warmer side of the relationship between Louis and Blackburn. When Louis and Blackburn first met, Louis was respectful and called his new teacher "Mr. Blackburn." Soon, though, the two began using the nickname "Chappie" for each other. Asked how the shared nicknames evolved, Guinyard explains, "Mr. Blackburn gave Joe Louis that name. He'd start calling him, 'Let's go, Chappie,' when they got ready to go to the training camp. And Joe would answer, 'Okay, Chappie,' and they struck it off just right with that. That was one of the things that brought them closer together."

While Guinyard concedes that Blackburn was uncompromising, he adds, "But Jack's kindness made Joe look up to him as a son, and that's the difference that I could see. Because being right there, I felt the same way about him." Blackburn, Guinyard adds, had his patient side. "He knew he was dealing with a kid."

About Blackburn's drinking Guinyard says, "Jack did not drink whiskey, he drank beer. But beer made him just as high as whiskey makes some people." Marshall Miles sums up Blackburn's drinking this way: "Well, he drank, but he didn't drink on the job. I used to take Jack out once in a while at night. He would drink a few beers, but that was it. It never interfered with his training. I didn't see it." Louis biographer Chris Mead, on the other hand, records this assessment from Louis' attorney and adviser Truman Gibson: "When he drank, he [Blackburn] was wholly unnatural."

Exactly what Jack Blackburn taught Joe Louis in those early days, as Louis made the transformation from amateur to professional fighter, is often discussed by boxing men. Though it in no way undermines Blackburn's monumental achievement, it's important to remember that Louis was already an accomplished amateur fighter when Blackburn took charge of him in June of 1934, when Louis was twenty years old.

Walter Smith emphasizes that Louis always had the stuff of greatness within him. To illustrate his point, Smith recalls Louis' first amateur fight against Johnny Miler, who was the light-heavyweight on the United States Olympic Team in 1932.

"At that time they never looked at the record of how many fights you had," Smith explains. "If you was an amateur in that class and they wanted a fight, they'd put you in the ring with this guy whether you were a novice or not. The first amateur fight Joe ever had was against the United States Champion—

the guy had just come back from the Olympic Games. . . . And he came back from the Olympic Games and they put Joe in the ring with him. He knocked Joe down seven times." Though the inexperienced Louis was severely outmatched, he "kept getting up," Smith says with admiration, "and that really showed the heart of a champion. That's when everybody knew he was going to be a good fighter."

Smith and his friends "used to kid" Louis about the devastating experience, Smith says. "Yeah, we used to kid him about it. Everybody kidded him about it. We told him he was just like an elevator going up and down. But he laughed just as hard as anybody else did."

Smith adds that Louis had expert coaching from the moment he walked into the Brewster Recreation Center in Detroit at the urging of his friend Thurston McKinney. Smith himself was a member of the Brewster center and boxed as an amateur from 1930 through the mid '30s.

Atler Ellis, who started the Brewster Center, was Louis' first trainer as an amateur. Atler Ellis was known as "Kid" Ellis when he boxed in Philadelphia. As the head of the Brewster Center, Ellis had already produced a record number of amateur champions in Detroit by the time he met the 18-year-old Joe Louis in 1932. At the same time that Ellis was guiding Louis through an outstanding amateur career, he was also a full-time employee of the Ford Motor Company.

Ellis was later aided in coaching Louis by Holman Williams, the superb middleweight whom Louis continued to admire and assist for years to come. "Louis loved him," Walter Smith says. "In fact, he called himself Holman's manager. He took care of Holman."

Together, Atler Ellis and Holman Williams taught Joe Louis what Smith calls "the Brewster style." Asked to define the style, Smith says, "Left jab, right hand, left hook. Boxing all the time. Moving back and forth. This is the Detroit style. You gotta have a good left hand. That's the Detroit style."

Smith recalls that as an amateur, Louis improved his hand speed by working out with lighter, faster boxers. Smith himself sparred with Louis early on. "Most of the time he sparred with small guys—like lightweights, welterweights and some middleweights. . . . He liked to box little guys all the time when he was first starting to train. Always boxed small guys. This is one reason: because he was big and he boxed little guys, he had a tendency to have real fast hands."

In 1933, Louis began working with trainer George Slayton, manager of the Detroit Athletic Association which ran the Brewster Center. By April of 1934, Louis won the National AAU light-heavyweight title, ending his amateur career of fifty-four fights with forty-three knockouts and four decision losses.

Asked what Blackburn changed in Louis' style, Walter Smith says, "He taught him balance. Balance and a good left jab, a *good* left jab. See, Joe Louis always had a hell of a left hook. He punched good. He was a helluva amateur fighter." Smith goes on to discuss the importance of proper balance: "As long as a man keeps himself on balance when he's throwing punches—that is one of the basic things of boxing. If you don't have good balance, your punches are not going to be effective."

Making a similar point, Freddie Guinyard says, "Blackburn worked on the whole body movement—to step in while throwing a punch." As an amateur, Guinyard says, Louis had relied on raw power. "Joe would stand back and he was so powerful that he could throw a punch and knock a man out, but Blackburn taught him if you step in with that punch how much more effective it would be."

When Blackburn began working with Louis, the trainer told his pupil, "You can beat anyone you can hit, but I have to teach you how to get in the proper position to do so."

Like Walter Smith, trainer Eddie Futch sparred with Louis as a member of the Brewster Recreation Center. With a scholar's precision, Futch provides unique insight into Blackburn's impact on Louis, arguing that what Blackburn took away from Louis' boxing style was as important as what he added.

"He [Louis] had his first seven fights in Chicago," Futch recalls. "Then he came home to Detroit and trained at the Detroit Athletic Association. I watched and asked questions of Blackburn and he was receptive, knowing I was a member. Blackburn was a mean person, as mean as he looked." Futch, though, treated Blackburn respectfully, so the two "got along well."

Before Louis began working with Blackburn, Futch says, he was "a mover. . . . Box and move." However, he adds, "When Blackburn took him over, I was kinda disappointed when I first saw him. I really was." Futch remembers looking at a revamped, more aggressive, less mobile Louis and saying, "I don't know whether that's gonna be too good or not."

Louis' sixth professional fight, a fourth-round knockout of Alex Borchuk in Detroit, made Futch further question Blackburn's handling of Louis. "He was in a couple of tough fights," Futch recalls. "One tough fight he got hurt. And that really made me think twice about what he was doing. . . . He boxed Borchuk and Borchuk hit him with a left hook and wobbled him. It looked like he was going to go down. But he withstood it and came on. But Louis was using that style that Blackburn had given him, taking away that bouncing on his toes."

In later years, Louis referred to the punches he took against Borchuk as the hardest he'd ever endured—harder even than those of Max Schmeling, who knocked him out in 1936. Describing the Borchuk fight in a 1937 interview, Blackburn said, "The punch of Borchuk's that Joe still remembers so well was some punch and make no mistake, I haven't forgot it myself." The punch, Blackburn added, "broke off one of Joe's molars."

Futch now sees that by the time of the Borchuk fight, Blackburn "had Louis fighting like a heavyweight." As an amateur, Louis moved more and took fewer risks, Futch says, "so Blackburn took that away from him. He got him sliding in, cutting the ring off, using that good left hand—not bouncing all over the place."

Blackburn also further developed the remarkable accuracy of punching that Louis already possessed. "Louis always, even as an amateur, was so accurate with his punches," Futch says. "Very seldom, if you watch Louis' fight pictures, he very seldom missed a punch. Rather than throw a bad punch, he wouldn't throw any at all."

Futch concludes, "Louis was taught how to cut the ring off—put the opponent where he could find him. And use that good left hand to set him up. And so that was what Jack Blackburn took away from Louis. It seems paradoxical sometimes, but that was actually a fact."

Futch is also careful to emphasize that Louis was not a passive pupil merely following Blackburn's orders. Just the opposite was true. Searching for the right word to describe Louis' fascination with boxing in the early days, Futch says, "He was so . . . intense. He was a student of boxing, most people don't realize that. They think he was just a puncher. But he was a student of boxing."

Blackburn himself said that Louis' seventh professional fight in September of 1934—the first to go the distance—offered an early clue to Louis' greatness. In a 1935 *Pittsburgh Courier* article, the trainer stated: "I first saw the earmarks of greatness in Joe during his fight with Adolph Wiator. It was Joe's first battle to go ten rounds, the others ending through Louis' hard punching in the second and third, except one which ended in the eighth. I soon saw that this was to be Joe's acid test. In the fourth, Wiator . . . hit Joe so hard that he actually stunned him. Joe was wobbly and I had to go and get him after the bell to help him back into his corner. I help[ed] rally him a bit during the rest period and told him to go in there and do his level best during the fifth and sixth. He responded well, trying hard, but

still the going was tough and the long distance was telling on
him. During the minute between gongs for the seventh and
eighth, I believe I talked more than any other minute of my
life."

No doubt employing a touch of melodrama designed to
please his newspaper audience, Blackburn stated that he then
reminded Louis of the home he wanted to buy for his mother—
and told Louis he'd never be champion if he didn't rally now. "In
the eighth, ninth and tenth," Blackburn continued, "Joe simply
murdered Wiator and won the decision. I told him to shoot his
left and outbox him, and not to use his uppercut. He followed
my instructions to the letter. I knew that Joe was wobbly and in
bad shape himself, and wanted him to preserve his strength. But
when Joe pulled through those ten rounds, I knew that I was
handling a great fighter."

Under Blackburn's guidance, Louis scored nine knockouts in
his first eleven fights. Louis' eleventh fight was against heavyweight Charlie Massera who was handled by an old friend of
Blackburn's, Ray Arcel. Massera was then ranked among the
top ten active heavyweights. Arcel describes the enthusiasm
Blackburn had by then developed about Louis' prospects.

"The first time I saw Joe Louis fight was in 1934," says Arcel.
"I went to Chicago with a young fighter by the name of Charlie
Massera. Louis had been boxing in Chicago when he came out
of the amateurs. I didn't know how good Louis was. In fact, I had
only heard about him. So I went to Chicago and I saw Blackburn. I hadn't seen him in a while and I was very glad to see him,
and he said to me, 'I got me a fighter now. Wait till you see the
fighter I got.'"

Here Arcel laughs as he contemplates the thrill and awe with
which Blackburn described the young Louis.

"I don't want to discourage you, Ray," Blackburn told Arcel.
"I'm glad to see you. But I got me a fighter!"

Massera was staggered in the first round, and fought defen-

sively in the second. Before the start of the next round, Blackburn told Louis to "cross the right to the chin," and Massera was
counted out in the third.

After the fight, Blackburn asked Arcel for his opinion of
Louis. *"You got a fighter,"* was Arcel's simple reply.

In the 1935 *Pittsburgh Courier* article, Blackburn portrayed
Louis as an earnest pupil who "obeys me and does exactly what
I tell him in the ring." Blackburn added, however, "Only once he
crossed me. It was during the fight with Reds Barry out in
Frisco." In that March 1935 bout, Blackburn stated, "I saw that
Joe had his number in the first round, but didn't finish him.
After the round I asked Joe why he didn't stop him. 'Well,
Chappie,' Joe replied, 'I promised them over the radio that I was
going to knock him out in the third round and I didn't want to
disappoint them.' So the fight ended in the third round."

By July of 1935, Louis was doing so well that Blackburn's
former opponent, the great heavyweight Sam Langford, was
inspired to compare Louis to another of Blackburn's opponents,
lightweight champion Joe Gans. "The Detroit Bomber," Langford told the *Chicago Defender*, using one of Louis' nicknames,
"is another Joe Gans who I think was the greatest fighter of all
time. . . . I consider him another Gans. He can hit, he is fast and
is no slouch at employing ring craft. . . . He is the marvel of the
age."

As Eddie Futch points out, Joe Louis' progress through the
heavyweight ranks was extremely fast. "Louis knocked out
Primo Carnera in June of '35," Futch notes, "eleven months after
he turned pro. And Primo Carnera was a recent heavyweight
champion. In September of that same year, he knocked out Max
Baer who was champion when Louis turned pro."

During these early fights, Louis relied heavily upon Blackburn's strategic advice in the corner. When he was having
difficulty landing punches agianst the slick boxing of Lee Ramage during their first fight in Chicago in December of 1934,

Louis told Blackburn in the corner after the sixth round, "I can't get a good shot at him." Blackburn, according to *The Ring*, replied, "Well, he's got arms ain't he?" The advice proved effective: by the eighth round, Ramage had trouble holding up his arms and Louis moved in for the knockout.

Looking back on the Ramage fight the following year, Louis told Jack Turcott of *The Chicago Tribune*, "After the third round, Blackburn told me to quit boxing him and work on his body. I started banging away at his chest and heart with rights and lefts, and in the sixth I landed a right on his elbow and noticed that I slowed his arm up. . . . Blackburn told me to watch for my opening when I went out in the eighth. I feinted a left to the body and crossed with a right to the chin. Lee went down, but he got up again." Ramage went down two more times before his handlers threw in the towel.

When Louis knocked out Ramage in the second round of their rematch in Los Angeles in February of 1935, promoter Mike Jacobs was in the arena. Shortly after that, Jacobs reached an agreement with Louis' managers, Roxborough and Black, that led to Louis coming to New York to fight more significant opponents, beginning with former champion Primo Carnera.

At this time, Blackburn publicly compared Louis to Jack Johnson. "I never saw a kid learn so quickly," Blackburn told the *Pittsburgh Courier* in March of 1935. "Moreover, he is a great boxer, a great puncher and a great judge of distance—and he don't waste any punches. His judging of distance is something you seldom see. He is very aggressive. In my opinion, he is the greatest fighter since Jack Johnson."

Though Primo Carnera's record was built on fixed fights and his abilities as a boxer were dubious, Louis and his managers took the gigantic Carnera seriously. They set up training camp in Pompton Lakes, New Jersey to prepare for the bout which was to be held at Yankee Stadium. Blackburn's prefight strategy called for Louis—who was nearly sixty pounds lighter than his opponent—to waste no time feeling out Carnera in the early going. Instead, Louis was to attack Carnera's body from the opening bell.

One of the visitors to Louis' training camp was Jack Johnson. According to Louis' autobiography, Johnson, still bearing a grudge against Blackburn, approached manager John Roxborough and said that if Roxborough fired Blackburn, he—Johnson—would be willing to take over as Louis' trainer. Louis reports Roxborough merely "cursed Johnson out" in response to the offer.

Louis also details Blackburn's behavior immediately before the Carnera bout: "Chappie kept talking to me—hypnotizing me with his tactics and reassurances. Chappie told me to work on Carnera's body till he dropped his guard, and then go to the head."

Covering the goings-on in Louis' corner during the June 25, 1935 bout, the *New York Sun* reported that Louis' handlers "were a peaceful group during the first two rounds and permitted their charge to make his own fight." The paper added that Blackburn did "all the talking" in the corner. Before the first round, Blackburn told Louis, "It is your fight, kid, and I want you to take a good peep at that big guy in this round. Keep stepping in, and jolt him once or twice, just for luck." After remaining quiet for two rounds, the *Sun* reported, Blackburn told Louis, "Now, kid, here is the fourth round right upon us, and I think you better go out there and ready that big guy for the big splash." After Louis was clearly in control following the fifth round, Blackburn, according to the *Sun*, "whispered" the following: "Here is the sixth round, kid, and you know you missed fire on this guy in the last two rounds. You have got this boy right where you want him, so let's get it over with. You just drop old Betsy on that fellow's chin, and we'll start the parade for home." That was all the talking Blackburn needed to do that evening: Louis scored a knockout in the sixth.

In a 1939 interview with Chester Washington, Blackburn looked back on the Carnera bout. "I remember when I handled him for the Carnera fight," Blackburn said. "I gave him signals like a baseball coach. When I wanted Joe to work on Primo's midsection, I kept pointing downward. Then when the time was ripe to shoot for the head, I pointed upward. Joe followed like clockwork. He never missed a signal. And he turned in one of the finest fights of his career against Carnera."

Before Louis' next bout, against Kingfish Levinsky in August of 1935, Blackburn exuberantly told a Chicago interviewer that Louis didn't merely defeat his opponents—he ended their boxing careers. "When Joe licks 'em," Blackburn said, "they're not merely licked. They're ruined! When Joe is finished with them, they never are the same."

Reviewing Louis' opponents, Blackburn said, "For instance, there's Donald "Reds" Barry of Washington, a fast, smart boxer that had bothered a lot of good heavyweights." After Louis knocked out Barry in three rounds, Blackburn asked, "What happened to Barry? He was flattened three or four times in succession after Joe was through with him." After Louis won a tough decision from Adolph Wiater, Blackburn said, "He was beaten several times by very ordinary fighters." And after Lee Ramage was twice knocked out by Louis, "Those two lickings took so much out of him that I understand he has announced his retirement from the ring." Blackburn concluded by saying, "Just look over Joe's record, and you'll find that very seldom is a fighter the same after the Bomber is through with him. The boy's just a natural-born ruiner."

Louis' fight against Levinsky was the occasion for one of the most often told of the handful of anecdotes that are always associated with Blackburn and Louis. During the training sessions for the fight, Louis recalled in his autobiography, he noticed Blackburn behaving "strangely," and discovered that it was because of drinking. On the day of the fight, while walking to the ring in Comiskey Park in Chicago, Blackburn told Louis, "Man, I don't feel good, been drinking too much." Louis responded, "You just walk up the steps with me one time, that's all you have to do." Louis added, "Chappie, if I knock him out in the first round, would you quit drinking for six months?" Blackburn agreed to the deal, but after Louis scored a first round knockout, Blackburn asked Louis, "Chappie, about that drinking, would you let me off the hook?" Freddie Guinyard confirms the story, adding that Blackburn "did stay off [drinking] for almost 30 days."

Louis finished 1935 with quick knockouts of two leading heavyweights, former champion Max Baer and Paulino Uzcudun.

After viewing a slow motion film of Baer's knockout of Primo Carnera, Blackburn and Louis prepared a defense against Baer's celebrated right hand. In a "secret" workout which was closed to reporters—though it was nonetheless described in *The New York Times*—Blackburn "put on the gloves with Louis and showed him how he should feint and shift when moving in." The *Times* added that "sparring mates have feinted him [Louis] into leads, and Blackburn has been anxious to correct this fault." The Associated Press also carried news of the "secret" workout, reporting that Blackburn was "attempting to show him how to give false signals to an opponent, make him drop his guard for a blow in the stomach and then get it in the head."

When Baer faced Louis, Jack Dempsey worked in his corner as chief second, but it didn't seem to help Baer. After he was knocked out in four rounds, Baer uttered his famous line, "When I get executed, people are going to have to pay more than twenty-five dollars a seat to watch it."

Following the fight, Edward Van Every of the *Sun*—who often played Boswell to Blackburn's sagacious Dr. Johnson—reported that Blackburn was now ready to begin comparing Louis to the great Sam Langford. Van Every wrote that since knocking out Carnera, Louis continually asked Blackburn, "How about Langford?" Following Louis' knockout of Baer, Blackburn told Louis, "Two more fights, and on the improvement you showed tonight

I'd say bring on Langford." Blackburn also told Van Every that he was upset that Baer had managed to land a few of his famous rights: "A fighter like Baer has no license to land any rights on a boy who has what Joe's got."

By this time, as Blackburn recalled in an interview with Van Every the following year, Louis' reputation was such that his opponents were often petrified before stepping into the ring with him. At the weigh-in for Louis' fight with Max Baer, Blackburn said, Baer "cracked so bad he ran right out of the boxing commission room." Listing Louis' other victims, Blackburn said, "Maybe Carnera didn't show it so much, but we knew he thought he was in for it as soon as we spied him. Paulino [Uzcudun] was the same way. King Levinsky looked like he would have to be carried into the ring."

In a column written after Blackburn's death, Van Every recalled that during this period Blackburn would say with pride, "Some day there's not going to be any more I can teach Joe. He don't make the same mistake twice. I see him do something wrong in a fight and then I take him in the gym and show him how not to do what he shouldn't do, and in the next fight he do it right."

In the winter of 1935—as Louis faced Uzcudun—Jack Blackburn was once again charged with murder when a Chicago Grand Jury indicted him on manslaughter charges in the shooting death of a man on October 20, 1935. According to court records, Blackburn testified before the grand jury on December 5 that he did not at the time of the shooting possess a gun and had not fired a gun. On December 15, Blackburn was indicted for perjury as well as manslaughter.

On March 3, 1936, the *New York Sun* carried a United Press report which stated in part: "The elite of Chicago's Little Harlem wedged into Judge Robert C. O'Connell's court room today to see Jack Blackburn, trainer of Joe Louis, tried on manslaughter charges. Blackburn and two others were accused of the fatal shooting of Enoch Hauser, Negro, in a South Side argument last fall. ... With Blackburn at the time of the argument were William Parnell and John Bowman. Blackburn and Parnell, it is alleged, argued with Bowman over purchase of a garage. The shooting, in which Hauser was killed and a child wounded, followed."

Strangely, no subsequent report on the trial appeared in the *Sun*, nor was the trial reported on in any New York or Chicago newspaper that I could find. Joe Louis biographer Chris Mead says that he also was unable to find a published account of the murder or the trial. I can only speculate, therefore, that Louis' managers may have used their considerable influence to keep Blackburn's problems out of the press.

On March 9, 1936, the charges against Blackburn, the court record states, were declared *nolle prosequi*, indicating that the prosecutor no longer wished to proceed with the case. Still, some old-time boxing men speak of Blackburn going to prison during this period. It's possible, of course, that Blackburn may have served some time behind bars while awaiting trial.

Blackburn was a free man as Louis prepared for his June 19, 1936 fight against Max Schmeling. Schmeling, of course, handed Louis his only defeat on the way to the heavyweight title. It's widely reported that before knocking out Louis in twelve rounds, Schmeling had spotted a "flaw" in Louis' style. "I see something," Schmeling told the press, pointing out that Louis momentarily dropped his left after he jabbed, leaving himself open to a right-hand counterpunch.

Recalling a visit to Louis' Lakewood, New Jersey training camp, Ray Arcel refutes this piece of boxing legend. "No, he didn't see anything," says Arcel. "Louis had just married, and he was in training in Lakewood. I went out to see how he was doing, and he looked pretty bad. I mean, he looked like he was nothing. So naturally, being close to Blackburn, I walked over to Blackburn and I said, 'Chappie, what's wrong with your fighter?'

He says, 'Ray, he's on his honeymoon, and she's here with him.' I said, 'Enough said, buddy.'"

Louis confesses in his autobiography that, while preparing to face Schmeling, he not only saw his new wife, Marva, but repeatedly snuck off to see other women as well. He adds that Blackburn literally chased some of Louis' female admirers away with a stick. At this time, Louis also took up golf for the first time—an activity Blackburn felt would be harmful to his boxing because it encouraged Louis to hold his hands low.

Freddie Guinyard recalls that Blackburn was very upset with Louis' behavior before the Schmeling fight. "Joe had gotten in the limelight then and everybody was coming around to see him and Blackburn didn't like that too much. He wanted Joe to train when he was in the training camp—not to socialize so much. So he would tell him. Joe would do it for a while. Then old friends would come around the training camp, you know, so Joe would go play golf with them. Or he'd go to the theater. That wasn't quite right, for a man in training to be up at 10:30 instead of going to bed at nine."

Asked about Blackburn's attitude at the time, Marshall Miles says "If it was up to him, Joe would never have gotten into the jams he got in—like the Schmeling fight. But you see, Joe had gotten out of hand and it took a lot to bring him back." Miles remembers arriving at Louis' camp one night while Louis was preparing for Schmeling and discovering that Louis was at a nightclub. "I could tell then he wasn't in shape," Miles says. "But couldn't anybody do anything with Joe right then."

Though Blackburn tried to hide his worries from most reporters, a trace of concern can, in retrospect, be seen even in his seemingly optimistic prefight comments. While telling Walter Stewart of the *New York World-Telegram* that Louis planned to try for an early knockout, Blackburn also revealed his anxiety about what could happen if the fight went into the later rounds. "There are sixty-four and a half different ways of lookin' at a fight before you fight it. But there ain't but one right way,"

Blackburn said. "Now, when you gets two big guys in there pitchin', some mighty strange things are likely to happen. A split eye has turned many a bum into a headline man, and that ol' Schmeling can bust hard enough to hurt anything he tags just right. We ain't intendin' this here fight to go no longer than we absolutely has to, and you can go to sleep on that. . . . No, siree—we goes fast when we starts, and we ain't givin' that Schmeling man no time to get warmed up."

Blackburn expressed his concern more directly to Edward Van Every of the *Sun*. In a 1938 column, Van Every revealed Blackburn's extraordinarily frank remarks which had been made "in confidence" on the eve of the first Schmeling fight in 1936. "When we first started working together," Blackburn told Van Every, "I told Joe: 'You got a punch, but punchin' ain't fightin'. You got to punch faster than the other fellow. You don't make a fighter in one year, or two years. Some day a two-year fighter is going to run into a boy he ain't going to knock right over. Then you need something more than just punchin'. Then you got to make the other boy lick himself a little bit first before going back to the punchin' stuff. Schmeling ain't one of them babies that licks themselves before they get into the ring.'"

Confiding in Van Every, Blackburn continued, "No matter what the world thinks or the boxing experts tell them, Joe is in for a real fight. Any cracks I may 'a' made about this one being easy, I takes it all back."

Blackburn also told Van Every that Louis had begun to believe the myth of his own invincibility. "The trouble with Joe is that you newspapermen have made him think he can just walk out and punch any one over and that Schmeling is the softest pushover of the lot. He's up against an opponent with a straight right hand that can do a lot of damage and he may need more than he's got in the way of condition, to say nothing of experience.

"Joe weighed in at 198, three pounds under what I aimed to have him and was almost down to 195 for a spell. Why? I'll tell you—too much having his own way. Just for one example—that golf stuff. Out on the links under the sun altogether too much. He don't listen to my orders on this, and when I sent the managers after him they have to keep after him for two or three holes before they can drag him off.

"Joe's likely to get hit on the chin with one of them Schmeling rights and what with his legs not being what they should be and his being only a two-year fighter—well, lots can happen that's not so good."

After the weigh-in for the 1936 Schmeling fight, Van Every overheard Louis tell Blackburn, "That German was sure a pretty cool bird . . ." Blackburn responded, "Chappie, it looks to me like you got a fight on your hands this time." Blackburn then told Van Every, "Of course, there's no question in my mind about Joe winning, and by a knockout, but beating a man who ain't licked before he climbs in the ring is lots harder than beating one who is. If Joe wasn't impressed by the way Schmeling kept his nerve, then he'd be a plumb fool, and Joe ain't no fool, not about this fighting business. You may think he ain't noticing much, but those sleepy eyes of his take in plenty. And he didn't overlook the fact that this Schmeling was acting just like a guy who is going into just another fight and what of it. It was the first time anything like this happened at a weighing-in since Joe started to be somebody with his gloves."

While Louis' other opponents were paralyzed with fear, Blackburn stressed, "This Schmeling was different. . . . You can't fool me . . . and I could tell by Schmeling's color and his eyes and other things that Joe was going to have to lick that boy before he got licked."

In his own account of his defeat by Schmeling, Louis goes out of his way to exonerate Blackburn from any blame. Before the opening bell, Louis recalls in his autobiography, Blackburn told him, "Don't go for the knockout yet. Keep jabbing him off balance so he can't get that right in, and for God's sake keep your left arm high." After Louis went down from a Schmeling right in the fourth round, Blackburn told him in the corner, "Keep your guard up, keep your guard up."

According to Lester Bromberg, writing in *The Ring* in 1954, Blackburn's first words to the defeated Louis while helping him back to his corner were brutally honest: "Chappie, you gonna keep gettin' knocked out if you don't do what I tol' you."

Louis had to be carried to his dressing room after the fight, *The New York Times* reported. While Blackburn tended to Louis' wounds, Louis said that he had sprained his left thumb in the fourth round and the right in the ninth. The injuries, Blackburn said, prevented Louis from punching effectively. The report continued: "As Louis sat on his dressing table, he put his face in his hands and cried like a child. His co-manager Julian Black and Blackburn finally soothed him and told him he was certain to do better the next time and not to be too down-hearted."

Freddie Guinyard recalls that following the loss Louis told him, "You know, it's a funny thing. After the second round, I didn't remember any of the fight." Louis' statement proves, Guinyard says, that from the second round on, Louis was fighting on instinct. "Now I do know that," Guinyard emphasizes. "That was told to me by Joe Louis." Guinyard adds that although Blackburn was extremely upset by the loss, "He didn't rub it in when Joe lost the fight."

"Chappie and I went over what was wrong; this time I listened," Louis wrote in his autobiography. "He told me Max was a different kind of fighter for me. He was a counterpuncher. He told me I kept dropping my left hand after a jab, and Max just kept shooting his right hand over it. He said we'd fix that all up."

Preparing Louis for his first comeback fight—an August, 1936 bout against aging former champion Jack Sharkey—Blackburn lectured Louis on the fine points of blocking and slipping the sort of right hands that Schmeling had used so effectively. In sparring, Louis practiced defending against right-handed on-slaughts and how to counter-punch effectively. Four days before Louis was scheduled to face Sharkey, though, Blackburn told Walter Stewart of the *New York World-Telegram* that he was not truly happy with Louis' condition. "He ain't the Louis of yesterday—not yet," Blackburn said. ". . . He's getting better all the time, but I'm not satisfied—not yet."

The day before the Sharkey fight, Blackburn again discussed the Schmeling loss with Bill Corum. "He should have knocked that Mr. Schmeling out right quick," said Blackburn. "I don't mean to talk smart, but I think I can still lick that Mr. Schmeling. I know he ain't going to bring any right hand all the way over from Germany and keep hitting me with it."

Describing Louis' current condition, Blackburn said, "I got him in good shape, but he makes me right mad sometimes the way he loafs along and takes things easy. But he still can belt 'em. Yes sir, when he hits 'em he still hurts 'em. He ought never to have been licked and he ought not be licked any more. But all you can do is tell him. You can't go in there and make him open up and fight."

Following Louis' third round knockout of Sharkey, Blackburn told the *Sun*, "I just told him to go out there from the first bell and kill 'im." Citing Louis' improved defense, Blackburn said, "He kept his left up this time. Sure he did. His left hand was all right the last time [in the loss to Schmeling]. He just got hit, that was all. He just forgot to duck. But did you see him duck and weave tonight? Oh, but Chappie was fine tonight."

Louis had impressive showings throughout 1936 and 1937, and by June of 1937 was ready to challenge heavyweight champion James J. Braddock, who had won the title from Max Baer in a stunning upset. Louis' account of Blackburn's role in his preparation for Braddock, and his subsequent historic one-round victory in the rematch with Schmeling, reads like a love letter of appreciation from a grateful son to his wise, dedicated father.

Though Blackburn remained skeptical up to the last moment that the white power structure would permit a black heavyweight to fight for the title, once the Louis-Braddock fight was signed, Blackburn stopped drinking and rededicated himself to making Joe Louis heavyweight champ. When Louis went on a month-long exhibition tour to polish his skills, he recalls, Blackburn told him, "All right, you son of a bitch, you made it to here, and I'm going to see you make it all the way. When I finish with you, you're gonna be a fucking fighting machine!"

Blackburn and Louis were "almost like one person" before the Braddock fight, Louis writes. Blackburn frankly set out Louis' flaws—his tendency to drop his left and his habit of attacking in predictable patterns. Blackburn also further developed Louis' skills as a counter-puncher.

Despite the hard work, some in the press criticized Louis' showing at his training camp in Kenosha, Wisconsin. Before the Braddock fight, Edward Van Every later recalled "the fault finding . . . was so extreme that promoter Mike Jacobs became unduly alarmed and a hurry call was put in for Harry Lenny." Lenny was a veteran corner man and manager who had worked with the legendary Joe Gans, as well as light-heavyweight champion Jack Delaney. According to Van Every, however, Lenny "could find little wrong with Louis." Today, those who were around the Louis camp say that Jacobs brought Lenny in because Jacobs was eager to have a white face in Louis' corner. Presumably, then, Jacobs wanted a white man to work with Louis for public relations reasons. In his autobiography, Louis refers to Lenny as a "cut man."

In a 1938 interview with Frank Graham, Lenny said of Louis: "He is the fastest puncher with both hands that I ever saw, and I have seen them all since [John L.] Sullivan. I even saw Sullivan, for that matter."

Blackburn was still clearly in charge of Louis' training, despite Lenny's presence. Two weeks before the fight, he told reporters, "We are working out a new defense. . . . We are working out something entirely new, and it will take a few more days to get the thing going." Knowing that he had instructed Louis to go easy in sparring, Blackburn added, "Joe is working along just the way he should be—that is to get himself right at the right time and not just to put on a training camp show. Just before the fight, I'll let Joe go to town and that's the way you'll know better how ready Joe really is."

Blackburn's last words to Louis before he went out to face Braddock in the ring in Comiskey Park in Chicago were, "This is it, Chappie. You come home a champ tonight." After Louis went down in the first round from a Braddock right, Louis stood up immediately rather than staying down to rest and gather his strength while taking a count. In the corner when the round ended, Blackburn presented Louis with one of the most famous between-round speeches in boxing history: "Why didn't you take a nine count? You can't get up so fast that nobody in the place didn't see you was down."

Analyzing the Braddock fight for Edward Van Every, Blackburn said that Louis was knocked down because of his failure to keep punching after ducking under Braddock's attacks. "If he'd 'a' had that down right," Blackburn argued, "he'd have knocked out Braddock in the first round. He got under Jim's right as pretty as you could ask, but was a little slow in shooting when he came up. Result was that Jim ripped through a do-or-die uppercut, which Joe should have beaten him to, as Joe was coming up, and down went Joe. Jim hit him right on the whiskers, all right."

In subsequent rounds, Louis recalls in his autobiography, he heeded Blackburn's advice and cautiously controlled the fight with his powerful jab and counter-punching. "Let him do the crowding," Blackburn advised. "He'll come apart in five or six rounds. Take it easy. I'll tell you when to shoot." By the eighth round, Braddock was an exhausted and defeated fighter, and Louis scored a knockout to become heavyweight champion.

In the dressing room after the fight, Louis reveals in his

autobiography, Blackburn helped himself to a souvenir. "I'm gonna take this right glove," he told Louis. "I earned it."

Reminiscing about Blackburn during the time of the Braddock fight, columnist Frank Graham wrote in 1942, "All the things he taught Louis were sound and clean. It also was characteristic of Blackburn that, at a weighing-in or in Louis' corner during a fight, he paid no attention to Joe's opponent save, in some cases, to greet him pleasantly. Whatever tricks he may have learned, in the rough-and-tumble days that he was fighting, about disconcerting an opponent before or during a fight, he kept in his bag. For some of Joe's opponents he had little regard, if any. For others . . . Jim Braddock in particular . . . he had a great liking.

"And when a fight was over," Graham concluded, "he went methodically about the business of getting Louis ready for the street, chuckling sometimes over what he had just seen in the ring but having little to say to those who crowded the dressing room."

Freddie Guinyard recalls that though reporters pestered Blackburn for quotes, he was often reluctant to be too expansive in public, telling writers that if he told them everything, he'd have nothing left to say to Joe Louis.

Blackburn's quiet wisdom again came in handy for Louis during the first defense of his title against the surprisingly difficult Welshman Tommy Farr. Before the fight, when reporters argued that Farr was an easy opponent, Blackburn said, "There ain't none of them soft until you have them counted out."

Lester Bromberg in *The Ring* reported that after Louis hurt his right hand in the third round, he asked Blackburn, "What do I do now, Chappie?" "Jes' keep firin' the left and fake with the right," Blackburn replied. "He'll still be lookin' for the right at the end of fifteen."

To Edward Van Every, Blackburn said, "When we discovered the Welshman [Farr] was a better fighter than we had looked for, that he wasn't easy to get positioned for a right hand, and Joe hurt his own right hand on top of that, I said to Joe, 'You've got to do the job with a straight left and beat him to the punch.' That was a beautiful job Joe went out and did."

Louis stated that he wouldn't feel like the heavyweight champion of the world until he defeated his conquerer Max Schmeling. He therefore approached the training for the Schmeling rematch with the utmost seriousness.

Before going to Pompton Lakes, Louis began his training for the June 22 rematch in the Catskill Mountains. As he left for the Catskills, Louis told the Associated Press, "Schmeling is in for a good slamming . . . He'll meet a different Joe Louis when he turns around to face me this time. I'm hitting harder. I think I am punching faster and I aim to beat him to the punch." To this statement, Blackburn added, "That's absolutely right. Beat him to the punch is right. Louis ain't goin' to fool us this time. He won't be scared of nothin'."

Blackburn discussed pre-fight strategy more expansively with Edward Van Every once he and Louis had arrived at camp. Blackburn began by saying that Louis' loss to Schmeling "was the best thing for Joe's future as a fighter—that he got a licking and just at the right time. Naturally, Joe had faults when he first fought Schmeling, faults that a young fighter is bound to have. He didn't figure to know what to do if he got hurt because he never really had been hurt, at least not by an experienced opponent. Then his head was getting a little the best of him about then. He knows now that this doesn't help you much when you're in trouble. There's a big difference between confidence and overconfidence."

Cataloging Schmeling's limitations, Blackburn said, "Schmeling is not the great fighter he thinks he is. As a matter of fact, he is just a cautious fighter with a good right. Being cautious is all right, but not too cautious. Joe and I were studying pictures [i.e. film] of his first fight with Max. In the fourth round when

Joe was nailed flush with the right and started to go down, what do you think Max was doing then? He was covering up. Is that a great fighter? Fight Max right and he is not a great fighter.

"Yes, sir, this time I feel different about Joe's chances than I did the first time. This time Joe can't miss. He knows how to fight Max this time and he has got the experience he needed. I had worries before that other fight, but not this time."

Blackburn's confidence was based not only on Louis' superior physical condition, but on this observation: "The only way Max can hit Joe with a right is to lead with it. And if you lead with a right to Joe, the lights go out right then and there."

Mannie Seamon, who became Blackburn's assistant in 1937 at the time of the Louis-Tommy Farr fight, described the atmosphere in Louis' camp before the second Schmeling fight. "We acted as if this was just another fight," Seamon told a reporter. "We never mentioned to Louis that he would have to guard his jaw to prevent Max knocking him out again. We got him thinking Schmeling was just another fighter he was going to stop when he got around to it." Seamon, who was in charge of Louis' sparring partners, added, "I got the best possible sparring partners and told them to do their best in the ring. No sparring partner was instructed to take knockdowns to help build up Louis' belief in his own punching power." Blackburn also had the sparring partners throw right hands at Louis so that he could practice defending against the weapon that had been so effective for Schmeling in their first fight.

Marshall Miles, who visited Louis' camp shortly before the fight, recalls the intensity exhibited by both Louis and Blackburn: "Joe, when he got into shape like he was getting into shape then, he didn't talk to people. You can tell a few days before the fight, he gets mean, he gets nasty, and he don't hardly talk to anyone. That's the way Joe was. But the last day of training for that fight, Jack [Blackburn] said to me, 'Well, Marshall. I did all I could. He's as good as hands can make him.'"

The day before the bout, Blackburn told Edward Van Every, "If

Joe Louis loses this time, it will be only because he has beaten himself. He's got everything he should have this time, so much so I'd be ready to let Schmeling have one free shot and have it first, if he'd let Joe have one in return. It's just a bit silly how you writers keep harping on Joe getting hit with right hands. That's all you watch for. If Schmeling had the same set of sparring partners Joe had, I'll bet Max would get hit with lots of more rights than Joe does. Even though Joe's legs weren't what they should have been in the first fight, the German had to use up more than fifty rights to keep Joe down. No, sir, we ain't afraid of Schmeling's right."

Adding that Louis had worked for the Schmeling fight "harder than for any other fight," Blackburn concluded, "He's been a good boy, a very good boy this time, and so he's good enough for me, which means he'll be too good for Schmeling."

In his dressing room before the fight, Louis told Blackburn that he planned to attack early, hoping to score a knockout in the first three rounds. To make sure Louis would be ready to take charge immediately, Blackburn had him warm up for a half-hour rather than the usual ten minutes.

After Louis destroyed Schmeling in one round in what might well have been the most famous fight in history, Louis told reporters, "Now I feel like the champion. I've been waiting a long time for this night, and I sure do feel pretty glad about everything."

In Louis' dressing room, a gleeful Blackburn explained how Louis had overcome Schmeling's right-hand leads: "Did you see what he did when Max got over his right? He fired right back with a right as fast as he was clipped. Joe did exactly like he was told. You can't escape getting hit when you go to a man or he comes to you. Joe, he took plenty [of right-hand punches] in training because he was being drilled to fire right back as fast as he was hit. As I told you down in the camp, the science of boxing is to avoid getting hit, but if you do get hit, hit the other fellow before he hits you again."

Following the fight, according to Van Every, Blackburn also said of Louis, "There's nothing more I can offer the boy."

Joe Louis knocked out four opponents in 1939, including "Two Ton" Tony Galento, who managed to floor Louis in the third round before being knocked out in the fourth. After Louis was criticized in the press for his performance against Galento, Blackburn sarcastically told Edward Van Every, "They [reporters] find so many faults with Joe, I'm beginning to wonder how come he ever happened to win the championship, or, at least, how he has happened to hold onto it."

Describing Louis' mature style, Blackburn said, "Joe is what you might call an aggressive counter-fighter. He ain't a counter-fighter that lays back for the other fellow to lead. He comes in at you and tries to make you try to punch him off in self-defense. He tries to beat you to that punch. If he misses his aim or the other fellow pulls the trigger faster than he does, then Joe gets beaten to the punch. He takes chances and anyone who takes a chance is going to get hit. So, Joe gets hit and, if he couldn't take it, well, he couldn't be where he is today, believe me."

Citing Louis' minor weaknesses, Blackburn added, "Joe showed two faults in the Galento fight, both of which he knows better than to commit, but he did 'em just the same. He pulled back a couple of times from Tony's hook when he should have moved in. Also he got up after being knocked down without taking the benefit of the count."

If Blackburn still sounded like a teacher reluctant to over-praise his star pupil, Louis also continued to speak of Blackburn like a grateful disciple. Louis' account of his victory over Bob Pastor in September of 1939 is typical of the generous tribute the champion always paid his mentor. In a version of his life story as told to Meyer Berger and Barney Nagler in *The New York Times* in 1948, Louis described Blackburn's role in the rematch with Pastor, who had gone the ten-round distance with

Louis in 1937 by running and fighting a very defensive bout: "Blackburn said to make him carry the fight to me this time," Louis recalled, "and I did. . . . He [Pastor] got in some good punches and Chappie didn't like it. When I got to the tenth and Pastor was still in there, Chappie gave me sharp talk. I knocked Pastor out in the eleventh. That's the way Chappie was at a fight. We'd talk things over. I'd say, 'I think I can reach this man with a right hand now,' and he'd say, 'I think so too'; or I'd say, 'I think I'll try and feint' and he'd say, 'Okay.' Whatever Chappie told me, it always came out right."

As early as November of 1939, Blackburn predicted that Louis would soon retire. In an interview with the *Buffalo Evening News*, Blackburn said that Louis would face all top contenders, including light-heavyweight champion Billy Conn and any others who "want the chance." Louis, Blackburn added, "is ready to give Max Schmeling and Tommy Farr return bouts too, but that completes the field. By that time Joe will be ready to retire."

Louis, of course, was not nearly ready to retire. After Arturo Godoy of Chile embarrassed Louis by using a crouching style to extend the champion to fifteen frustrating rounds in February of 1940, a rematch was set for June of the same year. Before the match, Blackburn told reporters that Godoy's defensive tactics wouldn't be effective again. "Godoy has to come up to hit Joe if he wants to win that title," Blackburn lectured. "And if he does a little more fighting this time, Chappie's going to nail him. Joe nearly had him with an uppercut in the thirteenth round of that first fight. But Godoy knew enough to grab Joe and hold on. He [Godoy] take a punch pretty well. . . ."

Blackburn explained his tactical approach to the fight to Lester Bromberg: "Joe's gonna get to Godoy fast this time. Believe me. That fella don't dare stand up to Joe because he know what would happen. But fightin' low-like, he'll be easy to handle anyway. Joe got two ways of openin' him up. Joe can whip 'em in the body fast . . . and bring his guard down. And he can hurt him by hitting him on the head. Don't mean the top of the head. That's too solid. But around the temples, that's the place. Joe ain't going to waste time trying for the chin. Got to admit this Godoy takes them pretty good there."

Blackburn also frankly admitted that Louis' approach to Godoy in the first fight had been a mistake. "We just didn't figure right," Blackburn conceded. "In most of Joe's other fights he could move along, waiting for a chance to feint and shoot that straight right. Or settin' up the guy with left jabs or left hooks. But we found out this one got to be handled different. We know now."

Louis knocked out Godoy in eight rounds in the rematch, demonstrating one hallmark of Louis' greatness: he always learned from his mistakes.

Louis was now defeating a string of opponents in what the press—with more than a little exaggeration—dubbed the "Bum of the Month" tour. But waiting down the road in July of 1941 was the very determined and clever light-heavyweight champion Billy Conn.

While preparing to face Conn, Louis had one of his rare disagreements with Blackburn. In an interview with Lewis Burton of the *Journal American* years later, Mannie Seamon explained that Louis decided to come into the fight below his normal weight. "Joe wanted to train down for Conn figuring he was a small fellow and very fast." Both Seamon and Blackburn disagreed, but they "couldn't budge" Louis. "He had his heart set on weighing below his usual fighting weight," Seamon said.

After twelve rounds, Blackburn and Mannie Seamon told Louis he was behind on points. Blackburn later recalled for *The Ring,* "After the twelfth, I told Chappie that this boy keeps beggin' to be hit by a right hand. He cocks his left for a hook and pulls it back 'bout four inches." Louis, of course, scored a thirteenth-round knockout, but it was, Louis always said, his toughest fight as champion. In 1948, looking back on his disagreement with Blackburn about his weight for the fight, Louis recalled, "I almost lost the title that night. I never argued with Chappie again."

Though Blackburn by all accounts was, to say the least, all business in the ring, Freddie Guinyard remembers that the trainer also encouraged lighter moments if he felt Louis needed to relax. "One time in the ring in Madison Square Garden," Guinyard recalls, "Chappie asked me had I talked to my man yet—meaning Joe. And I said, 'No, I didn't. Mr. Julian Black told me to stop kidding with him when we got into the ring. This was one of the big fights.' Blackburn said, 'Mr. Black is the manager, but when you get in this ring I'm the boss. And you can still talk.' Now my talk was just saying to Joe, 'Don't let this last too long because there's a good show up at the Apollo theater up in Harlem later. Let's get up there.'" Guinyard concludes with a hearty laugh. "Little things like that, you know, we'd kid. Joe would laugh or try to keep from laughing in the ring, you know what I mean? He was kind of in a hurry to get up there himself."

Before Louis' second fight with Buddy Baer in 1942—in a fight that benefited the Navy Relief Fund—Blackburn told the press, "He is far better than he was for Conn last summer. That time he worked too hard, took off too much weight. He'll be about 206 for this fight and I ain't never seen him hitting harder. I don't think Mr. Baer will be around as long as he was the last time." (Buddy Baer had Louis down in the first round of their 1941 fight, and went seven rounds before losing on a disqualification.)

About Louis' increased weight for the Baer fight, Blackburn added, "It's natural weight. . . . Joe isn't a boy anymore. He's thickening up some. But he'll be plenty fast for Baer and that extra weight will be poured into his punch. I've made sure that his legs are strong. He's been doing a lot of roadwork in the snow."

By this time, Blackburn's health was failing. Though he was only fifty-eight years old, he was troubled by rheumatism and arthritis. In an exchange reminiscent of Louis and Blackburn's conversation before the Kingfish Levinsky fight seven years earlier, Blackburn told Louis in the dressing room before the Baer fight, "You'll have to go in there without me tonight, Chappie. I just don't feel strong enough to keep going up and down those steps." Louis responded, "Come on, Chappie. I promise you you'll only have to go up and down once."

Louis, true to his word, knocked Baer out in the first round. After the fight, Blackburn told journalist Chester Washington, "Tonight out there against Baer, Joe didn't need much coaching. He has developed ring smartness. He's learned something in every fight. Now he's smart and as sharp as a razor. You don't have to tell him much. He works out most of his problems himself. And he's quick to sense a weakness in the fellow he's fighting."

Responding to press allegations that Louis was somehow slipping, Blackburn said, "Some of the experts think that Joe's punches are losing some of their old zip. But if they are, Joe makes up for it by more fighting brains and better ring generalship. Take my word for it when I tell you that Joe Louis today is not only the hardest hitter but one of the smartest fighters in ring history."

Louis joined the Army three days after knocking out Buddy Baer and then signed to meet Abe Simon in a fight that would benefit the Army Relief Fund. By now Blackburn was too ill with arthritis and fatigue to supervise Louis' training. Recuperating in Chicago, Blackburn told the Associated Press, "Joe knows what to do even if I ain't there. He'll get Simon inside three rounds." Blackburn's assistant Mannie Seamon took over as Louis' chief trainer for the Simon fight.

When Blackburn and Louis spoke by telephone before the bout, Blackburn reminded his fighter of the prediction. Blackburn's words were clearly on Louis' mind when he forecasted a quick victory: "I'm not saying what round it will be, but it will be early," Louis told the *Times*. "If I do that much for Chappie, it might speed his recovery."

After knocking Simon out in six rounds, Louis addressed Blackburn directly while being interviewed on the radio. "I hope you're satisfied, Chappie," Louis said. According to an Associated Press report, Blackburn, listening to the broadcast in Chicago, responded with a tear in his eye, "I sure am."

Louis had returned to Camp Upton in Yaphank, Long Island to resume his role as an Army private when he learned that Blackburn had been hospitalized with pneumonia in a Chicago hospital. Louis was granted a five-day leave and visited Blackburn in Chicago. Shortly after Louis' visit, Blackburn died of a heart attack.

On the day Blackburn died, Louis told the Associated Press, "Chappie did more for me than anybody else. I can't believe he's dead. Chappie made a fighter out of me. This is the worst shock I ever had in my life. Jack started me in the boxing game and followed me all the way through. He was my closest friend." Describing his recent visit with Blackburn in Chicago, Louis said, "We kidded a little bit, and I thought sure old Chappie was on the way to recovering. I can't figure it out—how he came to die."

Freddie Guinyard, who sent Louis the telegram informing him of Blackburn's death, recalls Blackburn's funeral by saying, "Oh man, it was a sad affair. That was one of the few times I seen Joe wipe his eyes." In February of the following year, when Louis' daughter was born, Louis named her Jacqueline in honor of Jack Blackburn.

At the time of Blackburn's death, Al Buck of the *New York Post* reported, the trainer was doing well financially: he owned three apartment buildings in Indianapolis and another in Chicago.

The funeral service for Jack Blackburn was held at the Pilgrim Baptist Church on Chicago's South Side. All reports indicate that over 10,000 people attended. Sammy Mandell, the first champion Blackburn ever trained, was there, as was Blackburn's great ring opponent Sam Langford. The pallbearers included Joe Louis, John Roxborough, Julian Black and entertainers Cab Calloway and Bill "Bojangles" Robinson.

While paying tribute to Blackburn in an interview shortly after the trainer's death, Louis focused on the same private training sessions that had fascinated Ray Arcel. "All that I am as a fighter, a champion, I owes to Jack Blackburn," Louis said. "He was teacher, father, brother, nurse, best pal to me and I'll never get over his going away from here. I'll be only half as good as I was. Oh, they say I'll forget Chappie as time goes on, but I know different.

"He was my spark-plug for nine years. That's a long time and I won't forget his confidence in my corner. How could I? Suppose I do try to forget his teaching, his coaching, his great advice when things went bad? Just forgetting would take a lot out of me, more than anybody would ever know. You ask me what one great thing he taught me stands out in my mind? It was the trick of balance, balance in setting to hit, balance in delivering a punch, balance after I landed, but most important, balance if I missed.

"Balance in action was his god. If I lost my balance in a hot mix-up against a dangerous hitter, Chappie warned me about it in the corner. He never scolded. He spoke so plain like. He was easy to understand because he had a way of showing you your mistake in his simple way. In all our nine years together, I never missed a single word of his advice. We never had an argument and I never once tried to tell him he was wrong and I was right.

"When I first came to him in Chicago, I guess I was as green as a cucumber. He didn't rush me. He didn't scold me. He didn't point out my mistakes like a showoff in front of the crowd. He didn't want to show up my blunders to the crowd.

"So he went downstairs away from them and he put the gloves on with me. That was real teaching."

CHARLEY GOLDMAN AND ROCKY MARCIANO
PHOTO COURTESY STANLEY WESTON, *THE RING*

CHARLEY GOLDMAN

Charley Goldman was just a perfect man," Ray Arcel says of Rocky Marciano's trainer. "He was lovely. He was the kind of a man you could actually live with, you know what I mean? And I say that in a sense that he was that friendly. He was that nice. I liked Charley a lot."

A formidable bantamweight during his fighting days between 1904 and 1914, Goldman guessed that he fought over four-hundred professional fights. At Stillman's Gym, Al Braverman recalls, Goldman, ten years the senior of Bimstein and Arcel, was a respected elder. "Charley was like the dean with his little derby. He was like out of another world. Charley was a beautiful man," Braverman says. "He was a picture. He had two cauli-flower ears and a gnarled little nose." Press agent Irving Rudd adds affectionately, "And of course central casting sent him over to play an ex-fighter."

Angelo Dundee talks about the toll all of Goldman's fights had on his hands. "His hands were a blob of bonebreaks and everything else. Charley had gnarled hands. I mean *gnarled*. I can't describe 'em to you. I mean everything was a lump."

Goldman, who usually sported a derby, thick glasses and cigar, is remembered as a quiet, patient, witty and soft-spoken man. He was just over five feet tall, and was inevitably described as "gnome-like." The phrase "gnome-like," however, suggests a small creature who lives underground guarding buried treasure. Nothing could be further from Goldman's sunny persona. Rather than hoarding his treasure-trove of accumulated wisdom, Goldman shared it generously.

"I loved him," newspaperman Harold Conrad recalls. "He was very helpful to me—very helpful to young writers because he took time, and he was a bright little guy. A total gentleman. A wonderful man he was." Conrad adds that Goldman always cared about his boxers. "He was really a very kind guy. And was very solicitous of the fighters, too—which was rare in those days. They were like beef, the fighters, to most guys."

Goldman's kindness and patience is shown in the description of his profession he gave to Jersey Jones of *The Ring* in 1953: "The part I like best is starting from the beginning with a green kid and watching him develop. Of course, all new kids don't make good. Some of them never get beyond the preliminary class. But that's what makes this business so fascinating. It's the gamble. You never know if you've got a future champion. But I've been pretty lucky. I can usually tell the first time a boy puts up his hands if he is worth bothering with, and if I think his chances aren't very good, I tell him so. No sense wasting his time as well as mine. But when I see one who looks like he has the stuff and is worth going along with, I don't mind how much time and work I put in with him."

Goldman's aphoristic sayings give the impression of being carefully crafted. "Training promising kids is like putting a quarter in one pocket and taking a dollar out of another," he often remarked. It's a memorable line which, like many Goldmanisms, has the air of having been perfected over time.

Jimmy Breslin, who knew Goldman during the Marciano era, says Goldman's lines came from "a thousand fight camps and a thousand comedians hanging around fight camps and his own street way. . . . He'd work on those lines."

Explaining Rocky Marciano's cool approach to boxing, Goldman said, "He goes in for a fight like I go in for a glass of beer." Asked to assess Marciano's greatness, Goldman replied, "He must be good, he always beats the other fella." His other recorded boxing aphorisms include: "The punch you throw will take care of itself. It's the next one you gotta have ready"; and, "If you're ever knocked down, don't be no hero and jump right up. Take a count."

Passing on a piece of indisputable wisdom about boxing and life in general, Goldman told A. J. Liebling, "Never play a guy at his own game, nobody makes up a game in order to get beat at it." Goldman warned readers of *Life* magazine, "People who wear jewelry get stuck up." On other non-pugilistic matters, Goldman advised his fighters to never buy diamonds off anyone on the street.

Before taking a glass of beer at the Neutral Corner, Goldman would offer this standard toast: "Protect your honor at all times." Most famously of all, perhaps, when asked if he was married, Goldman once answered, "No. I'm living à la carte."

When Marciano was about to fight Jersey Joe Walcott for the heavyweight title in 1952, Goldman told Liebling, "You know, there are two kinds of friends—the ones who are with you when you are winning and the ones who stick when you are losing. I prefer the second kind. But you got to take advantage of the others while you got them. Because they won't be with you long."

Jimmy Breslin also cherishes Goldman's response to a group of sportswriters who asked if he planned to give Marciano a rubdown after a workout. "I don't do that," said Goldman. "A good fighter doesn't need a rubdown and a bad fighter doesn't deserve one."

About Goldman's well-known habit of referring to his female companions as "nieces," Irving Rudd says, "Charley, believe it or not—I'm talking about Charley in the '50s with Marciano—whenever he had a young lady on his arm, I mean *young* lady, it was his 'niece.'" Ray Arcel recalls being introduced to so many of Goldman's "nieces" that he finally told Goldman, "Charley, you must have a terrible lot of uncles and aunts and nieces." And what did Goldman do on his dates? "I usually take them to the fights," he told *Life* magazine in 1951. "I get free passes."

It's said that toward the end of his life, Charley Goldman would tell people, "I was the trainer of Rocky Marciano." But no one in boxing needs to be reminded. Mention trainers to knowledgeable boxing men, and they inevitably point to Goldman's work with Marciano as one of the finest instructional feats in the history of the sport. Marciano is also quickly given credit, of course, for his sensational punch, passion to absorb knowledge, unequaled dedication to training and champion's heart.

Goldman himself was, in general, scrupulously modest when discussing his role in any of his pupils' successes. He even slyly claimed that training a fighter was mostly "luck and common sense." How so? "Luck in getting hold of the right material, and common sense in trying to develop it properly," he told *The Ring* in 1953. "It helps, of course, if the trainer has been a fighter himself. It makes it that much easier to understand the problems of the boys he is training. To say a trainer actually develops a boxer is bunk. Sure he can help bring out the best in a fighter, but if the boy hasn't the natural ability to start with, and the willingness to stick to business and work hard, all the teaching and training in the world won't do much good."

Goldman's patience as a teacher was as famous as his quick wit. Bill "Pop" Miller, the trainer who developed Tiger Flowers in the 1920s and honed the young Sugar Ray Robinson's skills at the Salem Crescent Gym in Harlem, was not known for praising his colleagues. Yet Pop Miller admired Charley Goldman's teaching skills, as he told *The Ring*. (The peculiar grammar used in Miller's quote is *The Ring*'s attempt to capture Miller's Virgin Islands accent.) "I spend hours teaching [fighters] how to block and slip a punch," Miller said. "Charley Goldman is the one trainer I see do de same t'ing. When I see trainer do that, I know he not just good cut and corner man. I know he knows his business."

Al Braverman also describes Goldman's persistence and generosity. "He'd stop, he'd help out somebody," Braverman says. "'Al,' he'd say, 'I think you're doing this wrong. You're not pivoting when you throw your right hand.' . . . He was a teacher. He would drill you, and spend a half-hour on the bag with you. They don't do that anymore." Goldman, a firm believer in teaching through demonstration, said simply, "It don't do no good to tell 'em. You got to show them."

Harry Markson of Madison Square Garden, who saw Goldman and Marciano work "from the beginning," sums up most experts' assessment of the relationship between the two: "Charley Goldman was, I believe, the leading factor in making Rocky Marciano the heavyweight champion he became," Markson says emphatically. "Marciano was a very crude, raw, wild-swinging puncher. What Goldman did, he did not change his style. What he developed—or worked on, or refined—as much as he could, was the talents that Marciano had. And made him a fighter who became an undefeated heavyweight champion. He worked to perfect not only his offense, but Marciano had much more defensive skill—developed much greater defensive skill than most people thought that he had. He was not hurt very often and in my opinion ninety percent of that goes to Charley Goldman who worked with him in the gym day after day after day, teaching Marciano how to fight."

Goldman often spoke of the folly of altering a fighter's natural inclinations. "There's one serious mistake some trainers make," he told *The Ring*. "They try to change a boy's style. It doesn't pay to meddle around with a natural style. If a kid is inclined to be a boxer, don't try to make a slugger of him. And vice versa. You can improve on what he has, but don't change it. I've seen many a great prospect ruined because somebody tried to make him something he wasn't cut out to be."

Goldman went on to illustrate his point with historical references: "Some fighters have unusual styles to start with. What you'd call 'unorthodox.' Like Harry Greb, Memphis Al Moore and Maxie Rosenbloom. They became great fighters because nobody tinkered with their natural styles, and they were allowed to develop normally."

As Jimmy Breslin says with admiration, "Charley Goldman was very smart."

Legend has it that Rocky Marciano and his best friend, Allie Colombo, arrived in New York in 1946 after hitching a ride on the back of a vegetable truck from their home town of Brockton, Massachusetts. Jimmy Breslin, in a column written when Goldman died in 1968, reported that when Marciano arrived in New York, Goldman greeted him with the words, "You look worse than the cabbages."

Legend also has it that when Goldman and Al Weill, who was to become Marciano's manager, first saw Rocky spar at the C.Y.O. gym in Manhattan, Goldman observed, "He throws punches from his behind." In a 1953 article in *Collier's* credited to "Charley Goldman with Tim Meany," Goldman wrote, "Al [Weill] and I have often looked at green kids who thought they could become fighters but I'll eat my derby if I ever saw anyone cruder than Rocky."

Marciano described his first encounter with Goldman and Weill in a speech at a 1966 testimonial dinner held to support the American Association for the Improvement of Boxing—an organization that Marciano founded with Steve Acunto: "Charley is the guy that told me to go ahead and get into professional boxing because when I went to New York, I only came for a tryout—to try out with the pros and see if I had enough ability to continue on in probably the roughest sport in the world.

"And finally, after working out for three days, in the C.Y.O. gymnasium down on 17th Street, I asked Dr. Goldman. I says, 'Do you think I should be a professional fighter?' And he gave me very sound advice; he told me, 'It isn't easy. It's rough. It takes a lot of work, a lot of sacrificing, a lot of bats in the nose, but,' he says, 'I think you might be able to do okay.' He says, 'You're a strong kid. That's about all I can say for you right now. You're strong and you're willing.' And he says—one thing else that I think made me make the big decision—he said, 'I can tell that you like it. You've gotta like it, otherwise you just don't belong in it.' And when he said that I had to agree with that. I did like it. And so I became a professional fighter."

Watching Marciano at the C.Y.O. Gym, Goldman also saw the one thing he always looked for in a prospect—a punch. "It's the short cut to the money," he liked to say. Marciano's punch, of course, was the right hand Goldman would later dub "the Suzy-Q." In 1952, Goldman told *The Ring* that upon first seeing Marciano, "I realized Rocco had something terrific. He could hit, and he did it all naturally, though without finesse or . . . polish." Goldman must have seen something else, too—what Rocky's younger brother Peter Marciano calls "something up around the chest area known as the heart."

Though Al Weill took on Marciano following his audition, neither Weill nor Goldman traveled to Providence, Rhode Island to be in Marciano's corner during the future champion's initial bouts. Early on, Marciano's boyhood friend Allie Colombo served as the fighter's trainer, running partner and constant companion—roles Colombo continued to play throughout Marciano's career.

Charley Goldman first saw Marciano in actual combat in August of 1948 when Marciano knocked out Jimmy Weeks in one round. It was Marciano's sixth professional bout. In the dressing room after the fight, according to Everett M. Skehan in *Rocky Marciano: Biography of a First Son*, a skeptical Goldman told reporters, "I can't give no opinion. The fight was too short. How do I know if the kid can box? But he's got a punch. That's important." According to Skehan, Goldman then declined Marciano's dinner invitation and told the fighter, ". . . I'll do my best to bring ya along. But I want you should know, you ain't any too young, and you got an awful lot to learn, kid."

The story of Marciano's crudeness and inexperience as a boxer at this time has often been told: At five-feet-eleven-inches, he was short for a heavyweight. At Brockton High School, Marciano had been center on the football team and catcher on the baseball team, and even had a tryout with the Chicago Cubs. Marciano's first experience with boxing came in the army, where his natural punching ability had produced knockouts. But Marciano was old to begin his professional apprenticeship, and at first Goldman doubted his pupil's potential. "Rocky was twenty-four when I got him," Goldman once said. "I always liked 'em younger, so I can teach 'em my way."

But in Marciano, Charley Goldman had the perfect pupil. "You have to remember that the man he was training was like possessed," Peter Marciano says about his brother. "It was like a dream for a Charley Goldman to train this man because this man was just like a sponge. He wanted to learn. He wanted to know. He was a perfect guy to guide, to teach how to fight." As Goldman himself told *The Ring* after Marciano had already become champion, "Marciano does what you tell him, and doesn't attempt to challenge the ideas of those who, by experience, should know more about training fighters than the fighters themselves know."

Goldman employed a variety of training techniques—some innovative, some old-fashioned. The objective was to develop Marciano's left jab and left hook while preserving his splendid right and honing his underrated defense.

About Marciano's defense, Angelo Dundee says, "He was a

much smarter fighter than people made him. Rocky could box when he wanted to. Rocky was able to get into these big guys and nullify them. Rocky had his own way of laying back on that right leg and takin' away the distance of the jab and not getting hit with the jab. So he didn't get hit as often as people thought he did."

Goldman spoke about the delicacy of the educational process in *The Sweet Science*. "The great thing about this kid is he's got leverage," Goldman began. "He takes a good punch and he's got the equalizers. He had leverage from the start, and when you teach a fellow like that, you have to go slow, because you might change the way he stands or the way he moves, and spoil his hitting. Everything new you show him, you have to ask him, 'Does it feel natural?' 'Can you hit from there?'"

Promoter Red Greb describes the discretion with which Goldman treated all his fighters: "When he had a fighter that made a mistake, he always brought the fighter close to his mouth, and he whispered in his ear. He said, 'I don't want to embarrass you. I don't want to embarrass you, but your feet are too spread apart. You look like an old woman,' he says. 'Get loose.'"

Goldman also had a knack for making a fighter believe that Goldman's ideas were actually the fighter's own. "He had a quiet way of doing things," corner man Lou Duva recalls. "He used to get Rocky to do things that Rocky did not even know he was doing." To correct Marciano's habit of spreading his legs too far apart when punching, for example, Goldman would tie Marciano's shoelaces together. "Rocky would fall down sometimes," Duva says.

Duva also mentions Goldman putting towels under Marciano's arms to force the fighter to throw straighter blows: when Marciano threw wide punches, the towels would fall on the floor.

"They really did those things to Rocky," Peter Marciano confirms. "I remember them tying Rocky's right hand behind his body." The point of that exercise was to develop the left hand.

Peter Marciano would watch as Rocky, right hand tied behind his body, would throw "left jab, left jab—bang!—left hook."

These labors did not transform Marciano into an elegant pugilist, but that didn't bother Goldman at all. "Some of the critics say that Marciano does not hit straight from the shoulder," Goldman told *The Ring* in 1952. "I know how he hits, and he knows. But I never have tried to change his natural style. Sure I could pretty him up, but the result would not be the real Marciano. I merely try to coach him to get away from his faults. I do not teach him a new way of hitting. The way he socks is good enough for me."

Charley Goldman's friend Ray Arcel recalls that even as Marciano piled up early-round knockouts fighting mostly in New England, "Nobody thought that Marciano could fight. Because, you know, you judge a fighter in the gym. He didn't look like a fighter. He was short and stocky and wild." Smiling at his own failure to immediately perceive Marciano's greatness, Arcel says, "I thought he looked like a bum. I never thought he could fight. I said, 'Where'd they get this bum from?'"

Arcel adds that in October of 1949, his friend Sam Silverman—who booked Marciano's early fights for Al Weill—told Arcel, "I got Marciano in with Ted Lowry." Knowing Lowry as a talented boxer, Arcel told Silverman, "Weill will stop talking to you." When Arcel went to Providence to see the Marciano-Lowry fight, he says, "I was astounded in the improvement that he made. And he beat Lowry."

In December of 1949, when Marciano was preparing for his Madison Square Garden debut against Pat Richards, Goldman "devoted very little time" to Marciano, according to Everett Skehan's biography. Goldman instead focused on leading heavyweight contender Cesar Brion, who ended up losing to Roland LaStarza in the Garden's main event after Marciano fought on the undercard.

By 1950, however, as Marciano moved up in class to defeat

fighters such as Roland LaStarza and Johnny Shkor, Goldman spent more and more time with Marciano. The following year, it was Goldman who stopped the bleeding over Marciano's left eye long enough for Marciano to score a knockout over Keene Simmons in a tough fight in Providence. "They bumped heads over on the other side of the ring but the sound of it came across the ring so loud I didn't wait, I just reached down for my bag," Goldman remembered. "I knew I'd have plenty of work."

During Marciano's fights, Al Braverman says, Goldman was, "very very meticulous, very, very quiet, very, very soft-spoken—but firm. Marciano would look right dead in his eyes—which is the right thing to do. Then you know you're getting through." Asked to describe Goldman in the corner, Jimmy Breslin recalls ". . . the glasses and the punched-in face and a white cardigan. A little guy in the ring, that's all. There would be very little talk." Though Al Weill and Allie Colombo were also in Marciano's corner, Breslin says, "Goldman had the say. . . . He was the one that talked. Nobody else. Weill used to lean against the ropes and scream."

Marciano's well-known dislike—if not hatred—for Al Weill was amply documented in Skehan's biography of Marciano. Skehan also quotes Marciano telling Allie Colombo in 1949, "The guy [Weill] treats Goldman like a dog. I don't know how he takes it sometimes." Colombo's response, according to Skehan, was, "Charley's happy. As long as he's got good fighters and a place to train them, Goldmann will always be happy."

How well did Marciano and Goldman get along? "They had a business arrangement, and it was going great," Breslin says. "And he was a very easy fighter to train. He would do exactly what you told him."

Everett Skehan wrote that before Marciano won the title, he said of Weill and Goldman, "No matter how well I do, they never give me a compliment." According to Skehan, Goldman's approach to Marciano was, "If he wins, that's reward enough."

While some fight men recall that Marciano sometimes

resented Goldman, Ray Arcel says, the two were "very, very close. They were like brothers."

In 1953, Goldman said that he and Marciano rarely disagreed. "The only arguments me and Rocky ever have is over that eatin' between meals," Goldman told *The Ring*. "I'll go up into his room and under his pillow I'll find a bunch of bananas he's hidin' from me. I've found a lot of fighters have to be made to eat certain things and to work hard, with Rocky it's just the opposite, you have to keep after him all the time to keep him from eatin' too much and workin' too hard."

Any account of Marciano's rise to the heavyweight title must, of course, give full credit to Marciano's legendary devotion to boxing. Angelo Dundee recalls, "He trained so hard, Rocky . . . 'Cause you know, he'd go away for three months, stay away from his family, stay away from everything and just train. That's what made the guy. His conditioning was fantastic." After he became champion, Marciano sometimes spent as long as nine months preparing for a fight. He would limit contact with his wife to infrequent brief strolls in the Catskills, next to the airport runway, at Grossinger's hotel, which served as training headquarters for his championship fights.

Former heavyweight champion Floyd Patterson is one of many who pay tribute to Marciano's extraordinary will. "He was the most determined heavyweight I have ever seen in my life," Patterson says. "That man got in the ring and there was no way he was going to lose. . . . Determination is based in the mind. How far can you go? What is your limit? With Marciano there was no limit."

The importance of Goldman's work in Marciano's corner is illustrated by Marciano's 1952 match against a much-ballyhooed fighter named Harry "Kid" Matthews. Matthews had been built up by his celebrated manager Jack Hurley's careful selection of opponents. So clever and cautious was Hurley in building

Matthews' record that Jimmy Cannon was inspired to write, "As a fighter, Matthews was a fictional character Hurley created."

Before the Matthews fight, Goldman and Marciano went to training camp at Greenwood Lake. Their mission was to further develop Marciano's left hand. "We worked and worked, on that left hand," Goldman told *The Ring* after the fight. "I kept telling Rocky, 'Don't go hooking this guy, because he's a fine boxer. Jab him, then hook. The jab is a punch which goes right through. It creates a reaction in the man hit, and sets him up for the hook.'"

Marciano and Matthews met in Yankee Stadium in July of 1952. Veteran trainer George Chemeres worked in Matthews' corner along with Hurley that night, and he recalls the fight vividly. "Matthews could box. He could move lateral and all that. But we didn't move lateral, we didn't run. We stayed right there," Chemeres says, describing the prefight strategy of crowding Marciano rather than running from him. Matthews fared surprisingly well in the first round, winning it on the cards of all three judges. When the round ended, Chemeres says, "the crowd really went up in the air because they didn't expect Matthews to do what he did—punch for punch."

This inspired a change in strategy by Goldman. Goldman later told his friend Chemeres that following the first round he had told Marciano, "Hey, this guy's not running. He's standing right in front of you. Go out there and stand still. Just get right up in front of him and stand still." Al Buck in the *New York Post* reported that between rounds Goldman also reminded Marciano, "Jab before you hook. The jab will set him up for the hook."

Goldman's advice proved effective. Marciano stood still, which surprised and "hypnotized" Matthews, Chemeres recalls. "Marciano walked out slow and he stood still and he threw a right hand," Chemeres says. "When Marciano threw the right hand, that startled Matthews and he stepped back and he spread his legs. Matthews went to step back to counter, and he damn near did a split and his hands were down to his sides." Marciano then "hit Matthews with a left hook and damn near took his head off," Chemeres remembers. Matthews "hit the bottom strand of the ropes and he was laying there and he was snoring, man," Chemeres says. "I hada jump in the ring and take his mouthpiece out. He got stopped, that was it." Immediately after the fight, Goldman gleefully told the press, "I knew he'd fool him with that left jab. I knew he'd fool him."

Before Marciano faced Jersey Joe Walcott for the heavyweight title in September of 1952, Goldman said: "There is no doubt in the mind of Marciano or myself that the boy will knock out Walcott. . . . Rocky hits too hard, with either hand, to lose to a fighter of Walcott's age. Sure, Jersey Joe is a wise boxer. He packs a punch, too. But he will not stand up with Marciano."

Sounding like a good mother pushing a child out of the nest, Goldman also proclaimed that Marciano was almost a finished fighter: "Marciano is now prepared to go on his own. I am not saying that there is nothing more for him to learn. But he has learned a lot, and he doesn't repeat mistakes.

"Certainly Rocky's footwork is not ideal. But he makes up for that with a lot of important assets. . . . They say Marciano is an open target, easy to hit. That argument I refuse to buy. Ask Matthews if Rocky is easy to hit. The boy may look like a sucker to some of the writers in the press rows, but take it from me, he just isn't a sucker.

"Rocky proved against Matthews that he can feint a man, that he can counter, that he can punch, and that he is a two-fisted fighter with a knockout in either right or left. I used to call Marciano a head hunter. Now he is a real fighter. He will feel a man out, and punch for body and head. Now Rocky Marciano can call his shots."

Following Marciano's victory over Walcott, Goldman reviewed the performance in *Collier's*: "Everybody, fans and experts, raved about Marciano's knockout of Walcott, but take it from me, Rocky was not at his best. . . . He wasn't overconfident, careless or anything like that, but he just couldn't believe that he, a kid from Brockton, Massachusetts, was really fighting for the heavyweight championship of the world."

Goldman then drew an analogy with his own boxing career: "I can appreciate how Rocky felt that night. The same thing happened to me when I had a great deal more experience under my belt than Marciano. Back in 1912, I boxed ten rounds in New York against Johnny Coulon, who was then the bantamweight champion of the world. I stayed the ten rounds with Johnny, but I was fighting in a trance. Any time a fighter meets his first champion, it's bound to have an effect on him."

Goldman went on to boast about the improvements Marciano was continuing to make: "He was always magnificent with his right hand but now he carries an equalizer in either hand. And he's learned to shorten his punches, too, to shorten them without sacrificing power." The fabled right hand with which Marciano knocked out Walcott to win the title, Goldman pointed out, "traveled no more than ten inches."

Two days after Marciano won the championship, Goldman was back in New York following his normal routine. Early in the afternoon he was at Stillman's. Later in the day, he went to the C.Y.O. gym to work with what he called "juveniles"—amateurs and pros in the early stages of their careers.

Asked by Jersey Jones of *The Ring* why he didn't take a vacation after Marciano's victory, Goldman said, "What would I do with a vacation? Boxing is more than a business to me. It's my pleasure and relaxation, too. I'm sort of lost without it."

After Marciano disposed of Walcott in one round in their May 1953 rematch, Dan Daniel of *The Ring* recorded an exchange between Marciano and Goldman in which Goldman offered an explanation of Marciano's quick victory. "You won your second scrap with Joe in the first fight," Goldman told Marciano. ". . . Remember Walcott's age, certainly around 40. An old guy like that, taking the punches to the body and head you landed at Philadelphia [in the first fight], was worn down to the point

at which he just could not take them again." Expanding on the
dangers of fighters continuing their careers as they approach
middle age, Goldman told Marciano, "The Joe Louis you fought,
Rocky, was a better conditioned man than the Louis who, after
a year and a half layoff, met Ezzard Charles. But against you,
Louis could not raise his hands. You made him run out of gas.
... The ring is not a place for old guys, and you have chased
three of them into retirement."

Once Marciano won the championship, Charley Goldman received more and more praise in the press—which annoyed Al
Weill. "Al Weill did not appreciate the praise that Goldman got
from most knowledgeable boxing people," Harry Markson of
Madison Square Garden recalls. Weill tried "to claim most of the
credit for himself," Markson says, "but believe me it was Goldman. Weill was a great fight manager, one of the best of his time,
but for teaching a fighter—especially one who was an apt pupil—
Goldman did what I thought was a remarkable job." "Marciano
loved Goldman and Weill knew it," Ray Arcel recalls. "I mean, if
it wasn't for that Weill woulda gotten rid of him."

Promoter Don Chargin, who spent time in Marciano's camp,
recalls, "Weill was funny, even though he always had Goldman
training his fighters, he didn't want Goldman to get too much
credit." But didn't newspapermen adore Goldman? "Oh they
loved him," Chargin says. "But he would become very quiet
when Weill was around. Goldman's favorite thing was when
they would ask about Marciano, and Weill was there, he would
defer everything. He'd say, 'You have to ask the manager.'" Did
Goldman resent having to give credit to Weill? "No he didn't,"
Chargin says. "Trainers, most of them, they never looked for
publicity."

Yet Goldman did get his fair share of publicity as revealed in
press coverage of Marciano's first bout with former champion
Ezzard Charles in June of 1954. Milton Gross' prefight column
in the *New York Post*, for example, relied heavily on Goldman's
words of wisdom to analyze the bout. "Charles isn't the type of

opponent where you can pick your spot and name your shot," Goldman told Gross. "Rocky hits hard enough to knock out a man with one punch, but in this one I can't see it that way." Goldman's words were prophetic, of course: Marciano won the fight on a decision.

And what would Marciano do if Charles came out strong at the start of the fight? Goldman was unworried. "It's an old-fashioned idea, this coming out to be the boss with the bell," he told Gross. "But Rocky ain't the kind to be bossed. Nobody's bossed him yet." Overplanning strategy before a fight can be a mistake, Goldman warned. "You can't plan one way and let yourself get caught. You go from round to round and do what you have to do. I figure Charles will change styles maybe two, three times. Rocky'll have to change, too."

Following Marciano's grueling victory over Charles, Dan Parker, in *The New York Mirror*, gave credit to Goldman: "Charley Goldman . . . tipped off the pattern and outcome of the fight in advance when he told me at Grossinger's last week that Rocky, who had been at the mountain retreat since early in January, had concentrated on getting his legs in condition for the battle. . . . A heroic dose of roadwork was the prescription old Doctor Goldman ordered and so Rocky was ready for the exact situation that confronted him." It's a measure of Marciano's dedication that he began training for the June bout five months earlier in January.

Goldman's comments again played a large role in press coverage of Marciano's final title defense—the 1955 bout against Archie Moore in which Marciano came back from a second-round knockdown to score a ninth-round knockout.

Before the fight, Goldman still spoke of Marciano as a student making steady progress. "I'm telling you," Goldman told the *New York Post*. "Rocky today is the best heavyweight I ever saw. He could lick any of 'em, and remember he hasn't hit his peak yet. He'll be better a year from now."

Speaking to columnist Milton Gross, Goldman said, "Rocky's improved one-hundred percent over last year. His combinations are coming natural now. Now he doesn't have to think how he's going to go after a man. After all the time I've been working with him it's become like a reflex to him." In response, Marciano himself sounded like a proud and eager disciple: "Charley's been praising me lately in workouts. He never used to do that. He used to tell me what I did wrong. Lately, he's been telling me only what I do right. I feel right doing it. I do something I never could do before without thinking about it beforehand and after I've done it I realize I did it without thinking about it."

Marciano's victory over Moore drew raves for both the boxer and his teacher. Red Smith wrote, "It was the champion's finest fight. . . . He would feint with a right and throw the left hook instead. At least once he feinted with the hook, then threw it and connected. These moves delight his teacher, Charley Goldman, for they are lessons patiently taught and painfully learned."

Following the fight, Goldman, insisting that Marciano had still not yet reached his peak, told Milton Gross, "All the boxing knowledge the other guy has is no help when Rocky starts swinging."

In 1957, after Marciano retired as the undefeated heavyweight champion, he told Dan M. Daniel of *The Ring*, "I have no yen to return to the ring. . . . I can thumb my nose at Charley Goldman. Not that I want to. Charley is the salt of the earth, the greatest in his line."

Of all the great trainers at Stillman's Gym, Charley Goldman had the most distinguished career as a professional boxer. *The Jewish Boxers' Hall of Fame* by Ken Blady sets out the stunning record: often fighting for a mere five-dollars a fight in the back of saloons or private fight clubs, Goldmann had 137 documented bouts, though he put the number closer to 300 or 400 at various times. When Goldman fought—from 1904 to 1914—

fights were officially dubbed "exhibitions," and usually no decision was rendered. Goldman's official record lists only four decision losses and two losses by knockout. He scored twenty knockouts during his career. Goldman guessed that he faced one opponent, George Kitson, more than sixty times, though the two fought so often that Goldman couldn't be certain how many times they actually met.

Born Israel Goldman in Warsaw, Poland in 1888, Goldman began to box while growing up in the tough Brooklyn neighborhood of Red Hook. He described how he got his start as a fighter on the streets of Brooklyn: "Little kids, they got it from the parents. The kids called you a Jew bastard, so you punched them in the nose. I got to love it. Every time somebody called me a name it meant I could have a fight without picking one."

Jimmy Breslin reported that Goldman's formal education ended in the fourth grade when a teacher hit him, and Goldman hit the teacher back. "Nobody had to tell me it was the wrong thing to do," Goldman said. "I ran out of the class and never came back. I'd leave the house every day and go to the back of a saloon and fight for change and then come home and say I went to school all day."

Soon Goldman was hanging out with "Terrible" Terry McGovern, later the ferocious bantam- and featherweight champion of the world. In imitation of McGovern, Goldman parted his hair down the middle and began wearing the derby that was to become his trademark. Asked why he continued to wear the derby, Goldman said, "You don't see many 'iron hats' these days, especially in boxing. . . . I guess I'm the only one around who uses a derby. But I've worn one so long I'd feel undressed without it."

Reminiscing about his childhood hero, Goldman said in 1956, "I was around with Terry McGovern, and everyday before and after he worked out, he'd bathe his face in brine. Everybody did it. Their skin got to be really leathery. It had to be or those fellows never would have been able to fight twenty-three and thirty rounds."

In 1904, Goldman, not yet sixteen years old and weighing 105 pounds, fought his first professional fight—a forty-two-round bout against Eddie Gardner, also known as "Young Gardner"— which Goldman said lasted for just under three hours. "I was sixteen when I went them forty-two rounds," Goldman said, "and at the end somebody shouted 'Here come the cops.' Everybody took off, including the promoter with the money. I think the promoter tipped off the cops."

He eventually fought for the bantamweight title against Johnny Coulon in 1912, but the fight was declared a no-decision. Goldman described the fight this way: "I was in a trance. He kept hitting me on top of the head and I couldn't put my derby on for a week after, until my lumps went down."

Describing his approximately sixty fights with George Kitson, Goldman told *The Ring* "I don't know how many rounds were fought in all. There were six fifteen-rounders in the lot. The rest ranged anywhere from four to ten rounds. One night we boxed twice. . . . Georgie and I got so used to each other that we could fight all night with nobody getting hurt."

Goldman's almost unbelievable ring record is always reported with gleeful high spirits, and Goldman himself never publicly discussed the pain and suffering he no doubt endured. The closest he came to the topic was when he told *The Ring,* "It was a tough business then. I fought many a scrap for $100 and less. Once, I traveled all the way from New York to Charleston, S.C., for a fifteen-rounder that paid me a guarantee of $125. Shucks, a preliminary kid picks up that much money now. But a dollar was a dollar then, and it covered a lot more territory than a sawbuck does today."

Goldman also provided a sample of the kind of between-rounds advice that was typically offered by his manager and corner man, Jack "Three-Fingered" Dougherty. "Quit fiddlin' around," Dougherty would tell Goldman. "G'wan in and knock the bum out."

In 1914, Goldman trained his first champion, Al McCoy, who upset George Chip to win the middleweight crown in April of that year. Despite his Irish ring name, Al McCoy was born Alex Rudolph. He fought under an assumed name to hide his boxing from his Orthodox Jewish family, who disapproved of pugilism as a profession.

McCoy was an obscure fighter who received a shot at the championship by accident when the champion's brother, Joe Chip, whom McCoy had originally signed to fight, fell ill. Champion George Chip was brought in as a last-minute substitute. The champion was out of shape and took McCoy lightly. The McCoy-Chip bout was a no-decision affair: the title could change hands only by knockout.

Remembering the fight, Goldman told Lester Bromberg in 1951, "I said to McCoy, 'It's no-decision, so he [Chip] will be satisfied to go the limit. I want you to go in with a right lead as soon as it starts and, when his guard comes up, hit him in the belly with your left—with everything you've got!' McCoy did just what I told him. I'll never forget the way Chip went down. It was like letting the air out of a balloon."

After the bout, McCoy became known derisively as a "cheese champion"—an unworthy titleholder. In defense of McCoy, Goldman said, "Never forget, they fought twice after that and Chip never knocked McCoy out."

Beginning in 1920, when the Walker Law was passed, Goldman teamed with Al Weill and the two worked together until 1925, ✓ when Goldman decided to leave boxing. "I got myself interested in a roadhouse near Newburgh, New York, and did all right with it, but I wasn't too happy," Goldman explained. "I had to get back to boxing. It gets into your blood and there you are."

While living outside the city, Goldman continued to help fighters from time to time, but it was while working with a heavyweight named Johnny Risko—also known as the "Rubber

Man"—that Goldman decided to return to boxing full time. "Not many people know it, but I might not be training fighters now if it hadn't been for Johnny Risko," Goldman said in 1953.

Looking back on Risko's two battles with the estimable Spanish heavyweight Paulino Uzcudun, Goldman recalled in 1958, "Paulino was hard to beat because he had a trick of getting down low, under the other fellow in close, and setting him back on his heels by pushing forward. He was short and strong and he was getting away with this against taller guys. But Risko was short, too, and just as strong, so we told Johnny that no matter how low Paulino got he was to get even lower, and push just as hard. They looked like a couple of guys looking for something on the floor most of the time, but Risko got lower and Paulino couldn't do anything about his own trick, so Johnny won."

Risko's greatest victory with Goldman in his corner was a 1928 win over future heavyweight champion Jack Sharkey in Madison Square Garden.

"Sharkey had licked Risko in Boston by nailing him time after time with right-hand leads," Goldman said. "We knew he liked to use this punch, so we kept Johnny moving to his left, away from Sharkey's right all through the fight, and that upset Sharkey and beat him."

Working Risko's corner against other leading heavyweights, Goldman found his passion for boxing returning. "Risko did so good every time I worked with him, I got my confidence back in the boxing game," Goldman said, "and I have stuck with it ever since."

After returning full time to boxing in the mid-1930s, Goldman worked with an impressive list of champions, including lightweight Lou Ambers, welterweight Marty Servo and featherweight Joey Archibald.

Though Ambers, Servo and Archibald were Al Weill's fighters, Goldman also worked with other managers' fighters. Over the years, he worked with and opposed many all-time greats, and in a 1951 interview in *The Ring*, Goldman analyzed their styles. It's an invaluable record of Goldman's view of several historic boxing figures.

Of Sugar Ray Robinson, Goldman said: "Ray is what we call a combination puncher. He usually throws them in threes— bang, a left hook, a fast right hand; bang, another left hook. To get his power he's got to be coming into you when he throws them. Since he has to be moving in to do his damage, the idea is to keep him backing up when you figure he's getting ready to throw that hard stuff. That's what we did with Servo both times against him. We broke up Robinson's style by keeping Servo low and charging in. We did pretty much the same thing with Kid Gavilan when he fought Ray the first time and he made it pretty close, too."

Analyzing Henry Armstrong, Goldman said: "Lou Ambers was a very good in-fighter, so we had him stay close to Henry and dig in little short punches. If you backed off with Henry when he was good, it was certain suicide. He'd crowd you, then throw a powerful overhand right that would knock anybody out." In 1957, Goldman told *Ring* editor and publisher Nat Loubet how Fritzie Zivic beat Armstrong: "Fritzie, one of the best all-around ring smarties, met Henry each time he 'took off' and stopped him cold with a flurry of his own uppercuts. He had figured out the only way to cause Armstrong trouble, and he had the equipment to do it."

Finally, Goldman paid tribute to Joe Louis: "Joe Louis was an awful guy to fight. Here's why: Louis would look terrible against a certain move one minute, but if your man tried the same thing again, he was likely to get his block knocked off."

While training fighters in the 1940s and 1950s, Goldman lived at Ma Brown's, a West 91st Street boarding house which special- ized in the care and feeding of young fighters. Steve Acunto, who served as a sparring partner for several of Goldman's light- weights, remembers that Goldman "was like a mother and fa- ther" to his young charges at Ma Brown's. "He kept his people in line. He just had a very effective way of coping with boxers, having been one himself. He knew all the pitfalls, what would be detrimental. . . . He was like a mother hen to all of them."

Trainer Ted Walker befriended Goldman during his visits to New York in the late 1940s, when Walker and his fighters stayed at Ma Brown's. Goldman, Walker says, was "open-minded, a very humble guy . . . just a fountain of information and good ideas."

Each day, Walker and Goldman would ride the bus to Stillman's. "Yeah, Charley Goldman had the little black derby, and sometimes on Sundays he'd put his vest on," Walker recalls with a laugh. "He was a great conversationalist." Describing Goldman's style of speaking, Walker, a resident of Carson City, Nevada, says, "Well, he was a lot of 'dese, dems and dozes' . . . laced with New York talk. A flatlander like me would notice that."

While Goldman freely offered Walker advice on such fine points of training as how to stop cuts, flatten bellies and control weight, Walker says Goldman preferred not to talk about boxing during his nonworking hours. Goldman was "an avid reader," Walker says. "He liked novels. Followed all sports, followed a lot of the other sports. I think he was a Yankee man. I would read beside him on the bus and up at Ma Brown's. I saw him reading a lot. Of course, that was the era we read *Collier's* and *Life* magazine and all those good weekly news magazines." Jimmy Breslin backs up the portrait of Goldman as a reader. "Charley read everything," Breslin says. And Goldman knew all the boxing writers. "He knew all the guys from all over the country. He knew the names."

As for Ma Brown, Walker remembers her fondly: "She prepared the meals for each fighter according to the instructions of the trainer. . . . She was a good cook. A good housekeeper. Demanded the fighters be disciplined, not coming in and raising hell and coming in at too late an hour at night. . . . She was strong-minded, kind of a cranky little lady, but very friendly once you got to know her."

Later, when Walker took a railroad flat nearby with a few of his fighters, he sought Ma Brown's company. "I became friends enough with her living nearby," Walker says, "and I would go up there and visit her once in a while. I'd go up and see her. One time I was in New York for seventeen weeks straight, and I'd get lonesome and I'd go up and talk to her. She'd come out on the front step and drag a couple of chairs out sometimes and we'd sit outside on her little porch."

Angelo Dundee remembers the time Charley Goldman fell in front of Ma Brown's. "Charley fell down those steps one time when it was icy," he says. "Broke his hand, and he fixed it himself." Describing how Goldman mended his own hand, Dundee says, "What he did, he got a rubber tube from a car, and he sort of shaped it and then he put strings through it—and then what he did, he had it . . . where it stayed in one place," Dundee explains, marveling at the ingenuity of his old friend. "I remember seeing it. It was black, black tubing. And he took care of his own broken hand."

Referee Joey Curtis, who fought as a lightweight in the 1940s as Joe Krikis, shared a room with Goldman at Madame Bey's training camp in New Jersey before fighting future lightweight champion Jimmy Carter in 1946. Curtis offers this highly personal memory of sharing a room with the trainer: "Charley Goldman had his own room, and they put a cot into that room. That was the worst mistake . . . I think I could've licked Carter if I woulda got my proper rest and my proper sleep. Because Charley Goldman, all night, snored. This little dwarf could snore so hard that he knocked buildings down. And I used to throw shoes at him, and I used to throw books at him. I says, 'Charley, give me a break. I got a tough fight comin'. Let me get some sleep. And every time I woke him up, 'Yeah, yeah, yeah.' That was my experience with Charley Goldman." Curtis goes on to say of Goldman, "He was a very, very happy guy. Always kiddin' you, always had a grin on his face. He was a very, very happy man."

A 1951 feature on Goldman in *Life* magazine described his living quarters at Ma Brown's: "The room decorated with fighter pictures, including a full-page one of himself from a 1909 *Police Gazette*, is also where Charley prepares his own liniment of egg whites, turpentine and vinegar." One photo in the magazine showed the thirty-two items Goldman carried to each fight in a small bag which he wore strapped to his waist. The bag, *Life* noted, was a gift from one of Goldman's fighters, and was "initialed Dr. C.G.—not as a gag but as a mark of respect."

Goldman said that he preferred having his paraphernalia strapped around his waist because "not having to fish around for my stuff saves me fifteen seconds, and in my business, that's a lot." Angelo Dundee remembers Goldman at ringside with his bag, his "little fingers working away . . ."

Another *Life* photo depicts Goldman playing cards with friends. Then aged sixty-three, Goldman—ever the splendid interview subject—told *Life* that the secret of staying young was spending time with young people. "They jump around," he said. "You play pinochle with old guys, and one fellow has rheumatism and another has a stiff back and the other guy reads obituaries."

After Rocky Marciano's retirement in 1956, Charley Goldman remained a part of the boxing scene. In 1963, when Sonny Liston had emerged as a seemingly unbeatable heavyweight champion, Ted Carroll of *The Ring* asked Goldman how Marciano would have done against Liston. Goldman began by treating Liston respectfully. "Results are what count and Sonny has given us results," Goldman said. He then stated that his instructions to Marciano in a match against Liston would be, "Hit him in the body, he's a big man with a lot of weight to carry around and since most of his fights have ended quickly nobody knows how much endurance he would have if a fight got into the late rounds."

Goldman, of course, left no doubt about who he thought would win. "I know a lot of people are saying it's a good thing Rocky retired before this guy Liston showed up. But they're forgetting that Rocky was exceptionally strong and an exceptional puncher, too. Not only that. Rocky had certain moves that nobody he fought ever got wise to." Ending with a series of classic Goldmanisms, the trainer said, "Rocky was no picture fighter and many a guy would say to me, 'Rocky don't look so good in there.' I'd come back with, 'That guy lying on the floor don't look so good either.'"

In the early 1960s, Goldman trained heavyweight contender Oscar Bonavena of Argentina—who later had memorable, tough matches against Joe Frazier and Muhammad Ali.

Displaying his skill for hyping his client, Goldman told *The Ring* in 1963, "I say he is faster than Marciano was at a similar stage of development. Now, don't have me saying that Oscar looks better than Rocky. Marciano had certain qualities which do not come along very often. He was a dedicated fighter. Too dedicated. Rocky led a Spartan life. When he trained he cut out movies, golf, late hours."

Returning to his present client, Goldman added, "Oscar is a trainer's dream. . . . Sometimes you get a complex job. You have to build the fighter's body as well as his skill. In this case nature richly attended to the body building. I just have to give him better know-how. A physique like Bonavena's is a God-send to any man, be he a fighter or a shoe salesman."

At the 1966 dinner for the American Association for the Improvement of Boxing, Goldman made a five-minute, impromptu speech. When introducing Goldman, Rocky Marciano said, in part, "He is considered the greatest teacher of boxing in the entire world. I have to say that he had to be because he brought a raw-boned, awkward clumsy 210-pounder to the title. . . . When you talk about boxing there really is not a more final word in my book. This man has been a father to me, a trainer, a brother, adviser—everything." This was, in all likelihood, the final public appearance that the boxer and his teacher made together.

The tape of Goldman's remarks reveals a sweet-sounding, solicitous elderly man not used to addressing formal gatherings. Then seventy-eight years old, Goldman's voice was soft and his accent was still pure Brooklyn. Spying one of his former fighters, Steve Acunto, then in his forties, Goldman said, "Steve, I know Steve a good many years. He was always all right, a nice boy."

About Marciano, Goldman said: "Rocky didn't win fights on account of the gymnasium work that he did. Every boxer does gymnastics and does roadwork and punches the bag and so forth. But every boxer never works in the gymnasium like Rocky. In fact, it wasn't so much the gymnasium workouts that Rocky did. It's the way he lived. Every fighter pretty near trains the same, but all fighters don't live alike. If you were there looking at Rocky's training and the way he lived, it was hard to believe that a man could sacrifice so much of life and his family life and keep fightin'.'"

As Goldman continued, Marciano's whispering voice interrupted him with a cue to end his remarks. "That's good, Charley," Marciano said gently. "All right. I know it's getting late," Goldman concluded. "I know you folks wanta get home. Thanks for inviting me. And all stay well."

After Goldman finished, Marciano added: "You wouldn't believe that this little man could be so rough in the gymnasium. He certainly demanded discipline. He certainly had the patience of a saint. And I just can't tell you what he did for me."

Legend has it that Charley Goldman died in his room at Ma Brown's, covered with one of Rocky Marciano's old robes. But this is probably not true. *The New York Times* obituary of Goldman reported that he passed away of a heart attack in 1968 at New York's Roosevelt Hospital. The day after Goldman died, Jimmy Breslin read an obituary in a newspaper and then wrote: "The story said he was eighty when he died. The story, of course, is a lie. Anybody who knew Charley Goldman could tell you he was a thousand years old."

Asked about the myth that Goldman had died wearing Marciano's robe Jimmy Breslin scoffs. "Nah. After you have 400 fights, you're not gonna fall in love with much of anything, are you?" Says Angelo Dundee, "I don't know that. I wasn't around. It could be because he loved Marciano. And besides, Marciano's robe covered him real well. He was a little man, but he was a big man. A magnificent man."

WHITEY BIMSTEIN

When you leave New York, you're camping out," said Whitey
Bimstein, one of the most celebrated trainers of his time, and a
quintessential urbanite. Bimstein once told A. J. Liebling, in
one of his most famous remarks, "I like the country. It's a great
spot." Asked if he enjoyed traveling overseas with his fighters,
Bimstein replied dismissively, "Out of town is out of town"—a
classic fight camp one-liner which originated with Bimstein,
Charley Goldman or Freddie Brown but became the property of
all three.

Given Bimstein's charmingly overstated disdain for leaving
the city, it's almost disappointing to learn from his daughter,
Adele Shapiro, that although Bimstein "loved New York, he did
enjoy the traveling."

Al Silvani, who worked as Bimstein's assistant in the late
1930s, says Bimstein was a "soft-spoken man, but he liked to
have his little drink now and then. You know, when you work
seven days a week, you wanta relax." Irving Rudd offers this

189

WHITEY BIMSTEIN PHOTO COURTESY ADELE SHAPIRO

summary of his long-time friend: "A good man in the corner, a nice, easy affable man to deal with. I think he liked his schnapps a little bit—not to any excess—but he wouldn't say no to a good belt. He trained them all."

Train them all he did. In the 1950s, Bimstein told a reporter: "Name the top fighters of any class, and it's a dollar to a punch in the kisser that I've worked over them sometime or another." He worked Harry Greb's corner against Gene Tunney in their second fight in 1923, and then worked Tunney's corner when the two met for the third time later that year. He was in James J. Braddock's corner with Joe Gould, Doc Robb and Ray Arcel when Braddock upset heavyweight champ Max Baer in 1935. On September 23, 1937, the night of promoter Mike Jacobs' "Carnival of Champions," Bimstein seconded four champions. In the mid-1940s, he trained Rocky Graziano for Graziano's three classic confrontations with Tony Zale. And in 1959, he guided Ingemar Johannson to his upset victory over heavyweight champion Floyd Patterson. At the same time, of course, he applied himself dutifully to countless other champions, contenders and journeymen.

Bimstein often called Gene Tunney the finest fighter he'd seen. "Tunney was cool, calm and collected. Nothing ever bothered him," Bimstein said. He also called Tunney "the most underrated heavyweight champion in history," adding, "in my book, Tunney could have licked them all from Sullivan to Marciano."

The easiest fighter to train, according to Bimstein, was lightweight champion Lou Ambers whom he described as "a trainer's dream" because "going to the movies is his dissipation." Bimstein also had special affection for James J. Braddock. "What a heart he had," Bimstein said of Braddock, whose journey from the relief rolls to the heavyweight championship earned him the nickname "Cinderella Man." Early in Rocky Graziano's career, Bimstein told a reporter, "Graziano's another Dempsey.

Just walks in there and starts to punch and when he lands, brother, something's going to fall."

Bimstein, a short former bantamweight with a small pot belly, was often likened in appearance—by Liebling and others—to an overgrown baby. His face was pink, and the small amount of hair on the sides of his bald head was white. One of Bimstein's fighters, Vinnie Ferguson, a middleweight in the 1950s, says, "He was just a loveable little guy. He was a little Jewish guy that you could take for Irish to look at him. He had very light skin, and he had grayish-white hair. Bald-headed guy."

While working a corner, Bimstein was rarely, if ever, photographed without a cotton swab hanging from his mouth. In fight camp pictures Bimstein is almost always mugging for the camera: in one he wears a hat backwards and smiles broadly, in another he stands with mock solemnity although his trousers have been dropped. With his half-smiling, half-sad face, Bimstein could easily pass for a comic from the silent screen era. Veteran journalist Harold Conrad says Bimstein looked "like a clown without make-up."

In the corner, though, Bimstein was tough and combative. "He would try to bull you," remembers Billy Graham, whose extremely controversial 1951 loss to Kid Gavilan earned him the title of "Uncrowned Welterweight Champion." Graham adds fondly, "I'd come back to the corner, and Whitey would start rousting me. 'You stupid, Irish blankety-blank, get out there.' . . . We'd fight in the corner, then he'd put the thing in my mouth, and I'd go out and take it out on the other guy."

Describing Bimstein between rounds, fighter Vinnie Ferguson says, "Whitey was one of the best psychologists in the world. . . . He would light a fire under you. He'd maybe tell you that the other guy insulted you or something. . . . He knew how to get things outta guys. . . . He'd say, 'This guy can't carry your gym bag,' or 'This guy is a baby compared to you.'"

Bimstein also used physical stimulation as a motivational tool. He sometimes poked lackadaisical boxers in the rear end with a pin and once prodded a fighter with a lit match.

Bimstein's prowess as a cut man was as celebrated as any fight second who ever lived. He received his first lessons in wound-closing from a New York police surgeon, and from Doc Bagley, the same master who served as role model to Ray Arcel. "I had the honor of working with Bagley, who was the first trainer to actually study medicine," Bimstein explained to *Boxing Illustrated* in 1960. "He originated the use of adrenaline chloride to stop bleeding."

Perhaps Bimstein's finest quasi-surgical achievement came on July 16, 1947 when Graziano—who had lost to Zale the previous year—knocked Zale out to win the middleweight championship. Of that first Zale-Graziano fight, Bimstein told a British newspaper, "Rocky was winning all the way till he was knocked out. It was one of the greatest fights I've seen . . . The other two were Dempsey versus Firpo and [Jackie 'Kid'] Berg versus Kid Chocolate." Shortly before the second Zale-Graziano bout, Bimstein said, "I don't think Zale ever got over the head punching he took in that [first] fight."

Following the brutal third round of the rematch—which Graziano described in his autobiography, *Somebody Up There Likes Me*, as "the worst round I ever lived through in the ring"— Graziano's right eye was swollen shut. "Get my eye open," he told Bimstein in the corner. "We were sure the referee was going to stop it," Bimstein recalled in 1960. "I had to lead him back to the corner after the third round. . . . I had only sixty seconds to make him see, stop the blood and give him back the confidence that had been leaking out of him with the blood. His right eye was so swollen it had to be lanced and drained. This done, I went to his left eye where the upper lid was split wide open. I was still working when the bell rang."

It's also widely reported that Bimstein used a silver dollar to apply pressure to bring down the swelling on Graziano's right eye. At the time of Graziano's death in 1990, W. C. Heinz wrote that it was actually one of Bimstein's assistants, Frank Percoco, who pulled a quarter—not a silver dollar—from his pocket and applied it to Graziano's eye.

When the referee wanted to stop the fight, Graziano wrote in his autobiography, Bimstein pleaded, "Give Rocky one more round? Just one more round." According to Graziano, the referee replied, "If this wasn't a championship fight, I would never a let him last out the third round. One more and if he don't come out of it, I got to stop it. They give you the chair for murder in this state." As the fight progressed and Bimstein continued to minister to Graziano, "The attending ring physician, who could have halted the bout with a nod to the referee, stared in open-mouthed admiration at his [Bimstein's] attempt to save Graziano," according to *The New York Times.*

When Graziano went on to score a knockout in the sixth round, he was caught up in such a blind fury that he had no memory of the knockout. He could only recall that, at the fight's end, Bimstein slapped him and said, "Rocky! Rocky! Come out of it! Rocky, you're the world champion!" Columnist Jimmy Cannon wrote that in the dressing room following the fight, Graziano, still sensitive to critics' charges that he had quit in the first Zale fight, asked Bimstein, "Whitey, did I ever show any dog?" Bimstein's reply: "Any one who says you're a dog is crazy."

It's part of the Whitey Bimstein legend that he never relinquished the coin used on Graziano's eye in the second Zale fight. Vinnie Ferguson confirms the story. "I really think it's the truth," he says. "I heard he had that silver dollar." Other fight men are more skeptical.

When Graziano lost the title to Zale by a third-round knockout in their rubber match in July of 1948, Bimstein was anything but sentimental about his fighter's performance. "I can't understand what got into him," Bimstein candidly told the press. "He seemed petrified when he got into the ring."

Bimstein's career was filled with feats that equaled his work on Graziano's behalf. Bimstein liked to talk about the time he seconded ten fighters in one night. "My sleeves were blood right up to the armpits," he said.

He also often described working in the corner of Paulino Uzcudun—the rugged Spanish heavyweight known as "The Basque Woodchopper"—in a twenty-round fight against Max Baer on July 4, 1931 in Reno, Nevada. "It was 110 in the shade, and right off I had a bathtub lugged down to our corner and stocked it with ice and water," Bimstein recalled in a 1953 *Newsweek* story. "I had eight one-gallon bottles of mineral water, and another bottle that was filled with brandy and un-chilled water for drinking. I had a great stack of towels and kept soaking them in ice water for Paulino. I also covered the soles of his feet with adhesive tape and kept pouring ice water into his shoes, so the burning-hot ring canvas wouldn't bother him."

The referee for the Uzcudun-Baer fight was Jack Dempsey. After Baer fouled Uzcudun during the early going, Bimstein often remembered, he told Dempsey, "Hey, Jack, tell Baer to stop fouling my boy." "Whitey, tell your boy to foul him back," Dempsey replied, creating the rules for what would become a classic, rule-bending brawl. "It was a lovely, eye-gouging affair from there in," Bimstein later said. After the match went the twenty-round distance, Bimstein said, "Dempsey thought Uz-cudun out-fouled Baer, and we got the decision."

Dempsey himself described the fight in an article credited to him in *Liberty* magazine. In the story, Dempsey said Bimstein's emergency room-style corner-work won the fight for Uzcudun. "Now Baer was much the better fighter that night and in fine condition," Dempsey recalled, "but at the end of twenty rounds he was a mess and Paulino looked as if he could go another twenty, so I gave the decision to Paulino. But Paulino didn't win that fight himself—Whitey Bimstein won it for him."

Bimstein revealed in a 1954 interview that he managed to antagonize Max Baer before the fight even started. "Baer was in Dempsey's headquarters before the fight, bragging about what he was going to do," Bimstein said. "While he was talking, I sneaked up and gave him a hot foot. He chased me all over the place."

Bimstein's talent for inspired improvisation in the corner was never constrained by how things might look to ringside observers. He only cared about winning, as demonstrated when he worked the corner of former middleweight champion Fred Apostoli against Melio Bettina in 1941. "Fred's getting quite a shellacking," Bimstein explained to Associated Press boxing writer Jack Cuddy, employing the present tense he often favored when telling stories. "He comes back to the corner after an especially hard round and starts to cry. 'What's the matter with me? I can't fight.' I don't find anything physically wrong with him, so just before I get out of the ring I haul off and poke him in the puss. 'Get out there and do your stuff,' I snarl. Well, sir, he goes out there and beats hell out of Bettina. At the end of the round he comes back smiling and says happily, 'That's what I needed. Sock me again, but hard, get me mad.' He went out there fighting mad and turned the tables on Melio, winning by a good margin." Showing a subtle appreciation for the ironies of a trainer's profession, Bimstein added, "Funny, he didn't get mad at Bettina for socking him, and he didn't get mad at *me* for socking him, but when I socked him he got mad at Bettina and it riled him to a fighting pitch."

Covering the fight for the *Journal American*, Bill Corum wrote, "Trainer Whitey Bimstein in Apostoli's corner banged and biffed Fred about between rounds as much as Bettina did while the official fight was in progress. It wouldn't surprise me if Bimstein didn't really win the fight. He kept prodding and driving Apostoli to keep him going, grabbing him by the hair and shaking him like an Apache dancer . . ."

Dan Parker of *The Daily Mirror* reported, "The going over Freddie [Apostoli] received in this heat was merely a warm-up for what was in store for him when he went to his corner. Whitey Bimstein . . . grabbed him by the hair, shook his head sharply until the press box was showered by Neapolitan dandruff, and fetched him half a dozen sharp belts on the back of the neck. As Freddie's anger mounted, I thought he was going to haul off and knock Whitey's bicuspids around to the back of his neck . . ."

At times there was an almost callous quality to Bimstein's tales of the brutality he'd witnessed in the ring. "I've seen fighters tagged on the chin and knocked so groggy that I've wondered if they'd even last long enough to make it to the corner," he once said. "Then I've seen them hit again and restored to their senses."

Despite his tough-guy public persona, Bimstein was also known for his concern for his fighters' welfare. Interviewed for a 1947 article about safety standards in boxing, Bimstein described his outrage at observing incompetent trainers: "There's too many places like the London gym I dropped into one day last year. I see ten fighters working out at the same time—and nobody taking care of them. No headgear, no bandages, no mouthpieces, nobody to see that they didn't overmatch theirselves when they sparred. For those ten kids, there's one handler, but he's a dope, just a towel swinger. He don't even have medicine and tools with him." By way of conclusion Bimstein added, "It's a tough enough game without leaving dopes to take care of the kids."

Bimstein had reason to be concerned with safety. In 1924, early in his career as a trainer, one of the first fighters he handled, a young bantamweight named Frankie Jerome, died as a result of blows received in a fight against Bud Taylor in

Madison Square Garden. Jerome had had over three-hundred fights and was managed by Billy Gibson who handled Benny Leonard, among others.

Frankie Jerome's given name was Frank Doherty. He took his ring name from St. Jerome's Catholic Church in the Bronx, which sponsored a gym where he learned to box. Jerome and Bimstein were close friends. Jerome was best man at Bimstein's wedding, and after Jerome's death, Bimstein reportedly named his son "Jerry" in memory of the boxer. Bimstein's son Jerry Barnes says, however, "I was supposed to be named after him. But I'm not so sure that was true."

After the boxer's death, Bimstein often spoke of Jerome, ruefully muttering, "If he'd lived, if he'd lived. . . ." Bimstein's grandson, Michael Shapiro, says, "My grandfather thought that Frankie Jerome was potentially the greatest fighter he ever saw."

In a 1950 interview with Barney Nagler of *The Ring*, Bimstein discussed the tragedy. "Three months before the fight Jerome drove his car into a wall in Central Park. Never said nothing to anybody about it. He was as game as the gamest in the ring, but funny thing about him, he didn't like medicine. He didn't like doctors. And he didn't like trainers who used iodine.

"Once he had a scratch on his hand and I wanted to put iodine on it and he screamed. This was a kid that took punches like nobody, but he didn't like iodine. So when he got hurt in the car, he don't tell nobody, but keeps fighting with a fracture at the base of the skull. But Bud Taylor hits him and he gets killed and everybody raps boxing." Bimstein described Jerome's death to A. J. Liebling by saying, "He died right in my arms, slipping punches."

Most people's memories of Whitey Bimstein focus on his sweetness. In a 1969 obituary in the *New York Post*, Lester Bromberg wrote, "He was so decent, so unmercenary that he might not have belonged in a business that often was, and is, a world of selfishness. He was an uncomplicated, most happy fella. He never worried, he never bore a grudge." Veteran boxing publicist Murray Goodman recalls, "If he liked you, you could do no wrong."

Jackie Graham, younger brother of Bimstein's welterweight Billy Graham, remembers that as sweet as he was outside the gym, Bimstein could be tough on his fighters. "When you saw Whitey in Stillman's Gym, he was a cantankerous, angry, belligerent, tough-looking guy. But the minute he walked through the doors out onto the sidewalk, he was an entirely different man . . . a very pleasant, likeable guy."

Bimstein didn't allow his fighters to loaf in the ring, says Jackie Graham. "When fighters were lookin' to steal rounds, if they didn't feel like working out that day, they'd fire some heavyweight punches at their sparring partner and that would stop the sparring partner from, you know, really working with him. It would slow them down. They'd be wary of getting off punches themselves for fear of getting banged around. But Whitey knew instantly. And he'd start yelling, 'Cut it out. Cut it out. Come on, get in there and work. Get in there and box!'"

Jackie Graham particularly remembers Bimstein's fondness for food. "If you saw him with a knife and fork in his hand you'd wonder . . . if he didn't have a shopping bag on the floor between his feet. He had an excellent appetite."

"Oh, did he love to eat!" Bimstein's daughter Adele says with a laugh. Her father and his friends "used to have contests all the time to see who could eat the most hot stuff—hot peppers, things like that. These guys would get together and their faces would turn red, and steam would come out of their ears because they had these big eating contests." Bimstein was a connoisseur of small, out-of-the-way restaurants where, seated in a back room, proprietors would serve their specialties to Bimstein and his fight crowd friends. Bimstein's grandson Michael Shapiro adds that the trainer "made the best potato latkes in the history of mankind. Through him I learned to respect onions and black pepper."

While at training camp Bimstein took a unique approach to controlling his fighters' food intake. "We'd sit down to dinner and whatever the fighter ordered for dinner, my grandfather would just reach over and start grabbing stuff off the guy's plate, and he would put it on his plate," Michael Shapiro says. "Then when he couldn't eat any more, he'd start putting stuff on my plate."

At other times, Bimstein would order the same spartan meals as his fighters. At night, however, certain his fighter was asleep, Bimstein would indulge in a private feast. "He'd sneak down and buy a whole apple pie and a quart of milk," the trainer's grandson reports, "and he would eat a whole pie and a quart of milk in his hotel room. But he wouldn't want the fighter to see it. I saw that on more than one occasion."

Jimmy Breslin remembers another detail about Bimstein's eating habits: "He always came back from a training camp and the first thing he did was go to the Horn & Hardart and eat vegetables. It was the one thing he missed in his whole life, automat vegetables."

Most who knew Bimstein mention his drinking. Jackie Graham recalls, "He could drink pretty good. And the best part of the whole thing is that he did not show it. If I saw him, I'd know he'd been drinking heavily, but if you ran into him, you wouldn't know it. He carried his whiskey that well." Vinnie Ferguson adds, "He liked to drink, but he could handle that drink, boy. You'd never know he was drinking. . . . Drinking was a plus for him, I think. Most people, it's a detriment. But with him, he liked to have his drinks. He was a social guy."

Billy Graham says, "Whitey was a boozer, but he knew what he was doing. He always knew what he was doing in the corner. I seen him one time—he was oiled, I'm telling you. And I was very nervous about it because the guy I was fighting was one of those bulldogs, you know. But Whitey took care of it, regardless of the juice he had. He was a beautiful guy."

Bimstein's grandson Michael offers a memory of Bimstein's surprisingly wholesome-sounding habit of combining his fondness for alcohol with a desire to spend time with his grandson: "On Sundays in particular, if it was a nice Sunday, we would go for a walk, and he would bar-hop. We would go into a bar and he would meet with people. You know, all friendly stuff. Everybody knew him. I'd sit there with my Pepsi and peanuts, and he'd have a shot. Then we'd walk for a while and he'd go see somebody else."

Tales of Bimstein's drinking should not diminish his image as a hard-working trainer. In a 1958 interview in *The Ring*, Bimstein discussed the frustrations of—and delicacy needed in— his chosen profession: "You'd never imagine what sets a kid off stride. I'll have a boy getting the knack of slipping and countering. . . . To see that he doesn't get hurt while learning, I'll make sure that he doesn't work with somebody too tough. Okay, now I have to go out of town with a main-event fighter. I'm gone a week, no more. But, when I get back, I discover the kid is gun-shy, he hasn't the confidence to do the things I taught him. I ask the kid what's wrong and he doesn't say anything. I ask around. I find out that, while I was away, he boxed three or four times with some murderous puncher who makes him a human punching bag. . . . All my work of months ruined."

In 1960, Bimstein again explained the stress of a trainer's life. "The average person has no idea how temperamental fighters get, especially when they're training," he told *Boxing Illustrated*. "And when they get to be big shots it goes to their heads like a hundred percent booze. You take a kid off the streets, a kid who never saw a bathtub or a knife and fork in his life, and make him a big shot. Then, brother, you've got trouble."

Whitey Bimstein was born Morris Bimstein on the Lower East Side of Manhattan. He had two brothers and two sisters. His formal education ended in 1910 when he graduated from Public School 62, located at the corner of Hester and Essex Streets. During his brief time as a student, Bimstein ran the sixty-yard dash on the school track team and played baseball and basketball. Early in life, he began hanging around gyms and learned how to box. Soon everyone was calling him Whitey. It's said that only family members called him Morris later in life. His one-time partner Ray Arcel, however, would call him Morris during rare disagreements.

As a young boxer, Bimstein demonstrated the worst imaginable training habits. Bimstein "had a passion for frankfurters and charlotte russes which he would indulge even a few minutes before a fight," A. J. Liebling wrote in a 1937 *New Yorker* profile, "and all his roadwork was done at a walk, selling boxing tickets to neighbors."

Liebling reported that Bimstein's father, who was in the garment business, was unhappy with his son's tough East Side friends, so he moved the family to the Bronx. But Bimstein soon found his way to a Catholic Church where a priest gave boxing lessons.

Bimstein's daughter Adele says her father "never spoke very much about where he grew up. He was the maverick in the family. All I know is that there was a lot of fighting. I don't think it was a closely knit family where there were a lot of things he could talk about. He almost never spoke about his family life." Bimstein never really knew his father, whom, she says, disappeared. "I don't know how old my father was when his father took off."

Remembering his fighting career, Bimstein told *Boxing Illustrated*, "I fought anybody who weighed up to 125 pounds, and ran like hell from those who weighed more. . . . I . . . had a bitter hatred for two things. I hated school and I hated training. It didn't make sense to me in those days that a fighter had to waste all that time fooling around with punching bags and getting up at dawn so that he could chase his shadow in the park."

Bimstein estimated that he had seventy professional fights. He was managed by Lou Brix, who would later give him his start as a trainer. After a brief stint as a boxing instructor in the

Navy, Bimstein returned to New York and devoted himself to becoming a trainer.

Bimstein explained in a 1939 interview with a Cleveland newspaper that he switched from fighting to working in corners when he discovered that seconding fighters was more remunerative and involved less physical sacrifice. "I'm one of those boxers who never trained, and I'm lucky to make three bucks a night," Bimstein confessed. "Well, one night I make six bucks by fighting two places. But what really turns me into a second is one night when I get moirdered [sic] over in Queens. I used to get a little cut on tickets I could sell before the fight, but this night some politician is having a clambake and I only sell six tickets to my own fight. My end is half a buck. The other guy gives me a great going-over and then my two seconds want a little something out of my money—so we settle on 45 cents worth of sandwiches and coffee, and I've got a nickel left. Next day I look at my shiner and that nickel and I say to myself, 'What the hell, Whitey, those seconds got everything you did except a black eye. Get wise and be a second.' So I'm a second from there on." Among the champions Bimstein worked with early in his career as a trainer were bantamweight Abe Goldstein and featherweight Louis "Kid" Kaplan.

As both a fighter and a trainer, Bimstein acquired a large variety of nicknames. He fought under the name "Johnny White." When he started working as a trainer, he was known as "Little Whitey," "Kid Whitey" and "Whitey the Trainer." The caption of a photo taken when Bimstein seconded British middleweight Ted Moore in one of his 1925 bouts against Tiger Flowers identifies Bimstein as "Whitey Bentley," though it's difficult to determine if this is a misprint or yet another pseudonym. Over the years, Bimstein's achievements as a trainer also earned him names such as "the Brains" and "the Surgeon."

A. J. Liebling's *New Yorker* profile affectionately recreated Bimstein's speaking style. Discussing the difficulty of controlling a fighter's weight, for example, Bimstein said, "Some of them lunatics put on a pound every time they take a deep breath."

In *The Sweet Science* Liebling immortalized Bimstein's analysis of heavyweight Tommy "Hurricane" Jackson: "He throws a lot of leather, like a noctopus." [sic] Equally entertaining—though more difficult to believe—is Liebling's account of how Bimstein tricked a fighter with fear of airplanes into flying to Honolulu for a fight: "Whitey got him aboard," Liebling writes, "by telling him the trip would take only fifteen minutes. He said Honolulu was in New Jersey."

Liebling also honored Bimstein by using one of his comments as the epigram for *Back Where I Came From*, an anthology of Liebling's writing about New York City. The epigram reads, "A New Yorker doesn't have to discover New York. He knows it's there all the time."

Asked if Bimstein was as amusing as Liebling's portrait suggests, Jimmy Breslin says, "He was a funny bastard, yeah. He once had a good line, Whitey. He said, 'Things are so fuckin' bad, I gotta go to a foreign country, Manila, to get a fight.' He called Manila a foreign country."

Bimstein's daughter, Adele Shapiro, who graduated from Hunter College and became a high school biology teacher in New York City, says her father "sounded like a real Damon Runyon character" with a quintessential New York accent. She goes on to candidly explain, "I guess I went through life—part of my life—being kind of snobbish—you know, kids do this—thinking that I was more educated than my parents were, and looking down on the way he would express himself and what he would say. And once in a while he would surprise me and I would say, 'Hey, this man is smart.' It takes us a long time to learn."

At home with his family, Bimstein rarely discussed boxing. "He kept it separate," his daughter says, adding that her mother was less than enthusiastic about boxing, "and she let us know about it." Bimstein's son Jerry Barnes, though, remembers that his father often spoke about his work. "His whole existence was boxing. But you know, it was kind of depressing," Jerry Barnes says. "You never really heard him talk about any other field." Asked if she remembers when Liebling's profile of her father was published in 1937, Adele Shapiro replies, "I don't know that I was ever aware of it. And I don't think my mother was much into it, so he didn't really show us these things. I never became aware of them until later on."

Was her father conscious of being a celebrity? "It was never a big deal, no. But he knew that when anybody ever needed a favor, Whitey always knew somebody—somebody to fix it, somebody to help someone get a job, someone to take care of a law problem. . . . People called him for help." Adele Shapiro confirms stories that Bimstein was one of the softest touches in boxing—that he always made loans he knew would never be repaid. "His hand was always in his pocket," she says.

While Adele Shapiro doesn't remember her father coming up with the sort of one-liners that delighted Liebling, she says he could be funny in other ways. "He loved children. I would go out on the street with him and he'd stop all the kids and he'd joke with all the children. He'd always play hide-and-seek with them. I'd be out walking with my father, and all of a sudden he wasn't there. He was hiding behind something, waiting for me to turn around and discover that he was gone. So he was like a big kid lots of times." With young boys, she adds, Bimstein would always conduct an impromptu boxing class. "All right, get your dukes up. Keep your dukes up," he'd say. Bimstein's son Jerry fondly remembers that his father would playfully "push me up against the wall, faking throwing punches at me. It got to be a game."

Bimstein's grandson Michael speaks warmly of a childhood filled with weekends and holidays spent at his grandfather's side at Stillman's Gym during the late 1950s. "I was like the gym's kid," Michael Shapiro recalls. "I was like the dog that was running around the place that everyone's petting. I was having the time of my life." One of the only times he got into trouble with his grandfather, Shapiro remembers, is when he made the mistake of touching the gun Lou Stillman always carried. As a child, Shapiro adds, he thought everyone in the fight world was a relative. "Dempsey was Uncle Jack. Graziano was Uncle Rocky. We used to bump into these guys all the time. Until I was thirteen years old, I used to think I was related to these guys."

Though Bimstein taught his grandson how to tape fighters' hands and give rubdowns, he rarely let the boy box. "Every now and then he'd let me get in the ring," Shapiro says. "He'd put a mask on me that was about as thick as a brick so that I wouldn't get touched up too badly."

Having Whitey Bimstein as a grandfather also had other rewards: Bimstein, accompanied by fighters like Rocky Graziano or Ingemar Johansson, would sometimes stop the local ice cream truck and buy ice cream for all the kids in the neighborhood. "So I got to be a pretty popular kid when I was growing up," Shapiro says.

Bimstein was also famous in his Bronx apartment building for helping children with their scrapes and cuts. "People used to call him," his daughter recalls. "We lived in an apartment house where everybody knew everybody else and if somebody's kid got hurt, they would call my father. Everybody knew he was good at that." She also affectionately remembers the "little bag that he brought with him wherever he went" which contained bandages, scissors and a variety of cut-closing ointments. "He also had some kind of special concoction that he kept in his bag all the time that they [his boxers] drank," Adele Shapiro adds with a laugh. "I don't know what was in it. It was his own special pick-me-up."

The experience of being interviewed for a magazine profile of her father altered Adele Shapiro's perceptions about him. "I recall somebody from *Collier's*, I think it was, came to interview us about my father. I guess he was getting negative vibes from whatever my mother or even I was saying, and he stopped me and he said, 'Young lady, I want you to know that everyone in this business has the highest regard for your father. And there is no reason for you to denigrate him in any way.' And he had a profound effect on me because I changed my whole attitude toward how I felt. And I said to myself, 'Well, I've got to look at this differently now.' And it changed me.'"

Like so many of his fellow trainers, Bimstein became an accomplished raconteur, an informal historian of the ring, always able to produce polished anecdotes for eager reporters. As one grateful writer put it, "Bimstein never gropes for the right answers. They jump out like popcorn."

In 1950, Barney Nagler, in an article for *The Ring*, asked Bimstein which of his fighters was the toughest to handle. Bimstein mentioned British middleweight Ted Moore, who he trained for a 1924 championship bout with Harry Greb. "Let's see, the middleweight limit was 158 pounds then," said Bimstein, "and three days before the fight I had Moore down to 160 pounds, so I watched the fellow very close. The next day, after road work, I take Moore onto the scale to weigh him and what do you think? How much do you think? How much do you think he gains overnight? He hit 169.

"I almost hit him with the scale. I said, 'What did you do?' He kinda looked away and said, 'I don't do nothing.' I knew something was wrong. This guy don't leave the house and, in those days, we had a bathtub and a shower in this here camp. I look around and I find empty beer bottles under the tub. He had drank the eight bottles of beer.

"It's now two days before the fight and this here guy is eleven pounds overweight. I worked the skin off him the next two days and got him down to weight. Made a great fight with Greb, too. Came near winning the title. This fighter was the toughest I trained."

Lou Ambers, by contrast, was easy to train, Bimstein told Nagler. Here is Bimstein's account of preparing Ambers for his

1941 rematch with Lew Jenkins after Jenkins had defeated Ambers for the lightweight title in 1940: "It was fun working with Ambers. You didn't have to drive him. My job with him was to keep him from working too much. I remember when he was going to fight Lew Jenkins the second time that Al Weill wasn't sure he wanted Ambers to keep fighting. Weill said to me to watch Ambers close. I did and I told Al he didn't have much left.

"Weill went to Ambers and told him, 'Lou, maybe you shouldn't fight Jenkins.' Do you know what? Ambers cried and said he wanted to fight. He knew he could lick Jenkins, even if he got knocked out the first time. Cried like a baby and Weill got soft and let him go in. He got knocked out. It was too bad. There was the best fighter a guy could train."

Bimstein went on to compare Ambers to Rocky Graziano: "Not that Graziano was bad, but there was a difference. Now, you take Ambers. I could put him in the ring in the gym with anybody. He would adapt his style for the guy. Let the guy run—he would chase him. Let the guy fight—he would fight him. This here Rocky is different. You gotta give him guys who punch with him or he don't like it. Give him a boxer in the gym and it's no good.

"Funny thing was how Ambers would get cranky when it came close to a fight. Nice kid, but he would get so cranky you couldn't go near him. Now, Graziano, he doesn't get cranky never. He gives you that happy-go-lucky impression right 'til the end. Only thing, Rocky was tough getting into the gym. When I got him in there he would work hard, but getting him in was tough."

Bimstein expanded on Graziano's training habits for writer Al Buck in *The Ring* in 1956. "In the beginning we had trouble getting Rocky in the gym. But once he started to make money, I had no trouble getting Graziano to work. Rocky can be very serious about money."

Billy Graham, who Bimstein trained at the same time he handled Graziano says, "Whitey was able to handle Rocky.

Graziano was a rough kid. He was a nice guy. He and I were pals. But he never stopped smoking." Bimstein would get mad when Graziano smoked, but Graziano continued—even in his dressing room before a fight. "Someone would come in with a cigarette," Graham remembers. "Graziano would go over and say, 'Gimme that.' He'd take a few drags on it and give it back. He was off the wall."

Of Bimstein's many experiences with heavyweights, the most exciting was the time he accompanied Paulino Uzcudun to Barcelona to face Primo Carnera in 1931.

Bimstein described the scene—with perhaps a touch of hyperbole—in an interview with the Associated Press years later. "We arrived there [in Barcelona] with bullets flying all over the place in the middle of a revolution. The Spanish boxing commission decided to delay the fight a week, hoping the revolt would quiet down. It was nothing to walk along the streets covered with hundreds of dead, and you couldn't tell when the fighting would break out anew.

"I remember one day we were at a sidewalk cafe. Just as I started to put my lips to a glass of vermouth a shot splintered the glass. Believe me, I got back to the hotel in nothing flat . . .

"The fight finally went on before a crowd of 80,000 spectators, 20,000 military police and 40,000 soldiers. A hitch developed at the last moment when Carnera wanted to use American gloves.

"The Spanish boxing commission insisted on Spanish gloves. 'Me no fight,' Carnera shouted in Spanish. The commissioner went outside and about a dozen soldiers walked toward Carnera. The big fellow backed up hurriedly yelling, 'Okay, me fight.'

"Carnera won the decision of the officials, Spanish and Italian judges with an English referee. When the verdict was announced, the revolution started all over again. The fans started to break everything they could get their hands on and shots were flying in all directions.

"We crawled under the ring where we found about three-hundred others and waited there until the soldiers had control of the situation. Even then we had to fight our way back to the dressing rooms. They continued rioting in the streets all night, and believe me, it was the happiest moment in my life when I left there the next day and headed for the good old USA."

Uzcudun was one of the fighters Bimstein spoke most warmly of when looking back on his career. "It was a pleasure to work with Paulino," Bimstein recalled. "He was always pleasant, considerate, good-natured and never worried or fret[ted] about a thing. He was the finest character among the fighters I ever met, square as they make 'em, game and tough, and in his prime a match for any of 'em."

Uzcudun revealed in a 1968 interview with *The Ring* that after he was knocked out by Joe Louis in Madison Square Garden in 1935, Bimstein told him, "If I were in your socks, I would pack it up, get out of here and don't come back." Uzcudun added, "To this day I cannot find an explanation for Whitey's words." Uzcudun's claim that he was never paid for the Louis bout only adds more mystery to this peculiar episode.

Perhaps Bimstein's greatest triumph in a heavyweight's corner came as one of James J. Braddock's seconds when Braddock upset Max Baer to win the title in 1935. As Bimstein told the story, Braddock won a decisive psychological victory during the weigh-in for the fight.

"We'd been tipped off that Baer was going to tell Braddock that Jim shouldn't be fighting him, but should be boxing his younger brother, Buddy. Max tried it but only got part way through his speech when Braddock pushed him aside and threatened to punch him."

Paying tribute to Braddock, Bimstein said, "You'll never find a gamer guy in the ring than Braddock. He may not have been a great fighter, even though he did become heavyweight champion of the world. But he was game to the last punch. He had a fighter's heart, if ever there was one." Bimstein, however, was uncharacteristically critical of Max Baer. "And just as game as Braddock was," he concluded, "that's how much of a dog Baer is, unless he's out in front. He's got a ticker about the size of a pea." Bimstein's grandson explains Bimstein's attitude toward Max Baer: "Baer wouldn't train. The guy would not train. He [Bimstein] would say that a lot."

Bimstein stood in a corner opposite Joe Louis nine times. He was in Braddock's corner when he lost the heavyweight title to Joe Louis in 1937, and recalled the fight this way: "Joe clipped Jimmy a pretty good shot on the jaw midway in the fifth round and we thought that would be the end. But when Jimmy came back to his corner and we asked him how he felt, he said, 'I'm okay, only the lights are bothering me. I can't see right.' The poor guy didn't realize he was losing. He thought the lights were hurting his eyes. That's why he went in again in the sixth and kept on punching even though he was getting the worst of it. Even when he was knocked out and we brought him back to his senses, the first thing he asked was, 'Did I make a good fight?' There may be better fighters than Braddock but there'll never be a gamer one."

In 1939, Bimstein again faced Louis as cut man for New Jersey bar owner "Two Ton" Tony Galento when Galento challenged Louis for the title. Before the fight, Joe Jacobs, Galento's manager, told Reuters, "With referees stopping fights for the least little thing nowadays, we thought it advisable to have Bimstein in our corner."

After Galento was knocked out by Louis in four rounds at Yankee Stadium, he brooded about the opportunity he lost in having Louis on the canvas in the second round. "Back in the dressing room," Bimstein later recalled, "he is sitting there with blood pouring from his eyes, his nose and his cheek. He won't let me touch the cuts. He won't let me take off his gloves. He pushes me away every time I try to do something for him, and bellows, 'You guys wouldn't let me fight my own fight. I'd've knocked that mug cold.'"

A year after the fight, Bimstein laid out the strategic differences he'd had with Galento: "I still think Tony Galento would have licked him if he obeyed orders. We had Tony bobbing and weaving in the first two rounds, and he had Louis dizzy. He even knocked Louis down. Then he thought he was John L. Sullivan and came up straight to slug, and you just can't do that with Louis. If Tony had fought the way he was told, he might have got in another shot that would have kept Louis down for keeps—and I don't think Tony was the greatest fighter in the world, either."

Reminiscing about the rotund Galento on another occasion, Bimstein confirmed Galento's *laissez-faire* approach to training. "What a guy," Bimstein said. "The first time I was called upon to take charge of him, I watched him work out, then we went back to his tavern for dinner. And what do you think he ate? A big platter of meatballs and spaghetti! Two days before he fought Max Baer. And two days before the fight they called me and told me he had a fight with his brother and that his brother shoved a broken glass in Tony's face and split his lip. We fixed that up and the day of the fight, at three o'clock in the afternoon, he ate more meatballs and spaghetti and drank a dozen bottles of beer. Baer walked right out, smacked him with a right in the mouth and dug a left hook into his stomach. After that was repeated a few times, Tony was through."

Bimstein had more success with another of Joe Louis' challengers, Arturo Godoy of Chile, who went the fifteen-round distance in losing to Louis in February of 1940. Godoy was so elated at having survived against Louis that he planted a kiss on the champion's head. Following the fight, Louis admitted that Godoy's bobbing, weaving and running was both annoying and frustrating. "His head kept worrying me all the time," Louis said, "bouncin' and bobbin' and buttin'. He was a hard man to fight. . . . Man's supposed to fight when he gets in the ring, ain't he? It ain't no honor to stay fifteen rounds with nobody."

During the prefight build-up for the Louis-Godoy rematch

later that year, Bimstein told the press that Godoy had been sick with a temperature of 103 degrees three days before the first fight. "Godoy was certainly in no condition to train that day. I finally decided to take Arturo out of bed—and in bed he was indeed—and have him don the gloves. Arturo boxed that day all right and he boxed well. In fact, he was never seen to better advantage in training." Bimstein didn't tell the fighter that he had cut the length of the rounds from three minutes to a minute-and-a-half each.

Visiting Godoy's camp a few days before the rematch with Louis, boxing writer Lester Bromberg overheard Bimstein and Godoy playfully exchanging insults. "If you don't come for a walk with me, I'll stiffen you," Bimstein told Godoy who answered, "You mean it? I no worried for Joe Louis, but I plenty afraid for you, you shrimp." Following this bit of repartee, the two left for a walk "arm in arm," according to Bromberg.

Bimstein explained Godoy's prefight strategy against Louis this way: "Godoy will fight his fight after the first round. He can do one thing well that Louis can't do at all and that is change his style to meet any emergency. Louis is strictly a stand-up fighter who sets up a guy with a left and then knocks his brains out. If he is feinted out of position by a crouch or a weave, his one-track mind doesn't work so well and he has to step back and start over again. I won't say what tricks Godoy plans to use in the fight. He is practicing a lot of things and he has a very good chance to win. I think we know how Louis will fight. He has been training for hooks so that he can come up under Godoy's crouch, but he may find that Arturo is using an entirely different style."

Bimstein admitted that Godoy had run from Louis in their first fight. "Yeah, we ran away in the fourteenth round because we were tired," Bimstein said. "But this time we will be in great shape." Despite Bimstein's enthusiastic arguments in favor of Godoy's chances, Louis easily destroyed Godoy in eight rounds.

Prefight hype aside, Bimstein respected Louis enormously

and once went as far as picking Louis to "flatten" Dempsey if the two had met. "Dempsey was made to order for Louis' style," Bimstein said. "Dempsey would have come rushing at Louis and it would be curtains. Dempsey had the heart to take a punch, but Louis hits too hard for anybody to come tearing at him."

Following the Second World War, Bimstein formed a partnership with Freddie Brown. Brown especially admired Bimstein's knowledge of the human body. "He could sense where there was a bruised muscle, and he had his own remedies," said Brown.

Together, Bimstein and Brown handled, among others, Tommy "Hurricane" Jackson, a perpetually promising heavyweight contender who inspired comparisons with Harry Greb and Henry Armstrong, though he never won a crown. Jackson was celebrated for his fantastic conditioning, ability to absorb punishment and a punching style that included a double uppercut that Bimstein and Brown called the "scoop" punch. Press coverage of Jackson's personal eccentricities seems racist—one more example of journalists making a black man the butt of bad jokes. Bimstein, however, appears to have had a sincere belief in Jackson's boxing potential.

In 1955, Jackson won two decisions from former heavyweight champion Ezzard Charles. In 1956, Jackson lost a twelve-round decision to Floyd Patterson in an elimination tournament created to find a successor for retired heavyweight champion Rocky Marciano. Jackson was knocked out the following year by Patterson in Patterson's first defense of his title in 1957 at New York's Polo Grounds.

Freddie Brown once recalled that he and Bimstein "had to argue with Jackson to keep him from overtraining." After one of Jackson's 1954 victories, Bimstein told *The Ring*, "The kid is like the old-timers in his training. Nothing is too much or too hard for him to do. Ask him to run two miles and he wants to jog twelve." One year later, Bimstein said, "I have heard it said, and seen it written that Hurricane Jackson trains too much.

Don't you believe it. Hurricane has so much energy he has to work it off. If he didn't train the way he does, he couldn't fight."

Despite Jackson's disappointing career, Bimstein paid tribute to him once again in 1960. "Hurricane Jackson has the kind of stuff only the truly great fighters have," said Bimstein. "He has more endurance than any fighter I ever saw, and he's very hard to hit."

Bimstein was in Ingemar Johansson's corner when he beat Floyd Patterson for the heavyweight title in 1959, earning Bimstein the status of a national hero in the champion's native Sweden. Veteran trainer George Chemeres, who traveled with Bimstein to Sweden in 1963, recalls, "They loved little Whitey Bimstein . . . he was really big over there."

Johansson first saw Bimstein working in Archie McBride's corner when Johansson defeated McBride in Sweden in 1957. Before facing Patterson for the first time, Johansson hired Bimstein as his co-trainer. Bimstein shared responsibilities with the fighter's Swedish trainer, Nils Blomberg.

After training Johansson for his third bout with Patterson— the March 1961 contest which Patterson won by a sixth-round knockout—Bimstein wrote "My Wacky Life with Ingo" as told to Barney Nagler for *Sport* magazine. What most surprised Bimstein was the Swede's practice of bringing his family and his girlfriend to training camp. "You can't knock a guy for wanting to be with his family," Bimstein stated, "but the way I see it, a training camp should be for getting in shape, not for being comfortable. Life should be tough on a guy working for a heavy-weight championship fight. He should get mean and hate every-body, which doesn't happen when a fighter has it too soft."

Also surprising was Johansson's practice of not eating meals in Bimstein's presence, and his habit of leaving camp to feast on ice cream and pickled herring. "I never saw a fighter do that before," Bimstein wrote. He was finally invited to eat lunch with Johansson prior to the second Patterson fight. "The whole family was sitting around the table," Bimstein recalled. ". . . 'Where the hell am I?' I said to myself, 'at a Thanksgiving party?'"

While Bimstein said Johansson was "perfect" for the first Patterson fight in 1959, he complained Johansson was too light for the rematch in which he was knocked out: "I could see from the start that Ingo had nothing. The tiger was out of him. He threw only one good right." After Patterson knocked out Johansson in the fifth round, Bimstein recalled, "He was as flat as one of those pickled herrings he ate in that training camp."

For the rubber match, which Johansson lost by eighth-round knockout, Johansson was overweight. According to Bimstein, "When he had Patterson down twice in the first round, he didn't have the fire to go after him. He was too slow and got hit himself and went down."

Writer Harold Conrad, who organized the promotion for the third and final Patterson-Johansson fight, recalls that Bimstein had problems getting Johansson to control his eating. "Johansson used to get up at night and eat," Conrad says with a laugh. "He used to go to the ice box, so Whitey taped it up. And Johansson just pulled it open and put all the tape back on it. He kept eating every night. And Whitey didn't get wise to it until about a week later."

Conrad also delights in describing what happened when, for publicity purposes, he arranged a public sparring session in Miami Beach: "Whitey said, 'Geez, who are we gonna get to work with Johansson?' So Angelo Dundee's in the Fifth Street Gym, and we went up to Angelo and said, 'You got somebody to work with this guy?' He said, 'Yeah, wait a minute.' He said, 'Hey, Cass!' This big, good lookin' kid bounces over—Cassius Clay. And Ange says, 'You wanta go a few rounds with the Swede?' Ali said, 'I'll go dancin' with Johansson.' . . . So we put him in there, and he hit the shit out of Johansson. He made him look like an ass. Johansson had two left feet. Now Johansson's getting pretty pissed off. He had a pretty good right hand if he could ever hit you. But he was missing Ali by a foot! He was going crazy. And by the third round, Whitey says, 'We gotta stop this shit and get outta here.' We stopped the thing and I took Johansson back to Palm Beach with a new neurosis."

Conrad recalls that Bimstein was quite impressed with the young Ali. "My God, look at this guy," Bimstein said to Conrad. "Look at that jab on this guy!"

Conrad adds that Bimstein was also a good babysitter. "I had my kid down there. All I had to do was give Whitey a bottle of scotch and a television and he took care of everything."

During the last few years of his life, Whitey Bimstein suffered from diabetes. Though the disease ultimately left him almost blind, he continued to work corners for as long as he was physically able. Lightweight contender Johnny Busso, who befriended Bimstein at Stillman's Gym remembers, "Whitey Bimstein, at the end he was blind. They just put him in the corner because he was an inspiration to a fighter.... He was like a folk hero. Like, 'Jesus, there's Whitey Bimstein.'"

Bimstein spent his final years at the Kingsbridge Veteran's Hospital in the Bronx. Interviewed at the hospital in 1966 by Leonard Lewin of the *New York Post*, Bimstein remained optimistic even though his left leg had been amputated. "Don't worry about me. I'm going to be all right. Another ten days they are going to fit me with one of those [artificial] legs and a month from now I'll be walking around." Eventually, Bimstein underwent another amputation. Asked how he and the other veterans at the hospital passed their time, Bimstein replied, "We all sit here and lie like hell."

Michael Shapiro, who visited his grandfather at the hospital almost every day after school, recalls that Bimstein staged several "escapes," sneaking out to visit old friends or to make an appearance at a New York gym.

Bimstein's daughter Adele recalls the time her father made an entrance at a dinner held in his honor shortly before his death in 1969. "He was sort of kept outside until they were ready to bring him in," she says. "And when they were ready to bring him in they flashed on some lights and played a little music. And he had been walking with two canes, and he had just learned to walk on two artificial legs. And as soon as the door opened and he came in, he took the canes, he raised them from the floor, and he walked with his hands up to show how strong he was as he came into the room. I thought that that was a very great accomplishment. He just wanted to show that he was in great shape."

MANNIE SEAMON

After Jack Blackburn died in 1942, it didn't take Joe Louis long to fill one of the most coveted jobs in boxing: The heavyweight champion chose Mannie Seamon as his new trainer.

Seamon had been Blackburn's assistant since 1937 and was superbly qualified for the assignment. He had been Benny Leonard's trainer while Leonard held the lightweight title from 1917 through 1925. Over the years, Leonard bestowed praise upon Seamon with a generosity rarely equaled in relations between boxers and their trainers. "My success in the ring of recent years," Leonard stated in 1923, "is largely due to my trainer and pal, Mannie Seamon."

Seamon's association with Leonard, together with his work with early ring greats like Leach Cross, Benny Valgar and Ted "Kid" Lewis, made Seamon one of the founding fathers of modern boxing. Seamon also managed fighters early in his career, and in 1932 trained future heavyweight champion Primo Carnera.

Yet in recent years, Seamon, who died in 1983, has not received the recognition he deserves. His achievements as trainer

MANNIE SEAMON AND JOE LOUIS PHOTO COURTESY FAE SEAMON

for Leonard and Louis alone qualify him for ring immortality. No trainer has ever worked with greater fighters. And as a corner man, repository of boxing wisdom and raconteur, Seamon was at least the equal of any of his colleagues.

Jack Blackburn hired Seamon as an assistant trainer in July of 1937, before Joe Louis' defense against Welshman Tommy Farr. At the time, Seamon and Blackburn had been friends for twenty years. Seamon's assignment was to hire and care for Louis' sparring partners—a task he performed to some acclaim.

Frank Graham, columnist for *The Journal American*, described Seamon as "dark-haired, round-faced, pink-cheeked and smiling," adding that he was "a cheerful figure in any fight camp" who "never has failed to take a man into the ring in his best condition, physically and mentally."

Graham, who devoted many columns to Seamon, wrote that before Seamon was brought in by Blackburn, "Joe's sparring partners, with the exception of George Nicholson, were hapless wretches who, totally unable to defend themselves, simply hired their brains out for beating purposes." Nicholson, the man who sparred more rounds with Louis than anyone else, eventually became Seamon's assistant along with Larry Amadee.

Graham wasn't the only writer to praise Seamon's work with Louis' sparring partners. Before Louis' bout with Tommy Farr, *The New York Sun* reported: "The pushovers he employed formerly as sparring partners are missing from Louis's camp this time . . . partly because of Mannie Seamon, who was hired to get spar mates for Joe and oversee them. . . . Seamon thinks the way to prepare for a fight is to fight."

Seamon also acted as a strict trainer for the sparring partners, making sure they adhered to the regimen followed by Louis himself. "Every man who wants to hold his place on the Louis sparring staff will have to go on the road with Joe and spar with others of the staff on days they are not working with the champion," Seamon told *The New York Sun* before the Farr fight. "Sparring partners are being paid good money here, and we have no place for those who are out of condition. Joe wants real work, which he can't get by knocking over slow-motion picture boys."

Asked about a sparring partner who received a beating from Louis after he'd knocked the champion down, Seamon said, "That's what he is in there for, to take a smacking around, if Louis feels that way. I tell these fellows when I hire them that they've got to go in there and expect to fight. They get twenty-five bucks a day for it, and if they don't want to go in and fight for that or take a pasting for it, I can get somebody else. Up to now, no one has squawked, and I think Joe has never had better men to work with since he started fighting."

Describing Seamon's role as Blackburn's assistant, Freddie Guinyard, Louis' boyhood friend who later became the champion's personal secretary, recalls: "Mannie Seamon would stand back. He was smart enough to stand back and let Jack Blackburn do the training. Then he would come up and say, 'Mr. Blackburn, don't you think you should try to make him do it this way?' He [Seamon] was a very smart person."

By the time he succeeded Blackburn, Seamon had already proven his worth as a corner man during Louis' sternest task—his 1941 bout with Billy Conn.

Seamon told Lester Bromberg of *The New York World-Telegram* that when Conn was hurting Louis in the twelfth round of that fight, Blackburn said to Seamon, "Maybe he needs a new voice in the corner, you talk to him this time." Seamon recreated his words to Louis this way: "Here's what I told Louis, 'Joe, you're laying down. Dig in there. The title is worth five million bucks to you.' When he heard that five million his ears pricked up. When the bell rang, I pushed him out and yelled: 'Now jump all over him.'"

After Louis knocked Conn down in the following round, Seamon, employing an ancient corner man's trick, climbed onto the ring apron and—in an attempt to discourage Conn from continuing to fight—shouted, "Stay down! Stay down!"

Seamon's version of his role in the first Louis-Conn fight was confirmed by Louis. In a series of articles in *The New York Times*—prepared by Louis in 1948 with the help of Meyer Berger and Barney Nagler—Louis stated: "He [Blackburn] let him [Seamon] do some talking to me in the first Billy Conn fight in 1941. Some trainers are stubborn and want to dictate even when they know they got things figured wrong, but not Chappie [Blackburn]. . . . When Billy was still there with me in the twelfth, Chappie and Mannie Seamon said, 'You got to knock this guy out. You're losing on points.'"

In later years, Seamon dissented from the widely held view that Conn would have defeated Louis if he hadn't gotten too cocky and tried for a knockout: "Most people think Conn got careless in the thirteenth round after he nailed Joe in the twelfth. That just isn't so. Billy fought a great and exceptionally smart fight. He wasn't careless. He was standing and slugging with Joe because that was all he could do. He had been hit around the middle so often and so hard that his legs just wouldn't move him. He could not dance any more and he got tagged. That's all."

Seamon was first called upon to act as Louis' trainer and chief second when Blackburn fell ill before Louis' 1942 defense against Abe Simon, whom Louis had knocked out in thirteen rounds a year before. Louis, then a private in the United States Army, prepared for the fight at Fort Dix, New Jersey, which Seamon pronounced an ideal locale for training a boxer.

The fight didn't seem to present much of a challenge for Louis, who was then at the height of his powers. Still, Seamon, acting as Blackburn's substitute, was under pressure to make sure all went well.

Walking down the aisle at Madison Square Garden before the fight, Seamon felt Louis punching him lightly on the back. When Seamon asked Louis what he was doing, Louis said, "I always did that to Chappie, Mannie." "Okay, Joe," Seamon replied. "Then go right ahead and keep doing it." Once the fight began, Louis was clearly in control. He had Simon down in the second round, though he may have become over-anxious in the third in an effort to make Blackburn's prediction of a third round knockout come true. Press reports described Louis as looking uncharacteristically amateurish in that round.

After Simon was again down in the fifth, Seamon told Louis in his corner, "Time's come! Go out and destroy him, Joe. He's finished and there's no sense hanging around here any longer. Last round, Joe. Make it short and sweet. . . . Go out and nail him! Don't let him get away!" Louis went on to score a sixth-round knockout.

After the fight, Seamon told the press: "Joe was overanxious and when he began to miss a lot I had to steady him. He'll do anything you tell him in the corner. After he dumped Abe for six at the end of the fifth, I knew it was time for the big push. The bell had saved Abe and I knew he'd come out pretty foggy."

How did he speak to Louis in the corner? "You've got to talk directly to a fighter," Seamon told reporters. "No, 'please do this, and please do that.' I told Louis after the third round, 'Joe you're wild. Settle down. Shorten up your punches. Walk right in and belt this guy.' He looked at me and said, 'Okay, Mannie.' After that it was easy."

For his part, Louis graciously praised Seamon. "I sure did quite a bit of missing in spots," Louis said, "Mannie Seamon, who was pinch-hitting for Jack Blackburn, deserves a lot of credit for steadying me when I went a bit haywire in the fourth. Mannie pointed out how I was over-anxious, and I was to let Abe come to me, but not let him crowd me to the ropes . . . Mannie slowed me down. He was right. My kind of fight was wrong. He done a great job. I was missin' too many punches tryin' to hurry the thing along too much."

Writing in *The Brooklyn Eagle*, Harold Conrad concluded, "the absence of Jack Blackburn, Joe's trainer, didn't seem to bother Joe."

Shortly after the Simon fight, Seamon received the following
note from Blackburn, who was looking forward to returning to
Louis' side for his next fight—a proposed rematch with Conn:

Hello, Mannie.

You surely did a fine job and I want to thank you
for the clippings you sent me. I had a bad time. But I
am glad to say I am on the way up again and doing all
I can to be able to make camp about May 20, then we
can talk it all over again. Mannie did you order
sparring partners gloves let me know in advance.

Hoping to see you soon,

From your Pal,
Chappie Blackburn

When Blackburn died in April of 1942, Joe Louis was given
leave from the Army to attend the funeral in Chicago. "After
the funeral, Joe asked me to hang around Chicago and meet him
that night at a night club I think he had an interest in," Seamon
recalled in a 1963 article in the *Police Gazette*. "I went to the
club and found Joe sitting at a table with his manager, John
Roxborough. Joe took me to an office in the back of the club
and told me he wanted me to take over as his head trainer."

According to Lester Bromberg of the *World-Telegram*, Seamon
was Blackburn's "personal choice" to be his successor as Louis'
trainer. Bromberg reported that Blackburn had known Seamon
since Seamon's days with Benny Leonard. Leonard's faith in
Seamon apparently impressed Blackburn who, Bromberg wrote,
"knew Benny and trusted him."

In 1948, Seamon—with the help of writer Harold Mayes—
prepared a series of autobiographical articles for the British
newspaper the *Sunday Empire News*. In one of the pieces, Seamon recalled that after Louis assured him he was the new
trainer, newspapers reported that someone else had been

chosen for the job. When Seamon approached Louis, the champion said, "I told you you have the job. The only man who can fix the job is me. Go home and forget the papers—they'll be mad at the fellow who gave them that bad story."

Seamon later recalled, "I felt honored that a Negro champion had chosen a white man to be his trainer. I finally achieved the thing I wanted—the greatest heavyweight that ever lived." In the *Empire News*, Seamon put it this way: "I was on top of the world. . . . And so I became trainer—aye, almost a father and mother—to the man who had placed his faith in me." Describing his love for working with Louis to Frank Graham, Seamon once said, "This is as nice a job as a guy ever had. I take money for it only because my family has to eat."

In September of 1942, a rematch with Billy Conn was announced, but never came off, and Louis spent the rest of the war touring bases and putting on exhibitions for soldiers in America and Europe. As for Seamon, he stored Louis' boxing paraphernalia in his New York apartment, and took a job with the New York Racing Association. When boxing writer Barney Nagler saw Seamon working behind a betting window at the Aqueduct race track on Long Island, he asked Seamon how he liked the work. "It's a job," Seamon replied.

While on tour in England, Louis sent the following note to Seamon. Louis' "Uncle Mike" was his promoter Mike Jacobs.

> Dear Mannie:
> Your boy is having a good time here in England really enjoying the work I was sent here to do—they are keeping me busy as hell but I love it. The boys' spirit here is just about the same as yours when I deliver one of those knock-out punches. Tell Uncle Mike I said I am in the best of health an [sic] when I return I will be in condition to defend my title knowing that I will not do so until after this Really Big

Fight is over with. Well, Mannie, drop a line an [sic] I
will be writing to you again.

After Louis was discharged from the army in 1945 and the Conn
rematch was set, Seamon and Louis met to discuss his conditioning program. Louis was thirty-two years old and hadn't had
a title fight in three years. Seamon told Frank Graham, "I felt
him out a couple of times, trying to see if he was tired of
training and wanted to put it off as long as possible but instead
of that he was as enthusiastic as a kid. He wasn't kidding me
either. I been around fighters long enough to know when they
are trying to kid me and I knew he was on the level. Well, that's
the way he's always been about everything, isn't it?"

The publicity build-up for the Louis-Conn rematch befitted
its status as what *The New York Enquirer* called the "biggest
sports event of the post-war era." Countless newspaper stories
detailed how Louis worked himself back into shape. Seamon's
motto for the enterprise was, "One thing at a time." The first
step was overall conditioning. When Louis began training, his
weight was 235, though it was publicly disclosed as 224. Marshall Miles, who took over as Louis' manager in 1944, recalls
that during the war, Louis "picked up a lot of weight" and had to
"take off an awful lot of poundage" before meeting Conn. To get
Louis down to his fighting weight of 208 pounds, Seamon took
the champion to a health resort in West Baden Springs, Indiana
for a regimen of roadwork, sulphur baths and steam cabinets.

In an interview with *The Boston American*, Seamon explained his idiosyncratic weight reduction program: "I realized
there was a great deal of inside fat clinging to Louis' bones. This
would slow him down and possibly cause his defeat if it were
not removed. I decided that sulphur baths would help. They
would loosen his inside fat and enable Joe to get rid of it. There
were also the steam baths which helped to get the champion
into condition.

"Each morning Joe went out on the road for a few miles. The

soles of his feet got sore, and I rubbed them for hours as I did Joe's ankles and legs. One day I asked the 'Brown Bomber' if he wished to wear a heavy rubber coat and rubber pants while doing road work. I felt this would aid him in his task of taking off weight. 'The sulphur baths and the hours in the steam cabinet are doing the job,' replied Joe. 'I will not need the rubber coat and pants.'"

As Louis lost weight, Seamon saw the champion's confidence return. Still, when Louis moved to Pompton Lakes, New Jersey to focus on boxing, trainer and fighter were uncertain of how many of Louis' boxing skills remained intact. "The only thing we were sure about all along was that Joe had his old punch," Seamon later confessed. Together, though, Louis and Seamon focused on taking small steps. Louis, Seamon said, would "work a whole day or two days trying to do just one thing. He'd concentrate so hard, he'd look bad doing other things."

To many of the reporters covering Louis' workouts, however, Louis looked rusty and slow in sparring sessions, and stories abounded that he could not regain his former glory. When some reported that Conn looked good in training, Louis' response was a classic example of his terse yet expressive style: "Conn's training for the newspapermen. I'm training for a knockout."

Seamon, a quotable man who was nearly as gifted a publicist as he was a trainer, answered Louis' critics more expansively. "Actually Louis was at his worst for the last Conn fight," Seamon explained. "He'd had six fights in six months just before that and was in no shape at all. He was too fine because he had had no rest and no recreation."

When former champions Jack Dempsey and Gene Tunney criticized Louis in the press, Seamon wasn't shy about taking them both on. "People who don't know shouldn't talk," Seamon said. "Why, being in the Army, Louis stayed in shape better than any idle champion in all history." Responding to Dempsey's comparison between himself and Louis, Seamon said, "How can Dempsey compare himself before his first Tunney fight with

Louis right now? Jack hadn't been living the way Louis has. If you want to know what I honestly think, I think the boys are a little jealous deep inside. They're only human and the idea of the Conn fight . . . doing better than their gate at Chicago has hurt their feelings." Seamon added that Louis was in "the best condition of any fighter that ever laid off four years—Jack Dempsey, when he fought Gene Tunney the first time . . . Jim Jeffries . . . any of them."

To add to his case, Seamon told reporters that Louis had been studying films of his 1941 bout with Conn. "There are things Joe knows about Conn that Conn doesn't know about himself," Seamon boasted. "We talk it over often. The things he's observed about that guy from the movies are amazing. . . . One day he laid out his tactics and—honest!—it's like a guy playing checkers. He talks about a whole series of moves."

Writers filing stories from Louis' camp naturally compared Seamon to Blackburn. "Seamon never can be to Louis as Blackburn was—nor can anyone else," wrote Frank Graham. "Nor is his position exactly comparable to Blackburn's. Jack was the boss and gave the orders and Joe obeyed them. . . . Joe has matured since then and no longer needs anyone to tell him when to run, when and how to box—and when to stop. . . . But just as he was wise enough to obey Blackburn, so he is wise enough to consult with Seamon, to ask his advice and to follow it when it is given. They work together smoothly along lines they have mapped out together and it is Seamon's job to watch him, check him, speed him up, slow him down and be sure at all times that he is comfortable and free of annoyance."

Comparing Seamon and Blackburn, Louis' former co-manager Marshall Miles says "He [Seamon] was sincere. He was crazy about Joe Louis. He would have done anything for Joe. . . . Joe had a lot of respect for Mannie and Mannie had a lot of respect for him. It worked both ways. . . . As far as the boxing part of it, Blackburn had gone through all that. And Mannie's job was really to see that he [Louis] got in shape—and the boxing, too. Mannie was a good one. . . . I could trust him."

Asked if the Louis camp was any different under Seamon than it had been under Blackburn, Freddie Guinyard says, "Mannie Seamon followed the same lines that Jack Blackburn did. He wasn't a stranger there. . . . He knew everything. He had been there five or six years in the training camp, so he knew. He just stepped in and pushed the wagon a little harder."

In an interview in the New York newspaper *PM*, Seamon evoked Blackburn when modestly assessing his own role in Louis' camp. "Blackburn once told me that no trainer makes a fighter," Seamon said. "The fighter must have it himself. All a trainer can give him is a bit of polish. Training a fighter is just like caring for a child. You've got to watch him all the time and make sure he doesn't overdo things or neglect them, either. If you see him doing something wrong, you tell him. If he's a smart fighter, like a smart child, he'll respond. If he hasn't got it, the best trainer in the world can't help him."

If Seamon was self-effacing in discussing himself, he was proud and confident when describing the precision with which he and Louis planned for the Conn fight. Days before the bout he told the press: "Joe will be ready next Wednesday night. Don't let any of these training exhibitions fool you. If Joe appeared slow or sluggish, he knew what he was doing at all times. Our whole training campaign has been worked out to the smallest detail."

To explain Louis' approach to his return to the ring, Seamon offered an elaborate analogy: "Here at Pompton Lakes it has been work and more work. Joe has been preparing himself much as a painter paints a house. Slowly, but surely he develops his strokes and gets a nice coat all over the house. . . . You wouldn't expect a painter to put one coat of paint on the house, then smear the house up so he would have to redecorate the house. Well, the same applies to Joe. He is coming into shape gradually, so that he reaches his peak the last day. We don't want him at peak form a week too soon and then have him go stale. . . . Don't worry about his shape. That is my job and I am not worrying at all. . . . Billy Conn probably thinks he will set a pace too hot for the champ to maintain. Well, Mr. Conn is in for a surprise. Joe will travel at Billy's speed and come up the winner."

Asked about Louis' apparent affection for Conn, Seamon said, "Sure he respects Conn but he also respects the heavyweight championship of the world. That's a $10,000,000 championship these days. He wants to keep that and he'll be as tough and as vicious as he has to be. . . . If that Conn makes one mistake Joe will nail him." Told that Conn's trainer/manager Johnny Ray had said Louis couldn't punch, Seamon responded facetiously, "I wasn't looking at the finish of the last fight. Who knocked Conn out—the referee?"

What Seamon didn't tell skeptical reporters was that Louis was sparring on a ring canvas that was three-quarters of an inch thicker than normal ring flooring. This was a ploy that Seamon used throughout Louis' later career. His theory was that if Louis trained on a thick—and therefore slow—canvas, he would be much speedier on fight night when stepping on thinner canvas.

Seamon also later confessed that he and Louis had "propagandized Conn" during the prefight build-up. "We agreed that Joe should talk about a quick knockout and worry Billy into thinking along defensive lines."

Seamon expanded on the psychological warfare in one of the articles he prepared for the *Sunday Empire News*. "During the training period, Joe had told the newspapermen that he was going out to 'kill' Conn, to make it another Schmeling fight," Seamon explained. "Conn heeded that, and his camp fell for the ruse. I know, because I had someone watching his training. That's something I always do. I don't always use the same man, so no one knows who it is. In training, Conn was backing up, working on the assumption that Joe was out for the kill."

Contrary to public statements, however, Seamon recalled, "I

had Joe training to box, not to go for a quick knockout. That gummed up Billy's whole works, and as soon as he went into the ring it knocked his plans and more important still, his morale, all to pieces."

Also unreported in the papers at the time was that Louis was suffering from pain in his elbows and nearly had to postpone the fight. This is revealed in notes Seamon made as an outline for an autobiography which was never completed. "How I saved the second Conn fight from being called off," Seamon wrote as a heading in his notes. "Both of Louis' elbows bothered him from playing golf or a case of arthritis. Used special methods of heat mixture every evening for hours."

While confident of victory, Seamon was also honest in his press statements when comparing the thirty-two-year-old Louis to his former self: "Nobody can expect him to be quite the fighter he was when he polished off Schmeling in their second fight, but I'll go on record that he'll be ninety percent of the best Louis you ever saw. And that will be more than enough."

Four days before the fight, Seamon again felt compelled to respond to the bad press Louis had been receiving. "The trouble with all that stuff is that they don't know what I know or what Joe knows, either," he told W. C. Heinz of the *Sun*, a sympathetic columnist. "There's nobody knows Joe Louis like Joe Louis knows himself, and they don't see the things that I've been seeing in the last few days that let me know that on Wednesday night Joe Louis will be the way he wants to be, which is right.

"In the last half dozen workouts I have seen him do certain things for the first time, things that he hasn't tried to do before and that nobody else notices because they aren't looking for them the way I am. Then I notice him do something for a minute or so when he's punching the bag, and I know what that means, too."

Recalling the build-up to the second Louis-Conn fight, Louis' co-manager Marshall Miles says that the Louis camp had heard that Conn "looked terrible" in training camp and "was over-weight." Asked if he was confident going into the fight, Miles says, "I wasn't concerned at all."

The pressure on Louis and Seamon, however, was enormous. Five thousand spectators came to Louis' camp to watch his final prefight workout. Despite his bravado, Seamon was concerned about Louis' performance. When W. C. Heinz asked Seamon why he didn't seem more relaxed, Seamon replied, "You're right. That's what my wife says. She says, 'You've trained good fighters before. What are you worrying about?' You know, I don't know why, but I am excited and I've gotta lot to do."

Seamon's attention to detail extended to every aspect of prefight preparation. In notes for his autobiography, Seamon wrote that he talked to one of Louis' managers, John Roxborough, about padding the ring for Louis' two fights with Conn. A thickly padded ring canvas, Seamon reasoned, would slow down and eventually tire the quick-moving Conn. Another small advantage was making sure Louis arrived late to the weigh-in for the second Conn fight. Seamon's notes read: "Came thirty [minutes] late. Photographers and newspaper had Conn all upset by time we got there."

The second Louis-Conn fight proved to be a profound disappointment. In *The New York Times*, Arthur Daley wrote: "If the Louis-Conn engagement had been an ordinary main event in the Garden the customers would have booed it out of the arena. . . . No one can blame Louis for it. He was willing to fight."

In one of his *Sunday Empire News* articles, Seamon recalled that after dominating Conn in the seventh round, Louis said in the corner, "I'm going to go out and let him have it this round and see if he can take it." Sensing that Conn was a shell of his former self, Seamon replied, "Okay with me, Joe." The result was an eighth-round knockout. After the fight, Seamon proudly told the press, "It's like I told you guys. I never lie. I told you we knew what we were doin'."

Describing Louis' tactics, Seamon said, "We decided use of a left jab would confuse Conn, who would be expecting Joe to rush out and try for an early finish. Jabbing also would knock some of the confidence out of Conn, because Louis' jabs have power behind them. The idea then was to connect with a right-hand shot at the first opportunity, and that is exactly what Joe did. Louis was in great shape, and he never was hurt during the bout."

Seamon also gleefully described the impact of Louis' performance on Conn: "With his best bet, his left, trumped, Billy didn't know what to do except run. Finding himself outboxed, Billy was confused and panicky and it was easy to work on his body and dress 'im up for the kill after that." Recreating the end of the bout, Seamon said, "Joe's overhand right to the jaw and a left hook to the jaw settled things for good in the eighth round. It was a long grind from the sulphur baths and steam baths at West Baden to the eighth round of the Conn bout at the Yankee Stadium, but the payoff wallops were good to see."

Louis, as was his habit, praised Seamon. "Mannie Seamon was just as smart as old Jack Blackburn in handling me for the fight. My trainer put me in the best condition of my career for this fight. . . . That training siege of mine surely paid off, and when I fight again it won't be hard to get in this good shape I'm in right now. That was tough, but I knew I could make it."

Mannie Seamon had clearly proven himself a worthy successor to the great Jack Blackburn.

Newspaper columnists often referred fondly to Joe Louis' trainer as a "long-time Harlemite," and Harlem is where Mannie Seamon got his start in boxing.

He was born Mandel Simenovitch in Chicago on August 15, 1897. The Simenovitch family came to America from Minsk, where Seamon's father had been a cabinetmaker. In Russia, one of his uncles, Aaron Simenovitch, was secretary and confidant to Rasputin—and a court jeweler to the Czar. In 1905, the Simenovitch family moved to 159 East 113th Street in Harlem.

Mannie Seamon was one of eight children in what his daughter Fae describes as a "very poor family." They went on home relief after Mannie Seamon's father contracted malaria in Panama while working as a laborer, helping to dig the Panama Canal. The father was never again healthy enough to work full time.

As a child, young Mannie and older brother Ben loved all sports, particularly baseball, which they played for the "House of David" team which was sponsored by a local synagogue.

While a student at P.S. 83 on 110th Street and Second Avenue, Seamon, as he once put it, "seemed to have an excess of physical energy"—a trait which produced "constant fistic clashes with . . . fellow students." When he got into a fight with a weaker boy who knew a bit about boxing, Mannie learned the hard way that skill can overcome strength during a fight. It was then that he decided to make "an exhaustive study" of boxing techniques.

In 1912, Seamon's new-found fascination brought him to the New West Side Gym on 54th Street between Eighth and Ninth Avenues in Manhattan. Later, when Billy Grupp opened his famous gym in a former dance hall on West 116th Street in Harlem in 1915, Mannie and his brother Ben began to hang out there, boxing and watching the celebrated fighters of the era at work with their trainers. While swapping stories with Frank Graham, Seamon once recalled the time Billy Grupp, himself a fighter, returned to the gym from a bout with a cut above his eye. Seamon watched as Grupp threaded a needle with cat gut, stood in front of a mirror and sewed up the wound. "I never saw anything like it," Seamon confessed.

Seamon, whose formal education ended in grade school, got an early start as a trainer. "I was rubbing Leach when I was 16," he once recalled, referring to celebrated Jewish lightweight Leach Cross. Cross, who practiced dentistry while pursuing his ring career, was known—not surprisingly—as "The Fighting Dentist." Cross was the boyhood idol of Benny Leonard who, in imitation of his hero, began to spar with his young friends.

Seamon was fond of describing his own short-lived career as a fighter by saying, "After two fights I decided that training and not boxing was my line." Seamon fought his first professional bout against Benny Valgar, the famous lightweight he was training at the time. When Valgar's opponent failed to show up for a fight in Long Branch, New Jersey, the matchmaker persuaded Seamon to go up against Valgar. Seamon adopted the ring name Frankie Wilson for the occasion.

"I make no secret of the fact that I didn't want to fight Benny," Seamon recalled in the *Sunday Empire News*. "You see, I was his trainer and knew what he could do. . . . I said to Benny: 'You know I can't fight, and I know I can't go more than a couple of rounds.' After Valgar jabbed away at Seamon for a round, the crowd cried out for blood, and Valgar moved in for the kill. "They told me afterwards that Jack Dempsey, who was at ringside, was laughing his head off," Seamon remembered. ". . . In the second round the towel was thrown in four or five times, but each time the referee threw it out. Then he got tired of counting up to eight and nine, time after time, and he stopped the fight." Seamon received eighteen dollars for his efforts.

The next time Seamon reluctantly stepped into the ring as a combatant, he was counted out. "As a result of that night," he stated, "when I see a fighter is knocked out, my heart goes with him, for I was hit so hard that I landed in the laps of the newspapermen. They carried me to the dressing room, and when I came out of my punch-sleep I announced my retirement."

Recalling the knockout on another occasion, Seamon said, "the ref gave me a count . . . that sounded like thirty, not ten. You can catch a cold on that floor. It's drafty and there are no blankets. That was enough for me. I became a trainer."

In his early days as a trainer, Seamon was not above stretching the rules to gain an advantage for his fighter. He once secretly cut one of the ring ropes to save a fighter who was about to be knocked out. "Newspapermen jumped into the ring, and me with them," Seamon recalled. "It took a full half hour to fix the rope and in that time, I had my fighter on his feet and raring to go."

When Seamon's bantamweight, Archie Bell, suffered a bad eye cut, Seamon put a gash in one of Bell's gloves. Spotting the damage, the referee ordered the gloves to be changed. This ploy—later adopted by Angelo Dundee, among others—gave Seamon ten minutes to work on his fighter's battered eye.

When making notes for his autobiography, Seamon listed a few less orthodox tricks of the trade, including putting a skunk in the opponent's training quarters and blowing a horn all night near where the opponent was sleeping. Another item on his list simply read, "itching powder."

While still a young man, Seamon trained several world champions, including bantamweight Johnny Ertle, junior lightweight Tod Morgan and middleweight Johnny Wilson. Another of Seamon's champions, Englishman Ted "Kid" Lewis, always remained one of his favorites. Lewis twice held the welterweight title—from 1915 to 1916 and from 1917 to 1919. Already the British featherweight champion when he came to America in 1914, Lewis fought a celebrated series of bouts with welterweight champion Jack Britton. *The Jewish Boxer's Hall of Fame* reports that Lewis served as heavyweight champion Jack Johnson's sparring partner while Johnson was preparing to fight Jess Willard, but was soon dismissed when he gave Johnson too much trouble.

Seamon paid tribute to Lewis in one of his pieces for the *Sunday Empire News*. "He met the best men at three weights—light, welter and middle—licked a lot of them and was never disgraced against the others," Seamon recalled. And one of Lewis' greatest gifts was his ability to "go up and down the scale and make all sorts of weights."

Seamon reported that Lewis "used to train as hard as anyone I've ever handled and to get down to a weight used to wear a tight-fitting rubber suit on the road every other day." The rubber suit had "no ventilation holes," however, and after work-outs, Lewis "would be bathed in perspiration." About the suit Seamon said, "I always had my doubts as to its effect on his general health."

Seamon concluded his homage to Lewis this way: "My firm conviction is that he was the best all-around fighter Europe sent to America in my lifetime. . . . He was one of the few men I have seen who could deliver a knock-out blow as he was back-ing away. . . . And what's more, bad hands never meant a thing to him. Never a squeal that he didn't want to go on. If one hand was damaged he would say: 'Mannie, I can take care of him with one hand'—and if both of them hurt him it was just the same. Because he knew that, provided you can punch, you can always hurt an opponent's body even with bad hands. The body gives a cushioning effect to soften the jolt. . . . He won by letting his opponents fight their own way and doing it just a little better than they did, and if anyone hurt him he never showed it."

The highlight of Seamon's early career came when he served as trainer for the great Benny Leonard during seven of Leonard's eight championship years from 1917 through 1925. Though Leonard had previously been handled by trainers George Engel and Doc Robb, Seamon was the trainer during Leonard's glory years. Also in the corner with Seamon were Leonard's brother Charlie and his manager, Billy Gibson.

Seamon always stressed that Leonard's success as a boxer resulted from his intellectual mastery of ring strategy. In an interview in the 1930s, Seamon said: "Benny often went to the gym even when he was not training. Because boxing was his life. He said he discovered new moves and tricks by watching other boxers work out. He was a thorough student of boxing."

Though Leonard is renowned for possessing punching power and ring smarts, Seamon described the early Leonard as a physically frail fighter—an observation that makes Leonard's later feats all the more impressive.

Summing up young Leonard in the *Sunday Empire News*, Seamon recalled, "Benny wasn't strong, and he knew it. He was easily hurt with good punches. In fact, he could be hurt a little more than the average fighter. That's what made him such a great boxer. He knew he had to be clever to keep out of trouble, and so he spent many hours learning to 'hide' and get away."

To compensate for his innate vulnerability, Leonard studied pugilism with exceptional devotion. He learned to change his style in the middle of a round, Seamon often pointed out, and was always thinking. "Leonard made the closest study of feinting of anyone I've ever dealt with, and I regarded him as the master mind of boxing," Seamon recalled in 1948. "When fighters make a man miss today, they move back—off balance. Not so Mister Leonard. He would sidestep and then move on quickly with a punch hard enough to knock his opponent's brains out. And that was something, for there's no doubt that of all the fighters I've ever had he was the frailest in physique."

Seamon revealed in a 1970 article in *The Ring* that although Leonard was "the greatest lightweight the game has seen," Leonard's brother, Charley, was actually more talented, although he had a profound aversion to training. "Charley could hit harder than Benny," Seamon recalled, but Charley would do anything to avoid hard work: "Oh, the dodges he went through. He would go out on the road, hide, stay out an hour, throw water on himself and come in panting, with fake perspiration."

Despite Charley Leonard's lack of diligence, he and brother Benny had many heated sparring sessions in the gym—sessions which Seamon believed were extremely important in forging Benny Leonard's ring toughness. Charley was "a very good puncher," Seamon recalled in the *Sunday Empire News*, ". . . and when the two of them got going in the gym there were no half-measures—it was a real fight every time. They just looked as if they were going to kill each other. Benny just had to stand there and punch because otherwise Charley would have said when he jabbed: 'You hit me and ran.'"

Seamon added that, early in Leonard's career, "clever as he was, Benny wasn't a great hitter." Describing his efforts to build Leonard's power, Seamon stated: "I worked on him for months trying to correct all the little things which make the difference, and then one day it came to him in a flash. It was a matter of hitting properly. His well-directed punches at one time wouldn't have cracked an egg—and then, as a result of all his gym work, suddenly without warning, he started hitting like a sledgehammer. It was just a matter of acquiring the knack . . . and once he'd got it, he never lost it."

Like all good trainers Seamon didn't try to impose uncomfortable changes on Leonard. "Had I tried to alter his style to cause him to find that punch," Seamon wrote, "it might never have worked. But it came, and I was happy."

Seamon also described a rather unusual training technique which Leonard employed to hone his celebrated defense: "He was a fast boxer, and so to keep up his speed I used to put two boys in the ring with him together. He either jabbed one and watched for the other, or feinted one and jabbed the other. If one missed him, as they often did, he knew he could take care of the other."

Elsewhere, Seamon revealed one of the reasons why Leonard worked so hard on defense—he was a good son: "His mother, who was a long-time invalid, did not want him to fight and feared that he would get hurt. Benny saw to it that he did not come home bearing marks of contest."

In an article prepared for *New Physical Culture* magazine in 1949, Seamon called Leonard "the perfect physical culturist," and told how he and Leonard stumbled upon the idea that a boxer should pay attention to what he eats. After Leonard's early fights, the boxer's fans would return to Leonard's mother's house for "a feast of stuff from the delicatessen shop." At one of these celebrations, Leonard consumed "a few sandwiches and pickles, a couple of hot dogs or so, and a few bottles of cream soda." Leonard got sick and Seamon took him to a doctor who, upon discovering what Leonard had eaten, told Seamon, "I thought you were a trainer! And you let him get away with stuff like that? His diet is as important a part of his training as his boxing." Seamon then for the first time began thinking about a fighter's diet—a process that resulted in new rules for Leonard, beginning with, "No more eating at 'celebrations.'"

In an interview from the mid-1930s, following Leonard's retirement, Seamon doted like a good Jewish mother on the excellence of the former champion's eating habits. "Leonard knew more about training, I believe, than any trainer," Seamon said. "Leonard was almost always making weight. He had the ability to get as much satisfaction out of a light meal as others would from a heavy meal. Benny would sit down to a dinner of one lamb chop, half a head of lettuce, half a grapefruit, a cup of tea with lemon and two slices of dry toast and get as much satisfaction out of it as another would from twice as much food. He could cut his food into very small bites and chew each small portion thoroughly. He would take twice as long eating the meal I have outlined as the ordinary fighter would in bolting twice as much. Many a fighter kids himself by working hard in the afternoon and then nullifying all his labors by taking on a heavy dinner."

All of Seamon's hard work on Leonard's behalf by no means went unnoticed. Seamon's scrapbook contains several yellowing newspaper stories celebrating Leonard's superb regimen and the young trainer who supervised it.

The earliest of these pieces is a tribute—torn from an unidentified newspaper—to Seamon's role in Leonard's victory over former champion Willie Ritchie in a nontitle bout on April 28, 1919 in Newark, New Jersey. In February of the same year, Ritchie had faced Leonard in a four-round, nontitle bout in San

Francisco. While no official decision was rendered, a majority of newspaper reporters at ringside gave the nod to Ritchie. Leonard won the rematch with an eighth-round knockout—the first time Ritchie had been stopped since his first professional fight in 1907. The following day the newspaper headline read, "Trainer Seamon Made It Possible for Leonard to Defeat Lad from Frisco."

In the article, Seamon, then twenty-two years old, is described as a "red-cheeked, good-natured, happy chap" who "made it possible for the champion to come back as strong as he did last night." To assure Leonard's victory, Seamon had "worked as no other trainer worked on a fighter." The article goes on to pay an extraordinary tribute to Seamon's role in Leonard's victory:

> And so when Mannie Seamon ages and looks back into the pages of pugilistic history, he will have every reason for feeling proud of what Leonard did last night, for it was Mannie who furnished the ambition and pep that enabled the champion to win. For days he boxed and rubbed the champion. Seamon's heart was in his work. He had made up his mind that Leonard would beat Ritchie, and he was doing all he could to put the title holder in a condition where he could have beaten any man his weight—and some heavier.
>
> It was Mannie who trained Benny for all his big fights in the East—and how Leonard must have missed him on the Coast. Seamon knows Benny and vice versa. They are boyhood pals, but Mannie could not spare the time or money to go to the Coast, so he had to stay back. But how Benny repented that he did not take him along, for had he done so he probably would have gone through the line of opponents in the West with lightning speed.
>
> It was Mannie who coached and urged and encour-

aged the champion last night. When things looked darkest, it was then that his smile came into play and made the champion feel like he was the biggest man in the world. Oh, yes, too much credit for last night's victory by Leonard cannot be given this trainer of trainers.

Another unidentified clipping from the same period reveals that in the seventh round of the Leonard-Ritchie fight, one of Ritchie's fans started taunting Seamon by shouting, "Where is Leonard's K.O. punch?" Seamon replied, "We'll show you in the next round"—and he was right. After Leonard scored an eighth-round knockout, the Ritchie fan left the fight "dumbfounded."

The regular routine of Seamon's work with Leonard was detailed in a 1923 *Evening World* article which described Seamon as "the youngest trainer in captivity"—a fellow whose "baby face belies his age" and who "practically grew up with modern fisticuffs."

Seamon, the paper reported, had "the last word in whatever goes on in the magnificent training camp of the champion." Each morning, Seamon awakened Leonard at seven a.m. for a cup of hot tea, followed—on alternate days—by four or five miles of roadwork. Afterward, Leonard took a hot bath and was given a forty-five-minute rubdown. Sparring took place at 2:30 in the afternoon, and was followed by another bath and a "corking rubdown for which Mannie has become famous." Seamon had studied massage at a New York hospital and was a licensed masseur.

"Leonard is never out of Seamon's sight," the report concluded. "He takes him for a stroll after dinner and sees to it that he is under the covers for a good night's sleep at nine o'clock.

"Mannie and Benny are just pals. They scheme out the plan of battle, and Seamon goes through with the signals like a football player. Nothing ever goes wrong. They work like a well-oiled machine."

Leonard himself is quoted as saying, "Seamon is a marvelous trainer, and I am forced to give him credit for my great showings in fights during the last three years. He is a tireless worker, knows his business from A to Z and most important of all he is a faithful pal."

Seamon and Leonard, despite their hard work, faced a fair share of close calls in the ring. Leonard's July 1922 fight with Lew Tendler proved to be surprisingly difficult—and it gave Leonard one of his worst scares and one of his finest moments in the ring. Going into the fight, Leonard was having difficulty making the lightweight limit, as he recalled for an article in the *World* in 1927: "I hurt myself . . . making weight for Lew Tendler in our first fight and I remember how weak I felt when, a few days before the fight, I was down to 131 pounds." Leonard went on to credit Seamon, though, for helping him recover his strength: "Little Mannie Seamon, my trainer, built me up in the next few days. Otherwise there would have been a new lightweight champion that night."

As it was, Leonard was almost knocked out after being momentarily paralyzed by one of Tendler's famous left hooks to the body. Leonard, however, in one of his best-known pieces of strategic improvisation, claimed that Tendler had thrown a low blow. In the few seconds that Tendler stopped fighting to argue with Leonard's allegation, Leonard was able to regain control of his body—and he managed to go the distance in the no-decision bout. Years later, when asked for the high point of Leonard's career, Seamon said, "Maybe the fight in which Lew Tendler appeared to have Benny in trouble, but was talked out of his advantage, was the highlight." Seamon also revealed that following the Tendler fight, Leonard had to pay a dentist's bill of $1,200.

The close call against Tendler inspired Leonard and Seamon to new heights of pugilistic scholarship, as Leonard himself recalled in a 1923 article for the *World* written after Leonard won a fifteen-round decision in a rematch with Tendler for the lightweight championship. The article was credited to Benny Leonard as dictated to a *World* staffer. "Mannie and I scheme out three or four days in advance my plan of battle," Leonard reported. "It will surprise you undoubtedly to know that four days before I fought Tendler in the Yankee Stadium I took Mannie, or better still, Mannie took me, behind closed doors. He enacted the role of Tendler, the Philadelphia southpaw, and I learned more about southpaws in the half hour or so that I spent with Mannie than during the whole months of training with a quartet of southpaws."

Leonard again expressed his gratitude to Seamon: "When I start training for a fight, my manager, Billy Gibson and myself give Mannie absolute charge. I can't wink my eye unless he says so—that's how much I am in his power. He watches me like a hawk in the ring and when the day's work is over, he takes me upstairs and points out my faults—and I have lots of them that bob up every now and then that need correcting. I'm not one of those boxers, even if I am a champion, who thinks he knows it all. I'm learning, and willing to learn all the time."

It's generally known that Benny Leonard, following the practice of champions of his day, often allowed nontitle bouts to go the distance, yielding a "no decision" result—and the opportunity for a lucrative title match in the future. When boxing writer Leonard Gardner asked Ray Arcel why so many of Leonard's no-decision bouts went the distance, Arcel responded, "He *had* to go easy! He couldn't get anybody to fight him if he didn't agree to carry them."

Arcel's observation is backed-up by notes that Seamon made for the memoir he never wrote. These notes included two pages in Seamon's handwriting listing some of Leonard's "business" fights.

About Leonard's 1919 meeting with Charlie Metrie in Detroit, for example, Seamon notes, "Gave his manager his word to carry Metrie, Metrie got fresh." The result was a Leonard knock-out in round seven. Seamon's notes also revealed that Leonard carried Phil Bloom in a ten-round bout in Detroit in October of 1919. Seamon described Leonard's November 1919 fight against Soldier Barfield by writing, "no fight unless Benny leaves punch home." The fight went the eight-round distance.

Yet it wasn't always easy for the great Leonard to carry his foes. Of Leonard's December 1919 second-round knockout of Mel Coogan, Seamon wrote, "was to carry Coogan." Apparently, Coogan wasn't easy to carry. About Leonard's 1920 third-round knockout of Johnny Sheppard in Paterson, New Jersey, Seamon notes, "Leonard tried to carry Sheppard . . . Benny['s] brothers bet he would finish the third." Once again, Leonard couldn't avoid a knockout even when he wanted to.

Seamon's notes also stated that Leonard held up Rocky Kansas in their June 1921 fight in Harrison, New Jersey. "Carried him for a title fight in New York," Seamon wrote of that bout, meaning, of course, that Leonard was setting up a lucrative championship bout. Of their meeting for the title in New York in February of 1922, Seamon wrote, Leonard "knocked Kansas down" and "had a tough time carrying him after that." Seamon's notes on that fight also stated, "won big bet carrying Kansas," though it's impossible to tell who won the bet. Of Leonard's eighth-round knockout of Rocky Kansas in July of 1922, Seamon wrote one word: "leveled."

The sight of Leonard boxing—even when not trying for a knockout—was a thing of beauty to Seamon. The trainer's comments on Leonard's ten-round bout with Jake Abel in December of 1919 read: "Leonard footwork . . . feinting . . . cleverness . . . ducking . . . so great to watch. Leonard never tried for K.O."

While it has been suggested that Leonard fought "business" fights with the great Johnny Dundee, Seamon denied this in an unidentified clipping included in his scrapbook. "Leonard always did his best against Dundee," Seamon said, "except for maybe the last two fights when Benny was slipping a little himself and was afraid to take any chances of trying for a knockout. When you are trying for a K.O. you are always open yourself, and Benny wasn't interested in taking those risks at that point in his career."

One of Leonard's most celebrated title defenses was his January 1920 sixth-round knockout of Richie Mitchell. Leonard went all-out for a knockout in the first round, sending Mitchell to the canvas three times. Incredibly, Mitchell fought back, and floored Leonard. In another famous piece of spontaneous defensive brilliance, Leonard gestured for Mitchell to come in and hit him again. Confused, Mitchell hesitated before charging—and Leonard had enough time to regain his composure.

Seamon's cryptic note on the Leonard-Mitchell fight reads, "30,000 to 1000 - 1 rd." Playing ring detective, it's possible to solve the enigma. A large clue is provided by Ray Arcel, who recalls one of Leonard's brothers placing a bet on Leonard to win the fight by a first-round knockout. While Leonard usually "studied a guy in the first round," Arcel says, Leonard went out against Mitchell with "full force." Seamon's "30,000 to 1,000 - 1 rd." note in all likelihood refers to Leonard's brother's bet—a wager of $1,000 at 30-to-1 odds that Leonard would win by first-round knockout. Also included in Seamon's note on this fight is the name "A. Roth." Though Seamon attempted to cross out the name, it remains visible. This probably refers to Arnold Rothstein, the famed gambler of the era, to whom Leonard reportedly boasted before the fight, "I probably can knock him out in one round."

The greatest mystery of Leonard's career remains his behavior in a June 1922 challenge of welterweight champion Jack Britton. Britton was thirty-seven at the time, and Leonard was favored to beat him easily. Leonard didn't seem to be himself in the early rounds, but in the thirteenth, he floored Britton with a left to the midsection. When Britton claimed he'd been fouled, Leonard did something very peculiar. He walked across the ring and swatted Britton on the head, though Britton had not yet gotten to his feet. Leonard lost the fight on a foul.

Next to his listing of this fight in his notes, Seamon wrote simply, "What a story." Fortunately, Seamon told his version in the *Sunday Empire News* in 1948:

> Leonard trained hard and was in great shape for the Britton fight, and I am sure he would have won. But for some reason which I do not know to this day he just didn't have to [win]. After the weigh-in, Benny's manager, the late Billy Gibson, told Leonard: "I'm sorry I've got to say this, but you can't win this fight tonight."
>
> Benny didn't ask any questions, and neither did I. Those were the instructions. Whether or not Gibson had made a bet I don't know, but this is something of which even the opposing camp, including Britton and his manager, Dan Morgan, had no knowledge.
>
> Leonard started to cry and said, "Gib, I'm in such great condition, and I know I can win. And my friends are betting on me. It's a terrible thing."
>
> I'm sure that if Gibson had told him earlier there would have been no fight. But at the New York Velodrome in the Bronx that night we had the awful sight of the clever Leonard having to stand flat-footed and let Britton jab him.
>
> Leonard looked so bad that as he was going out for the thirteenth round I said, "Benny, you're a little too flat-footed. It looks too bad. You've got to get on your toes and hit this fellow a few punches."
>
> Leonard walked out, hit Britton a vicious body punch, and Britton went down. The referee counted seven. Britton tried to get up, but it was obvious he couldn't.
>
> Then Leonard realized that he had to lose. Ice-cool, he walked over, and when the referee said "Nine"

with Britton still on the floor, he hit Britton a right
to the head and lost on a foul.

Whatever else he had done, he had saved his
friends, because ninety-nine percent of the wagering
was on terms of "Foul, no bet."

And so Seamon explained Benny Leonard's most peculiar
performance.

It feels wrong, however, to end a discussion of Seamon's work
with Benny Leonard on anything but a positive note. Seamon's
spoken memories of Leonard were filled with images of countless days spent in Harlem gyms surrounded by "all kinds of fans
and well wishers in the neighborhood who never lost an opportunity to see the clever Benny do his stuff." When asked if it
were true that Leonard loathed having his neatly combed hair
mussed in the ring, Seamon replied fondly, "He was very proud
of that patent-leather haircomb and mussing it was like taking
his purse away."

Seamon also spoke glowingly of Leonard's 1916 Kansas City
bout against Ever Hammer, in Hammer's home town. Leonard
called it "the fight I can never forget." Early in the fight, Seamon
remembered, Leonard was "smashed, bashed, belted and ham-
mered all over the ring. Only his superb condition and ring
generalship at crucial times saved him from a knockout." After
Leonard knocked out Hammer in the twelfth round, he said of
his aptly named opponent, "If like Mannie says, we're made out
of the things we eat, that guy must have been weaned on trip-
hammers!"

Perhaps Seamon's affection for Leonard is best summed up by
his remark the day after Leonard was floored by Richie Mitchell in Madison Square Garden and came close to losing the title.
"Benny," Seamon told Leonard, "I would have died if you hadn't
got up."

Seamon once told a reporter, "I don't think there were five
times in all the bouts I served him that I had to say anything to

Benny in the corner. . . . There was nothing to tell him. He knew the job before him so why interfere?"

Seamon said that Leonard always "fully realized his greatness," and recalled Leonard telling him, "Mannie, I know I'm great. I know I can beat anybody my weight because I've worked so hard to become good and made many sacrifices. I know that if I get knocked down I have to get up because so many people expect me to and because I have nothing to fear! I have so much reserve in my system because I always train faithfully." Leonard was "not a braggart," Seamon added. "He said this because he knew it, believed it and lived it. He was actually a superman in boxing trunks in his prime and so had complete confidence in himself."

Mannie Seamon's daughter Fae describes her father as an energetic man who could never sit still and often had trouble sleeping. "His mind was always working," she says. "The wheels were always turning." Seamon ended his letters and phone conversations with the phrase, "Keep punching." He greeted most people—even members of his own family—by saying, "Hiya pal." Other favorite lines were: "I hope I live longer than you, and I hope you live forever" and "I don't want to be a millionaire, I just want to live like one."

Though he was friendly with many in the fight game, he preferred the company of businessmen, doctors, lawyers and show business personalities. Among his friends were performers Count Basie, George Raft, Cab Calloway, Jimmy Durante and songwriter Irving Caesar. Seamon himself had something of a show business personality. When he walked into a room, he felt obliged to cheer-up everyone, to make everyone smile.

John Scott, the president of the Mountain Valley mineral water company, became friendly with Seamon in the 1940s, after Scott discovered that Seamon had been giving his fighters Mountain Valley water since his days with Benny Leonard.

Before pursuing a business relationship with Seamon, Scott, a former Associated Press sports reporter, checked with his old friend Red Smith, who described Seamon as "one of the gems" of the boxing world. "You can rely on Mannie—on anything he says," Smith told him. With Smith's endorsement, Scott engaged Seamon to write a pamphlet titled "Training Champions" which promoted Mountain Valley Water.

When Scott mentioned Seamon to Gene Tunney, who Seamon had trained for one fight—against Marty Burke in 1921—Tunney praised Seamon. "He was young," Scott recalls Tunney saying, "but he never gave you the idea he was inexperienced."

Scott remembers Seamon as a lively conversationalist. "He had an almost boyish enthusiasm. He approached a subject that he knew something about or was enthusiastic about almost like a new toy." Seamon, Scott adds, "was never down. I never can recall Mannie just feeling licked or depressed or worn out or anything like that."

Like many of his colleagues, Seamon collected funny fight stories. Perhaps his favorite involved a fighter who was not particularly intelligent. "I kept showing him how to feint his opponent out of position to set him up for a punch," Seamon said. "But when the fight started, he kept getting hit and the other fellow was blocking his punches. So when he came to the corner, I asked him: 'Why don't you feint?'" The fighter's response: "Faint! What do you think I am—a quitter?"

One night a fighter was losing so badly that Seamon threw in the sponge from his corner, but the fighter caught it and threw it back saying, "Not now, Mannie, I haven't got time. After the round is over." Asked in the corner why he threw back the sponge, the fighter replied, "I thought you threw it in for me to sponge my face off." "You win," Seamon replied, and he allowed the fight to go the distance.

Seamon also liked to talk about the time he went into a bar near Stillman's Gym with his heavyweight Lee Oma—not to drink, of course, but to meet someone. "A fellow at the end of the bar hollers out, 'Run down here Oma; it will be your road-work for today!'" Seamon remembered. "Lee yelled back, 'Sorry, the bar's too long!'"

Once, at a French airport with Joe Louis, Seamon spoke to an airport official in Yiddish. Afterward Louis said, "Mannie, since when you learn to speak French so good?"

One of Seamon's passions early in life was horse racing, and his greatest relaxation was to go to the track—an activity he pursued with his friend Benny Leonard. "That was his club," says Fae Seamon.

Despite the physical dexterity he displayed at fight camps, Seamon was all thumbs when it came to fixing things around the house, and he never learned to drive a car. Calm and coura-geous while working a corner, outside the ring he suffered from a fear of heights. While he was a formidable cut man, he dis-liked gory scenes in the movies or on television.

Photos reveal Seamon to be a handsome man who often wore an expression of intense concentration. He wore his hair slicked-back and was always a dapper dresser. In the Joe Louis years he favored elegant custom-made double-breasted suits. "If you are somebody, you should look like somebody," he often said.

In all his years with Joe Louis, Seamon never had a written contract. He believed that if Louis became unhappy, he should have felt free to make a change with no questions asked. Louis, of course, remained loyal to Seamon.

With Joe Louis' easy victory over Conn in their second fight in 1946, Louis once again assumed command of the heavyweight division. Seamon took control of Louis' training. The job called into play Seamon's almost obsessive passion for routine, detail, order and cleanliness. Fae Seamon remembers her father's ex-planation for his perfectionism: "In the ring, you only get one chance to do things right."

Seamon's devotion to Louis is apparent in descriptions of how he wrapped Louis' hands with what one reporter described as "a meticulousness and almost tender attention that is a treat to watch." "How does that feel?" Seamon would ask, after each step of the forty-five-minute ritual.

Louis' training camp was governed by Seamon's motto, "Prevention is Strength." "Cleanliness costs nothing, and I always carry around with me a clean sheet for a boxer to lie on, as well as a clean blanket to cover him while he rests after a bout," he explained in the *Sunday Empire News.* "I always use three towels—one for the boxer's face, one for the body and one for the legs. They are never switched, and I mark them A, B and C so that there shall be no doubt. . . . When I see dirty towels around the head of a fighter it makes me squirm."

In that article, Seamon lovingly lingered over the details of Louis' regular training regimen, which began when Seamon woke Louis at 5:30 in the morning: "He had nothing to eat, but just cleaned his teeth and gargled." During the winter, Louis then dressed in "shorts, a sweater, a track suit, a knitted skull cap, woolen gloves and heavy boots," Seamon recalled. "Then he went onto the road for about an hour, running and walking for about five-and-a-half miles. On the way, he would change from walking to running as he thought fit, and I never interfered with him in this, because, being a good worker, he knew just how much of each he needed. I followed in a car because I don't need all that work, and I don't like it, anyway. That's why they call me 'the automobile roadwork man.'" As he ran, Louis would bend down "to pick up loose stones, without halting," Seamon wrote, "because that's very good exercise for the back muscles."

After returning to camp, Louis would drink a glass of carrot juice, and then rest until ten a.m. when he'd have a meal of "apple juice, three or four lamb chops, ham or liver, two four-minute boiled eggs—no bread, no potatoes." Fifteen minutes after the meal, Louis had a couple of glasses of water. "On no account would drink be taken with the food," Seamon emphasized.

Afternoons consisted of a long walk, followed by a game of

cards or Ping-Pong. Then Louis would lie down until two o'clock.

At three in the afternoon, the champion would go to the gym where he'd shadow box five minutes; spar four to six rounds with two or three partners; spend three to six minutes on the speed bag; three to six minutes on the heavy bag; five minutes skipping rope; fifteen minutes on calisthenics; and five minutes having a medicine ball thrown into his stomach twenty-five times.

Seamon wasn't above playing games to build his fighter's ego. A few times, he confessed later in life, he fixed Louis' punching bag and gloves so that they would tear, leading Louis to imagine that his power had grown to superhuman proportions.

After Louis' workouts, Seamon recalled in the *Empire News*, "I would undress him, wrap him in a blanket and throw another over him, and put out the lights so that he was in a completely darkened room for fifteen minutes and could perspire freely. Immediately afterwards, I used to dry him thoroughly before he took a lukewarm shower—not cold in any cirumstances because that's how fighters get lumbago and stiffen up."

After giving Louis a massage and drying him off "with oil of eucalyptus, omega oil and a little drop of olive oil," Seamon would administer an eye wash and apply a foot salve, and the ritual would be complete.

Dinner was at 5:30 and consisted of two glasses of water followed by salad, soup with crackers, a "thick steak of about a pound, grilled medium rare—never well done—with corn or string beans." Louis then had tea with either lemon or milk, and then a quarter of an hour later a pint of vanilla ice cream.

The meal was followed by a half-hour of rest, two glasses of water, and an evening of cards, or—two days a week—a trip into town to see a movie. After a walk, Louis would be in bed by 8:30 or nine o'clock.

Seamon also labored to keep the monotonous grind of training as entertaining as possible for Louis. At camp, the two

CORNER MEN

often—as a gag—refused to shave until Louis' beloved Detroit Tigers won a baseball game. "One reason why Louis gets into such good shape in training is that his camp is always a happy camp," Seamon told the *Sun*. "Everybody connected with Joe has a genuine affection for him. And he feels the same way toward the fellows he works with."

Seamon also insisted that Louis had a "wonderful sense of humor," though he rarely displayed it in public. "Just because he doesn't smile when he is in the ring and doesn't show any elation after he wins, people quite naturally take him as a somber sort of fellow who doesn't know what it means to laugh," Seamon said. "But when he's with people he knows and likes he really lets go when somebody pulls a good gag. He'll laugh so hard you will think he is going to fall apart."

Though Seamon was able to indulge his fondness for humor in training camp, he did make some sacrifices. Normally a man who enjoyed a good cigar and a drink, Seamon always refrained from both while preparing Louis for a fight.

A few months after his victory over Billy Conn, Louis faced challenger Tami Mauriello. Before the fight, Seamon told reporters that Louis was in his finest shape since winning the 1938 rematch with Max Schmeling. Anticipating a slugfest, Seamon told Bill Corum of the *Journal-American*: "It's bound to be a punching fight right from the start, and Mauriello is the type that will keep getting up. It's going to take plenty of persuading to keep Tami down there for keeps. That means Joe will have to open up and punch with him, and when you do that you are apt to have to catch a few yourself. It could turn out to be a brawl on the order of Joe's fight with Galento, and you'll remember that Tony thumped him pretty good before Joe finally broke him up into little pieces."

The Louis-Mauriello fight was as brief and explosive as Seamon had anticipated. A Mauriello right staggered Louis in the opening seconds of the first round. Louis then quickly came off the ropes and floored Mauriello with a left hook. Moments later, a Louis combination put Mauriello down again—and the challenger was counted out for the first time in his career. In his autobiography, Louis described the Mauriello fight as "the last time I really felt like my old self. I had complete control, energy, power."

Following Louis' victory, Frank Graham again compared Seamon with Blackburn: "There may be, although there shouldn't, an inclination to look lightly on Mannie's value to Louis. Of course, Louis has matured since the day when the late Jack Blackburn did all his thinking for him around a training camp and now he has ideas of his own about his conditioning. But no visitor to his camp can fail to note the respect in which Joe holds Mannie and his ready obedience to Mannie's commands when he is in the training ring."

In late 1946 and in early 1947, Seamon accompanied Louis on exhibition tours to Central and South America. For Louis, whose financial and tax problems were burgeoning, the tours were a means of earning much-needed cash. For Seamon, they were an all-expense-paid opportunity to see the world. Seamon's scrapbook is filled with photos of himself, Louis, co-manager Marshall Miles and others in the Louis entourage sporting straw hats and flowered shirts and surrounded by admiring crowds. In the photos, Seamon is usually smiling or joking.

When Louis signed for his next fight, his opponent, Jersey Joe Walcott, was considered such a profound underdog that the bout was announced as a ten-round, nontitle affair. This was changed to a regulation title bout at the insistence of the New York Athletic Commission.

While preparing for the fight, Louis and Seamon had one of the few disagreements that Seamon would admit to publicly. Concerned about appearing overweight and out of shape, Louis began drying out a few days before the fight—not drinking liquids in order to artificially lower his weight. Later on, Seamon recalled that when he objected, Louis told him, "Look, Mannie, I want to weigh 212 pounds." When Seamon replied, "You're making a mistake. I would take a drink of water," Louis said, "If I make a mistake, I'll take the blame."

As all fight fans know, the first Louis-Walcott fight at Madison Square Garden on December 5, 1947 marked the beginning of the visible decline of Joe Louis' boxing skills. Walcott knocked Louis down in the first and fourth rounds. While Louis was the aggressor for most of the fight, he was unable to corner Walcott and land solid punches.

Before the judge's decision was announced, Louis, embarrassed by his performance, began to leave the ring, only to be restrained by Seamon who realized that had Louis left the ring he would have technically forfeited the fight. Ruby Goldstein, who refereed the bout, said in a 1973 *Ring* article, "Instead of waiting for the official decision [Louis] started to leave the ring. He would have gone on to his dressing room if he had not been stopped by Mannie Seamon."

Following the fight, Louis told the press, "When the bout ended, I started out. Mannie Seamon, my trainer, told me to wait for the decision and I did. That's all there was to it. I certainly didn't think I was a beaten fighter. I was just embarrassed because I figured my performance was not what it should have been."

When the decision was announced in Louis' favor, the crowd booed loudly. After Louis left the ring, Walcott's handlers raised his arm in victory. In his dressing room after the fight, Louis, according to several reports, said: "I should have listened to Mannie Seamon. I dried out for this fight against Mannie's advice. Next time I'll listen to Mannie; next time I'll take his advice." A rematch with Walcott was obviously in order, and Louis realized, with his declining skills, that it should be his last fight before retirement.

Seamon accompanied Louis on an exhibition tour of England, Belgium and France before Louis settled down to train for the

June 1948 rematch with Walcott. A photo from Seamon's family photo album reveals Seamon surrounded by his French relatives. A huge black man looms in the background: the man, of course, is Joe Louis.

Louis trained in earnest for the bout, intending to retire after a victory. One measure of Louis' seriousness is that—at Seamon's request—he gave up golf while training. Golf, said Seamon, "encourages a man to keep his hands low and for that reason it's anything but an ideal form of relaxation for a fighter." Seamon also worried that Louis exhausted himself on the golf course. "Instead of knowing when to stop, you play fifty-four holes in a day," Seamon told Louis. "So it's no longer exercise or relaxation." Seamon preferred that Louis play Ping-Pong. "That table tennis," he said, "it keeps you movin'. It's good for the eye and good for the mind and good for the reflexes. It's a helluva thing."

This time around, Seamon also insisted that Louis not worry about his weight. "Joe's not going to do ANYTHING ABOUT HIS WEIGHT," Seamon told columnist Ned Brown of the *Daily Sports Bulletin*. ". . . I'm going to throw the scales away. This time Joe Louis will train to get into CONDITION—not to hit a specified weight. I don't care what Joe Louis weighs for this fight. He can weigh 210, 212, 215 or he can weigh a TON. One thing I DO care about, however, and that is having Joe at the peak of his form. . . . Joe is eating and drinking with a healthy appetite. He's not worrying about his weight."

When Frank Graham checked in with Seamon at training camp, Seamon was outspoken in his confidence that Louis would defeat Walcott. "Louis underrated Walcott," Seamon said. "He knew, while the fight was going on, he made a mistake. He won't make it again."

Like Louis, Seamon would not speak disparagingly of Louis' opponents, although he made an exception for Walcott. The reason, perhaps, stems from the publicity surrounding Walcott's claim—prior to his first fight with Louis—that Louis had fired him as a sparring partner before the first Schmeling fight because Walcott had given him too much trouble in the ring.

It's clear that neither Louis nor Seamon forgot Walcott's charges. "They say Walcott will lick Louis this time," Seamon told Graham. "Walcott never will lick Louis. He had his chance. He caught him on a bad night, and he couldn't lick him and I'll tell you why he'll never lick him. He lacks something. He showed it the second time he knocked Louis down. The first time was all right. Louis has been on the floor more often than any other great fighter but when he gets up he is dangerous, and Walcott would have been a sucker to rush in at him that time. But the second time, there he was. That was Walcott's chance. The heavyweight championship was right in front of him. No matter what your seconds have told you to do, when you have a chance to win the championship, what do you do? You do the natural thing. You walk in and belt the champion. You don't run away. That's why Walcott will never lick Louis."

In the *Sunday Empire News*, Seamon remembered his strategic plan for the rematch: "Walcott, even though he preferred to run, had a good right hand, and I had noticed in their first meeting that Louis didn't seem to have an answer to it. . . . All Joe's sparring . . . was concentrated on making him keep up his hands. I put the punching bag up higher for the same purpose." Seamon's strategy also relied heavily on Walcott tiring out as Louis pursued him in the early going. The plan called for a late-round knockout by Louis.

Despite hard training and a careful game plan, the fight proved less than masterful for Louis, who was again knocked down, this time in the third round. As Louis chased the evasive Walcott, the Yankee Stadium crowd booed the lack of action, and in round ten the referee told the boxers, "Hey, one of you get the lead out of your ass and let's have a fight."

With Louis looking bad, Seamon tried to inspire him in his corner before the eleventh round. As Seamon recalled in the *Empire News*, he told Louis, "There's only five rounds to go and

I don't want you to forget that you're a million-dollar fighter. Don't let him get set this round. Go and hit him on the chin. Just get twelve inches away from him, and when you catch him with the first punch give him everything you have."

Louis went on to score an eleventh-round knockout. After the fight, Louis told the press, "He didn't hurt me when he knocked me down. All I was doing was waiting my chance and when Mannie told me I had him then I went out and got him." Seamon told reporters: "I knew Walcott was tired. I just told Joe to go get him and he'd knock him out. You could see it. Walcott was stretching his arms and dropping them. He wasn't feinting. He was tired. So Joe went out and got him."

A film of the post-fight press conference shows Seamon interviewing Louis. "I thought you hit him with my left hook, Joe," said Seamon. "Well, Mannie," replied Louis in his typical deadpan style, "I hit him with my right, too."

In Louis' account of his life in *The New York Times* a few months later, he again credited Seamon's strategic advice: "Mannie Seamon figured out with me that the way to take Walcott would be to box him until he got tired. We figured I wasn't as fast as him any more. We even got it down where we figure I would have to tap him out between the ninth and the eleventh or he would try to keep it going to take the decision."

Although Louis announced his retirement after the second Walcott fight, his need for money forced him back into the ring against Ezzard Charles, who had defeated Walcott in an elimination bout to become the new heavyweight champion. With only six weeks of training, Louis lost a fifteen-round decision to Charles at Yankee Stadium on September 27, 1950. A year later, Seamon told Lewis Burton of the *Journal–American*, "In fourteen years with Joe, the only argument I ever had with him was when Marshall Miles and myself wanted him to stay retired and not come back for Ezzard Charles. Joe said, 'I won the title in the ring; I got to lose it there.'"

Asked if he and Seamon were against Louis' comeback, Marshall Miles says, "Definitely." Miles also confirms reports that Louis had only six weeks to train for the fight. "That's right," he says. "Joe should've retired. I begged him. I begged him to retire, but he wouldn't do it."

Seamon again trained Louis for his October 1951 comeback against Rocky Marciano in Madison Square Garden. "Oh that was something," Marshall Miles remembers sadly. He adds that reports that Louis, then thirty-seven, was unable to throw right hands are accurate. "He wasn't hurt," Miles says, "he was just worn out." Seamon tried to build up Louis' right, Miles recalls, but even Seamon "couldn't do nothing." Louis was a "one-armed fighter," says Miles. "He was over the hill."

Going into the Marciano fight, however, Seamon and Louis had a plan. Knowing that Louis could not go the distance against Marciano, they had decided to try for an early knockout. In the dressing room before the fight, Louis' old friend Sugar Ray Robinson came by to wish him good luck. Much to Seamon's chagrin, Robinson told Louis, "Joe, you're an old man. Take it easy." It's impossible to know, of course, whether Robinson's words of caution affected Louis' performance, but Seamon was upset by what he perceived as Robinson's meddling. Seamon told the story to his family, but never repeated it in public.

Describing the Louis-Marciano bout in a 1963 interview in the *Police Gazette*, Seamon said: "I could tell early in the fight that Joe wasn't going to be able to handle Rocky. He wasn't punching with that old zing. Then in the eighth round, Rocky caught Joe with a barrage of punches and he went down.

"Joe lay under the ropes at Madison Square Garden, his head hanging over the rope apron. It was obvious he couldn't beat the count, so I climbed in the ring and helped him to his corner. Honest, there were tears in my eyes when I asked him if he was all right.

"'I'm okay, Mannie,' he said. 'But I'll tell you something, that Rocky hits pretty good.'"

After Louis' loss, Seamon defended him against reporters who insisted he retire. "Why don't you let Joe Louis alone?" Seamon said. "Why do so many keep insisting he hang up the gloves? What is he, an invalid? . . . Sure, he was knocked out by Marciano, but it was only the second time he's ever been stopped. And Marciano can knock out anyone he hits. If Louis had been taking a beating from the first round on, I'd be the first to advise Joe to quit. But in my book it was a fairly even fight until the knockout. . . . Why didn't these same critics yell for Joe Walcott to retire after Joe knocked him out?"

Asked how Louis felt after the knockout, Seamon said, "Fine. I sent him through a rigid drill the very next day and he responded very well. There was nothing wrong with him. I'd say that if a light punching guy like Joey Maxim had knocked him out, then I would have to admit Joe should quit. . . . I want to say again, however, that I'm not trying to influence Joe to fight again—but I am asking that his future be left up to him."

In late 1951, Seamon accompanied Louis when the former champion ended his boxing career with an exhibition tour for American troops stationed in the Orient. In 1963, looking back on Louis' decision to retire, Seamon said, "I lost the best job I ever had." Another time he put it this way: "If I live to be a hundred, I could never have as happy and peaceful a job as my fourteen years with Louis."

Seamon, of course, always rated Louis as the greatest heavyweight ever. Comparing him to Tunney and Dempsey, Seamon said: "Louis is a combination fighter-boxer, a combination rarer than an oyster. A fighter is a clouter; a boxer is a thinker. Once he'd been dealt a stiff shot on the chops, even in training, Dempsey's brain deserted him like rats desert a stricken ship. He became a raging killer. Tunney was a boxer; never a fighter."

In 1952, Seamon offered this comparison of Louis and Dempsey to Lewis Burton of the *Journal-American*: "Jack Kearns' managing was half of Dempsey. Louis would outbox and outpunch Jack Dempsey and knock him out the best day Jack ever saw. Dempsey made a reputation on big guys like Firpo and Willard, guys you could hit with everything. Louis'd knock them out in the first round."

In that same interview, Seamon surprisingly disagreed with Louis' own contention that the first Conn fight was his toughest as champion. "I think Tony Galento was even tougher," Seamon said. "Galento had him hurt three or four times. Oh, yeah! Galento was a good hitter, the son-of-a-gun." Asked to pick Louis' greatest fight, Seamon chose Louis' match with James Braddock. "He [Louis] was down right off the bat and he had to be great to take the title," Seamon recalled.

In the *Empire News*, Seamon attributed Louis' unparalleled greatness to two qualities—a devastating punch and the ability to finish an opponent when the opponent was hurt. "Once Joe had a fellow going, there were no half measures," Seamon stressed. "He just got in as many punches as opponents had encountered before. There was no trickery about it. It was just something Joe had which no one else has possessed. I doubt whether it could ever be cultivated successfully."

Analyzing Louis' punching power, Seamon said: "Joe had what I choose to call a corkscrew punch. . . . Louis had a natural ability to turn his wrist at the very moment a punch was reaching its mark, and that made it a whole lot more devastating. . . . A straight punch, hard as it may be, cannot be so damaging as one which causes the glove to be turned in that last split-second before it connects. The force of the blow, plus the turning effect, if used repeatedly, can tear the flesh of an opponent. That's why so many of Joe's rivals found they got cut more easily than they had ever realized."

But Seamon paid Louis perhaps his greatest compliment in a 1946 interview with Lewis Burton. He rated Louis ahead of Benny Leonard—the equivalent of a father praising one child at the expense of another. "As an all-around fighter—boxing and punching included—Joe is the better man," Seamon said. Though he refused to compare the two in any great detail,

Seamon added, "You don't realize what a truly great boxer Louis is."

Over the years, in addition to training boxers, Mannie Seamon had owned a gym in Harlem, a poolhall and a bar-and-grill near Stillman's gym. With Louis' permanent retirement, Seamon, who had once turned down the job of matchmaker at Madison Square Garden because "I thought I might lose some of my friends," no longer wanted to be involved in boxing. He did, however, attempt to market "Mannie Seamon's Training Gloves"—mitts used to teach boxing to young people to help them "build . . . self-confidence without getting hurt," as a promotional brochure explained. The business venture, however, did not succeed. When he was offered a large salary to move to Texas and help a manager interested in developing young fighters, Seamon declined the offer.

Eventually, he returned to his old job as a mutuel ticket agent for the New York Racing Association at Belmont and Aqueduct race tracks. Asked why Seamon didn't stay in boxing, his friend John Scott recalls Seamon telling him, "There's nobody I really want to work with. They seemed to destroy the mold after Joe Louis." Also in Seamon's mind, no doubt, was a desire to be with his family. He was sometimes so homesick while in Louis' training camp, that he accidentally referred to Louis by his wife's name, Lillian. "There he goes again," Louis would say with a laugh.

Sportswriters didn't forget Mannie Seamon, however, and they often sought out his opinions on the boxing scene. As a boxing oracle, Seamon proved very accurate. Before Muhammad Ali—then known as Cassius Clay—challenged heavyweight champion Sonny Liston, Seamon was one of the few experts to pick young Clay. "My friends may be apprehensive of my sanity," Seamon said in one article, "but let's analyze a bit: the challenger is bigger, faster and a better boxer than the champion. To offset these advantages, Liston has the 'old equalizer'—a deadly wallop—but it must land on target to be effective."

In the *Police Gazette*, Seamon said, "Liston's no superman you know. He can punch, that's for sure. But in the fights I've watched him in, he makes a lot of mistakes." Seamon summed up Liston's problem as follows: "I figure he's a guy who won't take advice. He knows it all. This is dangerous in any fighter. Joe Louis, as great as he was, never was that way. He'd listen when I discussed certain strategy with him." Cassius Clay, though, struck Seamon as a better pupil: "Now I understand this Clay kid, despite all his talking, is a good man in the gym. He might have a swell head, but you can talk to him—give him a little advice once in a while."

Seamon, who knew how to handle the press himself, also admired Clay's publicity skills: "Clay's a good fighter and he should get better. The kid's a great salesman, too. He keeps bragging about how he's going to knock out guys in three or four rounds. That's salesmanship. It helps sell fights. But he's going to need more than salesmanship against Liston."

Seamon's prediction proved eerily accurate: "Sonny will come out throwing bombs right from the beginning. That's his style. He'll never change. Clay, though, won't make the mistake Patterson made. He won't try to mix it with Sonny—at least not in the beginning. The kid will be moving, throwing that jab . . . If Clay can keep out of trouble in those early rounds, then he can open up."

Seamon did not, however, remain enamored of Ali for long. The August 1970 issue of *The Ring* featured the headline, "Louis Would Have Whipped Clay on Cassius' Best Day." Under that heading, Seamon stated, "I am not going to let myself be influenced by my belief that he made a terrible decision when he refused to be drafted. His religious and political beliefs interest me not one plugged nickel's worth. I want to judge him strictly as a boxer." As a boxer, Seamon stated, "Clay is not to be compared with Jack Dempsey, Gene Tunney, Jack Sharkey and

Tommy Loughran, among others." Specifically, Seamon faulted Muhammad Ali for needing a big ring to fully exploit his mobility and for not throwing body punches. He also suggested that Ali could not endure a pounding to the body. "Louis would have whipped Cassius on the best day of Clay's ring career," Seamon said. "In fact, the subject does not bear discussion."

After his retirement from the track, Seamon continued to lead an active life in New York City. He saw many friends and made frequent visits to the track and Yankee Stadium, where he preferred to sit in the bleachers with a regular group of friends.

In 1975 Seamon was honored at the 50th Annual Boxing Writers' Dinner at the Plaza Hotel. Also honored that night were Joe Louis, Muhammad Ali, Ray Arcel, Freddie Brown and Chickie Ferrara.

Seamon traveled to Las Vegas in 1978 for Frank Sinatra's famous dinner honoring Joe Louis at the Caesar's Palace Hotel. After the dinner, Seamon approached Louis—who was still on stage in his wheelchair—and affectionately planted a kiss on the fighter's forehead.

Until the end of his life, Seamon carried two photos along with pictures of his family—one of himself with Jack Blackburn and one of himself with Joe Louis. During the illness that preceded his death in 1983, Fae Seamon remembers consoling her father by telling him, "You had a great life." He'd had a fine family, trained two of the greatest champions who ever lived and traveled all over the world, she reminded him. "I know," Mannie Seamon replied, "but I'd like to do it again."

FREDDIE BROWN

You could put five-thousand people in a line-up, and you could say, 'Which guy is a trainer, a cut guy?' And there wouldn't be any other guy—he was right there, Freddie Brown." This opinion comes from Rocky Marciano's brother Peter, and almost everyone who knew Freddie Brown would agree that Brown's appearance embodied every cliché about how a corner man should look.

Referee Joey Curtis, who as a lightweight was trained by Brown in the 1940s, provides this portrait: "Freddie Brown was the picture of an ex-fighter—flat nose, cigar in his mouth, dirty sweater, Vaseline on his knuckles. . . . He looked like he was ready to get into the ring himself." Randy Gordon, who was editor of *The Ring* before becoming New York State Athletic Commissioner, says of Brown's ever-present cigar, "It was like always the same cigar butt—just chewed up and moldy." About his fabled cigars, Brown told Dave Anderson of *The New York Times* in 1980, "I used to smoke about eight a day. But the last few years I smoke and chew maybe three a day. Mostly chew."

Brown, who boxed as an amateur featherweight, was best known as cut man for Rocky Marciano and co-handler—with Ray Arcel—of Roberto Duran. His many other celebrated clients included Bob Pastor and Abe Simon, who both lost twice to Joe Louis; middleweight and light-heavyweight champion Dick Tiger; middleweight contenders Tony Janiro and Jimmy Archer; welterweight contender Gaspar Ortega; heavyweight champion Larry Holmes; and middleweight champion Vito Antuofermo. Asked to name his finest fighters, Brown once said, "There was so many I'd have to take a day off to think about them. But good guys all of them. Mostly."

Freddie Brown was in Rocky Marciano's corner the night Marciano took the heavyweight championship from Jersey Joe Walcott in September of 1952. "Rocky came back to the corner after the fifth round and explained he couldn't see," Brown told the *Police Gazette*, providing his version of the controversial fight in which Marciano was temporarily blinded while challenging for the title. "Some solution or something—I never did learn what it was—had gotten into his eyes. He was half blind." Brown then "grabbed the water bucket" and washed out Marciano's eyes in an effort to dilute whatever substance was blinding the fighter. "A couple of rounds later it cleared," Brown recalled, "and Rocky went on to flatten Walcott in the thirteenth round. If I had lost my head that night maybe Rocky would have lost the fight."

Looking back on the fight in a 1969 *Daily News* column, Gene Ward wrote, "Luckily for Marciano there was a cool head in his corner. . . . [Freddie Brown], the expert cut man, who had been hired by Weill only that morning for a fifty-dollar bill. He calmed Marciano and put him back together."

Brown's most famous piece of work in Marciano's corner has to have been the repair job he did on Marciano's nose after Ezzard Charles split it open in the sixth round of the second Marciano-Charles fight on September 17, 1954 at Yankee Stadium. Marciano's nose was "ripped lengthwise,' Brown once said. Echoing the opinion of most fight men, press agent Irving Rudd says, "Freddie Brown, you gotta say, saved the title for Marciano."

Brown described the scene this way for the *Police Gazette*: "Rocky and Charles' heads came together and when they broke, the blood was gushing down Rocky's nose. . . . At the end of the round, Rocky came to the corner and the gash was so deep it looked like he had two noses. I patched it up as best I could and told Rocky he'd better go out there and knock out Charles before the ring doctor decided to stop the fight. And that's just what Rocky did. He stopped Charles in the eighth round."

Explaining the need to remain calm at such a moment, Brown told Deane McGowen of *The New York Times* in 1962, "It got me scared just looking at the Rock's nose. But you've got to be right when you begin the repair job and you've got to be fast, otherwise the fight's lost." Going into the fight, Brown added, he had been prepared for problems because "Marciano's skin cuts as easily as tissue paper."

Asked how he treated Marciano's smashed nose, Brown told McGowen, "I used something nobody else uses to close the wound." When the writer for the *Police Gazette* asked Brown directly whether he'd used Monsell's solution, the *Gazette* reported, "The little trainer sidestepped the question, but there was a gleam in his brown eyes when he said, 'You know that stuff is banned now.'" "Monsell's solution was considered very dangerous," Brown once explained. "It coagulated the blood all right. It was like pouring cement into a cut. You had to cut it out later in the dressing room, and the resulting healing left too much scar tissue. That's why you see scar tissue on most of the older fighters."

The day after Brown's triumphant operation on Marciano's nose, A. J. Liebling asked Brown why Charles fought in the style he did. Charles "fought the way he fought because Marciano fought the way *he* fought," Brown replied. ". . . It's very hard to think when you are getting your brains knocked out." Boxing

Brown concluded, is "not like football. Rocky never gives you the ball."

Though he was considered gruff by some, those who knew Freddie Brown best say the opposite was true. Michael Katz, who covered boxing for *The New York Times* before becoming the boxing columnist for the *Daily News*, says Brown's appearance was deceptive. "He had the face of a gruff man and he had the voice of a gruff man. He had a cigar poked in his face all the time. And he looked like a tough, no-nonsense guy, and he was very direct, but I don't think of him as being a hard man or anything like that."

Larry Holmes, who had Brown in his corner when he won the heavyweight title in 1978, says, "Freddie Brown wasn't tough. Freddie Brown was an easy-going guy. When he was with me he was always easy. He would sit down, have breakfast with you, talk a bit about boxing to you." Holmes recalls that Brown, then in his seventies, would square off in a fighting stance to demonstrate his points. Holmes says Brown would "show you things . . . He would stand there. He would box your body. Do things like that."

Brown was actually a shy man, according to his long-time friend, Dr. Edwin Campbell, former Medical Director of the New York State Athletic Commission. "He was reticent, reserved," says Campbell, "but he was a very kindhearted and patient man who loved his boxers and dedicated himself to them."

Muriel Brown says her husband's early life was tough. He was born on the Lower East Side of Manhattan in 1907. Brown's mother died when he was young and his father remarried, leaving young Freddie pretty much on his own. One of his brothers took Brown to a local gym, where his fascination with boxing began. Freddie Brown estimated that he fought sixty fights as an amateur featherweight, and had only four losses.

A severe injury to his nose gave Brown headaches and breathing problems. "I went to a clinic. They took the bone out, but they didn't do a good job with my looks," Brown explained in 1966. "Maybe today, with plastic surgery, they wouldn't even have had to take the bone out." The result of the operation was the profoundly dented nose which became a boxing landmark.

Brown always maintained a sense of humor about his nose. "When people talk about it, I laugh," he said. "For years people have been wanting me to get it fixed. There are some doctors who have offered to fix it for me for free of charge so that they can show before-and-after pictures and help their practice. But I leave it alone. I breathe good now. As long as it doesn't cause trouble, why should I bother?"

Unable to continue his boxing career, Brown turned to training fighters, starting sometime in the 1920s at Seward's Gym on Hester Street in his old neighborhood. Aside from a brief stint as a patternmaker for I. Miller, manufacturer of ladies' shoes, Brown earned his living in boxing his whole life.

Muriel Brown recalls that though her husband was not raised as a religious Jew, he easily adapted to her practice of keeping a kosher home, and learned to recite his prayers when candles were lit on Friday nights. She describes him as a quiet man who didn't drink and was sure to telephone her if circumstances prevented him from returning home for their customary five o'clock dinner. She says Brown had little tolerance for rough language in the home, and she points proudly to a clipping from the 1950s about Brown's heavyweight Tommy "Hurricane" Jackson. "He told his mother I cursed him in the corner," Brown told the press. "Why I never say a dirty word, ask my daughters." If the trainer heard his girls uttering what he considered inappropriate language, Muriel Brown adds, her husband would try to literally wash their mouths out with soap. Freddie Brown was also a very prompt person, and he always paid his bills the day they arrived. "Ask the phone company," Muriel Brown says.

In the 1930s, Brown trained fighters managed by Jimmy John-

ston, including former New York University football player Bob
Pastor. "I was the first guy to show how you could lick Joe
Louis," Brown told Dave Anderson, referring to Pastor's performance in surviving the ten-round distance in his first fight
against Louis in January of 1937. "I made Pastor box," Brown
continued. "He had Louis crazy. . . . The fight was in the Garden
and Louis got it, but they booed the decision."

Describing Pastor's defense-minded fight, John Kiernan of
The New York Times wrote in 1937, "Some of the spectators
were a trifle disgruntled as they left the Garden. It's true that
they received a great run for their money, but they paid to see a
fight." Kiernan, however, praised Pastor for surviving. "He was
there to last ten rounds and make Louis look bad," he wrote.
"He achieved complete success in both efforts."

When Pastor faced Louis again in Detroit in September of
1939, however, the fighter was determined to prove he could
slug it out with Louis, who was now heavyweight champion.
Brown recalled for *The Ring* in 1961 that before the fight he
told Pastor, "Okay, Bob, now you box him like you did the other
time." Pastor replied, "No, Freddie, I'm going to make history
tonight." After Pastor mixed it up with Louis and landed on the
canvas several times in the early rounds, Brown told him, "I
don't know anything about history, I do know that if you don't
start moving around again you'll have your head handed to
you." Pastor resumed dancing and lasted into the tenth round.

Press accounts of Pastor's fights with Louis feature few comments from Freddie Brown. "He was Jimmy Johnston's trainer,"
journalist Harold Conrad explains. "Jimmy Johnston did all the
talking." Asked why Brown received relatively little publicity,
Nat Loubet, former editor and publisher of *The Ring* explains,
"Some people are born to be P. R. [public relations]. Other people
can be more knowledgeable. Now believe me, this guy was very
knowledgeable. But he was not good at selling himself, and he
never thought of it. He was happy with his job. He did not sell."

Loubet also confirms the image of Brown as a shy but compassionate man. "The feeling I always had about him was that he was held back, very passive, not a pushy kind of a man. He sort of became a brother—a relation—to the fighter. He would put his arm around the fighter and talk to him in a low voice, unlike many trainers who bulldoze fighters and who warn them if they don't do this and that they're not going to win. I think Freddie was more warm. He would hold back until the person had complete faith in him. That's the feeling I always had. Which is one reason he never sold—because he wasn't loud, you know."

Says Brown's friend Dr. Edwin Campbell, "He was so reserved, he never sought any publicity. He just shied away from any publicity." When Brown worked with a fighter, Campbell says, "Freddie stayed with the boxer constantly. He was like a shadow. Except when the boxer went before the cameras."

In a terse, Freddie-Brown-like construction, Jimmy Archer—brother and manager of Brown's middleweight Joey Archer—recalls, "Freddie said nothing or he said what was."

Most of Freddie Brown's former fighters speak of him as a patient instructor. Joey Curtis started training with Brown's post-World War II partner, Whitey Bimstein, after Curtis fought ten professional fights. Though Bimstein "did whatever he could to help me," Curtis recalls, Bimstein was busy each day at Stillman's Gym with the likes of Rocky Graziano and Billy Graham. Though Brown also had a hand in training Graziano and Graham, Curtis says that Brown seemed to have more time to help young boxers.

Curtis offers a comparison between the styles of Bimstein and Brown: "In the ring, some of the times I'd get upset with Whitey, because I'd come back into the corner and he'd give me more of a beating than the fighter would give me a beating. He said, 'Didn't I tell you to do this?' And as he tells you to do that he smacks you across the face. I know what he was trying to do. He was trying to get my attention. But I didn't like it. I didn't like the way he did things like that. And that's when I started drifting off to Freddie Brown."

Other fighters have opposite memories: they say Bimstein was affable and Brown was dour. Al Braverman, who worked as a sparring partner for Bob Pastor, says of Brown, "If he says hello to you, it costs you money. I never got a thank you—never."

Yet Joey Curtis, like many others, remembers Brown as a devoted trainer. "He'd sit down with you and reason with you. . . . Freddie was a very, very easy-going guy," Curtis says. "He'd sit down with you after you worked out at the gym. He would tell you you did this wrong, you did that wrong. 'Don't hit the bag that way. Do this, do that.' When he was in the corner with you, it was, 'Look this guy's getting to you. He's hitting you with a lot of right hands. Go to the left. Don't let this guy hit you on the chin. He's liable to knock you out.' He was very, very methodical—in his teaching and his coaching and the way he would tell you to fight a fight."

Gaspar Ortega, Brown's welterweight contender from the 1950s, says, "Freddie Brown was the one who had the patience. He always told me how to do things, how to move, how to get more points, how to throw combinations. He was something special." Ortega says Brown "was like my baby sitter." Together the two would play cards, go to the movies, take walks and work on Ortega's uncertain English language skills. Another favorite activity, the fighter says, was "windowshopping." Ortega says that Brown never discussed his work with Marciano or other fighters. "No, he never bragged about it. He was very modest."

When discussing his profession in interviews, Brown lamented changes in the boxing scene as early as 1958 when he told *The Ring,* "Years back, there were enough good clubs so that a manager could get good money for a fight. It would be enough so that he could say to me or any other trainer, 'Here, stay with this kid, give him a lot of time. Know how he lives. If he has any bad habits, show him why he has to get rid of them to get ahead."

Brown added, "The fight fan never knows what you have to go through with a fighter. Of course, when it was worth your while, you did it and the results showed. I had some dillies, but I got around them. In time, they became good fighters, some of them champs. . . . Now? If I have a kid for a week before a fight, I'm lucky."

Speaking with the *Police Gazette* in the mid-1960s, Brown again suggested that training fighters was becoming a lost art. "There are a lot of trainers today who are not teachers," Brown said. "Years ago a trainer had to teach as well as take care of his fighters. That's missing today. Most of the trainers around are amateurs. They aren't making a career out of their work. They spend maybe an hour with their fighters in the gym and then knock off for the day."

The problem, said Brown, was insufficient regulation by boxing commissions. "They issue licenses like they're selling bagels. It's harder to get a driver's license than it is to become a licensed second. At least they give you a road test and you have to know the traffic rules when you apply for a driver's license. To become a trainer or second, you don't take an exam or give a demonstration; you pay a fee and you're in."

By contrast, said Brown, "In the old days everybody learned the business from the ground up. It took time." Admitting that he made mistakes in his early days, Brown stressed, "but I didn't repeat mistakes . . . I kept learning my trade." The lesson Brown prized above all, perhaps, was the importance of poise. "I've seen so many cuts, I'm an expert," he once said. "I'm the coldest guy in the corner."

By the 1960s, Brown told Deane McGowen of the *Times*, the cut man's job had become easier "because the medical preparations today are quicker and better." Brown also said he'd seen a second slash open a puffed eye to suck out the blood that was causing the swelling. "It was done before modern boxing commissions, but it was always a dangerous thing to do. Some fellows used a small scalpel, others a razor blade, but the danger of infection or damage to the nerves was too great. Commission physicians see to it that cut men don't practice it anymore. The best thing for a badly swollen eye is the ice bag. But I've used a half dollar pressed against the swelling. It can help but the ice bag is best."

About the job of advising a fighter between rounds, Brown said, "Sometimes the fighter doesn't listen. When that happens, I finish my night's work in the ring by half-carrying him to the corner stool."

Asked by the *Police Gazette* to name the finest boxer he'd seen, Brown said, "Well, everybody gives the nod to Sugar Ray [Robinson] and I'm inclined to agree. But don't overlook Willie Pep. Maybe he wasn't as colorful as Sugar Ray, but Willie was smarter."

As Roberto Duran rose to prominence in the 1970s, Freddie Brown and Ray Arcel, as Duran's handlers, received more and more attention in the press. Brown supervised Duran's training on a day-to-day basis—a task that demanded great patience and endurance. Duran was frequently overweight when starting training and often responded to Brown's instructions with explosive displays of his temper. Muriel Brown tells stories of Duran throwing his meal tray onto the ceiling of an airplane when Freddie Brown suggested Duran skip dessert; Duran punching through a windowpane when Brown insisted he run; and Brown traveling to Panama to retrieve Duran to force him to go into training for a bout. In one instance, she says, Brown went to Duran's house only to be told that he refused to see his trainer because he was embarrassed by his oversized waistline. She also recalls her husband going to sleep the night before a fight believing that Duran had retired for the evening. When she looked out of her hotel window, however, she saw Duran dancing and singing with friends.

In a 1974 interview, Brown compared Duran's temperament to those of fighters he'd worked with in earlier days. "I had real tough guys like Graziano, Terry Young, [Joey] Archer—mean guys, but they were delights to work with. Did everything you told them, never a word. Today, well today . . . take this kid Duran. . . . You should see him use the hook I taught him. Anyway, sometimes we have differences, disputes. He thinks he knows best and he's just a kid. But he comes around. You get kissed and he apologizes. Believe me, it's different."

Despite all the headaches, Freddie Brown took pride in explaining what he'd taught Roberto Duran. "When I came into his camp in 1972," Brown recalled in 1979, "he was just a slugger until I taught him a lot of finesse. He's fast with his hands. He's colorful. He's the most colorful fighter in boxing today." In 1980, Brown put it this way: "I took the early Duran, who was strictly a slugger, and turned him into a smart fighter. Now he has two styles, both of which serve him well."

In his early years with Duran, Brown also waxed eloquent about Duran's greatness and unlimited potential. "He's a born fighter, he don't want to know nothin' when you get in there," Brown told Dave Anderson in 1978, after Duran had won a rematch with Esteban DeJesus and was about to go ten tough rounds with Adolfo Viruet. "He wants to win. He wants to destroy you." Brown then showed just how highly he rated Duran. "The only guy I've seen anywhere close to him," Brown said, "would be Henry Armstrong." About a proposed match-up with Alexis Arguello—a fight which never happened—Brown said, "Arguello's a good boxer, a good puncher. But he's a stand-up fighter, he takes punches. Nobody can take this guy's punches."

Brown went as far as to say that Duran was his finest fighter in an interview with the *Las Vegas Sun* in April of 1979, before Duran faced Jimmy Heair. "I would have to go with Duran as far as the greatest fighter I've ever trained," Brown said. "He not only can fight, but he's one of the smartest. He's learned his business. He's one of the most vicious fighters we've ever had. When he's in the ring, he wants you. He can knock people out with either hand. While the fighters are watching one hand, he's hitting them with the other one. There's no question he'll be the welterweight champion."

As for Duran's human side, Brown said, "He's a very moody guy. If you speak his language, he is so much easier to get along with. However, he loves crowds. He's aware of their presence. And they know him. Not only do they know him, they like to watch him. No matter how he looks, he's exciting. He's an entertainer. They better not take their eyes off him."

By the time Duran had moved up to the welterweight division and was preparing to face former champion Carlos Palomino in June of 1979, Brown was discussing Duran's weight problems openly. "Would you believe he once went up to 168 pounds?" Brown told the *Daily News*. What did Duran eat? "He likes everything, sodas mostly. That puts weight on. And he doesn't like to train unless he has a fight on. Eight different times I've had to take at least 25 pounds off him to get him down to the lightweight limit." Though Brown acknowledged that Duran didn't "figure to be as fast" as a welterweight as he had been as a lightweight, he added, "But he's quick. And I don't know how to say it, but he's smart."

Brown then summed up Duran's ring intelligence: "A lot of people don't think Duran is smart, but he's one of the smartest I've worked with, especially for a slugger. Look how he surprised everybody in the second bout with DeJesus. Everybody expected him to come out slugging, but he didn't. He came out boxing."

After Duran decisioned Palomino, Brown repeated his prefight theme. "He is not just a slugger," Brown told the *New York Post*. "He's not just a catcher. He don't put his face out there and say, 'Hit me.'"

Sports Illustrated reporter William Nack chronicled Duran's temperamental outbursts as Brown supervised preparation for

Duran's first fight with Sugar Ray Leonard in 1980. "Duran's a funny guy," Brown told Nack. "Hard to work with. He's definitely got a mind of his own. But he listens. He does. He listens."

Leonard, Brown said, would be Duran's sternest test—"the toughest without question." Watching Duran spar without genuine intensity, however, Brown despaired: "I'd rather have him work two rounds on the heavy bag than that. *That's just wasting time. . . .*" After Duran acknowledged that he'd been goofing off, Brown said, "He knows he did wrong. He apologized. Like I was saying, sometimes you love him; sometimes you want to kill him."

Brown's no-nonsense verbal style is embodied in this description of working with Duran: "It's not a game. I don't play games. When he boxes good, I tell him. When he boxes bad, I tell him. We get into fights all the time. There were times when I was about to give it up. You try to help him, try to help him throw punches right, to do things right, and sometimes he says, 'Let me alone.' So you walk out. One day he's one way, one day he's another. Some days you can't get nothing. You never know. You just have to leave him alone and go along. He listens, but he wants it his way."

In an interview with *The New York Times*, Brown said that by the time Duran was preparing to face Leonard, Duran had mellowed: "The first couple of years, he was very, very tough and did a lot of bad things. He'd go out and get women or go out to eat. He'd send his friends out to get him something to eat, but you can't watch him twenty-four hours a day. He's not bad now. He's not Tony Janiro. Him, you had to watch like a hawk." Janiro, it should be pointed out, was famous for being irresistible to women.

As the Leonard-Duran fight approached, Brown provided a prophetic analysis of what would transpire. "There's a lot of tension in this fight. But it favors experience," Brown told Leonard Gardner, whose report on the fight appeared in *Inside*

Sports. "Duran's been through all this before. But the tension's getting to Leonard. He's worried." After he lost the fight, Leonard admitted to being overwhelmed by both the media attention he received and Duran's baleful image. Brown had gotten it right.

Brown also succinctly summarized the celebrated lecture he and Arcel gave referee Carlos Padilla before the fight began. "I seen the guy work before," Brown told writer John Schulian. "He wouldn't let my fighter work inside and it cost him the fight. So this time I was straightening him out. I told him there'd be a Senate investigation if he didn't let these guys fight."

Despite Duran's victory, Brown still continued to complain about the referee. "Every time the ref broke 'em up," Brown told Schulian, "he pulled Duran away and held him while that damned Leonard sneaked a couple of punches in."

Though Freddie Brown by no means labored in obscurity on Duran's behalf, some of his friends say he didn't receive his fair share of publicity.

Press agent Irving Rudd, who handled the first Leonard-Duran match in Montreal, says respectfully that Brown was "a great cut man and a great corner man" and a "no-nonsense guy" with a "great face" despite a "forbidding scowl."

Rudd then tells a story which he feels explains why the press may have favored Arcel over Brown. A few days before the fight, a boxing ring was set up in a hotel lobby so that Duran and Leonard could spar separately in order to generate publicity. When Duran worked out, Rudd says, "it was mob city." As spectators and newspapermen pressed to get closer to Duran, Freddie Brown got upset. "Get back, you guys, geez, get back," Rudd remembers him shouting. "And I'll never forget this as long as I live," Rudd continues. "He turned to me—an old, friendly face—'Jeeze, I don't understand this, Irving. When I had Freddie Archer I didn't have these problems.'"

Quickly explaining that Freddie Archer was one of Brown's less celebrated fighters from an earlier era, Rudd says that

Brown's comment is evidence of the trainer's failure to grasp the ways of the contemporary boxing scene. "He just had no understanding of what this was all about," Rudd says. "It was beyond him, you know." Freddie Brown was not, to use a contemporary cliché, media savvy.

Contrasting Arcel and Brown from a press agent's point of view, Rudd concludes, "See, here's what we got: We got Ray Arcel—articulate and sophisticated. A guy who reads a book, a guy who mingles, who spent twenty years as a purchasing agent. Freddie Brown has a face like a boxing glove. Freddie Brown says to Irving Rudd in 1980, 'I can't understand this. I never had this problem with Freddie Archer.' So therefore if you're a newspaperman, are you going to seek him out for a story? Are you going to seek him out for a quote?"

Yet for all Brown's supposed lack of polish, boxing writer Michael Katz calls Brown "a classic talker" who could always be counted on for "a good quote." And Jimmy Breslin recalls the day the novelist Nelson Algren walked into a gym where Brown was working—and Brown was the only one who knew who Algren was. "That's a true story," Breslin emphasizes.

As Brown's work with Duran gained him new-found fame, Larry Holmes—who was not yet heavyweight champion—asked the trainer to join his camp. "I been with Holmes . . . since his first Shavers fight," Brown explained to Dave Anderson in July of 1980, referring to Holmes' March 1978 decision win over Shavers. "I'm his cut man, and I show him a few things," Brown continued. "I smartened him up on his left hand. How to move away. How to block with it a little better. He's improving. He's the best of the heavyweights today, by far. He reminds me a little bit of Jack Sharkey, smart and a good left hand," Brown said, making an allusion to the man who won the heavyweight title in 1932.

Brown was again in Holmes' corner when Holmes beat Norton for the title in 1978. Brown, like many others, rated the fight a classic. "I told Holmes he had to win the last round to win the fight," Brown recalled a year later. "Believe me, he was tired. Of course, you know what happened in the fifteenth round."

"The Holmes and Norton fifteenth round was one of the best I've ever seen," Brown told *The Las Vegas Sun.* "Whoever won the round, won the fight. They stood toe-to-toe for the fifteenth and Holmes won. I've never seen a fifteenth round like they fought that time."

Assessing Holmes in 1979, Brown said, "Holmes is a good boxer, but the competition isn't there. The other fighters are nothing. You'd have to say he stacks up as one of the best. But I don't think he could beat Ali in his prime."

Brown, in fact, seems to have been an admirer of Ali. Ali was "the best boxer among the big men I have ever seen," Brown told the *Police Gazette.* "He could have been much too fast for Louis. He'd probably beat Louis on points." Brown also once called Ali "the greatest publicity man there ever was."

Following Duran's surrender against Leonard in the infamous "No Más" fight in New Orleans, Freddie Brown fell into a lasting depression. At the weigh-in before the fight Brown denied that Duran had had trouble making the weight. "I feel just as good about this fight as I did before Montreal," Brown told the press. "I should feel better, because I know Duran's in better shape." Following Duran's shocking surrender, Brown was reluctant to speak to reporters. "He's been a great fighter," was all Brown would say. Later he told *Sports Illustrated,* "He just quit. I been with the guy nine years and I can't answer it. The guy's supposed to be an animal, right? And he quit. You'd think that an animal would fight right up to the end." Freddie Brown was devastated.

Randy Gordon, then an editor of *The Ring,* returned to New York on a plane with Brown after the fight, and he describes a heartbreaking scene. "Freddie cried like a baby on my shoulder.

Cried! I'm not talking about just complain, I'm talking about cried—real tears. Because to him old fighters were the best in history," Gordon says. "Because he had seen them all. Jack Johnson and Benny Leonard. And Harry Greb. All those guys. And he was always saying Roberto Duran could probably beat any one of them in his prime. . . . And then he went out and quit—something that Freddie Brown really could not understand any real fighter doing, much less Roberto Duran. And the whole ride home he sat with me and he cried. . . . He went into hiding after that. He went in, he locked the door," Gordon adds. ". . . And he locked himself away, and he was never the same again."

Brown's widow confirms the story. Fight men would call him on the phone, but he had no interest in even watching a fight. Actor Sylvester Stallone, who at the time was investing in boxers, called to ask Brown if he was interested in working as a trainer, but Brown refused. Stallone, it's often said, based the character of the trainer in his "Rocky" movies on Freddie Brown.

Though Brown had soured on boxing, he apparently retained an affection for Duran. Before Duran, in one of his comebacks, defeated Davey Moore to win the WBA junior middleweight championship in 1983, Brown sent this telegram to the fighter: "I know you can win this fight. Don't let me down."

Prior to Duran's match against middleweight champion Marvin Hagler later that year, Brown told *Sports Illustrated*, "I got to pick Duran. I got confidence in him. I know how much guts he's got, how hard he can punch and how much ability he has. Very smart. You can hit him, but you're going to get hit back." Comparing Duran's chances against Hagler to those of Vito Antuofermo—whom Brown trained for a 1979 draw with Hagler—Brown said, "Vito got right on top of him, pressing him, facing him, making him fight. Hagler doesn't like that. That's why Vito gave him all that trouble. Duran's a better in-fighter than Vito. Duran's a harder puncher and not as easy to hit. Vito was easy to hit. This is a real good fight for Duran." Duran did well in the fight, narrowly losing a fifteen-round decision to Hagler.

After the "No Más" fight, Brown and Arcel had a falling out. Brown aired his opinions publicly nearly three years after the fight when he spoke with Dick Young of the *New York Post* in June of 1984, on the eve of Duran's bout with Tommy Hearns. Saying that he'd invented the story that Duran quit because he was suffering from stomach cramps, Brown told Dick Young, "I couldn't stand the thought of him being disgraced. He was too great a fighter for that. So I said to him, 'Tell them you had bad cramps.' He had no cramps. He had nothing. He was in better shape than he was for the first fight with Leonard."

Brown also criticized Ray Arcel for allegedly telling television viewers that Duran had quit for no explainable reason. "I couldn't do that," Brown said. "If they knew in Panama he'd quit, they'd of murdered him when he got back, so I made the alibi."

Revealing his anger over how much he'd been paid for his work on Duran's behalf for the second Leonard fight, Brown told Young that he'd been given only a small percentage of what he'd been guaranteed. Of his $75,000 payment, Brown told Young, "That is not one percent. I expected four, maybe five percent. I did all the work."

Showing his bitterness toward Arcel, Brown added, "He'd show up a week or so before the fight. Ray had a nine-to-five job. I was with Duran all the time. I was with him since he became champion when he beat Ken Buchanan." Brown also criticized the way Duran's corner was run during the "No Más" fiasco: "It was wild. Everybody was talking at once. I couldn't get a word in edgewise. When I tried, Ray would push me away. Ray just kept yelling, 'Get him on the ropes, get him on the ropes.' That's nothing. You got to tell a fighter something. It's not enough to be on top of a fighter. You got to work. I wanted to tell him to move to the right. He was moving to the left and getting hit by Leonard's right. I couldn't make myself heard in that corner."

When Dick Young asked Brown if he'd come back to Duran's side if Duran asked him, Brown said, "It's too late now."

What remains most poignant about Brown's final years is the image of the trainer cutting himself off from the boxing world. Jackie Graham of the New York State Athletic Commission went as far as to offer Brown a free second's license if Brown would return to boxing. Brown, Graham recalls, "just shook his head and he said, 'No, no, nobody gets a free license, not even you can do that.'" Graham, of course, planned to pay for the license himself. But Brown refused the offer. "He wouldn't do it," Graham says. "He wouldn't come back."

Trainer George Chemeres remembers talking with Brown on the phone during the final years of Brown's life. "He was lonesome," Chemeres says. "But he never wanted to get back in boxing after that Duran thing. . . . And I talked to him, I tried to liven him up, and put some spark in him. I said, 'Why don't you get back in the gym?' 'Oh,' he said, 'I don't even want to go down to the gym. When I go down there all these new guys think I'm gonna steal their fighter.' You know, because he could have any fighter he wanted. . . . He had a lot of offers to be with a lot of fighters, but when he got out of it he never wanted to get back into it."

In August of 1986, at the age of 80, Freddie Brown returned briefly to the boxing world to receive the Cus D'Amato Award for "outstanding service in his field" from the New York State Boxing Commission.

Dr. Edwin Campbell says that although the "No Más" fight hurt Brown, he would not complain about it. "He wouldn't even talk about it," Campbell says. "When you asked him, he wouldn't talk."

Years after his death in 1986, some boxing men will tell you Freddie Brown was the best trainer at Stillman's Gym. Jimmy Archer, for one, argues the case based on what Brown did for Jimmy's brother Joey Archer.

"Freddie wasn't that good with beginners because he didn't have the patience," Archer says. "But he could add to a style." When Joey Archer began working with Freddie Brown, he had already been fighting professionally for five years. With a fighter as experienced as that, Jimmy Archer says, "there isn't much you can teach them." But, he adds, "in the course of a fight, there's a certain step you gotta take. It's all a matter of inches because it only takes an inch or two to miss a punch and an inch or two to land a punch. You may be an inch off. You're not landing properly. Maybe just grazing the opponent." Freddie Brown, with his "experienced eye" taught Joey Archer how and when to take that extra step.

One signature of a Freddie Brown fighter, Jimmy Archer stresses, was the art of clinching—controlling an opponent by properly holding and manipulating him. "You don't see any fighters walking fighters today. Rarely do you ever see a fighter spin another fighter. It's like a lost art because nobody knows how to clinch," says Archer. "Freddie Brown, all the fighters he trained—he made them boss in the clinches. And they're all masters at clinches." Archer cites Roberto Duran, a great in-fighter, as a prime example.

What exactly did Brown teach about clinching? "I mean there was no such thing as letting a guy just hold onto you," Archer says. "The proper thing, when you get into a clinch, is to have your hands on the outside. And you're maneuvering a fighter."

As an example of how Brown's lessons helped Joey Archer, Jimmy Archer cites his brother's 1964 decision victory over Dick Tiger. "Tiger was the aggressor throughout the fight, always trying to get in close on Joey Archer," he recalls. "And Freddie told Joey, 'Just keep the jab out there and keep him at the end of the jab.' And every time that Tiger went to move in close, Joey Archer's hands went outside of Dick Tiger, and he just maneuvered him around the clinches. . . . That was all because of the Freddie Brown technique."

Following Archer's victory over Tiger, Joey Archer told reporter Bob Waters, "Freddie Brown had it figured out. I got hit when I pulled back. Freddie said I shouldn't do that. When I did what Freddie said, I wasn't hit. And that right I almost decked him with? That was Freddie's idea, too."

Vito Antuofermo, whom Brown took to the undisputed middleweight championship of the world in 1979, agrees with Archer's point. "Especially inside, Freddie used to teach me a lot. How to hold a guy. He had a lot of tricks," Antuofermo recalls. Brown's advice also contributed significantly to Antuofermo's successful title defense against Marvin Hagler in their closely fought 1979 bout. Before the fight, Brown told Antuofermo, "If you stay on top of him, if you stay close to him, he won't be able to hit you." The strategy was good enough to earn a draw in a bout which most experts picked Hagler to win easily.

Boxing writer Michael Katz says, "I thought Vito Antuofermo was a hell of a lot better boxer than he was given credit for. He knew how to make a guy miss, how to roll with punches, he knew how to bob and weave. He had very limited skills and very limited talent, but I think Freddie got the most out of him."

Brown began working with Antuofermo just before he won the middleweight title, starting as Antuofermo's cut man before taking over as trainer. For Antuofermo, it was not Brown's knowledge that was most helpful: it was Brown's way of commanding a fighter's respect. "When he spoke to me, for some reason, it sunk into me," Antuofermo says. "When I used to go back in the corner, I'd feel like I was a little kid and I had the father there telling me to do it. If I didn't do it, he'd spank me. And he really made me do it. He had that kind of power for a fighter."

Brown and Antuofermo communicated perfectly. "He knew exactly what to say in order to motivate a fighter," says Antuofermo. "A lot of the stuff he taught me, I knew. I'd heard it before. But I never done it. I knew it, but in the fight, I would never do it. I would do it in the gym, but not in the fight. But he used to make me do it in the fight itself. That's what was great about him. He knew how to talk to a guy."

Brown also knew how to handle Antuofermo's psyche. "Most of the trainers," Antuofermo says, "get close to a fighter. It's good to get close to a fighter, like to be a brother, or to be a friend—but he wasn't a brother, he was a teacher." And Brown was strict. When he wanted a fighter to do something, Antuofermo says, "you had to do it. And if not, you just got yelled at or you got the fuck out of the gym. Or you was no good as a fighter. Sometime I did it just to please him. That's what made me fight better."

Antuofermo, who was notoriously vulnerable to being cut, also gives firsthand testimony about Brown's prowess as a cut man. Particularly memorable was Brown's work during Antuofermo's first fight with Hagler: "When I fought Hagler, I had seventy-five stitches around my eyes, under my chin, around my face. Seventy-five stitches. And you know he was able to . . . there was no blood." After the bout, Brown, then seventy-two years old, told reporters, "I'm getting old. Once I could close six cuts in a minute and not feel hurried."

Before his first fight with Hagler, Antuofermo was suffering from a cold, but Brown convinced him he'd be able to handle Hagler anyway. "If Freddie told me to go through a concrete wall, I woulda done it," Antuofermo says. "The way he talked to me in that fight, he actually brainwashed me. . . . I knew that Hagler's good . . . and I knew I was gonna have a hard time with him. . . . The way Freddie was talking to me made me want to fight this guy in the worst way. . . . He made me believe there was no way this guy was gonna beat me." Freddie Brown, Antuofermo concludes, "was the best . . . especially in the corner. He was the best of anyone I've seen."

AL SILVANI

It's safe to say that no other boxing trainer has led as extraordinarily varied a life as Al Silvani, the young man who started as an apprentice to Whitey Bimstein in 1936 and would become known as Ray Arcel's "right-hand man and left-hand man, too." Silvani went on to befriend Frank Sinatra and pursue careers not only as a leading trainer, but a boxing consultant and assistant director for over two-hundred Hollywood movies as well.

Silvani trained champions such as Rocky Graziano, Jake La Motta, Nino Benvenuti and Alexis Arguello. In 1954, he spent seven months in what was then Siam—now Thailand—where he developed professional boxers and served as director of physical training for the army and police forces. The King of Siam was so pleased with Silvani's services that he rewarded the trainer by sending him on a tour of Thai embassies around the world. In 1972, Silvani trained the Danish boxing team for the 1972 Olympics.

AL SILVANI AND ROCKY GRAZIANO in 1949.
PHOTO COURTESY AL SILVANI

In the show business end of his career, Silvani has taught boxing basics to actors like Paul Newman, Elvis Presley, Clint Eastwood and Robert DeNiro.

All of this prompted Howard Cosell, while attending a fight in Las Vegas in 1978, to tell his wife, "That's Al Silvani . . . the most famous trainer in the world." When Silvani protested, "Oh, no, Howard," Cosell insisted, "Yes, Al, you are the most famous in the world. Others are famous in the U.S."

Silvani's association with world champions, it turns out, was perfect preparation for his later dealings with world leaders and film stars. In 1954, upon being introduced to the King of Siam, Silvani knew exactly how to behave. "They took me up to see the King," Silvani recalls. "I said hello, and I shook his hand. Well, he's the King of Siam. You gotta be a diplomat and don't start to ask questions right away. You just say hello and let them talk."

Silvani remains a quietly self-assured man. Still active as a trainer, Silvani says, "I'm the oldest one from Stillman's, I'm the oldest one left," meaning that he's the oldest active trainer from Stillman's. "I'm still here and I just worked twelve rounds and I'm seventy-nine years old," Silvani says. "And I jump in that ring, and I'm the chief corner man."

Silvani is not a tall man, though he stands out in photos taken at Stillman's because he was tallest among the trainers. He boasts a healthy head of hair, and could easily pass for a man ten to fifteen years his junior. Despite his years in Hollywood, he retains the streetwise air of a New York City native. He also still possesses formidable physical strength and agility. When he asks me to stand up so that he can demonstrate the basics of self-defense, Silvani gently tosses me around the kitchen of his large Los Angeles condominium as if I were weightless.

Silvani's life story, appropriately, sounds like the plot of an old-fashioned, action-filled movie. His parents were Italian immigrants who lived on MacDougal Street in the Italian section of New York's Greenwich Village. Later, the family moved to the Bronx, near the Bronx Zoo. "The Italian were on one side," he recalls, "the Jewish on the other."

Silvani became interested in boxing because his older brother, Joe, was a professional fighter. Silvani remembers hanging around Stillman's, the Pioneer Gym and the basement of the St. Nicholas Arena, watching fighters like Mickey Walker and Gene Tunney. At St. Nick's, Silvani encountered a veteran fighter, Corporal Izzy Schwartz, who had held the New York version of the bantam- and flyweight titles. The sight of the aging boxer with two cauliflower ears and an unsteady gait "scared the living hell out of me," Silvani says.

In 1925, Silvani watched as his brother, a promising light-heavyweight, was seriously injured in a fight for which he hadn't properly trained. "I saw my brother get a concussion of the brain and retire at nineteen years of age," Silvani says. Though his brother never trained, Silvani once explained, "he still fought guys like Maxie Rosenbloom and Battling Siki. I realized how good he might have been if someone had taken care of him." So Silvani decided to become a trainer, and he headed for Stillman's Gym.

Was it tough to break in at Stillman's? "No. It was very simple for me for the simple reason that I was only twelve years old with my brother when I used to go to the gyms. And of course you're a copycat. You look. You learn things by looking at other people. So working in a corner was nothing or training a fighter was nothing because I had forty-five amateur fights. And of course you're not nerved up. I wasn't afraid of what I was doing." About the early days at Stillman's Silvani remembers, "I worked with Whitey Bimstein in '36 and '37, then Ray Arcel asked me to work along with him."

Being a trainer during the Depression, Silvani stresses, was difficult. Sometimes he'd make as little as five dollars a week. "It was a tough business then," he says, echoing Ray Arcel's words. "Just to make a living was difficult." At Stillman's Gym, Silvani explains, there was only one working shower, and the water "just sprinkled out." Training camps were equally rustic—"broken down shacks with no heat or hot water."

Asked to name the best trainers at Stillman's, Silvani replies, "All of us were good. When you work fifteen, twenty fights a week, you gotta learn to be good." From Arcel, Silvani learned to be polite to his fighters. "That's why I'm glad I worked with him," Silvani says, "because I learned . . . I don't get excited. If I dislike a person, I'd sooner have nothing to do with him. I keep it to myself. That's why I say we were all quiet. Like a Ray Arcel, when you talk to him, you never think he was a trainer in the toughest business that we had."

With Arcel, Silvani worked with countless champions, including Henry Armstrong, whom Silvani and Arcel seconded in his 1941 loss to Fritzie Zivic. "See at the time they fought, Henry Armstrong was on the way out and Fritzie Zivic was on the way up," Silvani says. Though Armstrong was "at the tail end of his career," Silvani adds, "he was what we call perpetual movement. He always threw punches. And he took a good punch. But he was always aggressive. He was a little better than the average fighter then because every second of every round he was always moving in at you. That's what made him."

Silvani went off on his own as a trainer when his heavyweight, Tami Mauriello, started gaining prominence in the early '40s. Leafing through his scrapbook, Silvani points to a 1943 headline about "Mauriello's juvenile trainer." "I used to be the juvenile trainer," he says with a laugh. At the time, he was thirty-three years old.

In this period Silvani met Frank Sinatra. "I'll tell you exactly where I met him," Silvani says. "New York City, West 49th Street in the Forest Hotel. Sinatra was sittin' in a bar and he comes over, 'Mr. Silvani, can I talk to you?'" Sinatra, always a boxing fan, was interested in learning to fight, and Silvani agreed to act as his boxing tutor. Sinatra was not yet at the height of his fame as a singer.

"I took him to Stillman's and taught him how to throw a punch and how to move," Silvani recalled. "He caught on quickly. Frank weighed only 119 pounds in those days, but he became a good fighter." Looking at an early photo of himself and the young, skinny Sinatra, Silvani adds, "Look at him, my arms are as big as his legs!"

In March of 1943, as a favor to Sinatra, Silvani asked Harry Markson, who then worked for promoter Mike Jacobs, if Sinatra could sing the National Anthem before Mauriello's fight against Jimmy Bivins in Madison Square Garden. "Are you crazy?" Markson said. "This fight is going on coast-to-coast radio. We can't have an unknown singer." Markson, however, eventually changed his mind and allowed Sinatra to perform before the fight. It's a story that Silvani cherishes, and he points with pride to the fact that the same story appeared in New York City newspapers back in 1943—and again in 1983 when columnist Dick Young repeated it in the *New York Post*.

In 1943, with Tami Mauriello's manager Lefty Remini in the Army, Silvani temporarily became the fighter's manager, as well as his trainer. "Al knows me better than I know myself," Mauriello told the press. "He knows my ways, my moods, my temperament and disposition."

Becoming Mauriello's manager put Silvani in a powerful position in the boxing world. "He was a white heavyweight, the leading contender of the world," Silvani recalls. "I used to get telegrams. We had, at that time, four-hundred fight clubs throughout the whole U.S.A. Well, the matchmakers and promoters would send you telegrams: 'We'd like to see Tami Mauriello fight. Pick your own opponent.'" Silvani naturally picked opponents he was certain Mauriello could defeat. "Who you gonna pick?" Silvani asks rhetorically.

In September of 1946, Mauriello faced Joe Louis in Yankee Stadium. Asked how a trainer prepared a fighter for the awesome Louis, Silvani replies, "You don't do nothing. You react the same way. You can't get nerved up. You just talk. You show 'em, 'If you do this, you're gonna lick him.' You gotta put that confidence in him. You can't say, 'My God! He'll hit you and he'll kill you!'"

Although a Mauriello overhand-right had Louis staggering into the ropes early in round one of the fight, Louis quickly composed himself and floored the challenger with a left hook as Mauriello prematurely moved in for the kill. Mauriello got to his feet after the knockdown, only to be knocked down again and counted out as he hung helplessly over the middle strand of the ropes. After the fight, Mauriello scandalized radio listeners with what was then considered a shocking comment: "I got too goddamned careless."

Remembering the Mauriello-Louis bout, Silvani says: "See, Tami shocked me because usually they [Louis' opponents] were always on the bicycle. And Tami came out and—boom! hit him a shot." Mauriello's mistake, Silvani says, was in overestimating how badly Louis was hurt.

Silvani also revives a controversy which began after the bout. Mauriello's corner claimed that referee Arthur Donovan—who at the time had worked eleven of Louis' title defenses—protected the champion when Louis was hurt at the outset of the fight. Repeating the argument, Silvani points to a newspaper account of the fight in his scrapbook: "Donovan leaped between the fighters, arms outstretched, as if under the impression that Louis was down. For an instant, Tami may have been deterred in continuing the attack. Suddenly Louis was up, moving forward; and Donovan was out of the picture."

Immediately after the fight, Mauriello's manager Lefty Remini angrily told reporters, "Tami had a chance to finish Louis when he knocked him against the ropes, and Donovan interfered. What the hell was his idea of stepping between the fighters and putting his arms around Louis and pushing Tami away when Louis wasn't down?"

Evaluating Mauriello as a fighter, Silvani today says, "Mauriello would have been an exceptionally great fighter, but he always had dates, always had to meet his friends. To train was not his business. But he had natural great ability and he had no fear."

Silvani speaks of Louis with great respect. He also counters the widely held notion that Louis slept in his dressing room before a fight. "People tell me that Joe Louis used to fall asleep in the dressing room," Silvani says. "Well, I tell 'em, yes he did, but he wasn't asleep. He wanted to be left alone. Because I'd be in there a couple of times helping other people when the door would open, and he'd lift his head up to look who was coming in. So that means he's not sleeping." No fighter is truly calm before a fight, Silvani stresses. "They all have their different methods of fright. They all have that fright inside. . . . They're not calm. That inside is moving on you. The outside looks different, but the inside. . . ."

At the same time he was training Mauriello, Silvani was helping Whitey Bimstein with Rocky Graziano. Silvani describes the first time he saw Graziano, who was brought into the gym by Graziano's boyhood friend, the fighter Terry Young. "Terry Young was a tough lightweight from around 10th Street and Second Avenue. Irving Cohen was the manager of Terry Young. And Terry Young had told Irving Cohen, 'This kid is a tough son of a bitch. He fights anybody out on the fuckin' street.' So he says, 'Take him in. Let's see him.' So he comes in with Rocco Barbella, and we wanta see. So we put him in the ring. Now don't forget, Terry Young is nothing but a lightweight. That's a 135-pounder. And Graziano was a 150-pounder. But Terry Young kicked the shit out of him in one round like nothing at all because a street fighter can't fight a fighter. And poor Rocky's bleedin' and all that. I took him in Mauriello's dressing room, and he's bleeding and I fix it. And he says, 'This is a tough business.' And that's the first time I seen him, and he got the shit knocked out of him. But he looked like he had guts enough. He wanted to fight. And Irving Cohen took him over, and I started to work with him at the beginning."

Silvani rates Graziano as one of the top fighters he's ever seen. "Graziano didn't have the neatest looking style," he says, "but he was a rough son of a gun and he had a good right hand. That's all he had. He'd always choke you with his left hand and hit you with the right hand and knock your head in."

Silvani worked two of Graziano's legendary fights with Tony Zale—the first and the third, both of which Zale won. Describing Zale's famous knockout of Graziano with a body shot in their first bout at Yankee Stadium, Silvani says, "Zale caught him with a right hand and he just sat down and his legs were paralyzed. He couldn't get up. He just sat. Yet his mind was all there. He was not knocked out completely with his mind." Describing their third fight, Silvani says, "Graziano got knocked out in the third round. It was no contest. That was in Newark. That I remember like it was yesterday. He got knocked out easy."

A happier—or at least more amusing—memory of Graziano involves the period when Graziano was training for a comeback fight against Sugar Ray Robinson in 1952. Always reluctant to do his roadwork, Graziano protested when Silvani woke him early one morning in training camp. When Graziano tried to go back to bed, Silvani threw a glass of "ice cold water" at the sleeping fighter. "He jumped out of bed and wanted to fight me," Silvani recalls with a laugh. "I said, 'Well, come on. I'm bigger than you are.' And he looked at me. He said, 'You think you can lick me?'" Silvani concludes, "he woulda killed me, but you can't show fright." After this incident, Graziano would introduce Silvani by telling people, "Meet my trainer. He'll fight any trainer in the world."

Describing Graziano as a person, Silvani says, "Rocky was an exceptionally fine guy, but he was born like I was born. Hey, I don't take no dirt." About his own fearlessness Silvani adds, "I was born with that all my life—not to be afraid. . . . I don't look for trouble, but I'm not gonna let people push me around."

Silvani also trained another great—and greatly controversial— middleweight, Jake La Motta. The controversy stems mostly from his 1947 performance against Billy Fox. La Motta, as he explained it in his autobiography *Raging Bull*, threw the fight in order to curry favor with organized crime elements who had promised him a shot at the middleweight crown in exchange for cooperation. La Motta maintained that only by throwing the Fox fight could he have been assured a shot at the mob-controlled title.

Rumors quickly spread among savvy bettors that the La Motta-Fox bout was not on the level. After the fix, La Motta received poor notices from the press. *New York Mirror* columnist Dan Parker wrote that Actor's Equity should have picketed Madison Square Garden to protest La Motta's inferior acting skills.

While Silvani was La Motta's trainer and manager at the time of the Fox fight, he insists he did not know La Motta planned to throw the bout. This is easier to believe when La Motta's reputation of trusting no one is considered, as well as his claim that no one truly managed Jake La Motta because he made all his decisions himself. Asked what Silvani did as his manager, La Motta says, "That was just a front—a front for me."

La Motta describes Silvani's role as his trainer this way: "He worked my corner. Actually, there wasn't really much he could do because I wouldn't listen to nobody anyhow. I did what I felt was right. Of course, he bandaged my hands, he took care of me in the corner. If you had a cut eye, he was good at that. He was good for cuts and stuff like that. And he was a good companion. A nice man to be around with. But as far as him telling me what to do, I wouldn't listen to him—I wouldn't listen to nobody. I just did what I thought right."

La Motta is quick to point out that his indifference to advice is not the ideal approach for all boxers. "Let me explain some-

thing," he says, ". . . Most fighters, I think need some instruc-
tion, they need somebody to tell them what to do. I think I just
happened to be one of the exceptions. Because I was maybe too
stupid to take advice or whatever."

Though the tainted Billy Fox fight is clearly an unpleasant
memory for Silvani, he brings it up himself and discusses it
openly. "A fixed fight, you smell it. . . . You smell that weeks
before the fight. I told that to La Motta. You smelled it all over.
You couldn't get a two dollar bet. You see, the two dollar bettor,
he smells everything. He smells everything that goes on."

Asked what it was like to be in La Motta's corner the night of
the Fox fight, Silvani makes reference to the film *Raging Bull*,
for which he served as technical consultant. "I had the contract," Silvani says. "I was his manager. So I should have known
everything that was on. And I was more innocent . . ." Here
Silvani's voice trails off. "But yet I was under contract. I had Jake
La Motta . . . his manager. . . . If you remember seeing *Raging
Bull*, I told the corner man that plays me there . . . he takes him
and slaps him across the face. See, I did that in the real fight.
Because he [La Motta] wasn't missing by one foot, he was
missing by three feet. So I asked, 'What the hell are you doing?'
Understand? I remember that well."

About Silvani's behavior on the night of the Fox fight, La Motta
says, "Was he in my corner? See, I don't even remember. I don't
think he knew anything, but he knew something was wrong. . . . I
think I fooled him, I fooled everybody. Nobody knew." Told that
Silvani remembers slapping him across the face between rounds,
La Motta says he doesn't remember being slapped.

Silvani's association with La Motta marked the last time he
managed a fighter. "I've been in boxing my entire life," Silvani
says. "You'd think I'd want to be a manager because you make
five times more money than any trainer. . . . See, because Jake
La Motta wouldn't say nothing before a grand jury about Billy
Fox. And they called me. I said, 'Hey, that's the end.' . . . I said,
'They can keep the money. I don't want it.'"

Investigations by the New York State Boxing Commission
and the District Attorney failed to prove that La Motta had
thrown the Fox fight, though he was universally considered
guilty by knowledgeable reporters and fight fans. When a doctor testified that La Motta had been suffering from a ruptured
spleen before the fight, La Motta was found guilty of concealing
an injury from the commission. He was fined one-thousand
dollars and suspended for seven months.

La Motta's victory over Marcel Cerdan for the middleweight
title in 1949 is a happier memory for Al Silvani. Going into the
fight, Silvani says, La Motta was unusually confident. "He was
talking to me after the roadwork," Silvani remembers. "He said
this to me: 'Al, what has he got to lick me? If he could lick me
they're gonna see the greatest fight they ever seen.' And that's
the way he spoke to me. And he only talked to me. . . . And he
proved it."

What about Cerdan's claim that he injured his left shoulder
after La Motta wrestled him to the ground in the first round?
Silvani is unimpressed. "He [La Motta] beat him every round,"
Silvani says. "But they said he hurt his arm when he fell on the
floor. He sat in the corner and he quit." Other ringside observers, however, attributed Cerdan's loss to his shoulder injury. Red Smith, for one, wrote, "it is difficult to believe La
Motta would have had a chance with a two-handed Cerdan."

Silvani, who was joined in La Motta's corner by trainer Al
DeNapoli, ignores the press criticism of La Motta and proudly
points to a photo from The Ring of himself with La Motta and
Cerdan after the fight. The caption reads, in part, "The gleeful
person behind La Motta is his efficient trainer Al Silvani who
had the new title holder in the greatest physical condition of
his career."

In 1950, La Motta was scheduled to fight his old friend Rocky
Graziano. Silvani, who had left Graziano's camp after Grazi-

ano's 1949 victory over Charley Fusari, recalls returning home one day to find Graziano waiting for him. When Graziano asked Silvani to train him for the proposed La Motta bout, Silvani says, he replied, "I'm with La Motta." A few days later the bout was canceled.

Silvani continued in La Motta's corner when La Motta defended his title in 1951 against old nemesis Sugar Ray Robinson in Chicago. Though La Motta handed Robinson his first professional defeat in 1943, Robinson had won four of their previous five fights.

Robinson's 1951 technical knockout of La Motta became known as the "Valentine's Day Massacre" because of the brutality of the beating suffered by La Motta. Silvani blames the loss on La Motta's difficulty making the 160-pound middleweight limit. For La Motta to make the weight for the fight, Silvani remembers, "I had to take him to the baths 'til two o'clock in the morning. Because he decided to eat a lot of shit. I said, 'What are you eating for?' He said, 'No. I wanta be strong.' He put on five pounds. He weighed 166 stripped."

Asked how Silvani helped him make the weight for the fight, La Motta says, ". . . He helped me out by being considerate and by understanding and stuff like that, but I had to do all the hard work. I had to do the starving. I had to do the exercise. And I had to go to the steambaths and things like that. So he was my companion. He was a morale builder."

Silvani disputes the version of the 1951 Robinson fight depicted in the film *Raging Bull*. In the film, La Motta—who never hit the canvas despite a savage beating—taunts Robinson, saying, "You didn't knock me down." "Where did they get that bullshit from?" Silvani asks. The truth, he explains, is that "La Motta collapsed in my arms."

Silvani also objects to the tone of the film. "You see, that's why I told Scorsese, the director, 'What was it? Ninety-eight percent violence, profanity and sex. Right?' So I grabbed Scorsese. I was the technical advisor on it. I grabbed Scorsese. I says,

'Marty. Don't you think we talked like human beings? What is all this profanity?' He put his arm around me. He says, 'Al, it's an exaggeration ten times the amount.'" Sounding exasperated, Silvani explains, "You see that's what people wanta see." In reality, he says, people in the fight game "gotta talk like human beings to each other. Because I need you, you need me."

Silvani also maintains that La Motta's speech was free from profanity. "He never spoke bad," Silvani says. "One thing about Jake La Motta, he would never speak bad about people— although he could beat them. I never heard him swear. He just fought. I believe a real professional doesn't do things like that. As far as I can remember, any good professional never talked about other fighters. It's a tough business. You don't talk about that he's a quitter. It's a person that doesn't know that says things like that. It's too tough a business to go with that."

If he disputes the film *Raging Bull* on several counts, Silvani does confirm one legend—La Motta often played possum during fights, pretending to be hurt to lure his foe into punching range. "He played a lot of possum," Silvani says. "He'd con you to come in at him. And lay against the ropes playing possum and all at once—and this is no exaggeration—he'd throw, seven, eight, nine, ten left hooks at you. From nowhere they'd come— boom, boom, boom. See, there was no fear in him. He weaved good and he had a good left hook. And he played that possum and all at once he'd come off the ropes and throw so many left hooks at you you didn't know what happened to you."

Silvani quit La Motta's camp following the 1951 loss to Robinson. "La Motta doesn't listen to me," he told the press. "He doesn't obey even when he does hear. I'm through with him." But when La Motta was scheduled to fight light-heavyweight Irish Bob Murphy a few months later, according to the *New York Daily News*, "La Motta swallowed his pride . . . to beg Al to return." The report concluded, "Jake appreciates that he'll need all the help possible from his corner . . . and crafty Silvani has guided him to some of his greatest victories . . ." Despite Sil-

vani's presence, however, La Motta, already past his prime, was
stopped in seven rounds.

"At the tail end he got lazy a little bit," Silvani says of La
Motta. "When he fought the light-heavyweight, he got stopped
in Coral Gables on New Year's Day in '53. He didn't train at all.
He said, 'What do I care? What has he got to lick me?' That's the
first fight he ever got knocked down. Because of no training. . . .
And don't forget he fought everybody and this is I think one of
his last fights. . . . Well, he was pretty old, but he was through
then. But he didn't train. He was down there with his wife. He
wasn't training. He wasn't doing no roadwork. We never went to
the gym."

Though Sugar Ray Robinson was La Motta's greatest rival,
Silvani admired Robinson immensely—and didn't even object
to Robinson's occasional dancing, retreating style. "To my mind
he was about the greatest of all times," Silvani says. ". . . I never
saw Sugar Ray even get cut. He was very fortunate that way.
And very seldom ever got hurt. See, Sugar Ray was a smarter
fighter than people were led to believe. When he fought Rocky
Graziano, he would go on the defense when he was being forced.
He was not cocky enough to go, 'Come on, let's go.' He was
smart enough to go on the bicycle. He did that in the last fight
with Jake La Motta. He was on the bicycle backwards so fast
you couldn't believe it. But that wasn't fright. That was his
style. Hey, he was smart enough to know when to move back."

Silvani also resents any comparison between Sugar Ray Robinson and Sugar Ray Leonard. "Sugar Ray Robinson had 274
fights. How could you put them in the same category?" Silvani
asks. "Mr. Sugar Ray Robinson fought the toughest guys in the
world continuously. . . . And don't forget, he fought fighters like
Jake La Motta six times. At that time you couldn't pick your
own opponent."

To illustrate Robinson's toughness, Silvani tells a story that
took place in 1949. Silvani was watching Robinson work out in a

Harlem gym when Robinson asked him to work with a veteran middleweight named Vern Lester. Lester, Silvani recalls, "was a pretty good middleweight at one time. He had a bad eye. He couldn't see. But he needed money, so Robinson accepted a fight in New Orleans to fight Vern Lester. To get him a payday, you know. He [Robinson] said, 'Al, would you work with him and come down?' So all well and good, you know, the guy is gonna make a payday. . . . I know he's giving the guy a payday. He's gonna carry him and all that. And I think it was about the fourth or fifth round. All at once he catches Robinson on the ropes. And he starts to throw punches at him and all that. And the bell rings and he's still throwing punches. I'll never forget it. I had to take him [Lester] to the corner. I said, 'What the fuck are you doing?' 'I think I got him.' All I know is that Robinson is giving him a payday. So I said, 'Jesus Christ, the bell rings and you're still fighting.'" When the bell for the next round rang, Silvani says with an appreciative laugh, "Ray comes out of the corner and puts his hands up like, 'Forget about it.' Ray hit him with a shot and knocked him dead. Boom! I'll never forget it. He puts his hands up . . . and boom! And that was the end of the fight."

Beginning in the 1940s, Silvani spent a great deal of time with Frank Sinatra as a friend, assistant and security man. Defining his role with Sinatra, Silvani explained in 1975, "I don't like the word bodyguard. But if somebody starts to cause trouble, I can take charge."

Sinatra, in return, helped Silvani get started in the movie business. Silvani first worked as a technical advisor on a film in 1956, when he prepared Paul Newman to play Rocky Graziano in *Somebody Up There Likes Me*. The filmmakers originally hired Tony Zale to play himself in the fight scenes with Newman, but Zale had to be replaced when he proved too life-like in the ring. "Being someone who had fought all his life, and seeing this guy in front of him that looked just like Rocky, well, Tony just couldn't hold back," Silvani once recalled.

Silvani, however, says actors such as Robert De Niro often train *harder* for a performance than some boxers do preparing for an actual match. "They're more dedicated than the fighter is," he says. "The dedication is to look good to the public." But Silvani is quick to point out the difference between acting and the real thing. "They all look good when they're shadowboxing. Now when you fight, what happens? See, when you get hit on the chin it's a whole different world. Have you got the guts to come back?"

Having served as assistant director on such films as *Kid Galahad* (starring Elvis Presley) and *Paint Your Wagon* (starring Clint Eastwood), Silvani reached the high point of his movie career when he played himself in *Rocky*. "That's Al Silvani, and he's the best cut man in the business," says actor Burgess Meredith, who plays Rocky's fictional trainer in the film.

At the same time he was making movies, however, Silvani continued to work in the corner of such champions as Floyd Patterson, Nino Benvenuti and Alexis Arguello. Silvani's efforts on Patterson's behalf in Patterson's 1965 fight with Muhammad Ali are still discussed by boxing experts. *The New York Times'* account of the fight noted that Patterson suffered from pain in his chronically bad back as early as the third round. "Al Silvani had to give him a big tug around the waist at the end of the fourth," the *Times* reported. "Silvani said he had pulled Patterson's back into shape before, but this time it didn't work. Silvani tried again after the eleventh, when Patterson was in visible agony."

Looking at a photo of himself embracing Patterson in the corner Silvani says, "See, I'm lifting him up. He hurt his back. So I just snapped his back into place. He couldn't sit down. And he went twelve rounds like that." Remembering the fight Patterson says, "He picked me up to attempt to snap it back in place. It was my vertebrae. I've always had difficulty with my back for many years. And it came out. And he tried, I guess, to get it back in, but he didn't succeed."

Another celebrated piece of Silvani corner work came when Nino Benvenuti defended his middleweight crown against Luis Rodriguez in Rome in 1969. After Silvani managed to control a gash on Benvenuti's nose, which later required twenty-two stitches to close, Howard Cosell told television viewers, "Benvenuti would have lost if it weren't for Al Silvani."

Silvani began to work with Benvenuti in 1968, the year after Benvenuti won the middleweight title from Emille Griffith, only to lose it back in the rematch. "They called me because he wasn't lookin' too good," Silvani recalls. "He was training bad. He was training at Grossinger's up in the Catskills. And they called me and that's when I come in. And I asked them to run the movies of the fights, and I explained to him what he did wrong the second fight. And what he should do against a Griffith. And he beat him pretty easy the third fight."

When Silvani began working with Benvenuti, however, he was treated like an outsider. "Although I'm an Italian-American," Silvani explains, to Benvenuti's Italian-born entourage he was "an Americano." When Silvani first arrived in Benvenuti's camp, he says, "nobody would talk to me." Silvani eased his way in by taking a cautious approach to making any changes in Benvenuti's style.

When working with an established champion—a finished fighter—Silvani proceeds slowly. When he first arrives in camp, Silvani says, he's often asked, "Why aren't you telling the fighter what to do?" But Silvani simply tells the fighter, "I want to watch what you're doing without me telling you. I want to see what's natural to you without me saying anything." Silvani explains, "You gotta see how they do it, then you show 'em how it's done. But you never open your mouth 'til you see them do what's natural to them. Then improve what they want to do."

When Silvani adjusted Benvenuti's style for his bout with Luis Rodriguez in Rome in 1969, he was mocked in the Italian press. Silvani, who saved the headlines, provides a translation: "The Methods of Al Silvani . . . Nino Became A Clown for Rodriguez" and "The Strange Trainer. He Wants To Change The Style and Spirit of Nino." The headlines made Silvani so angry that he swore in the press that if Benvenuti lost, he wouldn't accept one lire. But Silvani remained unchanged in his approach to the fight. "I had to teach him how to throw the left hook that knocked out Rodriguez," he explains. Benvenuti's victory, according to one press account, made Silvani "an overnight personality in Italy."

Asked to summarize his work with Alexis Arguello, Silvani says, "I saw that he had a good right hand and a pretty good left hand, but he didn't jab enough with it. And then when you're jabbing good, you learn to throw a hook from it. And that's what I added."

Though he eventually parted company with Arguello, Silvani remembers the fighter fondly. "See, he was born in Managua, Nicaragua. Well, he was born to poor people. And he was an exceptionally nice kid. And where he lived—he showed me where he lived—it was all dirt roads, right in the city. And the family was pretty big. He had all to do to eat. . . . But he and I, we always had a good friendship, we were always together."

Is Silvani, then, like a father to his fighters? "Well, not like a father—like a friend. See, they know that you're their trainer. . . . If they got the confidence in you, they're gonna listen to you. I'm not going to give them a long story or nothing. You just give 'em what you think is right and that's it."

Perhaps the extraordinary diversity of Silvani's career is best expressed by a story he tells about getting the job of technical advisor on John Huston's 1972 boxing film, *Fat City*.

Silvani went to Huston's Rodeo Drive office to be interviewed by the director. "Hello, Mr. Silvani," Huston said. "I'd like to know some of your background." Silvani simply handed Huston a scrapbook containing clippings about his career as a trainer. "He took that book," Silvani remembers, "sat down at his desk, and for the next twenty minutes he's just reading. Gets up, hands me back the book. He says, 'What can I tell you? You got the job.'"

Completing the anecdote Silvani shrugs modestly and says simply, "What can I say? He saw the stuff."

EDDIE FUTCH

Eddie Futch was so quiet you wouldn't even know he was there," says Angelo Dundee when asked when he first became aware of his old friend and rival. But by 1973, like everyone else in the boxing world, Dundee was well aware of Futch, who had by then trained Joe Frazier and Ken Norton for their victories over Muhammad Ali.

Futch, the understated, scholarly trainer who began his career in boxing as a stablemate of Joe Louis at the Brewster Recreation Center in Detroit in the early 1930s, is probably more celebrated for halting a bout than for helping hand Ali his two most significant defeats.

After fifteen brutal rounds of Ali and Frazier's 1975 "Thrilla in Manila," Frazier's vision was severely hampered. "The swelling in Frazier's left eye became so pronounced that he couldn't see out of the eye at all," Futch recalls, providing a meticulously detailed account of his thoughts. "And the right eye was beginning to close also. Well, the twelfth round wasn't a good round, but it wasn't as bad as the ones that would follow. And we had

311

to abandon the fight plan. The fight plan was to stay low and stay in close, work the body, and make Ali bring his hands down and then shift to the head. Well, after [Frazier's] eye began to swell so badly that he couldn't see . . . he had to pull back a step and stand up so that he could see better out of the right eye—which was right in Ali's range.

"And Ali . . . took advantage of it and he really started opening up with both hands. . . . I kept looking for signs of Ali beginning to flag. But he saw his opportunity and he kept exploiting it. . . . Ali threw so many punches in the thirteenth round that I said, 'Maybe Ali will just have to try to coast.' Put the pressure and it's possible he [Frazier] could catch Ali with the good left hook and turn this round around.'

"The fourteenth round was worse than the thirteenth. So I decided during the fourteenth round, I said, 'If he gets through this round okay, I'm not going to let him go out for the next round because I knew Joe as a great father. A great father. He had a good family. He loved those kids and those kids loved him. And they did a lot of things together. It was always a pleasure to see them together as a family—him and his children. I said, 'Now I can't let this man get hurt. All these kids are his life—and he is their life.' I said, 'If he wound up a vegetable, that would be one of the greatest tragedies of all time. . . . I just can't let this happen.

". . . At that stage, after fourteen rounds of *intense* battling and his strength starting to slag, his ability to throw off the effects of a punch . . . was diminishing. And these are the kind of fighters who get hurt seriously—those who won't go down, who will stay there and absorb the punishment when their body is just not capable of handling it anymore. And their mind tells them to stay up and their body just can't handle it. That's when I made my decision."

When Eddie Futch stopped the Thrilla in Manila, he believed Joe Frazier was ahead on points. "I thought that his work up through the tenth round had given him an edge," Futch recalls, "and that Ali was coming up to the point where the fight was almost even, but I thought Joe was still ahead."

Red Smith of *The New York Times* also had Frazier ahead—and also agreed with Futch's decision to halt the bout. Smith wrote: ". . . little Eddie was right to negotiate the surrender. Frazier's two-million-dollar guarantee wasn't enough to compensate him for another round like the last."

Sports Illustrated reported the dialogue in Frazier's corner after the fourteenth round as follows:

Futch:	"Joe, I'm going to stop it."
Frazier:	"No, no, Eddie, ya can't do that to me."
Futch:	"You couldn't see in the last two rounds. What makes ya think ya gonna see in the fifteenth?"
Frazier:	"I want him, boss."
Futch:	"Sit down, son. It's all over. No one will ever forget what you did here today."

Recalling the moment fourteen years later, Futch says, "When Joe came to the corner at the end of the fourteenth round, I said, 'That's it.' He sat down and I said, 'Joe, it's all over.' Then he jumped up and I gently pressed him on the shoulder and he sat down again. I said, 'It's over, Joe.'"

Immediately following the fight Joe Frazier himself said, "I didn't want to be stopped. I wanted to go on, but I'd never go against Eddie."

Ray Arcel's initial response to mention of his good friend Eddie Futch is, "He's a helluva trainer. . . . He knows every move that goes on in that ring. He's a throwback to the old-time trainers." When Futch's name again comes up, Arcel adds, "Eddie Futch is a quiet, unassuming man. He has a wonderful way about him. He never raises his voice. And he knows boxing from A to Z. He knows just what to do."

Still active as a trainer at the age of seventy-nine, Futch

displays the same awesome poise and storytelling mastery as
Ray Arcel. Like Arcel, Futch is elaborately polite, though an
underlying firmness makes it clear that he has little patience
for anyone who might try to take advantage of his courteous-
ness. Like Arcel, Futch analyzes fighters at length and tells
detailed anecdotes. He talks about famous contemporary fighters and fighters who would likely be forgotten if not for his
faithful memory. Futch also loves order—a quality that's apparent when he describes the careful way he cares for a boxer or a
fight he worked on forty years ago.

Eddie Futch is a compact, powerful-looking man, almost bar-
rel chested. From the gracefulness of his movements, it's easy to
sense he was a fine athlete as a young man. His gold watch and
fondness for rings reveal the wealth he's found later in life.
Above all, there is a genuine delicacy about this former amateur boxer. His face is broad and strong, but his eyelashes are
strikingly long and curled. He speaks quietly and expansively,
more comfortable providing a questioner with a short, elegant
spoken essay than a quick one-liner. Though he loves to laugh
and relishes the many ironies of the boxing business, Eddie
Futch doesn't make jokes. He is a professor rather than a show-
man.

Futch is extraordinarily careful in his use of the English
language. As he speaks, he seems to consciously strain to avoid
ending sentences with prepositions. This love of language is
evident also in Futch's fascination with poetry—a passion
which began while he was growing up poor in a one-parent
household in Detroit. Today, Futch's ability to recite the works
of nineteenth-century British poets from memory can put almost any Ivy League English major to shame.

Futch's verbal precision is abundantly on display in his description of first seeing Muhammad Ali, the man Futch faced in
so many key fights in his career as a trainer. "I thought he was
amazing," Futch says, as delighted and amazed as if remember-

ing his first meeting long ago with an intriguing but difficult woman. "He did so much with so little. He didn't do many things in boxing. He had a jab, a straight right hand and he threw the hook whenever he had the opportunity, but it was jab and straight right hand most of the time. And his defense was monolithic. He pulled back. He very seldom ducked, he very seldom blocked a punch. . . . And he never threw a body punch. Didn't know how to throw the uppercut."

Rather than succeeding with technical boxing perfection, Futch says, Ali got along on "his speed and his good reflexes and his big heart. He would try anything that worked." Explaining the immense gulf between Ali and more ordinary fighters, Futch says, "You see, a lot of guys have ability they don't use because they're afraid to take the chance." By contrast, Futch remembers seeing Ali spar after he'd first turned professional. Working with "guys who could hurt you," Futch recalls, Ali "had his hands down and they couldn't hit him." Futch remembers thinking, "The kid's got a lot of guts. Brash!"

Futch first stood across the ring from Ali in Madison Square Garden on March 8, 1971, when Joe Frazier and Ali fought for the first time. Futch had been working in Frazier's corner along with manager Yank Durham, who had guided Frazier since 1964, after Frazier won an Olympic Gold Medal and a year before he turned professional.

Futch began training Frazier in 1966. "I was working at the Post Office at the time," Futch recalls, "handling fighters but things weren't that good. So I had gone to the Post Office in about '63. I didn't intend to make a career out of the Post Office. I wanted everybody to know that. But at the time it was necessary."

Describing how he came to work with Frazier, Futch says, "I moved to California in '51. But I'd been all over the East. I did a lot of work in Philadelphia. Everyone in Philadelphia knew me, and knew that I always handled good fighters. So when I moved to the West Coast, *every fighter* who came to the West Coast from Philadelphia was sent to me by someone. Everyone would say, 'Go to Eddie Futch on the West Coast. It'll do you some good.' Joe Frazier was the last one in a long line.

"I didn't know Yank Durham. I didn't know Joe Frazier. I knew Joe Frazier as the Olympic heavyweight champion. That's all I knew about him. I'd never seen him fight; he'd had eight pro fights at the time. So I'd come highly recommended to Yank Durham. . . . And naturally we got together and Yank liked how I sounded, so he came on out, brought Joe out to the Coast. Yank didn't know any of the fighters on the coast. So he had to put his trust in me."

Smiling at the memory, Futch recalls that he and Frazier had an instant rapport. "The minute we met, we clicked. It was a combination that lasted. I was with Joe for twelve years."

Futch speaks warmly about Durham and Frazier, and with appreciation for the opportunity they gave him. They were "fascinating people to be involved with," Futch says. "It was something that just happens once in a lifetime." Of Durham, Futch says, "Yank was a good man. A good man. And I always respected the fact that he was a man who knew his own mind. He got a lot of flack coming all the way to California to enlist my aid when there were all those good trainers there in Philadelphia."

Emphasizing his loyalty to Durham, Futch later adds, "See, I didn't take any liberties with Yank. Yank was the manager. He liked me. Joe Frazier was the best fighter he ever had, and he was enjoying it. I wanted everyone to know that Yank Durham was a good manager—as long as he'd listen to me, and I could get the results." If he did his job well, Futch recalls thinking, "Mine'll come."

In his straightforward way, Durham called Futch's judgment into question in May of 1966 as Frazier was preparing to go into the ring against the first opponent Futch had chosen for him. The opponent was Chuck Leslie, a fighter Futch had trained and considered "a good journeyman" but "no match for Frazier."

"So the day of the fight," Futch recalls, "we're in the dressing room, I'd just wrapped Joe's hands. And Yank came to me. He'd been out wandering around. He was a very frank man. He came in and sat down. He said, 'Eddie, they say you put me in a bad match.' I said, 'Yeah, well that's interesting.' I says, 'What did they tell you about the fighter?' 'They told me you put me in with a runner. He's gonna run. He's gonna make Joe look bad.' So I said, 'Well, Yank. I'm glad you got that information, but I'm gonna tell you how it's gonna be. I used to train Chuck Leslie. He's not a runner. He's got a big heart. But he's gonna run when he gets in there and sees how *strong* Joe is, and how hard he hits. He's gonna run. But he doesn't know *how* to run. And in the process—him trying to use that tactic to elude Joe—he's gonna get hit with something. It's gonna hurt him, but it's not going to knock him down. But it's gonna bring the fight out in him then. When he gets hurt, he's gonna stop and fight. Then he's going to get knocked out.'"

A man who takes pride in displaying his hard-earned powers of reasoning, Futch slowly concludes the story. "It happened just like I said. *Just . . . like . . . I . . . said.* And Yank said, 'You musta written a script for this one.' He says, 'You're my man. I don't care what anybody says, you know what you're doing.'"

The memory of Frazier's third-round knockout of Chuck Leslie compels Futch to describe what took place immediately after the fight. "So the matchmaker came down to the dressing room. He says, 'We just had one fighter in the main event fall out for next week's bout. Your fighter didn't work hard. So why don't you consider taking the main event?' So Yank said, 'Who's the opponent?' He says, 'Memphis Al Jones.'"

Once Futch was alone with Durham, he recalls, "I said, 'I have never seen Memphis Al Jones, but I'll tell you how he is. Memphis Al Jones boxed Jerry Quarry. Jerry Quarry had him down in the first round with a left hook. And Jones got up and went the distance with him. So Memphis Al Jones weighs 201 pounds, I saw that, which tells me if he can do that with

Quarry—get up after he's knocked down and go the distance with him—and he weighs 201 pounds, it means he's tall. He's probably six-foot-three. And he's thin. Because at six-foot-three weighing 201 lbs, he's gotta be thin.'"

How could Futch be sure Jones was tall and thin? "Because the only kind of fighter who was going to elude Jerry Quarry's good left hook—it was a short left hook—was going to be a tall guy who's gonna pull back. So on the basis of what I saw—I saw the weight and I saw the result—I saw he's gotta be a tall guy. And he's gotta be thin, so he's vulnerable downstairs."

Based on these deductions, Futch told Durham, "I would take the fight, and send Joe to go to his body. Bang him around the body and make him bring that chin down. Bring those hands down. And then get him outta there." Again relishing the payoff to a story, Futch says, "I never saw Memphis Al Jones 'til the weigh-in. When he stepped on the scales, he was *exactly* the way I described him."

As Frazier went out for the start of the first round, Futch told him, "Stay to the body. Hook to the body. Throw the right hand to the body. Don't throw anything to the head. Get his hands down, then he's gonna have to bend down a little bit to protect his body, then you go to the head." Frazier never had to go to the head, however, Futch concludes, "He knocked him out with a body shot in the first round."

By this time, Futch realized just how great a fighter he was handling. "After I saw him fight the first two fights," Futch remembers, "I said, 'He can lick anyone in California.'"

When Eddie Futch started working with him, Frazier was already an Olympic champion with a string of eight consecutive early-round knockouts. What, then, did Futch add to Frazier's style? "Joe was a standup fighter when he came to me," Futch says. It was an approach which got Frazier into trouble in his twelfth professional fight against Oscar Bonavena. The fight took place in New York, and Futch, back in California, watched it on television. "Bonavena had Joe on the deck twice," Futch remembers. "If he'd had one more knockdown he woulda been counted out." Afterwards, Futch recalls telling Durham, "Yank, we've got to make this kid bob and weave because he can't walk in standing up straight like he's doing now."

Before Frazier faced another major test against heavyweight contender George Chuvalo in July of 1967, Futch got a leave of absence from the Post Office to work with Frazier full time. "I made him start to bob and weave," Futch says. "I put a rope from one of the ring posts to the other, and I made him bob and weave under the rope."

Expanding on the fine points of this addition to Frazier's style, Futch says, "I taught him how to do it so that he wasn't in rhythm. I said, 'You see that speed bag? As long as it's coming right straight back to you, you can close your eyes all night long and hit it. But if it wobbles a little bit, then you have to hesitate to find where it's coming from. I want your head to do that. And never let the man know which way you're coming. Your body is going forward, but your head, you gotta make it erratic. Make it a little erratic.'"

After Frazier began moving his head, Futch says, "a lot of punches slid off his head where before they were glancing blows—because of the way the head was bobbing. And he picked it up very effectively, and being a short fella, he needed that."

In 1967, after Muhammad Ali had been stripped of his heavyweight title following his refusal to be inducted into the United States military, the World Boxing Association staged a tournament to find a new champion. Though Joe Frazier was a top-rated contender, at Futch's urging, Yank Durham did not enter Frazier in the tournament. "I kept him out of the WBA tournament," Futch says, recalling that he told Durham, "There's ten fighters, eight are going to be in the tournament. There's gonna be two who are not in the tournament. Let Joe be one of the two. Out of the tournament will come one winner and seven losers."

Frazier was instead matched against his old amateur rival Buster Mathis in Madison Square Garden. When Frazier knocked out Mathis in the tenth round, he won the New York World Heavyweight Title. Though the title was all but meaningless, it established Frazier as the natural rival for Jimmy Ellis, who had won the WBA tournament with victories over Oscar Bonavena and Jerry Quarry. After Frazier defeated Bonavena in a rematch in December of 1968 and knocked out Quarry in June of 1969, he was matched against Ellis, whom he knocked out in five rounds on February 16, 1970, to win official recognition as heavyweight champion.

Though Frazier had reached his prime as a fighter, Futch recalls with admiration, "Joe wasn't the kind of fighter who would try to intimidate. He never tried to intimidate. I used to watch him in the center of the ring as he looked at his opponent. And he always had a little smile on his face—just a half smile. In fact, I used to think, 'Joe looks at his opponents like they're something good to eat. And he just can't wait to get to it.'"

It was not until 1969 that Yank Durham was able to convince Futch to leave his Post Office job to devote all of his time to training Joe Frazier. Though Frazier was by then declared heavyweight champion, Muhammad Ali and his many fans still, of course, considered Ali the one and only true champion. The Supreme Court's decision in favor of Ali set up the classic, money-making match between two undefeated heavyweight champions.

Ali and Frazier were each guaranteed $2.5 million for their 1971 showdown in Madison Square Garden—a fight which set new standards for prize money, hype and genuine excitement. Yet Futch speaks of the event with characteristic analytical dispassion. In Joe Frazier, Futch had a great-hearted and gifted fighter with the tools to expose whatever flaws the brilliant Ali may have been hiding in his career as an undefeated heavyweight. Though Ali had won victories over Quarry and Bonavena during his comeback, three years of enforced idleness had somewhat eroded his brilliance.

Asked if Frazier was genuinely annoyed by Ali's outrageous— and sometimes cruel—pre-fight antics, Futch says, "Joe was very sensitive, very sensitive. And that type of thing bothered him." Futch, however, was not inclined to take Ali too seriously. "He was a mouthy guy, a cocky guy," Futch says. "But if you really knew Ali, you knew that he was putting you on. He was putting you on."

Before explaining Frazier's strategy going into the fight, Futch carefully lists Ali's many assets: "Ali had this great speed, and he was a difficult man to corner because he had learned to move. And he had the ideal type of a jab for a fighter who pressed persistently like Frazier did. Ali didn't try to hurt you with the jab or stop you with the jab, he just wanted to knock you off balance so that you have to get set repeatedly to try to land something effectively against him." Cataloging Ali's other strengths, Futch says, "That jab and straight right hand and good reflexes and that acrobatic balance, that's what he had. . . . He had that good chin, big heart."

Faced with Ali's abundant gifts, Futch explains, "We nullified the jab partly by having Frazier bob and weave—slip punches and force Ali back to the ropes. Then Ali would have to bend his body to defend his body as best he could against the attacks that Frazier would launch when he got Ali against the ropes."

Futch felt that Ali would be especially vulnerable against the ropes. "Ali did not know how to throw the good right hand uppercut. He would stand up straight, and Frazier being a bobber and weaver, Ali would have to drop the right hand down and bring it up in the uppercut fashion. So that meant Ali—this 6'3" fighter, dropping his right hand down to throw the upper-cut—would leave his right side exposed for the length of time that it would take Frazier to land that devastating left hook."

This then was the heart of Futch's plan: Frazier would back Ali against the ropes and counter Ali's imperfect right uppercut with his own famous left hook—one of the best left hooks in heavyweight history.

Futch remembers telling Frazier, "Joe, here's a guy who doesn't know how to throw an uppercut. He stands up straight, drops his right hand and throws a punch. So the minute you see that right hand drop, you step in with a left hook." Futch then adds proudly, "That's the way Joe knocked Ali down. He knocked him down in the fifteenth round."

Futch goes on to describe the eleventh round of the fight, when Frazier hurt Ali "worse than the knockdown in the fifteenth." Says Futch, "This is the way it worked out. Frazier caught Ali with a hook in the eleventh round of the fight, and he was so badly hurt that the fight should have ended there. But Ali—his great presence of mind—just conned Frazier out of it. He exaggerated how much he was hurt and so Frazier thought, 'Well, no, I know he can't be hurt that bad, he's trying to con me. He's trying to draw me in so he can launch an attack.' So Frazier just walked calmly over to him instead of rushing over and taking advantage of the fact that he had him hurt. He just walked calmly over to him and when he got within range he started working again. But Ali by that time—being in great shape—had recuperated. You know it takes maybe three seconds for a well-conditioned fighter to shake off the effects of a single punch like that."

Returning to Ali's improvisatory con job on Frazier, Futch says with admiration, "That shows *presence of mind.* Great fighters have that." Following the fight, Futch says, the members of Frazier's camp kidded Frazier about his failure to capitalize when Ali was hurt in the eleventh round. "We always teased Joe about that later—about 'The Long Walk.'"

Describing the fifteenth round, when Frazier floored Ali with a classic left hook, Futch says, "In the fifteenth round, he not only caught Ali with a good left hook—he caught him right on the chin. The other punch—[in the eleventh round]—had been on the jaw about midway, but the punch on the chin, a couple of inches lower, is what took Ali down. But he got up, in fact, he recovered in about four seconds on the canvas, and he was up again and going about his usual tactics. But that was the thing that we had planned for that fight, to catch him in the act of throwing the uppercut—and stepping in and throwing the left hook. And it did work whenever Joe was able to seize that opportunity."

Futch takes pride in the calm that prevailed in Frazier's corner that night—and notes that announcer Don Dunphy, who handled the closed-circuit broadcast of the fight, also noticed the professionalism of their work. "Don Dunphy, when the camera panned over into our corner, in one of the rounds, Don Dunphy made one comment. He said, 'A cool corner.' Everyone was working efficiently. Everyone was doing his job and there was complete coordination in the corner. There was no tension that you could detect. I was always proud that that was the kind of corner that I usually was able to achieve."

When Eddie Futch speaks of Muhammad Ali, he sometimes sounds like a butterfly collector recounting the capture of a particularly prized specimen. On a personal level, however, Futch seems fond of Ali. As for Ali, shortly after losing to Ken Norton, he told reporters, "that Eddie Futch isn't as dumb as he looks."

Asked about his personal relations with Ali, Futch explains, "the press assumed that Ali disliked me." Sensing an opportunity for controversy, Ali played up the rivalry with Futch. In reality, however, Ali sought out Futch's company. "Privately, Ali was always trying to get me to go out with him, come up to his camp. He said, 'You're not too far from me. I'll send a limousine down to come and pick you up. Come on up to Deer Lake [where Ali trained] and spend the day with me.' And I had considered this several times, but I was always too busy."

Futch and Ali finally wound up spending a day together when they were both in Albuquerque, New Mexico for the 1974 retirement party of one of Futch's fighters, light-heavyweight champion Bob Foster. "Ali was there and naturally I was there," Futch recalls. "And after breakfast, everybody was going out to see the sights and whatnot. Well, I decided to just get some newspapers and magazines and go up to my room and just rest and relax and read the papers." While at the newsstand, Futch encountered Ali who said, "Why don't you come out with me?"

Describing the pleasant memory, Futch says, "We went to one of the Muslim restaurants. And that was quite an experience. Boy, was he popular with everybody there! *Everybody*! And he said, 'Did you ever have any of our bean pie?' So he went back into the kitchen and served it to me."

When the two visited a men's clothing store, Ali couldn't resist revealing Futch's identity. "The minute Ali went into the store, people lined up outside, you know, looking in. And the owner of the store came out to wait on Ali. So I decided I would pick up a tie and shirt, too. So I was making my selection back there. And Ali looked back and he said—to everyone in the store—'I bet you can't guess who I'm palling around with today.' And the fella said, 'No.' He said, 'Would you believe—Joe Frazier's manager?'" Laughing heartily Futch adds, "So he insisted on me coming up there and identifying myself."

A question about Ali's current woeful physical condition, however, brings a decidedly unsmiling reaction from Futch. "I'm saddened when I see him today because it didn't have to happen." Repeating his words, Futch says emphatically, "It didn't have to happen. I've had a lot of fighters. I've never had a fighter walking around like that."

Often, Futch says, fighters continue their careers long after they should retire. "They don't realize the body cannot throw off the effects of the punches they take at one age like it can when they're much younger. And that's what caught up with Ali. And it wasn't so much the fights—it was the training. The training. He would stand there and let his sparring partners bang on him."

As a lightweight amateur boxer at the Brewster Recreation Center in Detroit in the early 1930s, Eddie Futch was a gifted young athlete with precocious powers as a teacher and leader. "Eddie Futch was a good basketball player," remembers Walter Smith, a Brewster member who went on to work as a trainer for the Kronk Gym in Detroit. Smith, who pays tribute to Futch's skills as a star forward for the Y.M.C.A. Flashes, recalls, "Eddie started boxing late because he stopped playing basketball. Then he came to boxing." Very quickly, Smith adds, "Eddie got real good."

Futch remembers that both athletics and teaching came easily to him. "I was always an athlete. Boxing was my last sport. I started off as a track man in grammar school and high school. And I gravitated to basketball. I became president of the Leader's Corps at the YMCA where the principal director took seven young men and taught them the use of all the equipment and how to teach all the sports. I taught swimming. I taught basketball, softball. And all of the equipment—the rings and the horse—all of the equipment they used in the YMCA, I could teach it. I could lead any class in the YMCA."

As a member of the Leader's Corps, Futch taught at Detroit's Century Club. "The Century Club was made up of lawyers, doctors, preachers, professional men," Futch explains. "And when I came in to lead the class, they followed my directions just the same as if I was the physical director. That was the spirit of the thing."

Analyzing the appeal boxing held for him as a young man, Futch says, "I was always very competitive. To me, boxing is like any other sport. I go out there to outscore my man. If a knockout comes, it's incidental. It's not because I went looking for a knockout."

Freddie Guinyard, boyhood friend of the Brewster Center's star light-heavyweight Joe Louis, confirms the image of Futch as an unusually mature young man who was always looked upon as a leader. "Eddie Futch was a damned good boxer and also a leader of most of the fighters," Guinyard says, adding that Futch "was an inspiration to Joe Louis."

Asked to explain how Futch inspired Louis, Guinyard says, "Well, Eddie Futch was an inspiration to most of the fighters that came up during that time because he had a little more on the ball than the average. His education was a little better. And also his movements and knowing how to fight."

Helping out as an informal trainer around the gym, Guinyard says, the young Futch "never neglected anyone." Guinyard remembers Futch quietly watching sparring sessions and helping Brewster's trainers do their job. "He would say, 'Tell him to keep that left hand up when he gets ready to throw that right hand. Stop pulling it down. That's an opening.' You know, things like that."

As a young lightweight, Futch sparred several times with Joe Louis who was then on his way to becoming the national amateur light-heavyweight champion. "I boxed with Joe for his last national amateur tournament," Futch explains. At the time, Futch was working a split shift as a waiter at the Hotel Wolverine in Detroit. The arrangement let Futch off from work during the afternoon for training sessions at the Detroit Athletic Association.

Futch relishes the details as he describes being Joe Louis' partner for Louis' last sparring sessions as an amateur in late May of 1934. "Joe was leaving that evening for St. Louis where the national AAU [Amateur Athletic Union] tournament was being held. Well, I had boxed with him on a number of occasions, and it really was a tough job," Futch says with a laugh, remembering the harrowing prospect of facing Louis in the ring. "And I used to ask him, 'Why do you want to box with me? I know what you want—you want speed. But the middleweights are fast enough for you. You're a light-heavyweight. Get a middleweight, they're bigger and they're fast enough.' He said, 'No, no, no. I can hit those guys with everything. When I hit you with anything, I know I'm sharp.' So I sparred with him for that tournament."

Futch goes on to remember how, against Louis, "I had little things I could do, though I never told him how I could do these things and get away with them." Over the years, Futch developed a way to hit Louis with a sneak left hook. "You couldn't do it often," Futch says, "but you could do it once in a while. And he never could understand how I could hit him with that left hook. And he never could counterpunch on me."

Displaying his subtle understanding of the complex mechanics of boxing, Futch explains, "What I would do is I would feint him. See, I couldn't force him anywhere. But I could *lead* him there. I'd get into the corner myself, then I'd move out, and with him following me, lead him into the corner. I'm in front now; he's in the corner. Better yet, maybe a foot from the connecting rope. So then I'd feint the left hand to the body, like I was gonna jab to the body. But it'd just be a feint. And I would throw the left hook to the head—and I'd pivot on the ball of my left foot and pivot hard and fast. If I'd been in the center of the ring and done that I'd have been falling on the floor. But remember we're at the ropes now and when I pivot around, the ropes catch me and keep me from falling down. So we wound up . . . side by side. He's in no position to punch."

Telling the story, Futch still seems awed by the immense physical risk he took sparring with Louis. "If he had the opportunity to counterpunch, that left hook was like lightning," Futch stresses. "He'd come back so quick with it."

Futch was careful to use his little trick against Louis infrequently. "I would pick that spot, set that up, and do that," he says. "Now I couldn't do it often because I didn't want him to catch on to what I was doing."

Louis, however, always a clever boxer, eventually analyzed Futch's tactics. "So now one day he was waiting for it," Futch concludes. "So I got him in the top and I feinted, and he just put up his hands, and he didn't do anything. And I feinted again, and he didn't do anything. So the next time I feinted and he didn't do anything, I stepped back and said, 'What are you doing?' And he said, 'I'm trying to see where you throw that damn flukey left hook from.'" With a laugh, Futch adds, "I said, 'What do you care? I can't hurt you?' He said, 'But if you can hit me with it, someone who can hurt me can hit me with it.' I said, 'You'll never know while I'm sparring with you.'"

Louis went on to win the national amateur light-heavyweight championship and then turn professional in the summer of 1934. Shortly after knocking out former heavyweight champion Max Baer in September of 1935, Louis came to Detroit and visited his old amateur gym. "He always liked to come down to the gym and talk to the fellas and train there for a few days," Futch says.

While at the gym, Louis chose five of his former teammates to be his sparring partners. "And I was one," Futch says, "and we were all excited about it. So some of the fellas came to me and said, 'Are you gonna work with Joe?' I said, 'No, I'm not gonna spar with him.' They said, 'Why not?' I said, 'First place, now he's a heavyweight. He's the best heavyweight in the world.'" Besides, Futch told his friends, "His pattern is so clear. We all gave him a little problem when he was here as a light-heavyweight. That was a year ago. Now he wants to see how far he has come." When Futch's friends reminded him that Louis was offering to pay his sparring partners the lofty sum of ten dollars a round, Futch replied, "Yeah, but that's not going to be enough to pay your hospital bills."

In 1933, Futch won the Detroit Golden Gloves lightweight championship. He ended his amateur boxing career with a record of thirty-seven wins and three losses. When he was about to turn professional in 1936, a doctor detected a heart murmur and Futch, as his old friend Walter Smith puts it, "had to resort to training fighters."

With a wife and four children to support, Futch worked various jobs in Detroit in the late 1930s and 1940s, including a stint with the Ford Motor Company as a spot welder. But he always kept his hand in boxing, serving as the head coach of the Brewster Center.

Futch spoke of the hard times he endured as a black man trying to make his living as a trainer in a profile written by Gary Smith for *Sports Illustrated* in 1989. Futch described long nights of driving when blacks were not permitted to purchase a cup of coffee in roadside restaurants in the north; having to drop off his second wife—who was white—because gas station attendants would not sell to interracial couples; and many other appalling indignities. In Smith's article, Futch revealed his deeply-suppressed anger and his life-long effort to control it. Smith also recorded instances in which Futch, even in recent years, has lost his temper and demonstrated his well-preserved punching skills on those who have tried his patience.

When discussing great boxers of the '30s and '40s, Futch speaks of two fighters with reverence—Holman Williams and Charley Burley. Holman Williams coached Joe Louis early in Louis' amateur career, and was, Futch says, "the greatest pure boxer I ever worked with." Louis, grateful for Williams' help, later served as his manager. As heavyweight champion, Futch recalls, Louis "used to bring Holman Williams to training camp whether Holman had a fight or not. And Joe would bring a sparring partner for him, and Holman would spar while Louis was sitting at ringside, all gloved up, headgear, all set to go in the ring. But he would watch Holman spar three or four rounds and pick up ideas."

Holman Williams was "one of the great unsung black middle-weights of the 1940s," Futch said in a 1976 interview with Neil Allen of the London *Times*. Futch then went on to offer this portrait of Williams: "Not a great puncher, but you should have seen Jake La Motta after he fought Holman. Both eyes busted up, and his nose. Jake would march over everyone—remember how strong he was against Sugar Ray Robinson—but Holman just kept catching him with that rising jab as he came in. They still gave the decision to Jake." The "rising jab" Futch refers to was "a specialty of Holman Williams'" according to Futch. Neil Allen explained that the Williams-style jab "starts almost waist high and comes up the middle so that the knuckle of the glove lands under the chin like a back-handed uppercut."

Futch's memories of Holman Williams' excellence are shared by Futch's contemporary Walter Smith. "Holman was a boxer that looked good as anybody you ever seen box. But the people didn't appreciate that," Smith says, explaining that Williams was a subtle, defense-minded boxer. "But you never seen anybody in the ring as sweet as Holman."

Futch's other favorite from that period is Charley Burley, whom he once called "the finest all-around fighter I ever saw." Burley was another classic example of a black boxer who was too good to succeed. Burley began his career as a welterweight. He fought primarily as a middleweight, but was avoided by fighters all the way through the heavyweight division.

Making a succinct argument for Burley's greatness, Futch says, "As far as I'm concerned this fella could do it all. He could do it all. He could box; he could punch. The guys who beat him were all bigger fellas. [Future welterweight champion] Fritzie Zivic beat him once when Burley was just a kid coming up. Then they fought two other times and he beat Zivic in those two fights. Zivic bought his contract so he wouldn't have to fight him anymore. He was really something to see. He was a master at slipping punches, counterpunching. He walked to you with a good jab, feint and make you miss. He didn't move his legs too much, he'd just slide over, make you miss a punch, and he was right there on top of you with either hand punching."

In a professional career that lasted from 1937 through 1950, Burley was never given a shot at a title. In addition to his two victories over Fritzie Zivic, Burley defeated future middleweight champion Billy Soose in 1938. He also dropped two ten-round decisions in 1942 to future heavyweight champion Ezzard Charles, who at the time outweighed him by fifteen pounds.

One night in 1944, Futch recalls, future light-heavyweight champion Archie Moore was scheduled to fight in Hollywood, California, when his opponent dropped out. "They needed a substitute, so they called Burley down in San Diego," Futch says. "He was on the job, went home, got his gear, hopped on a bus, came up the 125 miles to Hollywood, went into the ring and gave Archie a good ten-round licking."

Moore never faced Burley again, but when journalist Neil Allen asked him to name the greatest fighter he'd ever faced, Moore—who had fought Rocky Marciano, among others—answered, "Guy named Charley Burley. Knocked me down twice and won over ten." Burley also faced Holman Williams seven times; each won three times and one of their bouts was declared a no-contest. Futch worked in Williams' corner against Burley in Cincinnati in 1942. "What a privilege it was to watch both men—the way they thought as well as fought," Futch told Neil Allen.

Futch also confirms the story that Sugar Ray Robinson ducked Charley Burley. "That's true," says Futch, though he doesn't wish to "damage the career of a great fighter like Sugar Ray Robinson. So I don't like to make comparisons. But when it comes up, if anybody asks me, I got to say, 'Yeah, Robinson didn't want to fight him.' I can't blame him. La Motta would never fight Burley. None of those middleweights [would]."

With a deep sense of injustice, Futch describes what happened when a well-connected promoter brought Burley, then the second-ranked middleweight in the world, to New York in an attempt to get him a title shot. Though Burley could not get booked into Madison Square Garden, Futch says, he was matched in the St. Nicholas Arena against "Showboat" Bill McQuillan, a fighter Futch had worked with. McQuillan was "a good journeyman," Futch recalls. "So they put Burley in with McQuillan. They wanted to see what he was like. They'd heard all these things, but there was no television in those days." Once again, however, Burley's great talent interfered with the progress of his career. "Burley knocked out McQuillan in one round," Futch says, "and was never heard from in New York again." Though Burley continued to be rated as a top middle-weight until 1947, he never came close to fighting for the title.

Futch, who was instrumental in Burley's election to the Box-ing Hall of Fame in 1983, says sadly, "It was such a shame, such a great fighter as this . . ." As his voice trails off, Futch says that Burley is not a bitter man. "He didn't seem to be bitter. He didn't show emotion as a fighter. . . . As a person he didn't show his emotions. At least I never saw any display."

Talk of the great middleweights of the 1940s prompts Futch to tell a story about Sugar Ray Robinson and Jimmy Edgar, a leading middleweight with whom Futch began working in 1941 in Detroit when Edgar was a teenager. Edgar, who fought Jake La Motta three times—losing twice and earning one draw—repeat-edly faced Sugar Ray Robinson while on an exhibition tour in 1943. Early in the tour, Edgar wrote to Futch, saying that it was fortunate that Futch had never matched him against Robinson in a non-exhibition bout. "I can't catch up with him," Edgar confessed.

But after a period of steady exposure to Robinson, Edgar's confidence grew. "About a month later," Futch recalls, "they're sparring every day, you know, two days and then one day off. 'Well,' Jimmy says, 'at least he can't hurt me. That's one good thing. I've taken his best shots.' And about a month later, he says, 'I'm starting to hit him once in a while.'"

Warming to the story, Futch says with intensity, "Well it wasn't too long after that, maybe another month, Jimmy says, 'Well, today it happened. I caught Robinson with a left hook and he started down. So I grabbed him and waltzed him around.

I didn't want to, you know, embarrass him in front of all those people.'"

After the incident, Edgar reported to Futch, all of the members of Robinson's entourage jumped on Edgar, telling him he shouldn't have gone easy on Robinson. "You shouldn't have done that," Edgar was told. "Do you know what he would have done if he had gotten you in that position? He would have let you fall, walked over you so that everyone could see you on the floor. Then come back and picked you up. That's what he woulda done to you." Recounting the story, Futch laughs in appreciation of Robinson's unapologetic toughness.

After Edgar had hurt Robinson, Futch adds, "Robinson started complaining about working with Jimmy. He'd say, 'He's too big. He's too big.'" When Futch approached Robinson's manager George Gainford about matching Robinson and Edgar, Gainford told Futch, "You gotta be out of your mind. Too tough a match." In Detroit, Robinson later told Futch, "Eddie, I'm gonna box Jimmy. I'm gonna make some money. But not now." Recalling Robinson's words, Futch adds, "It never happened. Never happened."

Distilling a general principle from the story, Futch says Robinson was "a greater fighter" than Edgar, "but there's always somebody, no matter how great you are, that's gonna give you a problem."

Sugar Ray Robinson again had an impact on Futch's career in 1950 when Futch's fighter Lester Felton was working his way toward the welterweight title. "I had word from New York that Robinson was having trouble making 147 pounds, and would move up to the middleweight division," Futch recalled for Red Smith in 1981. "Lester beat Kid Gavilan and I matched him with Ike Williams, a great lightweight who couldn't beat the top welters. I told Felton, 'We're going to make some headlines. When you beat Ike Williams, we'll challenge Robinson but you'll never fight him. He's not going to make 147 pounds again, but it will make you big.' Lester went home walking on air.

"Next day he was down in the dumps. 'I told my wife what we were going to do,' he said, 'and she said, "They'll make you fight Robinson."' I couldn't get that out of his head. He was depressed, didn't train, and just walked through the bout with Williams, who beat him. We would have been in line to fight for Robinson's vacant title."

This is when Futch decided to leave Detroit for California. "I knew I'd had it," he told Red Smith. "I stayed with him one more fight, and he beat Carmen Basilio in Syracuse easily. Then I took off for California."

The first champion Futch trained was welterweight Don Jordan, who won the title in a 1958 upset of Virgil Akins in Los Angeles. According to *The Ring*, Jordan was the fourteenth child born to a family of nineteen children in Los Angeles. Jordan first came to prominence after winning a ten-round decision over contender Isaac Logart in 1958. Following that fight, Jordan was interviewed by *The Ring*. Futch—described by *The Ring* as a "refined, well-spoken man"—also contributed a few comments. "Don's father Harold was a fighter in his youth," Futch said. "Good, too. Even today at fifty-seven, he can whip all his sons—Don included. That may be because Don would not strike back. But wiry Harold can drop anyone he hits right." In an early demonstration of his public relations skills, Futch added, "Here's an item that I believe is interesting. Don, who measures five-foot-nine, started his boxing career as a middleweight. He won the Junior Golden Gloves 160-pound championship, though he scaled off at 149 pounds."

Paying tribute to Futch, Jordan told *Ring*, "Fighting a tough calibre of opponents helped polish me up. Also the instructions of my present trainer, Eddie Futch, aided me. You might say the Futch Touch benefited me a good deal."

While Futch worked various jobs in Los Angeles during the 1950s and early '60s, he watched over visiting East Coast fighters such as middleweight George Benton and lightweight Eddie Matthews. It wasn't until he began working with Joe Frazier, though, that Futch stepped into the boxing limelight.

If Frazier's 1971 victory over Ali is Futch's most cherished memory of Frazier's career, then Frazier's 1973 upset at the hands of George Foreman is likely Futch's most painful memory. Going into the first Foreman-Frazier bout, Futch says, "I felt Foreman was a strong, hard puncher, a young fighter. And I thought Joe had too much ability and experience for him. And Joe felt the same way. In fact, I'd never seen him take any opponent so lightly as he took Foreman."

Futch arrived late at Frazier's Jamaica training camp before the Foreman fight. Futch recalls that Yank Durham "always liked for me to come in maybe a week after the camp opened because he said I always brought a fresh perspective to the camp. He said that sometimes he was so close to the action that he really couldn't determine what was really going on.

"But when I came in, I surveyed the scene, and I said, 'Yank, I don't like anything about this camp.' I said, 'It's not the kind of a camp that a fighter should be involved in when he's getting ready for the heavyweight title defense.' There was too much partying going on. It was in the wintertime and he [Frazier] was down there in the balmy Jamaica atmosphere, and the jetsetters from New York and from Philadelphia had come down to the hotel. . . . And there was just a big party going on. You know, poolside hijinks and things like that—things that took away from the concentration that should have been the basis of the training regimen. And a lot of things happened that I didn't like. But they were in full swing when I got there. I changed whatever I could change."

Seeing Frazier work with heavyweight Ken Norton, then a Frazier sparring partner, further worried Futch. "Norton had been Joe Frazier's sparring partner for three-and-a-half years," Futch says. "And Joe had always been able to handle Norton in the gym. And Norton started off tentatively, but he kept increasing in experience and ability, so he'd really give Joe good work. Now, I watched them work two days after I got down there and I said, 'Look, that's all. No more work with Norton.' So I knocked Norton off. I said, 'Okay, you're on a vacation now. Have yourself some fun 'cause you're not working with Frazier anymore.'"

During a private conversation with Norton, Futch recalls, "I said, 'I saw what was going on from my point outside the ring. What would you say was going on *in* the ring? Why were you able to work so effectively with Joe?' He said, 'He seems to have lost his drive.'" Speaking slowly for emphasis, Futch says, "And that turned out to be the key. Norton said, 'He seems to have lost his drive.' And it showed up in the workouts with Norton."

About Foreman's brutal two-round destruction of Frazier—during which Frazier went down an amazing six times—Futch says, "Joe was a little, strong hard-punching fighter going in against a big, strong, hard-punching fighter." Using his size and strength effectively against Frazier, Futch recalls, Foreman "would push Joe off. And when he pushed him off, Joe would double back three or four steps and Foreman would catch him trying to come back in. That would have been enough, but Frazier not having gone into the fight with the same intensity that he had exhibited in other fights, I think there was just too much to overcome."

Asked what he said to Frazier following the loss of his title, Futch says, "Well, we just went over—we didn't commiserate over the thing. . . . There were a few things that I thought that Joe needed to tighten up on and we went over those things."

As Frazier's career began a downward turn, another of Futch's fighters, Ken Norton, came to prominence with a startling 1973 upset of Ali. *Sports Illustrated* wrote that when Norton defeated Ali in their first fight in San Diego, "No fighter Ali has met, save Frazier, seemed less intimidated." Credit for Norton's excellent psychic state—as well as his tactical approach—must be given to Eddie Futch who, at the time, was the only trainer to have worked a winning corner against Muhammad Ali.

Futch began training Norton in California in 1968, following Norton's third professional fight. "I took him all the way," Futch recalls. "I was actually the manager because I had power of attorney and I made all the matches. I signed for both the Ali fights," Futch says referring to the first two Ali-Norton fights in which he worked as Norton's trainer.

Here Futch speaks with a trace of anger, acknowledging that eventually "there was kind of a bitter separation" between himself, Norton and Norton's managers of record. For the first Ali fight, Futch says, "I signed the contract, and I told the managers three days later: 'Oh, by the way, I signed Norton to box Ali.'" Laughing at the memory, Futch says, "Oh they were very happy, very happy. And they were happier yet after we got the win, but then between that fight and the second fight, other influences started talking to 'em and telling them how much better they could do. And so we split up after the second fight."

Returning to the more pleasant subject of Norton's upset over Ali, Futch says that he had no problem making sure that Norton was not intimidated by the legend of Muhammad Ali. "No, no," Futch says cheerfully. "Norton believed what I told him. Everything that I told him on his way up turned out to be right. I hadn't made any mistakes with him. He believed that what I said was true. I said, 'Now you can lick Ali,' and I explained to him why." Laughing at the memory, Futch emphasizes, "I'm telling you, he had supreme confidence going in because I had conditioned him mentally for that fight."

Futch says he realized Norton would pose problems for Ali when the two sparred in a Los Angeles gym. "They had worked two years before in the gym. And I saw that Norton had the style to lick Ali but he didn't have the experience. After that workout that day Ali came back to the gym the next day screaming that he wanted to box Ken Norton. And I wouldn't let Norton work with him. And Ali said, 'Why not?' I said,

'Yesterday you came in looking for a workout. Today you came in looking for a fight.' I said, 'When this kid fights you he's gonna get paid real well.'"

Again, Futch laughs with delight as he relates how he got the better of Ali. "So a year later when Ali was boxing Al 'Blue' Lewis in Dublin and Mac Foster in Tokyo, he called me and wanted to box Norton in some foreign site. And I said, 'No.' He said, 'Why not?' I said, 'He's not ready yet.' He said, 'Well, I'm gonna give him twenty-five-thousand dollars—that's probably more money than he ever saw in his life.' 'Yeah,' I said, 'three times as much as he's ever seen. But that's not nearly what he's gonna see when he fights you.' And so I wouldn't accept the fight. But when the opportunity came a year later I grabbed it."

Futch discussed Norton's 1973 twelve-round decision victory over Ali in a 1989 interview with Phil Berger of *The New York Times*. Futch began his discourse by again critiquing Ali's idiosyncratic style:

> The orthodox way a fighter carries his right hand is to position it in front of his jaw. Joe Louis did it this way. From that position, as you jab, the right hand is there to parry the other man's punches. Now Ali, who had a great jab, carried the right hand out to the side. But because his jab was so good, it served as an offense and defense. He got away with carrying the right hand out there.
>
> What most fighters did against Ali was to pull back and shoot the right hand over his jab. Or duck under it and come up with a left hook. But Ali was too fast to make those tactics work. I told Norton, 'The only way to hit Ali is to jab with him, jab for jab. The difference is that your hand's in position to catch the jab. His isn't.'
>
> Nobody ever tried to jab with Ali and, when Norton did it, it upset Ali's rhythm. Ali was being hit

with a jab. I told Norton, 'The minute you hit him
with the jab, step in and jab him again. Two, three
moves like that in an eighteen- to twenty-foot ring
should force Ali back against the ropes.

"When you get him to the ropes, don't go like the
others do with a left hook to Ali's head. Because
what he'll do is he'll lean back and stretch the ropes,
and the left will go in front of his face. You'll be off
balance and he'll pepper you. Rather than hook to
the head, work both hands to the body and make him
bring his elbows in to his side to protect his body.
When he does, his head will drop, his chin will be
there for you. Then hit him with the right." And
that's how Norton broke Ali's jaw. Ali kept leaning
into the right hand.

In retrospect, Futch disputes Ali's claim that his jaw was broken as early as the second round. "Look, his jaw didn't get broken
until the eleventh round. Angelo Dundee was a very smart man.
He made it appear that Ali had stayed in there like a warrior in
the second round. No way. He got hit with so many right hands
on that jaw if it'd been broken in the second round it woulda
been in splinters," Futch says, laughing fondly. "After watching
the replays over and over again, I said that jaw was broken in the
eleventh round because Ali got hit with a beautiful shot with the
right hand and I said, that's when the jaw went."

Futch and Norton parted company after Norton lost a controversial close decision in the rematch with Ali. Putting aside his
professional differences with the fighter, Futch says that he
thought Norton beat Ali each time they met; including their
third fight, which Ali won by close decision, with Bill Slayton,
Norton's new trainer, in Norton's corner. "I thought Norton won
all three fights," Futch says. "I thought he won *all three* fights."

Futch worked against Norton in May of 1977, seconding
heavyweight contender Duane Bobick—who was managed by

Joe Frazier—against Norton in Madison Square Garden. Futch still seems miffed at the memory of Norton destroying Bobick in one round. "That should've been just the other way around," Futch says. "Norton was just about ready to be taken at the time and Bobick was undefeated. I had about sixteen straight wins for Bobick." But like many other young, successful boxers, Futch says, Bobick "got to the point where he didn't wanta listen."

Describing the night of Bobick's loss to Norton, Futch says, "That night . . . Bobick had a lot of his Navy cronies in the dressing room, and they were talking old times and this and that when Bobick should have been warming up." Futch, however, was eager for Bobick to be loose in the first round because Futch felt Norton—because of his differences with Futch—would be eager to try for an early knockout.

"Come on, knock off this conversation, let's get busy," Futch recalls telling Bobick. "I want you to come out really warm against Norton because he's gonna come out after you because you're with me. He's gonna be fighting me instead of you. So you're gonna have to deal with a guy who's got a mission."

As Futch struggled to keep order in Bobick's dressing room, he was also able to observe Norton. "We had a monitor in our dressing room and we could see Norton—and Norton could see us," Futch remembers. "And I saw Norton and when he started out of the dressing room. He was sweating like a horse. And Bobick was bone dry because every time I started him off, I'd get called away—some commissioner wanted to see me or some major reporter came in or whatever. Every time I looked around, Bobick was back talking to his friends. He went out bone dry and Norton came out steaming and Norton went right out . . . [and] jumped right on Bobick. And Bobick just never got a chance to get started."

Futch still regrets that when fight fans think of Duane Bobick they inevitably think of his quick loss to Norton. "Now he'll be remembered for that fight instead of all the other, good performances that he had," Futch says sadly.

Talk of his troubled relationship with Norton prompts Futch to generalize about the lack of gratitude he feels is endemic to the boxing world. "There are so many things in boxing—so many things in boxing. It's a sport that I have been in for more than fifty years, but I'm not *of* boxing," Futch says, distancing himself from the more unsavory aspects of his sport. "I'm in it, but I don't like a lot of things in it. But I tolerate some things because that's the way it is. Ingratitude is one of them. The ones I've done the most for have been the ones who have been the most ungrateful." Ingratitude, Futch says, is "a part of the scene. And I expect anything, but I don't let it throw me. I go on to the next."

Clearly making reference to welterweight champion Don Jordan—though Futch does not mention his name—Futch says, "I took one fighter from starvation. Found him starving in Mexico City. Took him to the welterweight championship of the world in twenty months from the time I saw him down in Mexico City. And took him through two title defenses after he won the title. He was a big underdog going into the title shot—four to one underdog. And I took him through that, won a unanimous decision. . . . Then took him through two title defenses. And he walked away. They always manufacture reasons to dislike you."

Though Futch feels immense fondness and loyalty for Joe Frazier—whom he calls "one of the easiest fighters to handle I ever worked with"—he freely answers questions about the more unpleasant moments that became a part of their relationship.

After Yank Durham's death in August of 1974, Futch added the responsibility of being Frazier's manager to his duties as trainer. "When Yank died, five minutes later he [Frazier] called me," Futch explains. "He said, 'Eddie, Yank's gone, what shall we do?'" Futch, who was then preparing Norton for his rematch with Ali, gave Norton a day off and flew to Philadelphia to meet with Frazier and his lawyer to make a deal to take over as Frazier's manager.

Futch adds that Durham—who was aware of his health problems—had repeatedly asked Futch to succeed him. "I'd been with him about a year and Yank one day approached me and said, 'Eddie, if anything happens to me I want you to take all of my fighters.' . . . I bet you he said that to me at least eight or nine times. And the last one was in '73, July 4th of '73, when Frazier had just beaten [British heavyweight] Joe Bugner the night before. August 31st, Yank was dead."

Following Frazier's defeat of Bugner, Futch gave a frank assessment of Frazier's status as a boxer in an interview with Dan Hafner of the *Los Angeles Times*: "Joe worked hard. He was in good condition, but his zip wasn't there. . . . But I saw signs of the old Joe and a couple of more fights could bring out even more. I'm sure the Ali fight took something out of both fighters, but not as much out of Joe as Ali would like to have you believe. Joe seems determined to regain the title." Referring to Frazier's career as the lead singer for a band called "Joe Frazier and the Knockouts," Futch said, "When he was champ he thought he could mix the entertainment business with boxing. He knows better now. He disbanded his singing group and plans to concentrate on boxing. We'll just have to wait and see if he can make it back."

Frazier's first fight under Futch's management was a January, 1974 twelve-round rematch with Muhammad Ali at Madison Square Garden. The fight offered Frazier, then the former champion, the opportunity to put himself in line to fight for the title against George Foreman. Although Ali got the decision, Futch still does not accept the defeat. "When Joe lost that second fight against Ali in the Garden," Futch says, "I told him that if the referee had just done his job . . . Joe would have been a decided winner in that fight." Here Futch refers to the referee's inability to stop Ali from repeatedly grabbing Frazier behind the neck as Frazier charged in. "Joe was pulled in by the back of his head 113 times in a twelve-round fight," Futch says with the precision of a man who has studied the fight film and does not easily forget a loss—particularly one which he feels is unjustified. "And so I really didn't consider that a loss. Joe didn't consider that a loss."

In the summer of 1974, with Ali and Foreman scheduled to face each other for the title, Futch matched Frazier against Jerry Quarry in Madison Square Garden. Five years earlier, Frazier had knocked Quarry out in seven tough rounds. To assure an easier victory for Frazier, Futch says, "I changed him all completely."

Futch explains, "I wouldn't have done it if Yank were alive because that would have been a slap in the face. But Yank was gone and I'm in complete control now, I'm responsible. I put him in a fight with Jerry Quarry and he knocked out Jerry Quarry in the easiest fight he ever had—and it was one of the toughest fights he had before when they fought the first time."

Futch recalls telling Frazier before the Quarry rematch, "Now Jerry Quarry's lookin' for you to come out throwin' that left hook. Now you're the same height as Jerry Quarry, the same height. I've seen you stand up and box . . . use a good left jab and a good straight right hand. And that's what you're going to do against Jerry Quarry because he's gonna be looking for the hook all night."

About the fight, Futch says with pleasure, "Jerry was so confused. He was lookin' for the hook and getting hit with the right hand. I mean he was getting banged with it, too. Joe threw one hook the whole fight. . . . He jabbed and threw a hook to the body off the jab—and knocked Jerry Quarry down with it. And that's when we started to ask for Joe Louis to stop the fight. Joe Louis was the referee."

Futch's assistant trainer at the time, former middleweight George Benton, still marvels at the way Frazier surprised Quarry in that fight. "Joe was throwing the right hand at Quarry," Benton says, confirming Futch's account. "See, Joe never threw right hands before. And we had 'em throwing the right hands and it surprised the hell out of Quarry. Quarry couldn't believe it. 'Cause Joe never threw right hands."

Eddie Futch worked in Joe Frazier's corner for one more fight following Ali and Frazier's famed "Thrilla in Manila." The fight was Frazier's ill-fated 1976 rematch with George Foreman, the man who had taken his heavyweight title in two brutal rounds in 1973. Once again, Futch attempted to augment Frazier's style. Frazier suffered a fifth-round knockout, but Futch still enjoys describing his ideas about how to beat Foreman—even though the fight itself didn't correspond to the Futch master plan.

"In the second Foreman fight, Frazier did all right for the first few rounds, you know," Futch says. "But he did something every round that I had warned him against—and that was going to the ropes. I said, 'You cannot go to the ropes with this fella. He's too strong. He hits too hard. He'll find you on the ropes. And you'll block a few and you'll slip a few, but he'll keep throwing and one of them will get through. And if one punch gets through, as hard as he can punch, he'll hurt you. And when he hurts you, it'll be all over. Because then he'll just continue, you know.' So I said, 'You must stay away from the ropes.'"

At the age of thirty-two, however, Frazier found the ropes an inviting place to rest his weary legs—a point Futch himself recalls making in a conversation with his assistant trainer, George Benton. "One day in the gym while we were training for the fight, I continuously warned Joe to stay away from the ropes," Futch recalls. "George Benton was working with the sparring partner. So I called George over and I said, 'Come here, George. I want to ask you a question.' So he came around to my corner while Joe was sparring, and I said, 'You see him on the ropes there?' I said, 'Why is he on the ropes? You heard me telling him time and time again not to go to the ropes.' He said, 'I don't know.' I said, 'George, you were a good fighter. I worked with you in one of your fights. And I know how good a fighter you were. But you know what? At the end of your career, you went to the ropes, too. Near the end.' And I said, 'Why?' And he said, 'To rest my legs.' And he realized that that was the answer. Against Foreman, that's what failed him."

About the fight itself, Futch says, "In every round . . . [Frazier] went to the ropes at one point or another. He got away with it for almost five rounds. And in the center of the ring he made a monkey out of Foreman. He kinda toyed with him. He dropped his hands and slipped punches and things like that. And he hit Foreman with counter punches and all that. But then his legs would get tired and he'd go to the ropes momentarily to rest his legs. And he did it every round. He got away with it for four good rounds and in the fifth round he was getting away with it for a while, but he went to the well once too often. . . . He bobbed and ducked and slipped a few punches, but Foreman just kept banging until one shot got through and hurt him and then it was all over."

Frazier retired following the loss to Foreman, but in December of 1981, after more than five years of inactivity, Frazier, at age thirty-seven, attempted a comeback against journeyman heavyweight Jumbo Cummings. Futch's opposition to the bout—and his refusal to help Frazier come back—began a period of ill will in the relationship between the trainer and his fighter.

"The press has always been good to me because I deal squarely with them," Futch begins when asked about Frazier's comeback. "I want to be honest. And so one day they called me about whether I was going to work with Joe Frazier in the Jumbo Cummings fight. They said, 'Why not?' I said, 'Because he shouldn't be in there. I put him into retirement five years ago and he should stay there. He didn't get any better in retirement. I think it's a mistake and I won't be a party to a mistake."

Frazier, a proud man, didn't take well to Futch's criticism. "He was very upset with me," Futch says, discreetly understating Frazier's mood at the time. Speaking to Dave Anderson in 1983, Futch was more blunt: "When Joe tried a comeback in 1981, I told him it was a bad thing to do, that I wouldn't be part of it. He's hated me ever since for that." Futch's opposition to Frazier's comeback proved to be well-founded: though Frazier was repeatedly staggered, the fight ended in a draw and Frazier never fought again.

The unpleasantness between Futch and Frazier came to a

head in 1983 when Joe Frazier, acting as manager for his son Marvis, matched Marvis against heavyweight champion Larry Holmes, though Marvis Frazier had had only ten professional fights. Futch, who was Larry Holmes' trainer at the time, had known Marvis Frazier since Marvis was a boy. A few months before the Holmes-Frazier fight, Futch had attended Marvis Frazier's wedding in Philadelphia.

Asked if he had conflicted feelings about the Holmes-Marvis Frazier fight, Futch says, "Oh yes I did. In fact, Joe got very upset with me about that because I didn't approve of the fight and I said so to him." At Marvis' wedding, Futch says, there was talk of matching Marvis against Holmes. "So I expressed my opinion to Joe and told him I didn't think Marvis belonged in there with Larry at the time. And Joe got very upset. And during the preparation—after the fight was signed—he said some very uncomplimentary things about me which I just ignored."

One of Frazier's more derogatory comments about Futch was: "He never did nothin' for me except collect fifteen percent of my purse. Futch can't train nobody. He was just there to wipe me down."

Eventually, when Futch and Joe Frazier appeared together on a Las Vegas radio program before the Holmes-Marvis Frazier fight, Frazier tested the limits of Futch's patience. "So here we were side by side at the microphone," Futch says, "and I knew the things Joe had been saying about me in the press, but I just ignored them. I said, 'We had twelve good years together and now he's embarked on a new career and he thinks these things are necessary.' But I just ignored him. And I just hoped that that type of thing wouldn't come up in the interview."

Describing the radio program as if it were a boxing match, Futch says with an ironic laugh, "Joe started off tentatively and I tried to keep my answers non-inflammatory. By me taking this approach, Joe got a little bolder and a little bolder and finally he went over the line. And that's when I had to really open up. I opened up on him then. And listen, when I got through talking to him, I'm pretty sure he was sorry that he ever instituted that line of answers. I told him things about his career that *he* didn't know. That's right. I told him, 'You know, Yank Durham was my friend. And he was your manager. But I made so many decisions in your career that Yank followed.' I said, 'Why do you think Yank Durham who had never met me brought you to California in the first place? You came three-thousand miles away to a man who he had never seen.' And I said, 'A lot of the most important decisions in your career—I made them. But Yank was my friend and your manager and I never wanted to take the credit.'"

Retaining a whiff of resentment at Frazier's attack on his professionalism, Futch restates his case, "Yank would ask me *everything* about what to do with Joe Frazier. . . . But those decisions—Joe knew nothing about those decisions. And the instructions came from Yank. And I would tell Yank, 'This is what we must do with this fighter.'"

Asked how Frazier responded to the verbal onslaught, Futch says, "Well, he was shocked. I can tell you. These things I had to disclose to him because he said I worked all those years with him and I took this great amount of money and I never contributed anything to his career." Futch adds with satisfaction, "He was wrong. I made more money than he thought I made. I was with him for twelve years. Why did he tolerate me for twelve years if I wasn't contributing anything? . . . And it was so ludicrous because he wouldn't make any moves at all without calling me."

Looking back on Joe Frazier's handling of his son Marvis' career, Futch says it was a mistake for the father to train the son. Marvis' first trainer, Futch disciple George Benton, was actually more effective as Marvis' trainer—yet another example of the widely held dictum that great champions don't often become great trainers.

"Georgie Benton had Marvis doing what he should have done," Futch argues. "Marvis was a pretty good boxer. But Joe never really encouraged Marvis to box at all. When I retired Joe and left and went back to the West Coast, Marvis was just starting his amateur career. He hadn't had an amateur fight when I left. And George Benton was training him. I left all the fighters with George Benton. And Marvis was doing real well. He was winning all the amateur tournaments and all."

After Marvis Frazier was operated on for a pinched nerve in the back of his neck, Futch recalls, "He was set for a good professional career in the heavyweight division. Although he was a small heavyweight, he was a good boxer. But by that time, Joe had taken over. And George Benton's style and Joe's style were completely different. And George's style was the one that Marvis should've followed."

Joe Frazier wrongly tried to make Marvis fight in the inimitable Joe Frazier style. "Marvis just didn't have the equipment," Futch says. "He wasn't strong enough. He didn't hit well enough, you know, and he didn't think in terms of that perpetual motion, of that continued aggression that Joe would use. He just wasn't equipped for it. But that's the way that his father wanted him to fight. And being a new manager, a new trainer, you know, Joe thought because he was a great fighter he knew everything there was to know about boxing, but he didn't. And he was a classic example of the great fighters who are not very good trainers because they expect everyone to have their natural assets, their God-given talents—and nobody has them."

Futch also felt it was foolish to match Marvis Frazier against Holmes so early in Marvis' career. "Marvis has a lot of athletic ability," Futch told *Sports Illustrated* before the fight. "What's the hurry to fight for the championship? If he gets destroyed now, and he could very well be destroyed, it could even end his career."

Anyone needing a reminder of the cold and brutal ironies of a boxing trainer's life need only imagine what went through Futch's mind as he contemplated Marvis Frazier's first-round destruction by Larry Holmes. "When I saw Marvis at the weigh-in for that fight he was as tight as a drum," Futch recalls. "His teeth were clenched and you could see the muscles in his neck standing out—just at the weigh-in. And I said to Larry, 'Look, Larry, this kid's like my son. I saw him grow up from the age of six years old. And I don't want to see him hurt. I don't want you to hurt him. I want you to get rid of him as quickly as possible.' I said, 'I don't want to see him beat up. Get him out of there as quickly as you can. And Larry took that opportunity the very first time he [Marvis] made a mistake. He nailed him."

Marvis Frazier went down in the first round from a classic Holmes right cross. After Frazier regained his feet, Futch says, "Larry backed him into a corner and Larry threw a few punches and he motioned for the referee to come in to stop the fight because he knew—I had warned him, I said, 'I don't want this kid banged around.'"

Immediately following the fight, Futch and Frazier had a reconciliation of sorts. "I was walking through the lobby at Caesar's Palace and it suddenly dawned on me that I needed to make a call. So I went to the public phone and while I was on the phone I heard someone making a strange hooting sound. I didn't pay any attention, really, I heard it behind me and it was halfway across the lobby. And pretty soon, Joe Frazier walked up and tapped me on the shoulder. He stuck out his hand and said, 'Congratulations.'"

Asked if he and Frazier are friends today, Futch answers, "I see him. Not often. I was at his daughter's wedding. . . . He's beginning to lose some of that frustration and bitterness that he had after his career. You know, he's competitive, Frazier."

In 1981, Eddie Futch began working with three established champions, three of the finest boxers of the time—Larry Holmes, Alexis Arguello and Michael Spinks.

Futch began training heavyweight champion Holmes in April of 1981, before Holmes' ninth title defense when he faced Trevor Berbick. Holmes had until then been trained by Richie Giachetti. Holmes' first trainer was Eddie Butler. Over the years, when Futch worked in the same gym as Holmes, Holmes would sometimes ask Futch, "How do I look?" As Red Smith wrote in 1981, "Eddie would tell him what he thought and the answer wasn't always to Larry's liking."

Futch remembers watching Holmes train for his 1979 title defense against Earnie Shavers, one of the hardest punchers in recent heavyweight history. "Don't leave, I'd like to talk to you," Holmes told Futch. When Holmes asked for Futch's opinion, Futch said, "You look good and you're in great shape, but I don't like the way you're working." Futch told Holmes not to engage in such heavy brawls with his sparring partners. If Holmes exchanged punches in sparring, Futch reasoned, Holmes might—through force of habit—brawl with the dangerous Shavers rather than trying to outbox him. As it turned out, Holmes boxed well, but then briefly stood toe-to-toe with Shavers—and was floored before rallying to win by a technical knockout.

When Holmes split with Richie Giachetti in 1981, he called Eddie Futch. "I joined him two weeks before he boxed Trevor Berbick on April 11 [1981]," Futch explained to Red Smith, "but not to change him. I told him we'd try to polish the things he does well, and what few faults he has we'll try to eliminate."

Asked why he chose Eddie Futch, Holmes says, "I knew he worked with good guys like Joe Frazier and Ken Norton. . . . And I felt that he was the best [out] there."

Holmes, already the dominant heavyweight in the world when Futch started with him, assesses Futch's impact on him this way: "All Eddie always tried to do is improve on what I was working on. And that's the only thing he had to do. And he done that. A trainer with his ability does not come in and try to change a fighter. And he knew that much." Holmes does acknowledge, however, that Futch "tried to correct the mistakes that I made when I was trying to do what I was trying to do." Futch's main contribution, Holmes says, was his celebrated talent for analyzing opponents. Futch "would tell you what the opponent's gonna do," Holmes recalls. "That's the only thing that we talked about."

Eddie Futch was in Larry Holmes' corner when Holmes easily defended his title against Leon Spinks in June of 1981. Later that year, Futch observed challenger Renaldo Snipes in a sparring session and warned Holmes against Snipes' straight right hand—the same punch Snipes used to knock Holmes down before Holmes rallied to score an eleventh-round knockout.

When Holmes faced challenger Gerry Cooney in their much-publicized 1982 bout, Futch's role in Holmes' corner began to receive wider recognition. Futch, who considered Cooney a "novice" with only one punch—a powerful but unsubtle left hook—told Dave Anderson before the fight, "Cooney is young, strong and ambitious with power in his left hand, but Larry is a disciplined fighter. He does what he has to do to win." Speaking with Michael Katz of the *Times*, Futch accurately predicted a late-round knockout by Holmes. "He [Cooney] will have to set a great pace," Futch said, "and after that he will be ready to be taken."

Ray Arcel, who also worked in the Holmes camp for the Cooney bout, warmly praises his friend Eddie Futch as a man and trainer. "I was very friendly with Larry Holmes," Arcel explains. "It was Larry Holmes who asked me to come and work. And it was through the graciousness of Eddie Futch that I did work . . . because he could have squawked, but he never did." With a smile, Arcel adds, "Eddie Futch showed his class. Well, I knew Eddie . . . and he knew that I would never, you know, do anything to offend him."

Before the bout, Arcel explained his working relationship with Futch to Dave Anderson: "Whatever suggestions I have, I'll whisper it to Eddie before we go up into the corner between rounds and he can take it or not. Eddie's the boss." Futch and Arcel were joined in Holmes' corner by cutman Bill Prezant.

After Holmes dispatched Cooney according to plan with an eleventh-round knockout, Futch provided Dave Anderson with a post-mortem: "Cooney did some things I didn't think he could do. Like his left jab, he was pretty effective with it, he bothered

Larry with it. . . . I told Larry that Cooney would throw a lot of right hands in order to camouflage his best punch, his left hook. Ever since Cooney's people saw [Renaldo] Snipes knock down Larry with a right hand, I knew they'd be working on his right hand. I knew if I had been planning his fight, I would've told him that."

Following his victory over Cooney, Holmes decisioned Randall "Tex" Cobb, a tough journeyman heavyweight who lacked the skills to threaten Holmes and absorbed a brutal beating over fifteen rounds. In an interview with Michael Katz of *The New York Times* before the Cobb fight, Futch said Holmes viewed the bout "as just another fight against another fighter who's coming to take away what he has." Describing Holmes' challenger, Futch said, "Cobb's big, he's strong, he's tough and he comes to fight. He gives you three minutes every round and he never lets up, never takes a backward step." Holmes' response to Cobb's charges, however, would be lateral movement. "A bull always charges straight ahead, he can't charge in a circle," Futch told Katz, evoking a favorite image. "You step over, he loses you for a certain time, especially when you hit him with a jab at the same time."

Though Cobb didn't challenge Holmes' or Futch's full reservoir of boxing knowledge, Tim Witherspoon, a veteran of only fifteen professional fights, did. The Witherspoon bout was a surprisingly difficult test for Holmes, who won a split decision in May of 1983.

Before the fight, according to Pat Putnam of *Sports Illustrated*, Futch "slipped into the gym where Witherspoon was working out" and then presented Holmes with this analysis: "He's working on stopping your jab and your right hand. He looks like Archie Moore: His right arm is up and jack-knifed across his face, and he'll pick off your jab with his right glove. You're going to have to use your hook. As soon as your jab touches his glove, turn the hook over. The whole side of his head will be open."

Futch continued to work in Holmes' corner for the champion's defenses against such opponents as James "Bonecrusher" Smith and Carl "The Truth" Williams, but Holmes and Futch split-up before Holmes lost two controversial decisions in 1985 and 1986 to another Futch fighter, light-heavyweight champion Michael Spinks.

Rather than work with one of his fighters against the other, Futch chose to work in neither corner—a decision which angered Holmes. Holmes' frustration surely increased when Spinks presented him with the first two losses of his professional career, ruining Holmes' hope of equaling Rocky Marciano's record forty-nine consecutive victories.

Futch had warned Holmes that Spinks was a trickier, more effective fighter than he seemed. When Holmes would disparage the undefeated Spinks' abilities, Futch would say, "When I see a winner, Larry, I always study him." Asked whether he advised Holmes not to face Spinks, Futch says simply, "I stayed away from it."

Though Holmes maintains he's forgiven Futch for not training him for the Spinks bouts, he adds, "I was bitter because . . . he was out of a job, and I brought him in. And then after I brought him in, people started seeing him. Then he gets work from a lot of other people . . . because he's with the heavyweight champ. And my theory is: If you start with me, finish with me." Michael Spinks, Holmes concludes, "probably wouldn't have called on Eddie Futch until Eddie Futch started hangin' with Larry Holmes. And that was my thing."

At the same time Futch worked with Holmes, he was training another of the finest fighters of the era, Alexis Arguello. By the time Futch arrived in Arguello's corner, Arguello was already a master boxer. His career began at age sixteen in late 1968 as a bantamweight in his native Nicaragua. In 1974, he won the WBA featherweight championship—the first of his three world

titles. When he first came to the United States, Arguello was
under the tutelage of Al Silvani. In 1978 Arguello won the WBC
junior lightweight title with a knockout of Alfredo Escalera. In
1981 Arguello defeated Jim Watt to win the WBC lightweight
title.

Arguello was beloved by sports writers: he was a master
boxer, a powerful right-handed puncher and a model sportsman
who could always be counted on to praise his fallen opponents.
Most of his fights were covered on American television, where
Arguello was routinely hailed as an all-time great.

Futch began working with Arguello in 1981, before Arguello
defended his lightweight title in a memorable bout against Ray
"Boom Boom" Mancini. Futch urged Arguello to be patient
against Mancini, a young, aggressive and undefeated boxer
"who believed he could beat any fighter in the world." Certain
that Arguello was too experienced for his foe, Futch told Arguello, "You're going to have to lick him, to make him understand. I want you to use the jab . . . counter to the body early."
Arguello scored a fourteenth-round knockout—the sort of late-
round victory that Futch points to as a sign of Arguello's
methodical, calm greatness.

In 1982, Arguello moved up in weight in an attempt to become the first man in boxing history to win a title in four
weight divisions. His opponent was junior welterweight champion Aaron Pryor, the undefeated fighter whose hyper-aggres-
sive, windmill style evoked comparisons with the great Henry
Armstrong.

Before meeting Pryor, however, Arguello tested himself at his
new weight of 140 pounds by fighting Kevin Rooney, who
would later become the celebrated trainer of Mike Tyson.
Rooney, who then had a record of nineteen wins and one loss as
a professional, normally fought as a welterweight, but reduced
himself to 140 pounds to face Arguello.

Analyzing Arguello's second-round knockout of Rooney,
Futch told William Nack of *Sports Illustrated*, "Alexis' jab took

Rooney off balance. He couldn't use lateral mobility." Explaining how Arguello landed his picture-perfect right hand, Futch said, "You can beat that jab with a right hand all the way. He's so vulnerable to that." Futch also told Nack that Pryor would not be an easy fight for Arguello. "Aaron Pryor has a very different style," Futch said. "He's unorthodox. He's strong. He can present problems."

Futch, of course, knew what he was talking about. Aaron Pryor was a formidable fighter. He had won the title in 1980 with a fourth-round knockout of the great Antonio Cervantes. Since that time, he had successfully defended his title four times, all by knockout. Before facing Arguello, Pryor had thirty-one professional victories without a loss, and had only twice failed to score a knockout.

In retrospect, Futch says Arguello did not prepare properly for the Pryor bout. "That's a story in itself," Futch says. "We started off in Panama training for the fight and we went to Bogotá, Colombia about six days. And then left Bogotá and went to Palm Springs. Then left Palm Springs and went home because he and his wife were having a tiff. All this happened before the Pryor fight. Nobody realizes that."

Before the fight, however, Futch—in his role as unofficial spokesman for Arguello—sounded optimistic. "People see Arguello as a long, tall string bean," Futch told Michael Katz. "That's where they make their mistake. He gets away good, short shots. And when you're inside, you're right there for his body work, and there's no better body puncher around." Futch also listed Pryor's vulnerabilities for Dave Anderson: ". . . when Pryor throws those long punches his chin will be straight away. The moment Pryor crosses that perimeter and comes into range, that's when Alexis should get off. Most of all that movement that Pryor has is purposeless unless Alexis lets it bother him. Patience is the big thing for Alexis in this fight. And sooner or later Pryor is going to move within Alexis' range."

On November 12, 1982 in Miami's Orange Bowl, Aaron Pryor

knocked out Alexis Arguello in fourteen rounds in a fight comparable in brutality and excellence to Ali and Frazier's Thrilla in Manila. Though Arguello repeatedly hit Pryor with the right hand that had eliminated so many foes, Pryor proved that he had one of the great chins in boxing by absorbing Arguello's best shots and then swarming all over him.

Futch attributes Pryor's endurance to the contents of the famous suspect bottle from which Pryor drank before the start of the fourteenth round. The bottle was mixed by Pryor's trainer, Panama Lewis, who was subsequently banned from boxing after he was found to have removed padding from the gloves of boxer Luis Resto in a June 1983 bout against Billy Collins in Madison Square Garden.

Pryor's aggressive style nevertheless dominated the fight, with Arguello exchanging punches rather than boxing—and attacking Pryor's head rather than employing his characteristic body assault. The fight ended in the fourteenth round with Arguello helpless on the ropes, taking repeated roundhouse blows to the head. Before the fight was halted, Arguello took twenty-three straight punches from Pryor. He remained unconscious on the canvas for four horrifying minutes before being revived by two ringside physicians.

After the fight, Arguello blamed the loss on Eddie Futch, claiming, according to a report in The New York Times, that he had "overtrained." Before facing Pryor in a rematch in 1983, Arguello, true to his reputation as a gentleman, publicly apologized to Futch. "I was like a drowning man after the fight," Arguello told Ira Berkow of the Times in August of 1983, "I felt all alone, and I wanted to take somebody with me. Then I couldn't sleep because of what I said. I hurt Eddie, who was a good friend." Just over a month later, Arguello again apologized to Futch while speaking with Michael Katz of the Times. "I make a big mistake when I blamed Mr. Futch," Arguello said. "I have apologized. But you must realize I am a human being. I grabbed a piece of wood in the middle of the ocean. I lost a fight,

I lost an important fight, and had to blame somebody. It was a big mistake."

Futch appreciated Arguello's apology and the two eventually worked together again. "When he finally apologized to me," Futch says, ". . . it was a hard thing for him to do. But he realized how much face he had lost. He hurt himself more than he hurt me. Because so many people came to my support."

After Arguello—with a new trainer in his corner—was again knocked out by Pryor in a 1983 rematch, Futch recalls, "I just thought, well, that's the end of him." But three years later, Futch asks rhetorically, "Guess who asked me to take him back when he decided to make a comeback?"

When Arguello was considering a return to the ring at the age of thirty-three in 1986, Futch received a phone call from Arguello's manager, Bill Miller. "He said, 'Alexis Arguello wants to make a comeback. What do you think about it?' Futch recalls. "I said, 'Bill, I don't think he's got anything left. He looked so bad in that second Pryor fight.' And he said, 'Well, he's been training now for two or three months. And besides, he just definitely wants to make a comeback. So I asked him who should we get to train him, and he says, 'There's only one guy. Call him and see if he'll take me back.'"

Futch finally agreed to take a look at Arguello to evaluate how far the boxer had come. "Just come up and look at him and tell me what you think," Futch recalls Bill Miller saying. "And if you say, 'No,' there won't be any comeback." Futch went to see Arguello, "not expecting to find anything, just as a favor," but he found that the boxer looked "surprisingly good," and agreed to work with him again.

After Arguello scored a knockout in his first return bout, he faced former junior-welterweight champion Billy Costello. Before the fight, Costello said he'd quit boxing if he couldn't defeat an "old man" like Arguello. In the dressing room before the fight, Futch recalls, Costello's trainer Victor Valle angered Arguello by insisting that the fighter's hands be rewrapped.

"Boy, he had him sizzling he was so mad," Futch recalls. "And he came out and he lost the first three rounds. But then he started finding the range. Then he hit Costello with a right hand. All over."

Following the fight Arguello complained of chest pains, and a medical examination revealed that the fighter had a heart condition and would have to retire for good.

Eddie Futch began working in Michael Spinks' corner in Las Vegas on July 18, 1981. It was Spinks' seventeenth professional fight, and he was challenging veteran Eddie Mustafa Muhammad for the WBA light-heavyweight championship.

A few hours before the fight, Spinks' manager Butch Lewis contacted Futch to see if he would help the fighter. Telling the story to Phil Berger of the *Times* in June of 1988, Futch said, "I said, 'But, Butch, I don't know Michael Spinks.' But Butch had watched me work. He was a friend of Joe Frazier's and had known me from back then. 'Do it for me,' Butch said. And I did."

Spinks, however, was then trained by Nelson Brison, Butch Lewis' half-brother. "I told Nelson," Futch explained to Phil Berger, "that during the rounds I'd discuss with him what I saw and he would pass it on to the fighter. 'He's accustomed to your terminology,' I said to Nelson. 'You tell him.' And that's how we did it the first two rounds. Nelson would tell him what I said, but sometimes he'd forget something. So I'd say, 'Don't forget to tell him such and such.' Well, Michael heard that a couple of times and at the end of the third round, he turned to me and said, 'Why don't you talk to me? I can understand you perfectly.' I took over and steered him to the light-heavyweight title."

The team of Spinks and Futch was a natural pairing. Spinks, like Futch, approached boxing as a somewhat cerebral pursuit. He based his career on his ability to outsmart opponents with clever, sometimes unorthodox tactics. Spinks also possessed a formidable right hand, which was dubbed "The Spinks Jinx."

"We look at boxing in similar ways," Spinks said of Futch in a 1988 interview in *Penthouse* magazine. "Eddie's a strategist and so am I. He likes to spot weaknesses in a fighter's armor, and I'm good at that, too. He likes to have different things prepared for different situations—you know, if what you try at the beginning doesn't work, you try something else; and you're ready to do that because you've prepared for it. To me, that's what boxing is about, not seeing how much pain you can absorb."

After Spinks defended his WBA title once in 1981 and four times in 1982, he faced a formidable challenge in a title unification bout against WBC light-heavyweight champion Dwight Muhammad Qawi. A veteran of a five-and-a-half-year prison term for armed robbery, Qawi was only five-feet, six-inches tall, but lived up to his nickname, "The Camden Buzzsaw." Qawi won his title by chopping down the formidable Matthew Saad Muhammad, and then beat Muhammad again in a rematch in equally impressive fashion.

As usual, though, Futch spotted a weakness to be exploited. Discussing the Spinks-Qawi fight in a 1988 interview with Phil Berger, Futch recalled, "As the opponent jabbed, he [Qawi] would force him to the ropes and to his left, making him walk right into the looping right hand he threw. He did it expertly. He cut you off so you had to move to the left. He'd run the man into his right hand. The other thing he'd do, in the center of the ring, was drop his left hand to draw your right hand. As the man threw the right, [Qawi] would roll and take the right on his shoulder and fire back. He did that real well."

Futch knew how to take advantage of Qawi's style, and developed a three-point plan which he explained to William Nack of *Sports Illustrated*. First, Futch told Spinks, "Jab and move to the right and throw left hooks. . . . When he starts to corner you, you cut back left. Then go right again." Second, "Stay off the ropes and out of the corners. This is where Qawi is the most effective. If he can stop you along the ropes or in the corners, he can put good combinations together. He throws punches in bunches there." Third, "Don't throw right-hand leads, even if he tempts you by dropping his left. That's the best thing that Qawi does, rolls that left shoulder and catches the other fighter's right with it and counters with a right."

In the fight itself, William Nack reported, "Spinks followed the Futch plan closely enough." After Spinks encountered some trouble in the eighth round, Futch told him, "Make that jab sharper. You're laying it out there. You can't do that with this guy." Spinks complied and continued to put on a masterful display of boxing, negating Qawi's offensive onslaught for fifteen rounds.

Responding to fans who complained that Qawi didn't do much offensively, Futch told Phil Berger, ". . . that was because Spinks didn't let him do much."

During the orgy of publicity that preceded the Michael Spinks-Mike Tyson fight in June of 1988, Futch often pointed to the Spinks-Qawi fight as model for what Spinks would do to Tyson. Futch's argument made sense, as always, though the fight itself defied Futch's logic when Tyson destroyed Spinks in ninety-one seconds.

Futch clearly realized the formidable obstacle Spinks was facing. In 1986, before Tyson had even won the heavyweight title, Futch told *Sports Illustrated*, "Tyson has wonderful attacking abilities. His hands are tremendously fast for a man with that kind of upper body and he can really punch with either hand. God, he can punch. His right uppercut especially will take your head off. . . . He has intimidated his opponents, made them freeze and wait to be slaughtered." Asked how Tyson's strengths might be nullified, Futch said, "I think you have to go to him, back him up, never let him take you into the corners or onto the ropes, keep him in the middle of the ring where you can use mobility against him."

"Michael Spinks is going to have to box him, box him, box him," Futch told Phil Berger of the *Times*. "He must frustrate him: make him make mistakes and take advantage. Mike Tyson's been known to become frustrated." Futch also stressed that Spinks would not be a head-on target for Tyson. "Angles," Futch said. "He'll give him angles. Nobody has more angles than Michael Spinks."

A month before the bout, Dave Anderson of the *Times* reported, Futch told Spinks that he could neutralize Tyson with tactics similar—but not identical—to those Spinks had successfully used while upsetting Gerry Cooney a year earlier. "Remember when you came here last year for the Gerry Cooney fight," Futch told Spinks at their upstate New York training camp. "Remember I told you that your left hand was going to be the key to that fight. Well, your left hand is going to be the key to this fight, too."

Explaining how to adapt this approach against Tyson, Futch said, "With a bobbing, weaving fighter like Tyson, you use a different kind of jab. Not a hard jab. It's better to keep circling and just touch him with the jab, keep him off balance." Repeating a favorite image, Futch told Spinks, "You've seen the bull and the matador. If the matador is straight ahead, the bull can charge. But if you keep the bull off balance, he can't charge. The bull can't charge in a circle."

In an interview with Earl Gustkey of the *Los Angeles Times* shortly before the bout, Futch warned, "Above all, he [Spinks] must remember to *never* trade power for power with this guy." This, Futch says in retrospect, was exactly the mistake Spinks made.

Following Spinks' ninety-one-second loss, Futch told the *New York Post*, "He [Spinks] looked ready for the fight. I couldn't detect anything wrong. And don't let anyone tell you he was scared because he wasn't. I was as surprised as any of the twenty-thousand in the arena when he started trading punches. That wasn't part of our fight plan—he was supposed to stay away from him in the first round."

In a column headlined "Spinks Didn't Fight According to

Plan," Dave Anderson reported that Spinks' mistake was trying to earn Tyson's respect early by exchanging punches. "I didn't expect him to try to go out and get respect right off . . ." Futch said. "I had planned on a strategy that entailed more boxing and moving."

In 1987, Eddie Futch began working with WBA welterweight champion Marlon Starling shortly before his rematch with Mark Breland, who Starling had knocked out to win the title. Futch told columnist Jerry Izenberg of the *New York Post* that, before deciding whether to work with Starling, he and the boxer had a meeting. Starling, as willful and eccentric as he is talented, told Futch that he refused to leave home to go to a training camp before fights. Futch's response, Izenberg reported, was: "It's going to be my way or no way at all. That's the way it is. Take it or leave it. And let me tell you something, young man. Joe Louis went to training camp. Willie Pep went to training camp. If fighters like that needed a training camp, what makes you think Marlon Starling doesn't." According to Izenberg, Starling answered, "Don't get excited, man. I'll go, I'll go."

With Futch in his corner, Starling fought Breland to a draw in a controversial rematch that many observers gave to Starling. Starling then lost the WBA title in July of 1988 in another controversial match, in which he was knocked out by Tomas Molinares with a right hand thrown after a round-ending bell. Though the State of New Jersey declared the fight a no-contest, the WBA awarded Starling's title to Molinares.

In February of 1989, however, Starling challenged WBC champion Lloyd Honeyghan for his version of the title. As Starling prepared to face Honeyghan, Futch was concerned that his fighter was traumatized by the freak knockout, the first of Starling's career. But before the fight, Futch told Michael Katz of the *Daily News*, "I've been watching him very closely and I haven't seen any signs."

In his vivid account of Starling's brutally efficient nine-round knockout of Honeyghan, Jerry Izenberg reported that Futch was not pleased with Starling's performance in the early rounds. When Starling returned to his corner after the fourth, Izenberg wrote, Futch greeted him with this speech: "Don't say one word. He is going to beat you to death inside unless you get down to business. When he moves away from your left hand, throw the right. When he moves away from the right, throw the left. You're doing everything wrong. And stop letting him pound you inside. You're going to pay for it later in this fight unless you tie him up. Go out there and fight him the way you're supposed to, or else you better be ready to fight me when you have to come back here after the bell. And I mean it." Looking back on the fight, Starling later told Jerry Izenberg, "I was more afraid of him [Futch] than I was of Honeyghan."

After Starling and Futch split up, Starling criticized Futch in the press. Futch had his revenge, though, in the summer of 1990 when he seconded Maurice Blocker when Blocker defeated Starling to take the WBC welterweight title.

In 1985 Eddie Futch collapsed while working in boxer James Schuler's corner in an Atlantic City bout. Futch landed in a hospital for a week. Though doctors advised him to take things easier, Futch continues to work full time at his most stressful profession. This incident, along with an awareness of his advancing age, makes Futch feel compelled to pass on his comprehensive boxing knowledge—to share his wisdom. Futch discussed this obligation in an unpublished 1989 interview with Jack Fiske of The San Francisco Chronicle.

"It's a fact that in two-and-a-half years I'll be eighty," Futch told Fiske. "I'm thankful I'm able to work at the pace, have the stamina to be able to do something to help fighters. But, I'd be foolish and unrealistic to think I could keep up that pace."

Looking at the current fight scene, Futch fears that the sort of training skills he worked so hard to cultivate may be vanishing. "There are some good ones [trainers] around, but so many poor ones who walk off the street, put a towel over their arm and tell a kid, 'I can make you a fighter,'" Futch told Fiske. ". . . It's really a crime to see what they're doing. They used to have a second's examination; now all you have to do is answer a few questions, pay the fee and get a license."

Futch himself was a key contributor to a test given to per-spective trainers in Detroit in 1945. "I sent in twenty ques-tions," he told Fiske, "and the commission used all twenty. And it's still used with two, three changes. If you get a [trainer's] license in Detroit, you're qualified. There used to be a time when a second would come in [to Detroit] from out of town and decide the test was too tough, so he'd apply for a manager's license instead so he could be in the corner."

In recent years, Futch has acted as mentor to a number of former fighters who have become outstanding trainers. "I know that when you start getting up there in that age bracket any day I might not be able to do it," Futch told Jack Fiske, acknowledg-ing the huge strain of training fighters and working corners. "In that light, I know the time to do it well is limited and I want to pass along the knowledge I have to younger fellows."

Futch's disciples include Futch's former featherweight Luther Burgess, who now trains for the Kronk Gym in Detroit; George Benton, trainer of world champions Evander Holyfield, Mel-drick Taylor and Pernell Whitaker; Murphy Griffin, trainer of retired lightweight champion Ray "Boom Boom" Mancini; former Futch lightweight Freddie Roach, who took over WBA light-heavyweight champion Virgil Hill and WBC welterweight champion Marlon Starling; and Futch's former welterweight Hedgemon Lewis.

George Benton, who began helping Futch with Joe Frazier in Philadelphia in 1974, speaks warmly of his debt to Futch: "We were together close to ten years, me and Eddie. We got along tremendously. Beautiful man, beautiful man. We never had a difference of opinion about anything. Because I knew that he was knowledgeable about what he was doing. And he knew that

I was the type of guy who was knowledgeable about what I was doing—but I was still learning at the time, getting that experience with him. And I knew he knew what the hell was going on. I've been in boxing all my life, you know, but there's so many things I picked up from him."

Asked to name the most important lesson he learned from Futch, Benton responds with enthusiasm as he sits in the office of his Philadelphia Gym. "I would say the biggest thing I picked up from him was psychology." By this, Benton explains, he means the ability to bring out the best in a fighter by treating that fighter as an individual with unique needs.

"I'm telling you Eddie is a real psychologist when it comes to human beings," Benton says. "He knows what to say to you and how precisely to say it to you. . . . That's why he gets along with guys. It's easy to teach when you're this way. Because every human being is not the same. They don't think the same. . . . This is Eddie, he does that. I picked up a lot of things from him. Oh, so much. And man, we got along tremendously together, we never had an argument. Not even a disagreement."

Searching for the right words to describe the source of Futch's strength, Benton says finally, "See, what he said made all the sense in the world."

NOTES

Unless otherwise indicated, quotes in *Corner Men* are directly from interviews I conducted from April 1989 through August 1990. Excerpts from these interviews are always referred to in the present tense. Within the text of *Corner Men* I have given the source for other quotes and information whenever possible. The purpose of the following notes is not to provide the rigorous evidence required for a scholarly work. Instead, they acknowledge my debt to other writers, as well as provide the interested reader with more precise information on secondary sources already credited within the text.

INTRODUCTION   Jack Kearns' observations about trainers are from "In This Corner," *Newsweek*, January 19, 1953 (hereafter "In This Corner"). Freddie Brown's description of trainers is from *The Sweet Science* by A. J. Liebling (New York: Penguin Books, 1982). Angelo Dundee's summary of a trainer's job comes from a biographical sketch of Dundee by boxing historian Hank Kaplan provided to me by Dundee's office in 1980.

W. C. Heinz's description of Ray Arcel is often quoted. I found this version in a Proclamation by New York Governor Mario Cuomo declaring September 11, 1985 "Ray Arcel Day" in New York State.

Freddie Brown's "The first thing a trainer . . ." comment is from "Freddie Brown Still a Winner" by Mike Levine. *Heights-Inwood*, June 13, 1979.

Charley Goldman's remark is from "The Burning Seconds" by Lester Bromberg, *The Ring*, December 1961. Whitey Bimstein's comment is from boxing writer Sam Taub's "In A Ringside Seat" column. The column is in Bimstein's scrapbook which was provided to me by his daughter Adele Shapiro. The clipping is not dated. Ray Arcel's observation that a second only has forty seconds to work on a fighter between rounds is from "In This Corner."

Sugar Ray Leonard's remark about abusive seconds is from the HBO broadcast of the Pernell Whittaker-Azumah Nelson fight, May 19, 1990.

For information on early boxing instructors and trainers, see *The Manly Art: Bare-Knuckle Prize Fighting in America* by Elliot J. Gorn (Ithaca, New York: Cornell University Press, 1986).

Background on organized crime involvement in boxing in the post-World War II period can be found in *Beyond the Ring: The Role of Boxing in American Society* by Jeffrey T. Sammons (Chicago: University of Illinois Press, 1988).

ANGELO DUNDEE AND HIS MENTORS   Angelo Dundee provides a comprehensive account of his career in his autobiography, *I Only Talk Winning* (Chicago: Contemporary Books, Inc., 1985) written by Dundee with Mike Winters.

Dundee's version of helping Muhammad Ali during the first Henry Cooper fight and the first Sonny Liston fight are from Randy Gordon's interview with Dundee in *Sport*, June 1983 (hereafter "Gordon").

Dundee's speech to Sugar Ray Leonard after the twelfth round of his fight with Thomas Hearns is from "Dundee: Champ of Corner Men" by Phil Berger in *The New York Times Sunday Magazine*, November 19, 1981.

The Red Smith column containing Dundee's description of Ali as "opaque" and Leonard as "home cookin'" is from *The New York Times*, November 30, 1981. Dundee's words to Willie Pastrano during Pastrano's fight with Terry Downes are from Phil Berger's profile of Dundee.

Dundee's one-liners about the Ali-Foreman fight and the first Leonard-Duran fight are from various press accounts recorded in notes I wrote while serving as segment producer for Dundee's 1980 appearance on "The Dick Cavett Show" on PBS. His remarks about Duran's habit of using his head as a pivot while fighting are from *The New York Times*, November 20, 1980. The long quote about Leonard's loss to Duran in their first fight was reported by Jerry Lisker in the *New York Post*, June 21, 1980. Dundee's description of Leonard's victory in the rematch with Duran is from the *New York Post*, November 26, 1980.

Dundee's ambiguous endorsement of Ali's comeback against Larry Holmes is from my Cavett notes. The account of Dundee's words to Bundini Brown before the end of the Holmes-Ali fight are from *Sports Illustrated*, October 13, 1980.

The Dave Anderson column with Dundee's memories of watching George Foreman spar in Zaire is from *The New York Times*, March 18, 1975. Dundee's words about how Ali "truly enjoys what he does" are from Red Smith's *New York Times* column of November 30, 1979. Ali's tribute to Dundee is from "The Corner Man" by Gary Smith in *Sports Illustrated*, November 2, 1987.

I am indebted to both Gary Smith's and Phil Berger's profiles of Dundee for my assessment of Dundee's status in the contemporary boxing scene. They are both invaluable accounts of Dundee as a man and a trainer.

Wilfred Sheed's evaluation of Dundee is from *Muhammad Ali*

by Wilfred Sheed (New York: Thomas Y. Corwell Company, 1975).

Dundee's advice to Leonard before the second Leonard-Duran fight is from "The Big Belly Ache" by William Nack, *Sports Illustrated*, December 8, 1980. Dave Anderson's tribute to Dundee's role in Leonard's victory over Hagler is from "Michelangelo's Masterpiece," *The New York Times*, April 8, 1987. Sugar Ray Leonard's praise for Dundee's work during Leonard's fight with Marvin Hagler is from "'Everything I Did Worked'" by William Nack in *Sports Illustrated*, April 27, 1987.

Details of Charley Goldman's record as a boxer are from *The Jewish Boxers' Hall of Fame* by Ken Blady (New York: Shapolsky Publishers, Inc., 1988), as well as various articles about Goldman in *The Ring*.

STILLMAN'S GYM   I should point out that Al Braverman's reputation was tarnished by his connection with Don King's 1977 United States Championship Boxing Championship. This was a short-lived tournament which aired on ABC television until irregularities involving *The Ring* magazine ratings on which the tournament was based were exposed. The scandal—and Braverman's alleged involvement in it—are treated in *Sports Illustrated*, May 2, 1977. Braverman is now Director of Boxing for Don King Productions.

My physical description of Stillman's is based on several magazine articles, in addition to my interviews: "Stillman's Gym" by Quentin Reynolds, *Colliers*, June 18, 1938 (hereafter "Reynolds"); "Maison de Muscle," *Newsweek*, November 29, 1943 (hereafter "Maison"); and "Slaughter on Eighth Avenue" by Dan Parker, *Colliers*, January 22, 1944 (hereafter "Slaughter"). The atmosphere of Stillman's is evoked in Budd Schulberg's novel *The Harder They Fall*, reprinted in *In the Ring: A Treasury of Boxing Stories*, edited by Martin H. Greenburg (New York: Bonanza Books, 1987).

Stillman's remark ("The joint was so thick with fighters . . .")
is from "Final Bell Tolls for Stillman's and Owner Doesn't Care"
by Howard M. Tuckner, *The New York Times*, February 8, 1959
(hereafter "Tuckner"). Stillman's reference to the "Stock Exchange of Boxing" comes from Maison. The anecdote about
Gene Tunney's request to clean up Stillman's and Johnny Dundee's response to it is from "Three with Moore" by George
Plimpton, reprinted in *Reading the Fights* edited by Joyce Carol
Oates and Daniel Halpern (New York: Henry Holt & Co., 1988).
Stillman's management philosophy (". . . I treated 'em all the
same way . . .") is from Tuckner. Stillman's "I am the boss"
statement is from his obituary in *The New York Times*, August
20, 1969. Budd Schulberg's description of Stillman's voice is
from *The Harder They Fall.* Stillman's remark about his self-
defense skills is from Tuckner. Lester Bromberg's obituary of
Stillman appeared in the *New York Post*, August 21, 1969.
Stillman's tributes to Benny Leonard are from Reynolds and
Slaughter. Stillman's version of the "Racehorse" anecdote is
from Reynolds. The story about Tony Galento and Jack Demp-
sey is from Slaughter. The Beau Jack anecdote is from Maison.
Information about the Florio brothers is from "Florio's
Unique Record" by Al Buck, *The Ring*, November 1958.
Charley Goldman's remarks about depending on his fellow
trainers are from "Big Little Guy" by Jersey Jones, *The Ring*,
January 1953.
A. J. Liebling's description of the Neutral Corner Bar is from
The Sweet Science.
Stillman's comments on the closing of his gym are from
Tuckner. The 1967 interview with Stillman is from "How Still-
man Saved Money" by Ted Carroll, *The Ring*, May 1967.

RAY ARCEL   Red Smith's description of Arcel ("the first
gentleman of fist-fighting") is from "The Return of the Meat
Wagon," *The New York Times*, June 14, 1972 (hereafter "Meat

Wagon"). Damon Runyon's comment on Arcel is from Jimmy Breslin's column "Ray Arcel's Diet: Food for Thought," *Newsday*, January 19, 1989.

Arcel's lengthy description of his work with Peppermint Frazer is from Jerry Izenberg's "Boxing's last great trainer . . ." in *Sport*, January 1979 (hereafter "Izenberg"). Arcel told the same story to Red Smith in Meat Wagon. Arcel's account of Carlos Eleta's call about Roberto Duran is from Meat Wagon and Izenberg. Carlos Eleta's remark about Arcel and Brown is from Pat Putnam's account of the third Duran-DeJesus fight in *Sports Illustrated*, January 30, 1978. Arcel's summary of what he and Brown taught Duran is from William Nack's "From Hard Punches, A Life of Ease" in *Sports Illustrated*, June 16, 1980 (hereafter "Nack"). Arcel's memories of what he told Duran before the second DeJesus fight is from Red Smith's "Roberto Duran and These Two Crazy Old Men," *The New York Times*, May 9, 1980 (hereafter "Crazy Old Men").

Details about Dai Dollings are from Dan Parker's "Durable Dai—Some of His Training Secrets," *Collier's*, May 30, 1942. The description of Doc Bagley is from "Second's Out" by R. McCann, *Saturday Evening Post*, January 28, 1939. Tunney's memories of Bagley's work in his corner during Tunney's first fight with Greb are from *The Tumult and the Shouting* by Grantland Rice (New York: Dell, 1954). Arcel's memories of Dempsey are from *The New York Times*, June 2, 1983.

Arcel's account of taking weight off Charley Phil Rosenberg is from "A Weighty Problem" by Nat Loubet, *The Ring*, October 1950. Arcel's comment upon Bimstein's death is from Lester Bromberg's obituary of Bimstein in *The New York Post*, July 14, 1969.

Arcel's stories of facing Joe Louis with Nathan Mann, Johnny Paychek and Lou Nova are from "The Ring of Fear" by Ira Berkow, *The New York Times*, June 30, 1988. Arcel's article about lugging Buddy Baer from the ring was published in *The New York World Telegram*, January 10, 1942. Arcel's memory of the Louis-Ezzard Charles fight is from Michael Marley's column in the *New York Post*, August 30, 1989.

Dan Parker's profile of Arcel, "When Seconds Count" was published in *Collier's*, July 27, 1940. I found Arcel's description of the second Henry Armstrong-Fritzie Zivic bout in an undated clipping in Whitey Bimstein's personal scrapbook.

Arcel's anecdotes about Benny Valgar and Joe Baksi are from Murray Rose's column in *The Ring*. My copy of the column is not dated. Because no index exists for *The Ring*, I can only guess it is from 1952 or '53.

Newsweek's description of Arcel as a prosperous trainer is from "In This Corner," *Newsweek*, January 19, 1953. Arcel's remarks about Ezzard Charles' shyness are from W. C. Heinz's "The Strange Case of Ezzard Charles," *The Saturday Evening Post*, June 7, 1952.

The account of the 1953 assault on Arcel is from "The Slugging of Ray Arcel" by Tim Cohane and Harry Grayson, *Look*, January 26, 1954 and *The New York Mirror*, September 20, 1953. Angelo Dundee discusses the assault in *I Only Talk Winning*. Dan Parker's column on the incident appeared in the *Mirror* on September 22, 1953. For background information on organized crime's influence over boxing in the 1950s, I am indebted to *Beyond the Ring* by Jeffrey T. Sammons. Background information on Harry Kessler is from "Incorporeal" in "The Talk of the Town" section of *The New Yorker*, September 19, 1953.

Arcel's questions about Sugar Ray Leonard are from Nack. Vic Ziegel's account of Arcel's speech to Duran at the press conference announcing the first Leonard-Duran fight is from *Inside Sports*, June 30, 1980. Arcel's account of his speech to referee Carlos Padilla are from Red Smith's "Duran: He's Gotta Have Heart," *The New York Times*, November 23, 1980 (hereafter "Heart"). Angelo Dundee's remark about being "outwisdomed" by Arcel and Brown and Arcel's fears about Carlos Padilla are from Dave Anderson's "The Brain's Behind the Boxers," *The New York Times*, June 20, 1980. Arcel's remarks about

Dundee being influenced by Muhammad Ali are from *The New York Times*, June 19, 1980. Arcel's postfight evaluations of the first Leonard-Duran fight are from *The New York Times*, June 21, 1980 and *Sports Illustrated*, June 30, 1980.

Arcel's postfight comments on the second Duran-Leonard fight are from *The New York Times* and *New York Post*, November 25, 1980. Jerry Izenberg's account of Arcel's behavior following the fight is from "Fitting Laurel to a Class Act," the *New York Post*, October 28, 1988. Arcel's later thoughts on the second Duran-Leonard fight are from Ira Berkow's "No Night for Thespians," *The New York Times*, April 13, 1987 and "Tribute to 'The Meat Wagon,'" *The New York Times*, November 1, 1988.

Arcel's description of Duran's 1983 victory over Davey Moore is from *Sports Illustrated*, June 27, 1983. Arcel's statement about Duran knowing more about boxing than Arcel himself is from *The New York Times*, August 28, 1989.

Arcel's pre-fight remarks about the Holmes-Cooney fight are from *The New York Times*, June 11, 1982; the post-fight comments are from *The New York Times*, June 14, 1982. Arcel's memories of his post Holmes-Cooney fight thoughts are from "The Foreman-Cooney Fight In Perspective" by Thomas Hauser, *Boxing Illustrated*, May 1990.

Arcel's comments on other recent fights are from Ira Berkow's columns in the following editions of *The New York Times*: August 20, 1986; April 13, 1987; July 14, 1989; June 30, 1988. Arcel's reaction to the February 1990 Douglas-Tyson fight are from "Credit Tyson for Playing Turkey Part" by Dave Kindred, *The National*, February 12, 1990.

For more information on the Ray Arcel Medical Center see *Sports Illustrated*, February 11, 1985.

Bill Gallo's comments about the Ring 8 dinner for Arcel are from his column in *The Daily News*, November 6, 1988. Billy Soose's speech about Arcel at the Ring 8 dinner is from the Gallo column.

JACK BLACKBURN   The source of almost all of the newspaper interviews with Jack Blackburn cited in this chapter is the Joe Louis scrapbooks at the New York Public Library's Schomburg Center for Research in Black Culture. I am also indebted to three books for providing background on Joe Louis' career and Blackburn's role in it: *Joe Louis: My Life* by Joe Louis with Edna and Art Rust, Jr. (New York: Berkley Publishing Co., 1981); *Champion: Joe Louis, Black Hero in White America* by Chris Mead (New York: Scribner, 1985); and *Joe Louis: 50 Years An American Hero* by Joe Louis Barrow, Jr. and Barbara Munder (New York: McGraw Hill, 1988).

Details about Blackburn's family and early life are from "Here's Blackburn's Glamorous Record," by Chester L. Washington, *The Pittsburgh Courier*, July 20, 1935. Washington's brief account of Blackburn's life appeared in conjunction with the publication of a series called "How I Trained Joe Louis" which was credited to Blackburn and probably prepared with the help of Washington and his sometimes partner William G. Nunn (hereafter "Glamorous Record"). Various articles in *The Ring* mention that Blackburn's father was a preacher—a story confirmed in my interviews with Freddie Guinyard.

According to Washington, Blackburn faced Sam Langford six times. Peculiarly, the 1961 edition of *The Ring* record book lists three bouts between Langford and Blackburn under Blackburn's record, but five bouts between the two under Langford's record. Details of Langford's career—and his history with Jack Johnson and Jack Dempsey—are from *The 100 Greatest Boxers of All Time* by Bert Randolph Sugar (New York: Bonanza Books, 1984). Louis' remark about Langford and Blackburn fighting draws is from a Bill Corum column written at the time of Blackburn's death in April of 1942. Blackburn's praise for Langford as "the greatest of them all" is from an "On the Scoreboard" column by Lester Rodney, also written when Blackburn died. (The Rodney column is contained in the Schomburg collection.) The report that Joe Gans would not face Blackburn in a title bout is from Glamorous Record. Gans is reported to have made the statement to George Burton of the *Minneapolis Tribune*. The "Make him stop that" story about Blackburn and an unnamed heavyweight is from Lester Rodney's column. The report of Blackburn fighting six men in one night is from Glamorous Record.

There are several reports of Blackburn "loading" his gloves, including mention of it in *Joe Louis: 50 Years An American Hero* (hereafter "American Hero"). My account of Blackburn's 1909 shooting spree is from various newspaper accounts at the time. The 1917 "Man Who Came Back" poster was contained in Mannie Seamon's collection of boxing memorabilia. The figure of 167 total bouts for Blackburn is from a "Thumbnail Sketch" of Blackburn in *The Ring*, June 1940. This is also the source of the "fearless, clever" description of Blackburn's style.

Joe Louis' account of the Blackburn-Jack Johnson feud is from *Joe Louis: My Life* by Joe Louis with Edna and Art Rust, Jr. (hereafter "Rusts"). Blackburn's "Louis would whip Jack Johnson" comment is from *The Southern Broadcast*, May 11, 1935.

The description of Sammy Mandell's boxing style is from "Gone Are the Boxing Teachers" by Ted Carroll, *The Ring*, June 1953. Blackburn's comments about Mandell and Bud Taylor are from "How I Trained Joe Lewis to Beat Primo" [sic], an article credited to Blackburn in *The Louisiana Weekly*, July 27, 1935 (hereafter "How I Trained"). The account of the relationship between Blackburn and Jersey Joe Walcott is from *The 100 Greatest Boxers of All Time*. Walcott's comments are from my interview with him.

Chris Mead's *Champion: Joe Louis, Black Hero in White America* (hereafter "Mead") made me aware of the June 18, 1936 interview with Blackburn published in the *Honolulu Advertiser*. Anyone interested in a detailed and scholarly account of racial attitudes in boxing during the first half of this century should see Mead.

Blackburn's account of his initial conversations about Louis with Roxborough and Black is from "Louis' Rise Meteoric," *The Ring*, September 1937. Blackburn's words to Louis at Trafton's Gym ("You know, boy . . .") are from Rusts. Blackburn's "Joe needed correction in everything" comment is from How I Trained.

Background on Atler Ellis, Louis' first trainer as an amateur, can be found in "Kid Ellis, Ex-Philly Pug, Trained Joe Louis," *The Afro-American*, January 12, 1935, contained in the Schomburg collection. Ellis' role is also touched on in American Hero.

Blackburn's "You can beat anyone you can hit" remark to Louis is from American Hero. Blackburn's 1935 "I first saw greatness in Joe" is from "How I Trained Joe Louis to Beat Carnera, Part II," *The Pittsburgh Courier*, July 27, 1935. Blackburn's account of the Louis-Reds Barry fight is from another installment of How I Trained, published July 27, 1935 in *The Louisiana Weekly*. Langford's comparison of Louis to Joe Gans is from *The Chicago Defender*, July 20, 1935. The anecdote about the Louis-Lee Ramage fight is from an "A-Round and A-Bout" column by Bob Allen, *The Ring*, May 1957.

Blackburn's "I never saw a kid learn so quickly" comment is from "The Life of Joe Louis" as told to Washington and Nunn, *The Pittsburgh Courier*, March 2, 1935. The pre-fight strategy of attacking Carnera's body from the opening bell is from "Primo A Target for Louis," by Jack Turcott, the *Daily News*, October 17, 1935. The story of Jack Johnson approaching John Roxborough about replacing Blackburn is from Rusts—as is Louis' recollection of Blackburn's behavior the day of the Carnera bout. The *New York Sun*'s detailed account of Louis' corner during the Carnera bout is from "Seconds Allow Victor to Box in His Own Way," June 26, 1935. Blackburn's 1939 memories of the Carnera bout are from an otherwise undated *Pittsburgh Courier* column by Chester Washington found in a scrapbook kept by Mannie Seamon.

Blackburn's "When Joe licks 'em . . . they're ruined" comments are from "Joe Doesn't Only Run 'em, He Ruins 'em," a clipping in the Schomburg collection from a Chicago newspaper at the time of Louis' 1935 bout against King Levinsky. The story of Blackburn's pledge to quit drinking after the Levinsky bout is often told. The dialogue is from Rusts. *The New York Times'* account of Blackburn and Louis' "secret" workout before the Baer fight—and their viewing of the Baer-Carnera fight film—appeared on September 17, 1935. An A.P. report of the same incident appeared in the *New York Post* that same day. Baer's "When I get executed" remark is from Mead. Blackburn's comparison of Louis to Langford is from "Almost a Langford" by Edward Van Every, the *Sun*, September 25, 1935.

Blackburn's recollections of fighters being petrified by Louis is from "Uhlan's Nerve Impresses Joe" by Van Every, the *Sun*, June 17, 1936. Blackburn's "Some day there's not going to be anything more I can teach Joe" comment is from a Van Every column in the *Sun*, June 11, 1946.

The U.P.I. report of Blackburn's murder trial is from the *Sun*, March 3, 1936. Subsequent editions of the *Sun* carried no news of the trial. My account of the outcome of the trial is from the official court record as read to me on the phone by Dick Scalise of the Felony Courthouse, Circuit Court of Cook County in Chicago. The case numbers for Blackburn's trial on manslaughter and perjury charges were 76873 and 76874.

Blackburn's comments about the first Louis-Schmeling fight—"There are sixty-four and a half different ways . . ."—appeared in "Early Rush: Joe's Plan to End Bout" by Walter Stewart, the New York *World-Telegram*, June 16, 1936. Van Every reported Blackburn's very frank 1936 evaluation of Louis' chances prior to the first Schmeling bout in "Trainer Says Louis Is Ready, Dubious Before the First Schmeling Bout, Blackburn Now Expects Joe to Win," the *Sun*, June 21, 1938. Blackburn's comment to Louis after the weigh-in for the first Schmeling fight—"That German is a pretty cool bird"—is from "Uhlan's Nerve Impresses Joe," the *Sun*, June 17, 1936.

Blackburn's advice to Louis during the course of the first Schmeling bout is from Rusts. Lester Bromberg's report of

Blackburn's comment to Louis after the loss is from "Crafty Seconds," *The Ring*, November, 1954 (hereafter "Crafty Seconds"). *The New York Times'* account of the scene in Louis' dressing room after the fight is from June 21, 1936.

Blackburn's remarks prior to the Louis-Sharkey fight—"He ain't the Joe Louis of yesterday . . ."—are from "Louis Guards Chin Now," Walter Stewart, the New York *World-Telegram*, August 4, 1936. Blackburn's "He should have knocked out Mr. Schmeling" statement is from Bill Corum's *Evening Journal* column of August 17, 1936. Blackburn's postfight analysis of Louis-Sharkey is from "Bomber Still a Sepia Sphinx" by James M. Kahn, the *Sun*, August 19, 1936.

The account of Louis and Blackburn's intense preparation for the Braddock fight is from Rusts. Edward Van Every's report on Harry Lenny's role in Louis' camp is from a June 11, 1946 column in the *Sun* in which Van Every recalled Blackburn's role in Louis' career. Lenny's comments to Frank Graham are from Graham's column in the *Sun*, February 25, 1938. Blackburn's "we are working out a new defense" remarks are from an unidentified clipping in the Schomburg scrapbook. His "Joe is working along just the way he should be" remark is from Van Every's column in the *Sun*, June 11, 1946. Blackburn's final words to Louis before the Braddock fight are from Mead—as is Blackburn's famous "why didn't you take a count" speech. Blackburn's memories of the Braddock-Louis fight—"If he'd 'a' had that down right . . ."—are from a "Louis to Weight Under 200," a prefight report on the Louis-Tommy Farr bout by Van Every in the *Sun*, July 28, 1937. Blackburn's advice to Louis between rounds in the Braddock fight is from Rusts—as is the story of Blackburn taking Louis' right glove as a souvenir.

Frank Graham's tribute to Blackburn—"All the things . . ."— is from a column written at the time of Blackburn's death in 1942. The undated column is contained in Mannie Seamon's scrapbook. Bromberg's account of the exchange between Louis and Blackburn during the Farr fight is from Crafty Seconds.

Blackburn's "There ain't none of them soft . . ." comment prior to the Louis-Farr fight is from a Van Every report in the *Sun*, August 27, 1937. Blackburns memories of the Farr fight—"When we discovered the Welshman . . ."—is from a Van Every report in the *Sun*, May 12, 1938.

Louis' comment to the A.P.—"Schmeling is in for a good slamming"—is from "Negro Positive He Will Win by Knockout," in the *Sun*, May 10, 1938. Blackburn's "that's absolutely right" remark is from the same report. Blackburn's argument that Louis' first loss to Schmeling was "the best thing for Joe's future" is from "Blackburn Confident Louis Will Win" by Van Every, the *Sun*, May 12, 1938. Blackburn's subsequent comments—". . . Schmeling is not the great fighter," etc. are from the same interview. Blackburn's comments on the impact of age on the fight are from "Time Works in Louis' Favor" by Van Every, the *Sun*, June 6, 1938.

Mannie Seamon's account of the atmosphere in the Louis camp before the second Schmeling fight is from an undated article in the Seamon scrapbook. Blackburn's comments to Van Every the day before the fight—"If Joe Louis loses this time . . ."—are from "Trainer Says Louis Is Ready," Van Every, the *Sun*, June 21, 1938.

The account of Louis and Blackburn in the dressing room before the fight is from Mead. Louis' "Now I feel like the champion" comment is from "Louis Rejoices in Feeling he is Now Champion," Van Every, the *Sun*, June 23, 1938. Blackburn's postfight comments are from the same article. Blackburn's "There's nothing more I can offer the boy" statement is from a Van Every column in the *Sun*, June 11, 1946. Blackburn's "They find so many faults" comments and his lengthy description of Louis' mature style are from "Trainer Defends Joe Louis," Van Every, the *Sun*, July 1, 1939.

Louis' comments about the second Bob Pastor fight are from a version of Louis' life, as told to Meyer Berger and Barney Nagler in *The New York Times,* November 10, 1948. Blackburn's comments prior to the second Godoy fight are from "Louis Told Not to Worry, Squatters Have to Come Up" by Lester Scott, *New York World-Telegram,* June 18, 1940. Blackburn's remarks to Lester Bromberg prior to the second Godoy fight are from the *New York World-Telegram,* June 12, 1940.

Seamon's comments about Louis' weight prior to the first Louis-Conn fight are from a Lewis Burton story in the *Journal American* in the Seamon scrapbook. Blackburn's account of the fight is from Crafty Seconds. Louis' "I almost lost the title" comment is from the Berger/Nagler *New York Times* account of Louis' life.

Blackburn's remarks about the second Buddy Baer fight—"He is far better than he was for Conn . . ."—are from the Seamon scrapbook. The story of the Louis-Blackburn exchange prior to the second Baer fight is from Mead. Blackburn's postfight comments are from a *Pittsburgh Courier* column by Chester Washington which appeared after the second Buddy Baer fight and is included in the Seamon scrapbook.

The account of Blackburn's words to Louis before the second Abe Simon fight is from the Seamon scrapbook. Louis' "I'm not saying what round it will be . . ." remark is from *The New York Times,* March 25, 1942. The story of Blackburn responding to Louis' words over the radio is from an A.P. report dated March 28, 1942. Louis' reaction to Blackburn's death—"Chappie did more for me . . ."—is from an A.P. interview dated April 24, 1942 which appeared in *The New York Times.* Al Buck included the interview in "Louis Pays Tribute to Jack Blackburn," his *New York Post* column which also reported that Blackburn was doing well financially at the time of his death. The account of Blackburn's funeral is from various reports in the Seamon scrapbook. Louis' lengthy tribute to Blackburn is from a Hype Igoe column which appeared at the time of Blackburn's death. It is included in the Schomburg Joe Louis scrapbook.

CHARLEY GOLDMAN   Goldman's description of his profession ("The part I like best . . .") is from "Big Little Guy" by Jersey Jones, *The Ring*, January 1953 (hereafter "Jones").

Goldman's aphorisms come from various sources. "Training promising kids . . ." is from Goldman's obituary in *The New York Times*, November 12, 1968. "He goes in for a fight . . ." is from "Fight Trainer," *Life*, February 12, 1951 (hereafter "*Life*"). Goldman used the "Rocky must be good . . ." line often. "The punch you throw . . ."; "If you're ever knocked down . . ."; and "Never play a guy . . ." are from *The Sweet Science* by A. J. Liebling. (Hereafter *Sweet Science*.) "People who wear jewelry . . ." is from *Life*. The remark about buying diamonds on the street is from "The One-Minute Angels" by Mark Kram, *Sports Illustrated*, February 17, 1975 (hereafter "Kram"). Goldman's standard pre-beer toast is from "For Charley" by Jimmy Breslin, the *New York Post*, November 12, 1968 (hereafter "Breslin"). The "traveling à la carte" comment is from Lester Bromberg's obituary of Goldman in the *New York Post*, November 12, 1968. Goldman's ". . . two kinds of friends . . ." speech is from *Sweet Science*.

Goldman's habit late in life of reminding people he trained Marciano is from Kram. Goldman's "luck and common sense" speech about training fighters is from Jones. Pop Miller's praise of Goldman is from "Gone are the Boxing Teachers," by Ted Carroll, *The Ring*, June 1953. Goldman's "It don't do no good to tell 'em . . ." line is from *Life*. Goldman's comments about not changing a fighter's style are from Jones.

Goldman's "worse than the cabbages" and "punches from his behind" remarks to the young Marciano are from Breslin. Goldman's account of meeting Marciano is from "How Marciano Can Be Beaten" by Charley Goldman with Tom Meany, *Collier's*, January 17, 1953 (hereafter "Goldman/Meany"). Marciano's 1966 comments about Goldman are from a dinner held for the American Association for the Improvement of Boxing. A tape of the evening was provided to me by the organization's president,

Steve Acunto. Goldman's 1952 memories of first meeting Marciano are from "Improved Rocky Menaces Joe" by Daniel M. Daniel, *The Ring*, October 1952 (hereafter "Improved Rocky").

Goldman's remarks following the Jimmy Weeks fight are from *Rocky Marciano: Biography of a First Son* by Everett M. Skehan with the assistance of Peter, Louis and Mary Anne Marciano (Boston: Houghton Mifflin Company, 1977). (Hereafter "Skehan.") Goldman's "Rocky was twenty-four when I got him . . ." comment is from the *Times'* obituary of Goldman. Goldman's "Marciano does what you tell him . . ." quote is from "Marciano Has Problems," *The Ring*, January 1953.

Goldman's speech about teaching Marciano carefully is from *Sweet Science*. Goldman's "Some of the critics . . ." comments are from Improved Rocky.

For a full account of Marciano's resentment of Al Weill, see Skehan. Skehan explores Weill's conflict of interest during the time Weill served both as matchmaker of Madison Square Garden and Marciano's undercover manager (while Weill's son Marty was manager of record). Skehan also treats Weill's alleged connections to organized crime, as well as Marciano's own fascination with mob figures such as Frankie Carbo. I could find no record of any comments by Goldman on either Weill's reported organized crime connections or Weill's conflict of interest.

Marciano's exchange with Colombo about Goldman is from Skehan, as is the account of Goldman spending little time with Marciano before the Pat Richards fight.

Goldman's memories of Marciano's fight with Keene Simmons are from "Crafty Seconds" by Lester Bromberg, *The Ring*, November 1954. His remarks about Marciano's eating habits are from "Food for Thought" by Ted Carroll, *The Ring*, August 1953.

Goldman's analysis of the Marciano-Harry Matthews fight is from Improved Rocky. Al Buck's account of the fight appeared in the *New York Post*, July 29, 1952. Goldman's prediction of victory in the first Marciano-Walcott fight is from *Improved Rocky*. Goldman's review of the Marciano-Walcott fight is from Goldman/Meany. Goldman's remarks about returning to New York after the fight are from Jones. Goldman and Marciano's exchange about the second Walcott fight is from "Power vs. Cleverness" by Dan Daniel, *The Ring*, October 1953.

Goldman's remarks prior to the first Marciano-Charles fight are from Milton Gross' column in the *New York Post*, June 17, 1954. His postfight comments to Dan Parker are from *The New York Mirror*, June 19, 1954. Goldman's pre-fight analysis of the Marciano-Moore fight are from the *New York Post*, September 20, 1955. Goldman's and Marciano's comments to Milton Gross are from the *Post* of the same date. Red Smith's analysis of the bout is from *The New York Herald-Tribune* from the same date.

Marciano's 1957 quote about thumbing his nose at Goldman is from "Marciano Says: 'I Could Return . . . But—" by Dan M. Daniel, *The Ring*, May 1957.

Details about Goldman's professional record as a fighter are from *The Jewish Boxers' Hall of Fame* by Ken Blady (hereafter "Blady"). Goldman's ". . . they called you a Jew bastard . . ." remark is from Blady. Goldman's account of leaving school is from Breslin. Goldman's explanation for his derby is from Jones. Goldman's memories of Terry McGovern's habit of soaking his face in brine is from "Too Eager To Learn" by Lester Bromberg, *The Ring*, September 1956. Goldman's remarks about his early fights with Kitson and Gardner; how tough boxing was in those days; and the behavior of his manager are from Jones. His memory of fighting Coulon for the title is from Blady.

Goldman's version of the McCoy-Chip fight is from "What's Behind the One Round Knockout?" by Lester Bromberg, *The Ring*, January 1959. His comment about leaving boxing to run a roadhouse is from Jones.

The importance of Goldman's work with Johnny Risko in reviving his training career is from "Johnny Risko: 'He Fought 'Em All," *The Ring*, April 1953. Goldman's memories of the

Risko-Uzcudun fight are from *The Ring,* July 1958. Goldman's account of the Risko-Sharkey fight is from "Fought 'Em All."

Goldman's analyses of Robinson, Armstrong and Louis are from "Ace Trainer Analyses Styles," [sic] *The Ring,* April 1951.

The description of Goldman's quarters at Ma Brown's is from *Life.* Goldman's observations about Sonny Listen are from "How Good Is Liston?" by Ted Carroll, *The Ring,* October 1963. Details from Goldman and Bonavena are from "Argentinian Scores Six Knockouts, Has Master Trainer in Goldman," *The Ring,* February 1965.

In "The One-Minute Angels" Mark Kram wrote: "And then one day they found him [Goldman] in his room, dead and wearing an old robe of Rocky's." *The New York Times* obituary of Goldman from November 12, 1968, however, reported that he died at Roosevelt Hospital.

WHITEY BIMSTEIN   Bimstein's "When you leave New York . . ." line is from my interview with his former fighter, Vinnie Ferguson. Bimstein's ". . . a nice spot" remark is from "The Man in the Corner" by A. J. Liebling, *The New Yorker,* March 20, 1937 (hereafter "Liebling"). The "out of town" line is from Lester Bromberg's obituary of Bimstein in the *New York Post,* July 14, 1969.

Much of the material in this chapter is from Bimstein's scrapbook which was provided to me by his daughter, Adele Shapiro. When possible, I indicate the date and source of Bimstein's comments. Unfortunately, the newspaper and magazine pieces were often clipped in a way that excluded that information. In the following notes, I identify specific sources when possible.

Bimstein's "Name the top fighters . . ." speech is from an Associated Press story headlined, "Boxers Today Too Pampered." The story is dated July 4, though no year is included. Bimstein's praise for Gene Tunney as "calm, cool" etc. is from Bill Gallo's obituary of Bimstein in *The Daily News,* July 14, 1969. Bimstein's statement that Tunney was "the most underrated heavy-

weight champion" is from Mel Beers' profile of Bimstein in
Boxing Illustrated, April 1960 (hereafter "Beers"). His memories
of Doc Bagley are also from Beers.

Bimstein's memories of the first Zale-Graziano fight are from
an undated interview in the *Evening News* of London and Beers.

Rocky Graziano's account of his second fight with Zale is
from *Somebody Up There Likes Me* by Rocky Graziano with
Rowland Barber, (New York: Simon and Schuster, 1955). Bimstein's memories of the fight are from Beers. W. C. Heinz's
account of the fight is from "Graziano: Champion for Life's
Underdogs," *The New York Times*, May 27, 1990. The description of the ringside physician's admiration for Bimstein's work
on Graziano's eye is from the obituary of Bimstein in *The New
York Times*, July 14, 1969. The obituary also reported that
Bimstein "never relinquished" the silver dollar used on Graziano's eye that night. Bimstein's remark about Graziano's performance in the third Zale fight is from the *New York Post*, July 11,
1948.

Bimstein told the story of working Uzcudun's corner against
Max Baer in "In This Corner," *Newsweek*, January 1, 1953.
Bimstein's conversation with referee Jack Dempsey during the
bout is from several undated scrapbook clippings. Dempsey
remembered the fight in "The Seconds," an article credited to
him in *Liberty*, March 8, 1941.

Bimstein's account of the Apostoli-Bettina fight is from an
undated interview with Jack Cuddy of the Associated Press.

Bimstein's memory of seeing fighters "tagged on the chin and
knocked so groggy . . ." is from the *Times* obituary. His remarks
about the conditions in a London gym are from "Boxing: Training Troubles," *Newsweek*, January 13, 1947.

Bimstein's friendship with Frankie Jerome and the fact that
he named his son after the fighter are from conversations with
Bimstein's family. His habit of saying of Jerome, "If he lived . . ."
is from the *New York Post*'s obituary. Bimstein's explanation for
Jerome's death is from "Lou Ambers Best; Moore Toughest" by

Barney Nagler, *The Ring*, September 1950 (hereafter "Nagler").
"He died right in my arms . . ." is from Liebling.

Bimstein's account of the frustrations of training fighters
("You'd never imagine what sets a kid off stride . . .") is from
"Fadeouts: What Causes Promising Prospects to Fadeout?" by
Lester Bromberg, *The Ring*, July 1958.

Details about Bimstein's youth are partly derived from Liebling. Bimstein's 1939 account of his poor training habits is
from a Cleveland newspaper. The name of the newspaper and
the exact date of the article were destroyed. Bimstein's various
nicknames are mentioned in numerous items throughout his
scrapbook.

Liebling's description of Hurricane Jackson and the story of
the fighter whom he tricked into flying to Hawaii are from *The
Sweet Science*. Bimstein's epigram for Liebling's *Back Where I
Came From*, is from *Back Where I Came From* (Berkeley, California: North Point Press, 1990).

Bimstein's memories of training Ted Moore and Lou Ambers
are from Nagler. His comments about Graziano's training habits are from "Training Is the Bunk?" by Al Buck, *The Ring*, June
1956.

Bimstein's account of the Uzcudun-Carnera fight is from an
undated Associated Press interview in Bimstein's scrapbook.
Uzcudun's account of Bimstein's behavior following Uzcudun's
fight with Joe Louis is from "Paulino Hints He Was Doped In '32
N.Y. Bout" by Paulino Uzcudun as told to Jose Alvarez, *The
Ring*, August 1968. Bimstein's homage to Braddock is from an
undated and otherwise unidentified interview with W. W.
Edgar. Bimstein's account of Galento's behavior in the dressing
room following his loss to Joe Louis is from the *London News
Chronicle*, October 24, 1946. His description of Tony Galento's
training—and his bout with Max Baer—is from "Meet the Second" by James R. Fair, an undated and unidentified article in the
scrapbook. Bimstein's comments about Godoy's two fights with
Joe Louis are from various unidentified clippings. Bimstein

expressed the opinion that Louis would defeat Dempsey in these clippings.

Freddie Brown's appreciation of Bimstein's talent for healing is from the *New York Post* obituary.

Bimstein's comments on Hurricane Jackson's training is from "Hurricane Blows Toward Crown," *The Ring*, June 1954. His remarks about Jackson "training too much" are from "Training is the Bunk" by Al Buck, *The Ring*, June 1956. His comparison of Carter to great champions is from Beers.

Bimstein's memories of training Johansson are from "My Wacky Life with Ingo," by Whitey Bimstein as told to Barney Nagler, *Sport*, August 1961.

Bimstein's comments from the Kingsbridge Veteran's Hospital come from Leonard Lewin's interview with him in the *New York Post*, August 24, 1966.

MANNIE SEAMON   A majority of the excerpts from interviews with Mannie Seamon are from his personal scrapbook which was provided to me by Seamon's daughter, Fae. In many cases, the name of the publication from which the clippings were taken; the date of the publication; or the name of the writer are not included in the scrapbook. The following notes provide whatever information was available to me.

Benny Leonard's 1925 tribute to Seamon is from "Leonard Praises Mannie Seamon Who Trains Him" by Benny Leonard ("as dictated by the world's lightweight champion to a member of the *Morning World* sporting staff"), the New York *World*, September 3, 1923. Frank Graham's physical description of Seamon is from an undated New York *Sun* column which appeared shortly before Louis' March 27, 1942 fight with Abe Simon.

Graham's comments about Louis' sparring partners before Seamon arrived in Louis' camp are from a different undated Graham column. *The New York Sun's* assessment of the quality of Louis' sparring partners—and Seamon's remarks about their efforts—are from an undated article by James M. Kahn which appeared before Louis' August 30, 1937 title defense against Tommy Farr. Seamon's remarks about sparring partners to *The New York Sun* are from "Louis to Weigh Under 200" by Edward Van Every, July 28, 1937.

Seamon's description of his role in the first Louis-Conn fight is from a Lester Bromberg column in the *World Telegram* which appeared at the time of the second Louis-Abe Simon fight. Seamon often told the anecdote about telling Billy Conn to "stay down" when Louis knocked Conn down in their first fight. Louis' account of Seamon's role in the first Conn fight is from Louis' version of his life story as told to Meyer Berger and Barney Nagler in *The New York Times*, November 10, 1948. Seamon's analysis of the first Louis-Conn fight is from an un-dated article by Tom O'Reilly of the New York newspaper *PM* writen before the second Louis-Conn fight.

The story of Louis lightly punching Seamon on the back before the second Abe Simon fight, as well as Seamon and Louis' accounts of the fight are from various press accounts included in Seamon's scrapbook. Harold Conrad's line about "the absence of Jack Blackburn" is from *The Brooklyn Eagle*, March 28, 1942.

Blackburn's note to Seamon thanking Seamon for his work with Louis for the Simon fight was published in a Frank Gra-ham column at the time of Blackburn's death in April of 1942. Seamon's account of Louis offering Seamon the job of training Louis is from "There'll Never Be Another Joe Louis" by Mannie Seamon as told to Jim Moriarity, the *Police Gazette*, December 1963. Lester Bromberg's report that Seamon was Blackburn's "personal choice" to be his successor as Louis' trainer is from an undated *World-Telegram* column in the Seamon scrapbook.

The articles Seamon and Harold Mayes prepared for the Brit-ish newspaper the *Sunday Empire News* appeared in the summer of 1948. The account of Seamon's conversation with Louis about stories that Louis wanted someone else as his trainer is from the "I Cured the Fist that KO'd Walcott," article in the *Empire News* series. Seamon's remark that he "felt honored" that a black man had chosen him as his trainer is from an unidentified article in the scrapbook. Louis' wartime letter to Seamon from England was reprinted in a Lewis Burton column in the *Journal-American*.

Seamon's extended remarks to *The Boston American* about Louis' weight reduction program prior to the second Conn fight are from an article by Jack Conway. Seamon's account of Louis studying films of the first Conn fight are from a report by Lewis Burton. Seamon described his pre-fight strategy for the Conn rematch in "Corkscrew was Louis' Secret," the August 29, 1948 installment of his series in the *Empire News*. Louis' "Conn's training for the newspaperman . . ." comment was reported by Tom O'Reilly in *PM*. Seamon's response to criticism of Louis by Dempsey and Tunney is from an unidentified scrapbook clipping. Frank Graham's comparison of Seamon and Blackburn ("Seamon never can be to Louis as Blackburn was . . .") is from a December 15, 1945 *Sun* column. Seamon's "Blackburn once told me that no trainer makes a fighter . . ." comment is from the interview with Tom O'Reilly of *PM*. Other pre-fight comments by Seamon are cited as completely as possible within the text.

Seamon's "We decided use of a left jab . . ." comment following the second Louis-Conn fight appeared in *The New York Times*. Seamon's ". . . Billy didn't know what to do except run . . ." remark was reported by Edward Van Every of the *Sun*. The trainer's description of the end of the fight ("Joe's overhand right to the jaw . . .") is from a Jack Conway article in the *Boston American*. Louis' praise for Seamon—"Mannie Seamon was just as smart . . ."—is from an unidentified scrapbook clipping.

Details about Seamon's early family life were provided to me by Fae Seamon. Seamon's description of his youthful "excess of physical energy" is from "What Fighting Does to a Man's Body," *New Physical Culture*, January, 1949. Seamon described his short-lived career as a fighter in the "I Cured the Fist . . ." installment of his *Empire News* series.

Seamon's description of cutting the ring ropes to save an

injured fighter and the anecdote about Archie Bell's cut eye are from a January 17, 1964 interview in *Boxing News*.

Seamon's tribute to Ted "Kid" Lewis is from the "K.O. Kid Trained in a Rubber Suit" article in the *Empire News*. Lewis' career is described in detail in *The Jewish Boxer's Hall of Fame* by Ken Blady.

Seamon's discussion of his early work with Leonard is from the July 11, 1948 *Empire News* article. Seamon's memories of Charley Leonard as a fighter are from "Louis Would Have Whipped Clay on Cassius' Best Day," *The Ring*, August 1970. Seamon's memories of Benny Leonard's eating habits early in his career are from "Benny Leonard the Perfect Physical Culturist," *New Physical Culture*, April 1949. Seamon's mid-1930s description of the way in which savored his training meals is from an interview with journalist Wilbur Wood of the *Sun*.

The source of the lengthy unidentified newspaper description of Seamon's role in Leonard's 1919 victory over Willie Ritchie is included as completely as possible in the text. The *Evening World* piece about Seamon and Leonard appears to be from the mid-1920s.

Leonard's "I hurt myself making . . . weight for Lew Tendler in our first fight . . ." observation is from an article credited to Leonard in *The World*, June 2, 1927. The account of Leonard's performance against Lew Tendler in their first fight is from Bert Sugar's *The 100 Greatest Boxers of All Time*. A slightly different account of that fight appears in *Leonard the Magnificent* by Nat Fleischer, a book Fleischer published himself in 1947. Leonard's detailed description of his collaboration with Leonard at the time of Leonard's second fight with Tendler ("Mannie and I scheme out three or four days in advance . . .") is from "Leonard Praises Mannie Seamon Who Trains Him," *The World*, September 3, 1923.

The material on Leonard's no-decision fights is from the notes Seamon made for an autobiography. Seamon's account of Leonard's mysterious behavior in his 1922 fight with Jack Britton is from "Champion, in Tears, is Told to Lose," in the *Empire News*.

Seamon detailed Joe Louis' training regimen in the August 22, 1944 *Empire News*. Seamon's remarks about the good feelings in Louis' training camp ("One reason why Louis gets into such good shape . . .") is from an interview in the *Sun*, December 29, 1945.

Louis' description of the Mauriello fight as the last in which "I really felt like my old self" is from Louis' autobiography, *Joe Louis: My Life*, written with Edna and Art Rust, Jr.

Seamon gave his account of warning Louis about drying out prior to the first Walcott fight is from the *Empire News*, August 29, 1948. Ruby Goldstein's account of Seamon's role in keeping Louis in the ring prior to the announcement of the judge's decision is from *The Ring*, July 1973. Louis' comment ("When the bout ended . . .") is from a column by Curley Grieve contained in the scrapbook. Louis' "I should have listened to Mannie Seamon . . ." statement is reported in Ned Brown's column in the *Daily Sports Bulletin*, June 26, 1948.

Seamon's comments about golf encouraging "a man to keep his hands low" are from the *Empire News*, September 5, 1948. Seamon's words of warning to Louis were reported in a column by Ed Sullivan. Seamon's remarks about Louis not worrying about his weight prior to the second Walcott fight are from an undated Ned Brown column in the *Daily Sports Bulletin*. Seamon's disparaging words about Walcott prior to the Louis-Walcott rematch are from undated Frank Graham columns from Seamon's scrapbook. Seamon's strategy for the rematch is from the *Empire News*, September 5, 1948.

Comments by Louis and Seamon following the second Walcott fight are from the *Herald Tribune*, June 26, 1948. Louis' tribute to Seamon's role in Louis' second victory over Walcott is from Louis' life story as told to Meyer Berger and Barney Nagler, *The New York Times*, November 12, 1948.

Seamon's account of arguing against Louis' 1950 comeback against Ezzard Charles is from "Louis Trainer High on Charles" by Lewis Burton, the *Journal–American*, March 9, 1952.

Fae Seamon told me the story of Sugar Ray Robinson's visit to Louis' dressing room prior to the Marciano fight. She said her father never told the story in public because he did not wish to embarrass either Louis or Robinson. Seamon's "I could tell early in the fight . . ." description of the Marciano-Louis fight is from "There'll Never Be Another Joe Louis" by Mannie Seamon as told to Jim Moriarity, the *Police Gazette*, December 1964. Seamon's "Why don't you let Joe Louis alone . . ." comments to reporters following Louis' loss to Marciano are from an unidentified column in the scrapbook. Seamon's statement that he "lost the best job" he ever had when Louis retired is from the 1963 "There'll Never Be Another Joe Louis" article.

Seamon's comparison of Louis and Dempsey is from an unidentified column in the scrapbook. Seamon's comments about Jack Kearns' role in Dempsey's career are from "Louis Trainer High on Charles" by Lewis Burton. Seamon's description of Louis' extraordinary power and "corkscrew punch" are from the *Empire News*, August 29, 1948.

Seamon rated Louis over Leonard as "an all-around fighter" in a 1946 Lewis Burton column published prior to the second Louis-Conn bout.

Seamon's prediction of Cassius Clay's victory over Sonny Liston ("My friends are apprehensive of my sanity . . .") is from an interview with the North American Newspaper Alliance before the first Clay-Liston fight. Seamon's "Liston's no superman . . ." remarks are from "How Sonny Liston Can Be Beaten" by Lawrence Martin, the *Police Gazette*, February 1964. Seamon's "Louis Would Have Whipped Clay on Cassius' Best Day" article appeared in *The Ring*, August 1970.

The story of Seamon kissing Louis on the forehead at the 1978 Las Vegas dinner was told to me by Fae Seamon.

FREDDIE BROWN   Brown's remark about his cigar smoking is from "Holmes, Ali and a Trainer" by Dave Anderson, *The New York Times*, July 7, 1980 (hereafter "Holmes/Trainer").

Brown's memories of the first Marciano-Walcott fight and the second Marciano-Charles bout is from "Why Bad Trainers Can Kayo Boxing" by George Roberts, *National Police Gazette* (hereafter "Roberts"). The article is from a scrapbook provided to me by Muriel Brown, the trainer's widow. The article is not dated, though it seems to be from the late 1960s. Gene Ward's column on the Marciano-Walcott bout appeared in the *Daily News*, June 24, 1969. Brown's description of Marciano's nose being "ripped lengthwise" in the Charles fight is from "A Constant Pro in a Changing World" by Bob Waters, *Newsday*, August 5, 1974 (hereafter "Waters"). Brown's comments to Deane McGowen of *The New York Times* are from a column which was reprinted in the program for the February 17, 1962 fight between Sugar Ray Robinson and Denny Moyer at Madison Square Garden (hereafter "McGowen"). Brown discussed the second Marciano-Charles fight with A. J. Liebling in *The Sweet Science*.

Brown's remarks about breaking his nose while an amateur boxer are from "The Noses Have It at Archer's Camp" by Stan Isaacs, *Newsday*, July 8, 1966 (hereafter "Isaacs").

Brown's comment about the first Louis-Pastor fight ("I was the first guy . . .") is from Holmes/Trainer. John Kiernan's account of the fight is from "The Ten-Round Flight," *The New York Times*, January 30, 1937. His account of the second Louis-Pastor bout is from "The Burning Seconds" by Lester Bromberg, *The Ring*, December 1961.

Brown's 1958 reflections on the changes in boxing are from "Fadeouts: What Causes Prospects to Fadeout?" by Lester Bromberg, *The Ring*, July 1958. His comments from the 1960s are from Roberts. His discourse on treating cuts is from McGowen. His remarks about staying calm are from Waters.

Brown's account of what he taught Duran are from "Freddie's Been Around" by Dan Pattison, *Las Vegas Sun*, April 2, 1979 (hereafter "Pattison"). His comments about Duran as a "born fighter" are from "Streetfighter From Panama" by Dave Anderson, *The New York Times*, April 25, 1978. Brown's comment on Duran's eating habits prior to the Palomino fight are from "Duran: Biggest Problem Could be his Weight," *The Daily News*, July 21, 1979. His analysis of the Duran-Palomino fight is from the *New York Post*, June 23, 1979. Brown's comments on Duran's preparations for the first Sugar Ray Leonard fight are from "From Hard Punches, A Life of Ease" by William Nack, *Sports Illustrated*, June 16, 1980. Brown's "The first couple of years" comment on Duran is from *The New York Times*, May 28, 1980. Brown's remarks to Leonard Gardner are from "Roberto Duran and Those Crazy Old Men," reprinted in *Reading the Fights* (New York: Henry Holt, 1988). Brown's account of his remarks to referee Carlos Padilla is from "On Roberto Duran" by John Schulian, reprinted in *Reading the Fights*.

Brown's comments on Larry Holmes are from Holmes/Trainer. His account of the Holmes-Norton fight is from "Freddie Brown Still a Winner in Late Round of Boxing Career," by Mike Levine, *Heights-Inwood*, June 13, 1979. Brown's 1979 comparison of Holmes to Ali is from Pattison.

Brown's prefight comments about the second Leonard-Duran fight are from *The New York Times*, November 26, 1980. His post-fight comments about Duran being "a great fighter" are from the *New York Post*, November 26, 1980. Brown's "he just quit" analysis of the fight is from *Sports Illustrated*, December 8, 1980.

Brown's telegram to Duran prior to Duran's fight against Davey Moore is from *The New York Times*, June 18, 1983. Brown's prefight look at the Duran-Hagler fight is from *Sports Illustrated*, November 7, 1983.

Brown's comments to Dick Young about the second Leonard-Duran fight are from "Blowing the Lidd off No Más," the *New York Post*, June 13, 1984.

Joey Archer's comments on Brown are from *Newsday*, October 17, 1964. Brown's comment about the first Autuofermo-Hagler fight is from *Sports Illustrated*, December 10, 1979.

AL SILVANI   Silvani is referred to as Ray Arcel's "right-hand man and left-hand man, too" in several articles which appear in Silvani's scrapbook. Silvani himself also used the phrase during my interviews with him. Howard Cosell's comment about Silvani's fame is from an entry in Silvani's scrapbook dated November 9, 1978. No source is given.

Harry Markson's account of Silvani's 1943 efforts to have Sinatra sing the National Anthem appeared in Dick Young's *New York Post* column on November 10, 1983. It was also reported in a clipping dated March 10, 1943 from an unidentified New York tabloid included in Silvani's scrapbook.

Tami Mauriello's reaction to Silvani taking over as the fighter's manager is from *Ringside Sporting News*, September 22, 1944. Mauriello's reaction to being knocked out by Joe Louis—"too goddamned careless"—is from *Champion: Joe Louis, Black Hero in White America*. I am also indebted to that book for my description of the Louis-Mauriello bout. The newspaper account of referee Arthur Donovan's actions during the fight are from unidentified clippings in Silvani's scrapbook. They all seem to be taken from various New York newspapers on September 19, 1946. I found Lefty Remini's postfight comments in an unidentified clipping in Mannie Seamon's scrapbook.

Jake La Motta's account of the tainted Billy Fox fight is from *Raging Bull: The True Story of a Champ* by Jake La Motta with Joseph Carter and Peter Savage (New York: Bantam Books, 1980). Dan Parker's comment on the fight is from *Raging Bull*. For my account of the aftermath of the Fox fight I am indebted to *Raging Bull* and *Beyond the Ring* by Jeffrey T. Sammons. Red Smith's comment on the La Motta-Cerdan fight is from his *New York Herald-Tribune* column, June 17, 1949.

La Motta's efforts to make up with Silvani before La Motta's

1951 bout with Irish Bob Murphy are from Hy Turkin's *Daily News* column, June 23, 1951.

Silvani's remarks about whether or not he was Sinatra's "bodyguard" are from a September 17, 1975 clipping from an unidentified New York newspaper. The clipping is from Silvani's scrapbook.

Silvani's account of Tony Zale sparring with Paul Newman during the making of the movie *Somebody Up There Likes Me* is from an unidentified scrapbook clipping.

Silvani's comments following the 1965 Clay-Patterson fight are from *The New York Times*, November 23, 1965.

Howard Cosell's tribute to Silvani's role in the 1969 Benvenuti-Rodriguez fight is quoted in "Silvani: He Finds Success In A Corner," *The Los Angeles Herald Examiner*, April 27, 1978.

EDDIE FUTCH   Red Smith's comments on the third Ali-Frazier fight are from "Joe Was Still Coming In," *The New York Times*, October 2, 1975. The dialogue in Frazier's corner at the conclusion of the fight is from *Sports Illustrated*, October 13, 1975. Frazier's postfight comments are from "Battered Frazier's Pilot Ends Brutal Manila Bout" by Dave Anderson, *The New York Times*, October 2, 1975.

For a full account of Futch's lifelong interest in poetry—and details about his youth—see Gary Smith's profile of Futch, "Dear Mike," *Sports Illustrated*, February 27, 1989. Smith's account of the development of Futch's psyche—his temper, his experiences as a black man in America from the 1930s to the present—seems definitive to me. Rather than reiterating Smith's work, I decided to focus mostly on Futch's role in boxing history in my own chapter on his career.

I've presented Futch's account of his role in Joe Frazier's career largely in Futch's own words. Unfortunately, Joe Frazier declined to be interviewed for this book.

Futch's 1976 memories of Holman Williams are from "Watch Out for the Trademark of Futch" by Neil Allen, *Times of Lon-*

don, March 13, 1976. For details about the career of Charley Burley, I am indebted to *The 100 Greatest Boxers of All Time* by Bert Randolph Sugar (New York: Bonanza Books, 1984). Futch's memories of Lester Felton are from "Pals in the Bear Pit" by Red Smith, *The New York Times*, June 12, 1981.

Don Jordan's remarks about Futch—and Futch's anecdotes about Jordan—are from "Don 'Geronimo' Jordan" by Fred Eisenstadt, *The Ring*, November 1958.

Sports Illustrated's description of Ken Norton's preparedness for his 1973 victory over Muhammad Ali is from "Bury His Heart at Wounded Jaw" by Dan Levin, April 9, 1973. Futch's discussion of his prefight strategy for Norton's victory over Ali is from Phil Berger's "Notes on Boxing Column," *The New York Times*, October 4, 1989.

Futch's assessment of Frazier following Frazier's 1973 victory over Joe Bugner is from "Futch Admits Frazier Hasn't Regained Peak" by Dan Hafner, *The Los Angeles Times*, July 15, 1973.

Futch's memories of Frazier's bitterness over Futch's refusal to take part in Frazier's 1981 comeback attempt is from "One Boxing Trainer's Triangle" by Dave Anderson, *The New York Times*, November 27, 1983.

Futch's assessment of Marvis Frazier's chances against Larry Holmes are from "No Chip Off the Old Block" by Pat Putnam, *Sports Illustrated*, December 5, 1983.

Red Smith's account of Futch's early conversations with Larry Holmes is from "Pals in the Bear Pit." Futch's prefight comments on the Holmes-Cooney fight are from "Holmes in Six" by Dave Anderson and "Champion, at 212 1/2, A Strong Favorite" by Michael Katz—both from *The New York Times*, June 11, 1982. Ray Arcel's description of his working relationship with Futch during the Holmes-Cooney fight are also from Anderson's column. Futch's postfight remarks on the fight are from "Gerry Cooney's Road to a Rematch" by Dave Anderson, *The New York Times*, June 14, 1985.

Futch's comments on Holmes' career prior to Holmes' fight

with "Tex" Cobb are from "Holmes' Trainer Sees No Contenders" by Michael Katz, *The New York Times*, November 26, 1982. Futch's prefight evaluation of Tim Witherspoon is from "Holmes Really Had a Spoonful" by Pat Putnam, *Sports Illustrated*, May 30, 1983.

Futch's thoughts on the Arguello-Kevin Rooney bout—and his appreciation of Aaron Pryor—are from "His Pryorities are in order" by William Nack, *Sports Illustrated*, August 9, 1982. Futch's predictions of an Arguello victory in the first Arguello-Pryor fight are from "Arguello-Pryor Fight 'Has to Be' Great" by Michael Katz and "The Hawk and the Dove" by Dave Anderson—both in *The New York Times*, November 12, 1982. Arguello's claim that he overtrained for the first Pryor fight is from *The New York Times*, February 2, 1983.

Arguello's "I was like a drowning man" comment about blaming Futch for the loss to Pryor is from "Arguello Gets Another Shot" by Ira Berkow, *The New York Times*, August 1, 1983. Arguello's "I made a big mistake" comment is from Arguello Fights History Second Time Around" by Michael Katz, *The New York Times*, September 8, 1983.

Futch's account of the first time he worked with Michael Spinks is from "In the Corners, a Kid vs. the Old Man" by Phil Berger, *The New York Times*, June 24, 1988. Spinks' appreciation of Futch is from *Penthouse* magazine, July 1988. Futch's analysis of Dwight Muhammad Qawi is from "Spinks and Trainer Plot Strategy for Title Fight," *The New York Times*, June 26, 1988 (hereafter "Spinks and Trainer").

Futch's three-point plan against Qawi is from "A Crowning Achievement" by William Nack, *Sports Illustrated*, March 28, 1983. Futch's comment about the Spinks-Qawi fight to Phil Berger is from "Spinks and Trainer."

Futch's praise for Mike Tyson's "attacking abilities" is from "Mighty Mike Shoulders A Heavy Task" by Hugh McIlvanney, *Sports Illustrated*, November 24, 1986. Futch's "Michael Spinks is going to have to box him, box him, box him . . ." comment is from Spinks and Trainer. Futch outlined Spinks' strategy for Dave Anderson in "Spinks' Left Hand," *The New York Times,* May 27, 1988. Futch's comment to Early Gustkey from "Man Behind Spinks," *The Los Angeles Times,* June 24, 1988. Futch's postfight comment to the *New York Post* is from Mark Di Ionno's article, June 29, 1988. Dave Anderson's "Spinks Didn't Fight According to Plan" column is from *The New York Times,* June 28, 1988.

Jerry Izenberg's report of Futch's initial dealings with Marlon Starling and Futch's role in Starling's victory over Lloyd Honeyghan is from "Fear of Futch Sets Starling On Title Track," the *New York Post,* February 6, 1989. Futch's "I've been watching him [Starling] . . ." remark is from "Marlon-Lloyd: More than a Spat" by Michael Katz, *The New York Daily News,* February 2, 1989.

Futch's description of his efforts to pass on his boxing wisdom to younger trainers are taken from an unpublished March 17, 1989 interview with Futch by Jack Fiske of *The San Francisco Chronicle.* I am grateful to Mr. Fiske for providing me with the article and allowing me to use it in this book.

INDEX

Abel, Jake, 245
Acunto, Steve, 164, 186, on
  Charley Goldman, 181; on
  Stillman's Gym, 36-7
Akins, Virgil, 334
Algren, Nelson, 281
Ali, Muhammad (born Cassius
  Clay), *xiii, xiv, xvii,* 1, 3-4, 6,
  9-10, 11, 12-17, 22, 99, 100,
  107, 185, 215-16, 263-4, 282,
  311, 314-15, 319, 323-4, 355,
  336-9, 342, 343, 356; on
  Angelo Dundee, 15; *vs* Henry
  Cooper, 3; *vs* George Foreman,
  11, 13-14; *vs* Joe Frazier, 311-
  13, 319-23, 342; *vs* Larry
  Holmes, 12-13; *vs* Sonny
  Liston, 4, 263-4; *vs* Ken
  Norton, 338-9; *vs* Floyd
  Patterson, 306-7
Allen, Neil, 329, 331
Amadee, Larry, 220
Ambers, Lou, *xv,* 37, 180, 190,
  206-7
American Association for the
  Improvement of Boxing, The,
  164, 185
Anderson, Dave, 13, 100, 102,
  106, 267, 227, 281, 345, 351,
  355, 361; on Angelo Dundee,
  17; on Tyson *vs* Spinks, 361-2
Antuofermo, Vito, 102, 268, 283-
  4; on Freddie Brown, 287-8

Apostoli, Fred, *vs* Melio Bettina,
  195-6
Arcadia Gym, 119
Arcel, Ray, *xiii, xiv, xvii, xix,*
  xxi, xxii, 19, 20, 25-6, 34, 38,
  55-110, 138, 156, 189, 192,
  201, 246, 265, 268, 276, 291,
  293-4; on Jack Blackburn,
  113-14, 131-2; on Angelo
  Dundee, 20; on Eddie Futch,
  313, 351; on Charley
  Goldman, 159, 162, 170, 174;
  on Benny Leonard, 244; on
  Rocky Marciano, 168; on
  Stillman's Gym, 32, 39, 41-44,
  48; on Lou Stillman, 41, 50
Archer, Freddie, 280
Archer, Jimmy, 50-51, 268; on
  Freddie Brown, 273, 285-6; on
  Stillman's Gym, 35
Archer, Joey, 35, 51, 277, 285; on
  Freddie Brown, 287
Archibald, Joey, 180
Arel Andy, *vs* Willie Pep, 8-9
Arguello, Alexis, 277, 291, 306,
  308, 349, 353-8; *vs* Billy
  Costello, 357-8; *vs* Ray "Boom
  Boom" Mancini, 354; *vs* Aaron
  Pryor, 354-7; *vs* Kevin
  Rooney, 354-5
Armstrong, Henry, 181, 213, 277,
  294; *vs* Barney Ross, 80; *vs*
  Fritzie Zivic, 88

401